The Bloomsbury Introduction to Popular Fiction

The Bloomsbury Introduction to Popular Fiction

Edited by
Christine Berberich

Bloomsbury Academic
An imprint of Bloomsbury Publishing Plc

B L O O M S B U R Y
LONDON · NEW DELHI · NEW YORK · SYDNEY

Bloomsbury Academic

An imprint of Bloomsbury Publishing Plc

50 Bedford Square
London
WC1B 3DP
UK

1385 Broadway
New York
NY 10018
USA

www.bloomsbury.com

BLOOMSBURY and the Diana logo are trademarks of Bloomsbury Publishing Plc

First published 2015

© Christine Berberich and contributors, 2015

British Library Cataloguing-in-Publication Data
A catalogue record for this book is available from the British Library.

ISBN: HB: 978-1-4411-7201-3
PB: 978-1-4411-3431-8
ePDF: 978-1-4411-5567-2
ePub: 978-1-4742-3258-6

Library of Congress Cataloging-in-Publication Data
A catalog record for this book is available from the Library of Congress.

Typeset by Deanta Global Publishing Services, Chennai, India
Printed and bound in India

To Lucas Finnegan Stefanuti –
tall, dark and devastatingly handsome.

Contents

Acknowledgements

This book has been much longer in the making than initially anticipated. To my Commissioning Editor at Bloomsbury, David Avital, many thanks for his immediate enthusiasm about this project, and to him and Mark Richardson for thorough support and constant understanding for shifting deadlines. And special thanks to Bran Nicol for getting me started on this project in the first place.

To my contributors a resounding 'thank you' for agreeing to write the chapters, for being passionate about the project and for producing exciting work that sheds new light on old and new genres, authors and their work.

My mother has – as always – supported me in this project, even in adversity and through traumatic months. She has taught me to persevere, and to keep pushing, even when the going got tough, and when giving up seemed a more enticing option. Hellmut Bauscher always provided friendship, support and advice – and will be so sorely missed. My colleagues and friends both at Portsmouth and further afield have supported me with good cheer, open ears and much patience: Patricia Pulham, Páraic Finnerty, Holger Kreiling, Frank Becker, Stefan Hartz, Arthur Aughey, Simon Barker, Antonio Cavaliere, Patrick Parrinder and Sophia Wood provided chocolate, trips to the museum, advice (in word, by phone, by email), wine, cups of tea, reading of drafts, general distraction or child-minding on countless occasions.

And finally, my son Lucas – who always keeps me on my toes and pushes me that extra little bit, even if it is sometimes over the edge, and who makes it all worthwhile.

Southsea, April 2014

Contributors' Details

Christine Berberich is a senior lecturer in English Literature at the University of Portsmouth. She has published widely on the topic of Englishness, and authors as diverse as Ian Fleming, J. K. Rowling, Kazuo Ishiguro, Julian Barnes and W. G. Sebald. Her book *The Image of the English Gentleman in Twentieth-Century Literature: Englishness and Nostalgia* was published in 2007 (Ashgate). She is co-editor (with Arthur Aughey) of *These Englands: Conversations on National Identity* (Manchester, 2011), (with Neil Campbell and Robert Hudson) *Land & Identity: Theory, Memory, and Practice* (Rodopi, 2012) and (also with Campbell/Hudson) *Affective Landscapes in Literature, Art, and Everyday Life* (forthcoming; Ashgate). She is, with Neil Campbell, series editor of *Place, Memory, Affect* with Rowman & Littlefield.

Joanne Bishton is a lecturer in American Studies at the University of Derby. Her research area is concerned with how representations of lesbian figures in popular fiction challenge traditional understandings of genre and authorship. She is currently completing her PhD on the fictional writing of Sarah Waters. She has published a chapter on 'Queering the Speaking Subject in Sarah Waters' *The Little Stranger*' in *Cross-Gendered Voices* (eds Rina Kim and Claire Westall; Palgrave, 2010) and journal articles on Waters' work in *ABC: The Journal of American, British and Canadian Literature* and *The New Horizons PGR Edition Response E-Journal*.

Neil Campbell is professor of American Studies and research manager at the University of Derby, UK. He has published widely in American Studies, including the books *American Cultural Studies* (with Alasdair Kean) and, as editor, *American Youth Cultures*. He is a co-editor of *Issues on Americanisation and Culture* (2004), *Land & Identity* (2012) and *Photocinema* (2013). He has published articles and chapters on John Sayles, Terrence Malick, Robert Frank, J. B. Jackson, D. J. Waldie and many others. His major research project is an interdisciplinary trilogy of books on the contemporary American West: *The Cultures of the American New West* (Edinburgh, 2000), *The Rhizomatic West* (Nebraska, 2008) and *Post-Westerns: Cinema, Region, West* (2013).

Stefania Cioccia is a reader in Modern and Contemporary Literature at Canterbury Christ Church University. She is the author of *Vietnam and Beyond: Tim O'Brien and the Power of Storytelling* (Liverpool University Press, 2012) and co-editor of *The Invention of Illusions: International Perspectives on Paul Auster* (Cambridge Scholars Publishing, 2011). In the field of crime writing, she has worked mostly on postmodern revisions of the genre, such as Paul Auster's metaphysical thrillers or Mark Haddon's *The Curious Incident of the Dog in the Night-Time*. She has recently developed an interest in American women writers in the noir tradition in the 1940s and 1950s.

Ben Clarke is assistant professor of twentieth-century British literature at the University of North Carolina at Greensboro. He is the author of *Orwell in Context* (2007) and co-author, with Michael Bailey and John K. Walton, of *Understanding Richard Hoggart* (2012). He has published on subjects such as public houses, mining communities, Englishness, Edward Upward, Virginia Woolf and Western anthropological accounts of Taiwan. He is currently working with Sue Owen on an intellectual biography of Richard Hoggart.

Ben Dew is a senior lecturer at the University of Portsmouth. His research is concerned with the intellectual history of the Enlightenment. He has published articles on Bernard Mandeville, David Hume and eighteenth-century historical writing, and is the editor of *Politics and Tea*, part of the Pickering and Chatto collection, *Tea and the Tea-Table in Eighteenth-Century England*.

Juan Elices is a senior lecturer in English Literature and director of the Language Centre at the University of Alcalá (Spain). He has conducted extensive research on theory of satire, dystopia, alternate history and censorship. His publications include *Historical and Theoretical Approaches to English Satire* (Munich: LINCOM Europa, 2004) and *The Satiric Worlds of William Boyd: A Case Study* (Bern and New York: Peter Lang, 2006) and a number of scholarly articles on authors such as Steven Barnes and Walter Mosley. His current research interests focus on sociological and literary manifestations of the Irish economic boom and on the role of the Irish family.

Alice Ferrebe is a senior lecturer in English at Liverpool John Moores University. She is the author of *Masculinity in Male-Authored Fiction 1950-2000*

(Palgrave, 2005) and *Literature of the 1950s: Good, Brave Causes* (Edinburgh University Press, 2012). While harbouring an enduring interest in issues of literary gender, much of her research is now focused upon British writing of the immediate post-World War II period, and particularly the intersections between fiction and visual art during that period.

Monica Germanà is a writer and senior lecturer in English Literature and Creative Writing at the University of Westminster. Her research interests and publications concentrate on contemporary British literature, with a specific emphasis on the Gothic, gender and popular culture. Her first monograph, *Scottish Women's Gothic and Fantastic Writing*, was published by Edinburgh University Press in 2010. Recent publications include *Ali Smith* (Bloomsbury, 2013), co-edited with Emily Horton, and *Apocalyptic Discourse in Contemporary Culture* (Routledge, 2014), co-edited with Aris Mousoutzanis. She is currently working on *Bond Girls: Body, Dress, and Gender*, a monograph exploring the politics of body and dress in Ian Fleming's narrative and subsequent cinematic adaptations (Bloomsbury, 2015).

Bran Nicol is professor of English Literature at the University of Surrey. He writes on twentieth-century British and American fiction, crime fiction and film and cultural theory. His books include *The Private Eye: Detectives in the Movies* (Reaktion, 2013), *The Cambridge Introduction to Postmodern Fiction* (2009), *Stalking* (Reaktion, 2006) and the co-edited collection *Crime Culture* (Continuum, 2010).

Patrick Parrinder's books include *James Joyce* (1984), *Authors and Authority* (revised edn, 1990), *Shadows of the Future* (1995) and *Nation and Novel* (2006), and he is general editor of the ongoing 12-volume *Oxford History of the Novel in English*, of which three volumes are now published. He has also written extensively on science fiction and, in particular, H. G. Wells, and was general editor of the Wells editions published by Penguin Classics. He is currently writing on science and nineteenth- and twentieth-century utopian fiction. He is an emeritus professor of English at the University of Reading.

Christopher Pittard is a senior lecturer in English literature at the University of Portsmouth. He has published numerous articles and chapters on Victorian culture and popular fiction (including the monograph *Purity and Contamination in Late Victorian Detective Fiction* [Ashgate, 2011]), and won the 2006 VanArsdel Prize for his work on Arthur Conan Doyle and the

Strand Magazine. Pittard is a member of the editorial boards of the *Journal of Popular Culture* and *Clues: A Journal of Detection*, and is a faculty member of the Dickens Project at UC Santa Cruz.

Petra Rau is a senior lecturer in Modern Literature at the University of East Anglia. She is the author of *English Modernism, National Identity and the Germans, 1890-1950* (Ashgate, 2009) and *Our Nazis: Representations of Fascism in Contemporary Literature and Film* (Edinburgh University Press, 2013). She is also the editor of *Conflict, Nationhood and Corporeality: Bodies-at-War* (Palgrave, 2010) and the forthcoming *Long Shadows: The Second World War in Literature and Film, 1943 to the present* (Northwestern University Press, 2014). Her research interests are representations of war and fascism, the theory and practice of commemoration and, more recently, travel writing. She is currently working on a monograph on travel writing about Central and Eastern Europe.

Andy Sawyer is a librarian of the Science Fiction Foundation Collection at the University of Liverpool Library. He is Reviews Editor of *Foundation: the International Review of Science Fiction*. He has published numerous essays on aspects of science fiction and fantasy, has contributed to many reference books and is a frequent reviewer in the field. He co-edited (with David Seed) the collection of essays *Speaking Science Fiction* (Liverpool University Press, 2000). His 'Foundation Favourites' column of highlights from the Science Fiction Foundation Collection has appeared in the British Science Fiction Association's *Vector* since 2003. He most recently co-edited (with David Ketterer) *Plan for Chaos*, a previously unpublished novel by John Wyndham (Liverpool University Press, 2009; Penguin, 2010) and (with Peter Wright) *Teaching Science Fiction* (2011). He was the 2008 recipient of the Science Fiction Research Association's Clareson Award for services to science fiction and was Guest Curator of the British Library Exhibition 'Out of This World: Science Fiction But Not as You Know It' (2011). He is currently researching the science fiction of the 1950s.

Lena Steveker teaches British Literary and Cultural Studies at Saarland University in Saarbrücken, Germany. Her main research interests are contemporary British literature and popular culture as well as early modern English drama. She has published several articles on cultural memory, trauma, ethics and identity in British literature. She is the author of *Identity and Cultural Memory in the Fiction of A. S. Byatt* (Palgrave, 2009), and she co-edited the essay collection *Heroism in the Harry Potter Series* (Ashgate, 2011). She is currently writing a monograph on theatre and news culture in early modern England.

Carl Tighe is the author of three novels and two collections of short fiction. He is the winner of several literary awards: City Life Writer of the Year 2000, the Author's Club Award, the All London Drama Award. He is also the author of *Gdansk: National Identity in the Polish German Borderlands*, *The Politics of Literature: Poland 1945-89* and *Writing & Responsibility*. He has a long association with the magazine *Ambit* and with *The Journal of European Studies*. His book *Writing the World: Writing as a Subject of Study* will be published in 2014.

Maryan Wherry is an Independent Scholar and writing specialist. She holds a PhD in American Culture Studies and has taught composition, history and popular culture. She has published essays in US women's history and popular romance and edited the Love and Romance issue of the Journal of American Culture. She is a voracious reader of popular genre fiction, particularly the romance.

Gina Wisker is professor of Higher Education and Contemporary Literature at the University of Brighton and head of its Centre for Learning and Teaching. Her principal research interests are in twentieth-century women's writing, particularly postcolonial writing and popular fictions, and she has published *Postcolonial and African American women's writing* (Palgrave Macmillan, 2000), guides to Sylvia Plath, Virginia Woolf, Toni Morrison and Angela Carter (Hodder, 2000–3), a companion to Margaret Atwood's *Alias Grace*, and another to *The Handmaid's Tale* (Continuum, 2003, 2011), *Key Concepts in Postcolonial Writing* (Palgrave Macmillan, 2007) and *Horror* (Continuum, 2005). In 2012, Palgrave Macmillan published her *Margaret Atwood, an Introduction to Critical Views of Her Fiction*. Gina also teaches, supervises, researches and publishes in learning and teaching areas, specializing in postgraduate study and supervision and has published *The Postgraduate Research Handbook* (2001, 2008, 2nd edn) and *The Good Supervisor* (2005, 2012, 2nd edn) (both Palgrave Macmillan). She is currently completing *Getting Published* (Palgrave Macmillan, 2014) and starting *Contemporary Women's Gothic Fiction* (Palgrave Macmillan, 2014).

Introduction: The Popular – *L*iterature versus *l*iterature

Christine Berberich

The story goes that, one day in 1997, the Russian editor, translator and academic Grigory Chkhartashvili travelled on the Moscow underground with his wife who was so engrossed in a book that she would not talk to her husband. He tried to catch a glimpse of the title – but all he could see was a brown paper cover. When they were back above ground, and his wife was speaking to him again, he found out that she had, in fact, been reading a, in her words, 'trashy' crime novel (Hobson 2003, n.p.). Her reading matter clearly embarrassed her – hence the brown paper cover; she realized that a crime novel, no matter how engrossing or engaging, would be considered 'beneath' her status as a well-educated, high-brow Muscovite (see Finn 2006, n.p.). Chkhartashvili's response was singular – and very determined: he sat down and dashed off a series of detective novels that his wife would not have to be ashamed to be seen reading in public. Published under his *nom de plume* Boris Akunin – after the nineteenth-century Russian anarchist Mikhail Bakunin – his Erast Fandorin mysteries (there are now 13 titles in the series; see, for example, *The Winter Queen* [1998]) have become bestsellers not only in his native Russia. In an interview Chkhartashvili/Akunin explained that 'The style I used at the beginning [of the series] was anarchistic. Russian literature was either very high or low. I mixed literature with entertainment' (Thornhill 2013, n.p.).

The case of Akunin and his popular detective serves as a perfect opener for this study on popular fiction. As an author, Akunin was acutely aware of a pre-existing snobbery about literature not only in his own country. 'Popular' literature, the kind that seemingly provides only pure entertainment or escapism, has traditionally been derided and sneered at. In order to fulfil his wife's demand for 'intelligent, well-written entertainment for the highly literate and book-hungry Russian public' (Hobson 2003, n.p.), Akunin created successful works of pastiche, weaving together all the elements that he enjoyed himself in Russian and world literature, both of the 'high' and the 'popular' variety: 'Prince Andrei Bolkonsky from Tolstoy's *War and Peace*, Pechorin from Lermontov's *Hero of our Times*, Sherlock Holmes and James Bond – and threw in others of his own distilled from his knowledge of oriental culture' (Thornhill 2013, n.p.). The result is a highly successful series of historical detective whodunits that work on a variety of levels for different readerships: they are entertaining; they are engaging; they toy with literary and historical allusions that, however, need not necessarily be understood to enjoy the plot of the stories; in short, they serve the 'high' and 'low' end of the market Akunin mentioned in the interview. In the process, Akunin has created his very own brand – that he is now set to continue and expand with the creation of a new series of historical detective novels centred on the crime-solving nun Sister Pelagia (see, for example, *Pelagia and the White Bulldog*, 2007). Sherlock Holmes, James Bond, Father Brown and Miss Marple thus meet in nineteenth-century Russia – much to the delight of millions of readers worldwide.

Vague, Temporal, Shape-shifting: Pro and Contra Popular Fiction Today

So what is *popular* fiction, and why has it come under so much fire and been neglected for such a long time that it requires both a justification and defence? The following section provides some working definitions of the term popular fiction that also take in, simultaneously, some of its most common criticisms and defences.

At the most basic level, it is tempting to say that popular fiction indicates writing that is precisely that: *popular*, that is, read and, crucially, *enjoyed* by many readers. However, it is not that simple. The term 'popular' contains a variety of different and, potentially, contradictory meanings, and is one weighed down with ideological meaning. Raymond Williams' *Keywords* of 1976 defines 'popular' as, historically, 'belonging to the people', 'widely favoured' or 'well liked' but points out that it has always held the connotation of being 'low' or 'base' as well as containing 'a strong sense of setting out to gain favour'. Williams outlines that by the nineteenth century the meaning of the term had shifted more towards 'being seen from the point of view from the people rather than from those seeking favour or power from them'. Interestingly, though, he differentiates that '**Popular culture** was not identified by *the people* but by others, and it still carries two older senses: inferior kinds of work . . . and work deliberately setting out to win favour . . . ; as well as the more modern sense of well-liked by many people . . .' (198–9). 'Popular' thus always, and inevitably, has political connotations as it refers to the people and the distribution of power in society. As such, it has been a contentious term ever since its inception, with some fearing the power of the masses, while others are lamenting the manipulation of the people through those (few) in power, theories that will be further assessed in Chapter 2.

Scott McCracken's definition of popular fiction as 'fiction that is read by large numbers of people' comes with an important further discrimination: 'Contemporary popular fiction is the product of a huge entertainment industry . . . that markets and sells popular narratives for film, radio, television and periodicals as well as in book form' (1998, 1). Popular fiction can thus never be studied in isolation but has to both take in other cultural forms (here, in particular, film and TV) and acknowledge the power balance between writers, publishers and the market. Critics often use this link between popular fiction and its modes of production to disparage its worth. Increasing commercialization of narrative, it has been argued, has led to repetitive formulas being applied to writing: what was sold was replicated over and over again in varying forms and shapes but generally according to the same pattern (see, for example, Palmer 1991, 38). Walter Nash rightly points out that readers of popular fiction 'do not want [the same book] *again*, though [they] may want *more* [of the same kind]' (1990, 2). Popular fiction, the critics say, thus produces predictable texts, knitted according to the same pattern, with few, if any, deviations. It aims to employ those winning formulas to 'sell big' and do so in the shortest period of time: it hopes, in short, to produce bestsellers, those books that sell best in the shortest period of time. And this issue links to the temporality and spatiality of popular fiction, another common criticism: what is popular today is not necessarily popular tomorrow, and what is popular in one culture might not translate into another. Popular fiction is thus generally rooted in a time and, more often than not, a place. In our fast and furious world, allusions to trends and fads peculiar to their time might not be understood a decade, let alone a century, later. Jane Austen's early nineteenth-century readers would have understood the hidden social messages in her description of dresses more easily than twenty-first century readers; Helen Fielding's allusion to Lottery instant tickets in her bestselling *Bridget Jones' Diary*, so topical at the novel's 1996 publication, might be lost on readers a mere 20 years later. Critics use these points to highlight the lack of longevity of popular literature. A real 'classic' text, they argue, transcends time and space and gives new meaning to new generations of readers. However, this argument should be countered by saying that while today's popular success might not be appreciated for its narrative style or linguistic accomplishment in a hundred years' time, it can then, nevertheless, still tell new generations about what our society cherished, celebrated or felt strongly about at a certain point in time. As Clive Bloom puts it, popular fiction is the 'fiction that most becomes its period and which is most caught in its own age' and that, as such, it is the 'barometer of contemporary imagination, a type of acute pathological and sociological exemplary instance which sums up all that is interesting culturally ... and all that is ephemeral artistically' (2002, 15). It offers readers a window to a particular time and place and, as such, should be seen as part of our cultural heritage.

One final working definition comes from Christopher Pawling who refers to popular fiction as the 'significant other' of canonical literature, the 'paraliterature' surrounding the small core of intellectual literature that is 'crucial in helping to constitute the dominant literary culture' (1984, 2). This shows that, when it comes to literature, there appears to be a differentiation into Literature, a small cluster of acknowledged, high-brow, canonical writing enjoyed by a highly educated minority, and literature, the mass of narrative that is produced for the largely uncritical mass readership, a point that will be similarly expanded on in Chapter 2. This, of course, is an over-simplification and generalization – but one that has marred the reputation of popular literature for decades and that finally needs to be done away with. In the words of Tony Bennett and Graham Martin: 'there are many good reasons for studying popular fiction. The best, though, is that it matters' (1990, ix). Popular fiction, as McCracken has said, 'can tell us much about who we are and about the society in which we live' (1998, 1) and as such should be a valuable addition to any literary or cultural syllabus. But the already oversimplified division into Literature and literature outlined above has, in recent years, been further complicated as the boundaries between the two, ever tenuous, have become increasingly blurred. Jim Collins, for example, refers to the advent of postmodernism and its creation of works of literature that freely mix ingredients of so-called 'high' and 'low' origin, creating a more hybrid style of writing that had something that could appeal to anyone, and at a variety of levels. He explains that a number of postmodern writers have become so celebrated – through a combination of critical and commercial success – that they 'have the brand-name recognition once enjoyed by writers of bestsellers' (2010, 3). Collins explains this phenomenon with the all-pervasiveness of contemporary culture, where writers appear on chat shows, their books are advertised in supermarkets, the adaptations of their works turned into commercial success stories on the big or small screen. His example is Michael Ondaatje's 1992 novel *The English Patient* – by itself upon first publication not a huge popular success. After receiving the Booker Prize, however, its sales increased; it was then turned into an award-winning feature film that spawned the 'film-tie-in' reissue of the novel (3). This example could be extended to many other novels, such as Kazuo Ishiguro's 1989 Booker-winning *The Remains of the Day* or, prior to that, Thomas Keneally's *Schindler's Ark* (1982). In fact, similarly, McCracken contends that, in the twenty-first century, there is a general 'decline of authoritative texts', (1998, 11) which means that the defining of boundaries is increasingly difficult. Mukerji and Schudson agree that the 'rigid conceptual barrier between "high", or estimable, culture and popular, or representative, culture has broken down' because 'literary and art critics have come to recognize how much high culture and popular culture have in common as human social practices' (1991, 1). Mukerji and Schudson claim that this division into high and popular culture has been an artificially maintained *political* rather than an aesthetic distinction. For Jerry Palmer, there might still be such a distinction, but he, too, emphasizes that it is one that is artificially maintained and that is ever changing, alternating with different trends and fashions that should, ultimately, negate the existence of a barrier between 'high' and 'low' literature altogether (see 1991, 110).

This Collection

The following collection of essays, all written by experts in their fields, aims to highlight and celebrate the multifaceted diversity of popular fiction and to show that we are all, as Henry Jenkins, Tara McPherson and Jane Shattuc have shown, 'connected to its pleasures and politics in our everyday existence through a diversity of experiences' (2002, 26). Politics and everyday experiences change – and so does popular literature. Literary trends and popular successes come and go; new genres emerge, are celebrated, and sink into ignominy again. The study of popular fiction is consequently the study of an ever-changing, ever-involving and ever-dynamic field that can be, as shown above, difficult to pin down. Christopher Pittard's and Christine Berberich's chapters that open the collection will give a historical overview of popular developments – from serialization and lending libraries to technological innovations leading to mass and consumer culture, the power of book clubs and literary prizes and the seemingly all-pervasive power of politics and ideology on public taste. As the twentieth century was the century that not only saw the emergence of successful and best-selling genres in popular fiction but also saw their implementation for production and marketing purposes, it seems appropriate to offer insightful introductions to the most popular of popular genres. Maryan Wherry introduces the quintessential popular genre, the romance, outlining the various trends and (sub-) developments in romance writing that range from pure titillation and the achievement of the ultimate happy ending to offering advice to the active and busy woman of her day. Alice Ferrebe charts the adventure story with its roots in escapist empire writing and its development towards the modern creation lad-lit. Andy Sawyer's chapter offers an insightful overview of the history of science fiction, one of the most successful twentieth-century popular genres that always aims to be several steps ahead of the actual technological and scientific developments of the day. Stefania Ciocia focuses on crime writing and the ever popular detective novel – from the nineteenth century on a frontrunner in the popularity stakes and with many unforgettable literary creations ranging from Agatha Christie's Miss Marple to the hard-boiled detectives of Raymond Chandler or Dashiell Hammett and the contemporary craze for Scandic Noir and Italian detectives. Ever since the eighteenth century, Gothic writing has had a big impact on literature, and Gina Wisker's chapter discusses the enduring legacy and popularity of horror fiction that now encompasses werewolves, vampires and their slayers. Children's books nowadays account for a substantial part of annual book sales, but as a recognized 'genre' children's writing is not only relatively new, but also, as Lena Steveker discusses in her chapter, an example of 'cross-over' literature in that new books for children are now often simultaneously marketed for adults. Monica Germanà, finally, discusses one of the 'newest' popular genres, the graphic novel, introducing two texts, Marjane Sartrapi's *Persepolis* and Art Spiegelman's *Maus*, that have successfully contributed to further blurring the boundaries between so-called 'high' and 'low' literature.

The final section of the book is dedicated to a series of case studies that offer more in-depth discussions of individual popular authors, the influence of politics on literature and individual popular trends. Ben Clarke assesses the work of H. G. Wells, and here, in particular, Wells' take on popular versus élite culture. Patrick Parrinder discusses one of the founding fathers of the spy and adventure genre, John Buchan. No book on popular fiction should be complete without a mention of one of the most popular creations of the twentieth century, James Bond, and Juan Elices' chapter offers unique insight into Ian Fleming's Bond series by discussing its reception – and censorship – in Francoist Spain, a chapter that clearly shows the troubling connection between popular culture and (abused) political power. Joanne Bishton offers a subversive take on the traditional 'boy-meets-girl' romance by discussing Sarah Waters' popular (and critically highly acclaimed) lesbian neo-Victorian romances. The hard-boiled detective is one of the most iconic twentieth-century literary creations, immortalized even more through his adaptation into film; Bran Nicol's chapter is dedicated to the discussion of one of the founding fathers of the hard-boiled detective, Dashiell Hammett, and argues that Hammett's writing contributes to the blurring of boundaries between literary and popular fiction. Like the romance, writing about wars has always been popular among readers of all ages, and Petra Rau's chapter critically examines the notion of using stories of wars and fighting for entertainment. The last two case studies are given over to two commercially particularly successful 'sub-genres': Neil Campbell assesses the contemporary craze for vampire writing with his case study of Stephanie Meyers' *Twilight* series while Ben Dew discusses the relatively new phenomenon of fanfiction with his study of popular rewrites of Jane Austen classics. Finally, Carl Tighe outlines the problems contemporary writers have to face – in learning their craft, in finding inspiration, in negotiating changes in style and use of language, in surviving in the market. The book ends in a brief forward-looking speculation about the challenges faced by popular fiction: as the genre chapters and case studies will have shown, popular fiction has come a long way in the twentieth century. In the increasingly multi-media driven and digitized twenty-first century it faces new challenges that will, inevitably, further reshape our reading experiences and our attitudes towards literature and popular culture.

Works Cited

Akunin, Boris (1998), *The Winter Queen*. London: Phoenix.

—(2007), *Pelagia and the White Bulldog*. London: Phoenix.

Bennett, Tony and Graham Martin (1990), 'Series Editors' Preface', in Tony Bennett (ed.), *Popular Fiction: Technology, Ideology, Production, Reading*. London: Routledge, pp. ix–x.

Bloom, Clive (2002), *Bestsellers: Popular Fiction since 1900*. Basingstoke: Palgrave Macmillan.

Finn, Peter (2006), 'A Case of Crime and Reward: Mystery Writer a Star in Russia'. *Washington Post Foreign Service*, 23 April: n.p., http://www.washingtonpost.com/wp-dyn/content/article/2006/04/22/AR2006042201064.html, accessed 21 November 2013.

Hobson, Charlotte (2003), 'He Wore a Corset of Durable Whalebone'. *The Telegraph*, 27 April: n.p., http://www.telegraph.co.uk/culture/books/3593380/He-wore-a-corset-of-durable-whalebone.html, accessed 21 November 2013.

Jenkins, Henry, Tara McPherson and Jane Shattuc (2002), 'Defining Popular Culture', in H. Jenkins, T. McPherson and J. Shattuc (eds), *Hop on Pop: The Politics and Pleasures of Popular Culture*. Durham, NC: Duke University Press, pp. 26–42.

Keneally, Thomas (1982), *Schindler's Ark*. London: Coronet Books.

McCracken, Scott (1998), *Pulp: Reading Popular Fiction*. Manchester: Manchester University Press.

Mukerji, Chandra and Michael Schudson (1991), 'Introduction: Rethinking Popular Culture', in C. Mukerji and M. Schudson (eds), *Rethinking Popular Culture: Contemporary Perspectives in Cultural Studies*. Berkeley, CA: University of California Press, pp. 1–61.

Nash, Walter (1990), *Language in Popular Fiction*. London: Routledge.

Palmer, Jerry (1991), *Potboilers. Methods, Concepts and Case Studies in Popular Fiction*. London: Routledge.

Pawling, Christopher (1984), 'Introduction: Popular Fiction: Ideology or Utopia?', in C. Pawling (ed.), *Popular Fiction and Social Change*. Basingstoke: Macmillan, pp. 1–19.

Thornhill, John (2013), 'Lunch with the FT: Boris Akunin'. *Financial Times: ft.com/life & arts*, 1 March: n.p., http://www.ft.com/cms/s/2/77f7ca96-80d4-11e2-9c5b-00144feabdc0.html#axzz2lHzBNP5f, accessed 21 November 2013.

Williams, Raymond (1976), Keywords: A Vocabulary of Culture and Society. London: Fontana/Croom Helm.

Part I

History

1

The Victorian Context: Serialization, Circulation, Genres

Christopher Pittard

Introduction

In George Orwell's 1939 novel *Coming up for Air*, the middle-aged narrator George Bowling revisits memories of his pastoral childhood, an escape from the rapid developments of urban modernism. Bowling's development is rendered in terms of reading Victorian popular fiction: he recalls reading 'boys' penny weeklies – little thin papers with vile print and an illustration in three colours on the cover – and a bit later it was books. *Sherlock Holmes, Dr Nikola, The Iron Pirate, Dracula, Raffles*' (1990, 90). Later, Bowling refers to his 'Dick Donovan days' (1990, 125), a reference to the late Victorian writer of crime fiction representing an earlier stage of cultural development.

Bowling's memories not only demonstrate the importance of Victorian popular culture as a source – and demonized other – of modernism but also repeat the terms in which popular fiction was viewed as a site of suspicion by guardians of a higher culture. No account of popular fiction can afford to overlook the Victorians, because the period provided much of the modern apparatus of popular culture, for instance developing the terms of genres such as detective and science fiction, and the alignment of such texts with commodity culture and excessive consumption. The nineteenth century saw not only the birth of modern popular literature, but also of the popularity of literature more widely: between 1800 and 1825, about 580 books were published annually, rising to over 2,600 by the middle of the century and over 6,000 by 1900 (Davis 2002, 201). That modern indicator of popularity, the bestseller list, was a Victorian creation, first appearing in the journal the *Bookman* in 1895; likewise, the cult of authorial celebrity and literary merchandizing took hold from the mid-century: by the *fin de siècle* interviews with authors were a regular feature of popular journals like *The Strand Magazine*. Study of the Victorian period allows us to historicize our concepts of popular fiction: Charles Dickens, a recurrent figure in this chapter, may now be considered a central figure of the Western canon, yet in the nineteenth century was closely associated with the realm of popular literature and, as Juliet John has shown, mass culture. An understanding of the politics and poetics of these categories therefore needs to understand their historical contexts.

The discussion that follows will be split into two mutually informing sections. In the first half, I consider the modes of dissemination of Victorian popular fiction, in particular the influences of serialization and the institutions through which novels were circulated. These are not incidental circumstances but have a real impact on the development of popular culture between 1837 and 1901. In the second half, I move from questions of production and publication to those of genre, outlining the key forms of popular fiction as they developed in the nineteenth century.

Serialization and Circulation

The single-volume novel, purchased from a dedicated bookseller as a discrete artefact, is a comparatively recent invention. The pre-twentieth-century history of popular fiction is one of serialization, a form of publication dating back to the seventeenth century and reinvented in the early nineteenth century. In the first half of the century, many novels were published as separate instalments known as numbers. The prominent author working in this mode was Charles Dickens, nine of whose novels were published in 20 monthly instalments of 32 pages (not including the extensive advertising sections included in each number) that sold at a shilling each. The final two numbers were usually packaged together as a double issue, but this format still necessitated a lengthy commitment from readers. Yet John Sutherland notes that, despite Dickens' enormous popular success and the distinctive mode of publication (allowing for a prototypical form of literary brand identity; the green cover of a Dickens number was immediately recognizable), monthly serialization in this fashion only accounted for a small proportion of Victorian publishing, with only 15 part-issued shilling serials a year in 1837, falling to five in the 1840s, and only one by 1870, Dickens' unfinished *The Mystery of Edwin Drood* (Sutherland 1995, 87). While Dickens made a success of this mode, by the mid-nineteenth century it had fallen out of fashion, and a new mode of serialization took its place.

From the 1850s, novels were increasingly serialized as weekly or monthly instalments in newspapers and magazines, where the text would share space with a wealth of other material. There were material reasons for such a shift: newspaper tax had been reduced to a penny stamp in 1836, allowing for expansion in newspaper and periodical printing; production accelerated with the repeal of the tax in 1855. As an example of this rapid expansion, in 1864, *Mitchell's Newspaper Press Directory* listed 1,764 periodicals published in the UK; this had risen to 3,597 by 1887 (Davis 2002, 202). The sheer expansion in the periodical press makes any survey of it necessarily selective; key titles in the market for serialized fiction included *The Argosy* (1865–1901), *Temple Bar* (1860–1906) (these journals being particularly associated with sensation fiction) and the newspapers the *Illustrated London News* (established in 1842) and the *Graphic* (1869–1932). Again, Dickens was a key figure: his twopenny papers *Household Words* (1850–9) and *All the Year Round* (1859–95) serialized a number of prominent novels, including Elizabeth Gaskell's *Cranford* (1851) and *North and South* (1855), both in *Household Words*; *All the Year Round* saw a shift towards tales of crime, sensation and the supernatural, including Wilkie Collins' *The Woman in White* (1860) and *The Moonstone* (1868), Charles Reade's *Hard Cash* (1863) and Edward Bulwer-Lytton's *A Strange Story* (1862).

Far from being an incidental feature of distribution, the breaking up of narratives into regularly released segments had a discernible effect on their interpretation and the cultural work they performed. Serialization could amplify the underlying political ideology of a text; as John Sutherland notes, while the serialization of Harriet Martineau's *Illustrations of Political Economy* (1832) embodied a somewhat patronizing instinct to spread the economic and intellectual demands made upon 'readers of a distinctly lower class than the author', by contrast, the regularity of instalments of Dickens' novels foregrounded equality and community (Sutherland 1995, 89). This sense of community also had implications for national identity; while booksellers had suffered in the economic slump of the 1830s and had reduced their provincial distribution networks, newspapers and magazines offered a more flexible and truly nationwide medium (Sutherland 1995, 90). Novels no longer had to be sold through the regulated, London-centric book trade; their instalments could be found at any venue that sold newspapers, a rapid distribution that outstripped more conventional modes of book dissemination. Serialization may have created reading communities of people waiting for the next instalment, but it was also an important component of what Benedict Anderson calls the 'imagined community' of nationhood. Yet while critics such as Krishan Kumar (2003) have discussed Victorian literature as being a formative influence on national identity, such studies tend to reinforce the category of the literary canon. One example from late Victorian culture, however, vividly illustrates the influence of popular culture (and its serialization) in forming national identity. Arthur Conan Doyle, while writing series fiction for *The Strand Magazine* (discussed in more detail below) in the 1890s and 1900s, took a trip to the European continent, later writing that 'Foreigners used to recognise the English by their check suits. I think they will soon learn to do it by their *Strand Magazines*. Everybody on the Channel boat, except the man at the wheel, was clutching one' (quoted in Pound 1966, 63). 'Clutching' is an intriguing choice of verb; in the liminal space of the channel, the English urgently hold on to their identity through vehicles of popular culture.

The serial form of the Victorian popular novel also reinforced a certain kind of capitalist ideology. Linda K. Hughes and Michael Lund argue that the serial novel fulfilled middle-class desires for cheap luxury, and that 'the part [of a novel] was a thing to be had for the time being, yet also promised more to come, and the richness of detail and expansion of the text over time suggested a world of plenitude' (1991, 4). Serialization thus simultaneously embodied both the here-and-now of ownership – the reader possessed the material form of the instalment as a commodity – and the promise of later (narrative) returns associated with investment and middle-class values of delayed gratification. Hughes and Lund likewise compare the Victorian fashion for serialized fiction to the expanded timeframes suggested by evolutionary models explained by Charles Darwin in *On the Origin of Species* (1859); both depend on the gradual development of a narrative over time, forming into a certain pattern of significance (1991, 8). There are limits to how far this analogy can be taken – the serialized novel was, ultimately, a designed system with a particular narrative goal, whereas Darwinian natural selection is not an end-oriented process – but the point about how the material form of fiction in the nineteenth century harmonized with wider thinking about society, economics and science is a useful one.

Once a novel had completed its run as a serial, its next manifestation was in volume form. Most novels in the mid-nineteenth century were published in three-volume editions (the so-called triple decker), priced at 10s 6d per volume, or 31s 6d for the complete text. This pricing scheme, inaugurated in 1821 with the publication of Walter Scott's *Kenilworth*, remained stable (to a degree that seems unusual today) until the mid-1890s (Roberts 2006, 1). At its height in the mid-nineteenth century, however, the three-volume novel was prohibitively expensive for much of its readership, and thus the dominant paradigm of mid-Victorian volume reading habits was not one of ownership but of borrowing. The key institution in this respect was Mudie's Select Library, established in 1842 by Charles Mudie. Mudie's business model was simple: customers, having paid an annual subscription of one guinea, could borrow as many volumes as they wanted from one of the many branches established in London, Birmingham and Manchester. The only restriction was that only one volume could be borrowed at a time, both to maintain circulation and to allow the same novel to be lent to three readers simultaneously.

Mudie's practice of investing heavily in new stock made the library a valuable concern for publishers, who were able to increase their print runs and extend their catalogue of novels, since the Select Library offered a virtually guaranteed audience. In return, Mudie could negotiate substantial discounts on the otherwise expensive triple decker (Roberts 2006, 2). The co-dependence of publishers and Mudie's Select Library was brought into focus in the early 1860s when publishers such as Blackwood's and Longmans co-operated to keep the library financially viable after a cashflow problem caused by Mudie's business practice of investing heavily in circulating stock and opening new branches (Finkelstein 1993, 21). But this relationship also gave Mudie's Select Library a disproportionate amount of power in determining the success or failure of a novel, and indeed Mudie saw the library as functioning as a kind of moral censor, refusing to stock material deemed immoral or controversial. This was a serious threat; a novel not made available through the library would almost certainly fail to reach a wider readership. The author George Moore, incensed by Mudie's exclusion of his novel *A Modern Lover* (1883) on moral grounds, launched a notorious attack on the institution in his pamphlet *Literature at Nurse* (1885). While Moore's argument was that Mudie's standards of morality were Puritanical, inconsistently applied and had consequences for artistry (Moore claimed to write on behalf of authors 'whose artistic aspirations are being crushed beneath the wheels of these implacable Juggernauts' [1885, 4], the circulating libraries), there was a class element to his critique. Moore argued that 'All I seek to prove is how absurd and how futile is the censorship which a mere tradesman assumes to exercise over the literature of the nineteenth century, and how he overrules the decisions of the entire English press' (1885, 17). Moore's disdain for the 'mere tradesman' indicates an investment in Romantic ideals of literature as existing beyond the marketplace, of 'Literature' with a capital 'L' as opposed to fiction determined either by the vagaries of popular taste or by the demands of the moral censor. This was to be 'Literature' in the same vein as Matthew Arnold famously defined 'culture' in *Culture and Anarchy,* as 'a pursuit of our total perfection by means of getting to know, on all matters which most concern us, the best which has been thought and said in the world' (190), a category that could hardly be said to coincide with the popular culture sold – and bought – by the market and the masses.

It is tempting to see Mudie as dictating the terms of mid-Victorian reading, and while his influence on the form, content and dissemination of Victorian literature was significant, his reach was not all powerful. Although some competitors in the circulating library market were easily seen off (the Library Company Ltd, for instance, which was founded in 1862 and went bankrupt in 1864 [Finkelstein 1993, 22]), others had greater staying power. The passing of the Public Libraries Act in 1850 saw the rise of free libraries; in the same year, there were almost 610 mechanics' institute libraries, with a circulation of 1,820,000 volumes each year (Davis 2002, 208). Mudie's most significant competitor, however, was W. H. Smith, a company dating from the later eighteenth century, which had established its first railway bookstall at Euston station in 1848, and later expanding into a lending library service in 1860 with 185 nationwide branches by 1862. W. H. Smith's success was partially due to its location; the railway was increasingly becoming the predominant venue for the reading of popular fiction (as Andrew Lang put it in 'Realism and Romance' [1887], 'However much we may intellectually prefer the old books, the good books, the classics, we find ourselves reading the books of the railway stall' [Lang 2000, 99]). W. H. Smith were especially successful in their collaboration with the publishers Chapman and Hall in producing 'yellowbacks', reprints of popular novels sold at two shillings each, a range which encompassed both popular fiction and titles that would eventually enter the literary canon (such as Hugo, Twain and Balzac).

The yellowback is in many ways paradigmatic of mid-Victorian popular culture, in that it crystallized a number of concerns about readership and cultural consumption. The first of these, described in more detail below, was the tendency of the yellowbacks to feature controversial material; sympathetic portrayals of crime were one such theme, but the yellowbacks also offered cheap reprints of French novels associated with decadence and moral turpitude. When, in Mary Elizabeth Braddon's *Lady Audley's Secret* (1862) the hero Robert Audley is described as reading French novels (Braddon 1998, 35), his choice of reading matter indicates a certain kind of louche effeminacy. But the yellowback, in its very title, played on the proximity between popular fiction and questions of materiality. Just as the twentieth-century term 'pulp fiction' referred to the rough paper stock on which such fiction was produced, the name 'yellowback' was a literal description of the appearance of these reprints, the yellow colour scheme of the wrapping relieved only by the novel's title (more often than not in bold red type) and a lurid cover, usually depicting a key dramatic moment in the text and consciously designed to grab the eye of the railway station browser (in contrast to the monumental and solemn spaces of Mudie's branches, in which texts were unostentatiously bound; while there was some overlap of audience between Smith's and Mudie's, these audiences were targeted in very different ways). Such novels, printed and sold cheaply, were not built to last, and relatively few survive today in proportion to their popularity and rate of production. The connection between the physical quality of such texts and the morality of their contents was a regular theme of critics of popular culture; for instance, in 1874 the journalist James Greenwood conducted an investigation into what he termed 'Penny Packets of Poison' (that is, penny dreadfuls, discussed below). Greenwood bought 12 of these publications and examined them closely, in terms of both content and, strikingly, physical form:

> Nasty-feeling, nasty-looking packets are every one of them, and, considering the virulent nature of their contents, their most admirable feature is their extremely limited size. Satisfactory as this may be from one point of view, however, it is woefully significant of the irresistibly seductive nature of the

bane with which each shabby little square of paper is spread. I have been at pains to weigh them, and I find that the weight of each pen'orth is but a fraction more than *a quarter of an ounce*. The 'Leisure Hour' weighs nearly eight times as much, as do the 'Family Herald' and one or two other penny publications of a decent sort. (1976, 358)

Here, moral and artistic quality becomes equated to physical weight, the 'shabby little square of paper' compared unfavourably with such solidly made and respectable periodicals as *The Leisure Hour* (1852–1905) and the *Family Herald* (1843–1940). Greenwood's methodology may seem to anticipate more recent work in book history, cultural materialism and thing theory, in which the physical manifestations of the text are not mere incidentals but crucial aspects of the experience of reading and interpretation. Yet there is a dimension of moral judgement in Greenwood's analysis missing from more theorized models of reading the object, and likewise an unspoken hierarchy between popular and canonical culture determines his analysis. The novels of (for instance) George Eliot were rarely, if ever, reviewed in such materialist terms, and even if a particularly handsome edition was commented upon, this was certainly not taken as a reflection on its literary content. Even though Greenwood contrasts the penny dreadful to the more 'decent' *Leisure Hour*, he still compares one example of popular literature with another. In *Culture and Anarchy* (1869) Matthew Arnold had written of high culture and its effects in ethereal terms of 'sweetness and light'; popular fiction, by contrast, remained a resolutely physicalized experience.

By the *fin de siècle*, however, serialization, as it had existed in the mid-nineteenth century, was no longer the dominant mode of literary dissemination and was gradually being replaced by one-volume novels (facilitated by advances in printing technology and falling costs in production) and the rise of the short story. Even where journals continued to serialize texts, the nature of serialization was changing. A crucial example of this can be seen in *The Strand Magazine*, launched by the editor George Newnes in December 1890 (the first volume being dated 1891). Newnes had already made a success of magazines such as the miscellany *Tit-Bits* (launched 1881), aimed at the wider readership created in the late nineteenth century by the effects of the 1870 Education Act. While it is easy to overstate the impact of educational reform in creating a new *fin de siècle* audience, it was nonetheless important: in George Gissing's novel of literary life, *New Grub Street* (1891), the editor Whelpdale (modelled loosely on Newnes) describes his market as 'the quarter-educated; that is to say, the great new generation that is being turned out by the Board schools, the young men and women who can just read, but are incapable of sustained attention' (1998, 460). The question of sustained attention was central to Newnes' strategy. He had realized that earlier models of magazine serialization were a double-edged sword: while a successful serialization could guarantee an ongoing readership, it could be potentially alienating for a reader to enter a complex narrative halfway through. Newnes thus developed a different model, one where the same characters would appear from month to month, but in self-contained narratives. This new mode made a distinction between the *serial* and the *series*, and the most famous example of the latter was Arthur Conan Doyle's *The Adventures of Sherlock Holmes* (1891). Holmes had already appeared in two novels, with only moderate success; the short story format, however, secured Doyle's popularity. Likewise, the impact of the *Strand* on popular publishing in the 1890s was profound: it provided the model for several other magazines launched in the last decade of the nineteenth century, including the *Ludgate Monthly* (established 1891), the *Idler* (1892), the *Windsor Magazine* (1895) and the *Harmsworth Magazine* (1898). All combined family-oriented features journalism with popular fiction, developing and reinventing the genres that had proved popular through the nineteenth century.

Popular Genres

What, then, were these genres? At the beginning of Victoria's reign, the dominant forms of popular literature were the sporting papers, tales of the supernatural and narratives of crime. These latter genres drew on the tropes established by Romanticist Gothic, in particular the novels of Ann Radcliffe (such as *A Sicilian Romance* [1790] and *The Mysteries of Udolpho* [1794]), and although sporting narratives emphasized the hale and hearty rather than the deviant and decrepit, the gothic nevertheless found its way into the most famous of these texts, Charles Dickens' first novel, the hugely successful *The Pickwick Papers* (1837). *Pickwick* had originally been intended as a series of illustrations of comic sporting episodes by Robert Seymour with an accompanying text by Dickens, but Seymour's suicide in 1836 allowed Dickens to change the project and to reduce the sporting component in favour of broader adventures. The gothic, however, was never far away in Dickens' popular fictions: it appears in *The Pickwick Papers* most obviously in the famous claim of the 'fat boy' that 'I wants to make your flesh creep' (1986, 179) and in the novel's use of associated genres such as crime fiction in the embedded story 'The Convict's Return'.

Dickens had already written narratives of crime in his earlier collection of stories and journalistic scenes, *Sketches by Boz* (1833–6); one such narrative blending reportage with imagination was 'A Visit to Newgate', a tour of the infamous London prison starting with factual accounts of its condition, appearance and inhabitants, and concluding with a remarkable fictionalized account of the thoughts of a prisoner awaiting execution (a theme Dickens would return to in *Oliver Twist* [1837]). Dickens chose his subject wisely; Newgate occupied a prominent place in the cultural imagination of the early nineteenth century, not least in the popular subgenre of the 'Newgate Novel', a collection of fictionalized accounts of the lives of criminals whose deeds had already been recorded in the *Newgate Calendar* (a moralizing series of narratives detailing the crimes and punishment of inmates). Where the *Calendar* sought to teach a moral lesson, the Newgate novel had a tendency to make the criminal the sympathetic hero. The most prominent writer of such fiction was Edward Bulwer-Lytton, whose works *Paul Clifford* (1830) and *Eugene Aram* (1832) caused controversy in their supposedly glamorizing portrayal of criminals. A similar controversy dogged William Harrison Ainsworth's novel *Jack Sheppard* (1839), a hugely popular crime serial first published in *Bentley's Miscellany*.

Closely related to the Newgate novel, but largely aimed at a younger audience, was the penny dreadful, a term denoting less a specific periodical format than a wide expanse of populist material published from the 1840s onwards and dealing primarily with narratives of transgression and criminality. As John Springhall points out, there was a class dimension to this generic labelling, demonstrating 'how an increasingly puritanical middle class came to misrepresent or distort the nature of popular reading, to feed a fear of working-class cultural activities that they had themselves helped initiate' (1994, 331). Although the dreadfuls reinvented earlier Gothic narratives of the supernatural (particularly in the case of James Malcolm Rymer's *Varney the Vampire* [1845–7]), the form was closely associated with crime fiction. Like the Newgate novel, penny dreadfuls were seen as an endorsement of criminality, occasionally featuring in criminal trials such as that of Alfred Saunders in 1876, charged with stealing from his father. Saunders' case, and that of popular fiction more widely, was not helped by the admission that he stole the money to buy papers which 'dealt with the adventures of pirates and robbers' (quoted in Springhall 1994, 338). The most successful of these cheap crime serials was G. W. M. Reynolds' *The Mysteries of London* (1845–55), a startlingly expansive narrative taking in body-snatching, violent crime and disturbingly (for an early Victorian readership) republican sentiment. The importance of Reynolds' serial lies not only in its massive popularity (selling a million copies in its 10 years) or extensive range but also in its delineation of the gradations of popular fiction, from the respectable to the sensationalist. Dickens made his opinion clear in 1859 when he described Reynolds' serial as 'bestiality' written under the pretence of being 'a story of incident' (quoted in Slater 2009, 470). Dickens himself had already laid the foundations for later popular fictions of crime: his novel *Bleak House* (1852–3) features Inspector Bucket, the first major appearance of a police detective in English literature.

The question of the uses of popular fiction, and its implications for an emergent concept of 'cultural health,' became more urgent by the 1860s. By this point, a new genre had emerged which moved crime from the streets to the home and which located deviance not in urban delinquents but in the middle-class family. Novels such as Wilkie Collins' *The Woman in White* (1860), *No Name* (1862) and *Armadale* (1866), and Mary Elizabeth Braddon's *Lady Audley's Secret, John Marchmont's Legacy* (1862) and *Aurora Floyd* (1863) were grouped together under the term the 'sensation novel', a genre Kathleen Tillotson famously defines in epistemological terms as a 'novel with a secret' (Tillotson 1969, xvi), usually one relating to bigamy, fraud and madness. The term 'sensation fiction' had a double meaning. Such novels were commercial sensations, selling thousands of copies, and marked the creation of a reading community that, dangerously, crossed boundaries of class (as W. Fraser Rae put it in 1865, sensation fiction had succeeded in 'making the literature of the Kitchen the favourite reading of the Drawing room' [1865, 204]). This led to the accusation that authors like Collins and Braddon wrote novels solely to answer commercial demand. As Henry Mansel argued in the *Quarterly Review*: 'No divine influence can be imagined as presiding over the birth of his [the sensation novelist's] work, beyond the market-law of demand and supply; no more immortality is dreamed of for it than the fashions of the current season ... [such novels are] called into existence to supply the cravings of a diseased appetite' (1863, 483). Mansel's bodily metaphors suggest the second meaning of sensation, the aim of these novels being to elicit a physical sensation in their readership, a reinvention of the shocks of late-eighteenth-century gothic and of the flesh-creeping ambitions of Dickens' fat boy. Sensation fiction created a physiological rather than a cerebral reaction, a distinction between feeling and the process of thinking that would characterize later detective fiction.

Sensation fiction provides a particularly useful example for the study of Victorian popular culture, because the extensive debates surrounding its propriety, its sympathetic portrayals of deviance and criminality, and its suspicious proximity to the demands of the market consolidated the terms of earlier Victorian questions about popular fiction. Like the debates on the Newgate novel or the penny dreadful, critics of the sensation novel relied on the creation of a passive reader, one who would fall prey to the thrills of the narrative. Such a debate can be theorized through Pierre Bourdieu's work on how cultural taste legitimates social and class differences. In his discussion of modern culture, Bourdieu identifies two broad categories of response: the 'taste of reflection', an educated, objective and detached form of reading, and the 'taste of sense', which is uneducated and subjective (1989, 6–7). Reflective readers are not wholly seduced by the pleasures of the text, whereas sensational readers give themselves up and become passive receptors of that text's political unconscious. In terms of the sensation novel and Victorian popular culture more widely, Barbara Leckie has compared the category of readers of sense to the Victorian idea of 'vulnerable' readers, a category that inevitably included women, the young and the working class, all seen as susceptible to the moral threat of popular fiction (Leckie 1999, 23). Although more recent criticism (by Kate Flint and Jennifer Phlegley) has noted how sensation fiction made a case for female reading as an active and reflective response, the sensation novel was nevertheless seen as a threat to be policed by those readers (usually middle-class men) who were supposedly able to resist the temptations of narrative.

The sensation novel is usually closely associated with the 1860s, although one might point to the persistence of the genre into the 1870s and early 1880s (especially with Collins' later works), or alternatively note that by 1870 the shift from sensation to detective fiction was already well under way, as exemplified by Collins' *The Moonstone* (1868). The history of the development of detective fiction in the later nineteenth century is dominated by the figures of Arthur Conan Doyle and Sherlock Holmes, whose careers are sufficiently well documented to avoid detailing here. But such a history, however seductive, overlooks the conditions of production and of reception of popular fiction in the 1880s and 1890s. The first appearance of Holmes, in *A Study in Scarlet* (1887), was only a modest commercial and critical success; his second appearance, in *The Sign of Four* (1890), fared marginally better, and as noted above, it was not until Holmes appeared in the *Strand* in 1891 that his success was assured. The biggest sensation of the late Victorian period was not Doyle, but rather Fergus Hume's *The Mystery of a Hansom Cab* (1886; published in the UK in 1887). Hume's novel is best understood as a transition between the familial secrets of the sensation novel and the ratiocination of detective fiction, ending the process that started with *The Moonstone*; although Hume's novel starts with a body discovered in a Melbourne cab, the murder plot is not the real focus, and the interest of the novel turns on the mystery of the prosperous Frettlby family and the bigamous secrets that connect them to the Melbourne slums. The *Illustrated London News* reported that *The Mystery of a Hansom Cab* had enjoyed British sales of 300,000 copies in less than 6 months, and by October 1888, it was still selling thousands of copies weekly; the *News* commented that 'Persons were found everywhere eagerly devouring the realistic sensational tale of Melbourne social life. Whether travelling by road, rail, or river the unpretending little volume was ever present in some companion's or stranger's hands' (Anon. 1888a, 410). Hume had created not only a publishing phenomenon, but also a reading community, a feat he struggled to replicate in later crime novels such as *Madame Midas* (1888) and adventure narratives such as *The Blue Talisman* (1912). Hume's dedication to the novel form (some short stories for the *Idler* aside) may have played a part in his lack of subsequent success; from the 1890s to the early twentieth century, the periodical short story was the dominant form of detective fiction. The relationship between the genre and *The Strand Magazine* was symbiotic: in the 1890s the *Strand* featured crime stories by Arthur Morrison, Grant Allen, L. T. Meade, Robert Eustace and Dick Donovan, built upon the commercial success secured by Doyle's fiction; the serialization of *The Hound of the Baskervilles* in 1902 gave the *Strand* added sales of 30,000 copies (Jackson 2001, 93). Rather than being sensationalist narratives of crime, these stories kept the promise George Newnes had made in the very first issue of the *Strand*; to provide nothing but 'cheap, healthful literature' (Newnes 1891, 1).

Newnes' idea of 'healthful' literature and the *Illustrated London News'* image of readers 'devouring' Hume's text are noteworthy. Victorian detective fiction, like much popular fiction, was figured as a commodity, to be consumed and discarded. An article in *The Pall Mall Gazette*, 'The Function of Detective Stories' (1888), emphasized these ephemeral qualities:

> Detective stories are not things to be sipped at and lingered over; they must be swallowed at one great gulp. . . . In the five minutes' interval between closing the book and forgetting it, we should say to ourselves 'That's a good story,' or 'A first-rate story,' or 'An A1 story,' according to our mood and our vocabulary; if any more particular or exhaustive criticism suggests itself, the book is not a perfect specimen of its class. (Anon. 1888b, 3)

This paragraph consolidates a number of modern prejudices against popular fiction, starting with the correlation of reading popular fiction with the act of physical consumption: before junk food, there was junk fiction. More significantly, however, popular fiction appears here as the antithesis of criticism; fiction which can be submitted to 'exhaustive analysis' is not, by definition, popular. Finally, the detective novel is imprisoned within the constraints of genre, couched in the late Victorian language of eugenics ('a perfect specimen of its class'); its greatest successes are those novels that remain precisely within the conditions of genre. There is, however, an irony in this article appearing in *The Pall Mall Gazette* at this historical moment: at the same moment that it was criticizing detective fiction in terms borrowed from Arnoldian ideals of high culture, the *Gazette* was also a major source of sensationalist reportage on the Whitechapel murders in the autumn of 1888.

The other major generic development of the later nineteenth century was the rise of modern science fiction, exemplified by the work of H. G. Wells. The very concept of science fiction was a characteristically Victorian one: the term itself was coined by William Wilson in 1851 in his *A Little Earnest Book upon a Great Old Subject*. The year is fitting: the 1851 national census had revealed that for the first time the majority of the population in the UK now lived in urban rather than rural spaces, while in the same year the Great Exhibition offered a utopian vision of technological advancement. Wilson's term, while seemingly contradictory (one might, not unproblematically, oppose the 'fact' of science to the 'fancy' of fiction), was of a piece with the wider convergence between Victorian narrative fiction and scientific enquiry. To take two examples, George Eliot's *Middlemarch* (1871), a post-Darwinian portrait of a pre-Darwinian community, contrasted differing modes of scientific knowledge, while Thomas Hardy's *A Pair of Blue Eyes* (1873) offers a literally cliffhanging episode in which the hero discovers a trilobite fossil and muses on the implications of the new timescales unfolded by nineteenth-century evolutionary biology and geology. But as Gillian Beer has argued, the interplay between Victorian fiction and science was not a one-way influence; novelists may have drawn on scientific enquiry, but biologists such as Darwin had presented their discoveries by using narrative techniques of rhetoric and metaphor.

If novels such as those by Eliot and Hardy were 'science fiction' in a sense of interplay between these two terms, the later nineteenth century saw the rise of what Wells called the 'scientific romance'. Earlier texts such as Mary Shelley's *Frankenstein* (1818), Bulwer-Lytton's *A Strange Story*, the short stories of Edgar Allan Poe and Jules Verne's *Journey to the Centre of the Earth*

(1862) and *Twenty Thousand Leagues under the Sea* (1870) had presented fantastical science fiction plots, but Wells' *fin de siècle* methodology was more naturalistic, if not necessarily explanatory. As Wells put it, 'It occurred to me that instead of the usual interview with the devil, or a magician, an ingenious use of scientific patter might with advantage be substituted. . . . I simply brought the fetish stuff up to date, and made it as near actual theory as possible' (quoted in Brantlinger 1988, 234–5). Thus while time travel had been used as a plot device in texts such as Edward Bellamy's *Looking Backward* (1888) and William Morris' *News from Nowhere* (1890), both of these had gestured towards mesmerism or dreaming to explain the extraordinary events of the narrative. By contrast, Wells' *The Time Machine* (1895) focused on the mechanized process of time travel and rejected the utopic visions of Bellamy and Morris in favour of a more dystopic extrapolation of concerns about evolutionary degeneration. The time traveller of Wells' novel travels into the far future to find humanity divided into the decadent Eloi and the degenerate Morlocks, and while the narrator sides with the Eloi, Wells resists any easy judgement on the superiority of one race over the other. The Morlocks may be illiterate and bestial, but the Eloi are childlike, superstitious and weak. Here, Wells satirically maps late Victorian concerns over class onto concerns about the direction of evolution. Bellamy and Morris, in their own distinct ways, suggest a model of evolution and historical change that tended towards progress and perfection, influenced by Herbert Spencer's model of biological evolution as improvement; Wells, on the other hand, realized that Darwin's model of biological change never implied values or a direction of movement. In this regard, much science fiction of the *fin de siècle* reflected the pessimism that had replaced the evolutionary optimism of the 1860s. By the 1880s, the other side of the narrative of progress held cultural sway; if cultures and bodies were demonstrated to have evolved from prior states of being, did this not also imply the possibility of regression and decay? Two texts, both taking *Degeneration* as their title, summed up this current of thought. Max Nordau's *Degeneration* (1892) found evidence of artistic degeneracy in the art of the Pre-Raphaelite brotherhood, the naturalist novels of Zola and the plays of Ibsen, while Edwin Ray Lankester's *Degeneration: A Chapter in Darwinism* (1880) considered more biological manifestations of decay.

If science fiction had a tendency to focus on the future, the closely related genre of imperial adventure presented a different kind of time travel. Late Victorian depictions of empire, Anne McClintock argues, depended on colonized territories being seen as anachronistic spaces, existing in some previous time zone; thus, 'imperial progress across the space of empire is figured as a journey back in time to an anachronistic moment of prehistory. . . . Geographical difference across *space* is figured as a historical difference across *time*' (1995, 40). The key figure here is H. Rider Haggard, beginning with *King Solomon's Mines* (1885), but the themes of imperial decay and gender anxieties implicit in this novel become explicit in his next, *She* (1887), describing the discovery of a near-immortal empress who rules by fear and wishes to depose Queen Victoria as head of the British Empire. Patrick Brantlinger identifies novels like *She* as belonging to a subgenre of 'imperial gothic', a term which (like science fiction) has a certain contradictory quality, in this case contrasting the Darwinian scientific underpinning of imperialism with a fascination with the occult. Brantlinger identifies three conditions of imperial gothic: the threats of 'individual regression or going native; an invasion of civilization by the forces of barbarism or demonism; and the diminution of opportunities for adventure and heroism in the modern world' (1988, 230). The threat of individual regression clearly relates to the degenerationist concerns addressed by Wells and other science fiction authors, while the invasion plot was a key concern of not only imperial gothic, but also *fin de siècle* gothic and science fiction more widely. Novels such as Wells' *The War of the Worlds* (1897), Richard Marsh's *The Beetle* (1897) and Bram Stoker's *Dracula* (1897) all played out fears of modern Britain (in Wells's text, standing in for the world) invaded by exterior, savage forces. Yet in relation to Brantlinger's third condition, there is a sense in these novels that modernity has lost a sense of adventure that can only be recovered through the (re)appearance of the ancient or the other. Andrew Lang, the dedicatee of *She*, made this point clear in 'Realism and Romance': popular fiction is such because it bypasses the intellectual responses of canonical realism and (for Lang) speaks directly to a pre-civilized desire for narrative excitement. While much popular fiction of the nineteenth century demonized the savage and the other, for Lang the success of such fictions depended on the exploitation of such states.

Conclusion

Returning to Orwell by way of conclusion, George Bowling recalls joining Mudie's Select Library:

> And what I read during the next year or so! Wells, Conrad, Kipling, Galsworthy, Barry Pain, W. W. Jacobs, Pett Ridge, Oliver Onions, Compton

Mackenzie, H. Seton Merriman, Maurice Baring, Stephen McKenna, May Sinclair, Arnold Bennett, Anthony Hope, Elinor Glyn, O. Henry, Stephen Leacock, and even Silas Hocking and Gene Stratton Porter. (Orwell 1990, 125)

Bowling ends this list of popular Victorian and Edwardian writers with a challenge: 'How many of the names in that list are known to you, I wonder?' (Orwell 1990, 125). He raises two methodological points in the study of Victorian fiction. The first is the attempt to situate popular fiction in its historical context, to try to recover a literary network in which Silas Hocking is a household name (as indeed he was). The second, and somewhat more difficult task, is to register the sheer plenitude of Victorian popular fiction. This chapter has only been able to offer a partial introduction to these riches and could easily have included discussion of Ouida's romances or the visionary popular fiction of Marie Corelli; even the survey of Victorian crime fiction might have been extended to such obscure titles as Ben Hayward's *All Else of No Avail* (1888) (a novel anticipating Doyle's more famous 'The Final Problem' [1894] in its destruction of both detective and criminal at Niagara Falls). Such novels are largely forgotten now and only recalled to us through the review pages of the Victorian press, and they provide a sobering reflection on how our understanding of nineteenth-century culture continues to be mediated through ideas of canonicity and what constitutes a text worthy of reprinting. The increasing availability of previously obscure texts through digital humanities projects will no doubt have an effect on how we understand and gain access to the popular culture of the nineteenth century. Yet there are also costs associated with such projects. This opening of the vast resources of Victorian popular fiction through digitization, valuable though it is, may end up obscuring the terms in which such fictions were discussed: as material artefacts and as physical pleasures.

Works Cited

Anderson, B. (1991), *Imagined Communities*, rev. edn. London: Verso.

Anon. (1888a), 'The Author of Madame Midas'. *Illustrated London News*, 6 October, 410.

—(1888b), 'The Function of Detective Stories'. *Pall Mall Gazette*, 22 September, 3.

Arnold, M. (1993), *Culture and Anarchy and Other Writings*. Cambridge: Cambridge University Press.

Beer, G. (2000), *Darwin's Plots: Evolutionary Narrative in Darwin, George Eliot and Nineteenth-Century Fiction*, 2nd edn. Cambridge: Cambridge University Press.

Bourdieu, P. (1989), *Distinction: A Social Critique of the Judgement of Taste*, trans. Richard Nice. London: Routledge.

Braddon, M. E. (1998), *Lady Audley's Secret*. London: Penguin.

Brantlinger, P. (1988), *Rule of Darkness: British Literature and Imperialism 1830-1914*. Ithaca: Cornell University Press.

Davis, P. (2002), *The Oxford English Literary History Volume 8: The Victorians*. Oxford: Oxford University Press.

Dickens, C. (1986), *The Pickwick Papers*. London: Penguin.

Finkelstein, D. (1993), '"The Secret": British Publishers and Mudie's Struggle for Economic Survival 1861-64'. *Publishing History* 34, 21–50.

Flint, K. (1993), *The Woman Reader 1837-1914*. Oxford: Clarendon.

Gissing, G. (1998), *New Grub Street*. Oxford: Oxford University Press.

Greenwood, J. (1976), 'Penny Packets of Poison', in P. Haining (ed.), *The Penny Dreadful: Or, Strange, Horrid and Sensational Tales!*. London: Victor Gollancz, pp. 357–71.

Hughes, L. K. and Lund, M. (1991), *The Victorian Serial*. Charlottesville: University Press of Virginia.

Jackson, K. (2001), *George Newnes and the New Journalism in Britain 1880-1910: Culture and Profit*. Aldershot: Ashgate.

John, J. (2010), *Dickens and Mass Culture*. Oxford: Oxford University Press.

Kumar, K. (2003), *The Making of English National Identity*. Cambridge: Cambridge University Press.

Lang, A. (2000), 'Realism and Romance', in S. Ledger and R. Luckhurst (eds), *The fin de siècle: A Reader in Cultural History c.1880-1900*. Oxford: Oxford University Press, pp. 99–104.

Leckie, B. (1999), *Culture and Adultery: The Novel, the Newspaper, and the Law 1857-1914*. Philadelphia: University of Pennsylvania Press.

McClintock, A. (1995), *Imperial Leather: Race, Gender and Sexuality in the Colonial Contest*. London: Routledge.

Mansel, H. L. (1863), 'Sensation Novels'. *Quarterly Review* 113, 481–514.

Moore, G. (1885), *Literature at Nurse, or Circulating Morals*. London: Vizetelly.

Newnes, G. (1891), 'Introduction'. *The Strand Magazine* 1, 3.

Orwell, G. (1990), *Coming Up for Air*. London: Penguin.

Phlegley, J. (2004), *Educating the Proper Woman Reader: Victorian Family Literary Magazines and the Cultural Health of the Nation*. Columbus: Ohio State University Press.

Pound, R. (1966), *The Strand Magazine 1891-1950*. London: Heinemann.

Rae, W. F. (1865), 'Sensation Novelists: Miss Braddon'. *North British Review* 43, 180–204.

Roberts, L. (2006), 'Trafficking in Literary Authority: Mudie's Select Library and the Commodification of the Victorian Novel'. *Victorian Literature and Culture* 34, 1–25.

Slater, M. (2009), *Charles Dickens: A Life Defined by Writing.* New Haven: Yale University Press.

Springhall, J. (1994), 'Pernicious Reading? The "Penny Dreadful" as Scapegoat for Late-Victorian Juvenile Crime'. *Victorian Periodicals Review* 27(4), 326–49.

Sutherland, J. (1995), *Victorian Fiction: Writers, Publishers, Readers.* Basingstoke: Palgrave.

Tillotson, K. (1969), 'The Lighter Reading of the Eighteen-Sixties', introduction to W. Collins, *The Woman in White.* Boston: Houghton Mifflin, pp. ix–xxvi.

2

Twentieth-Century Popular: History, Theory and Context

Christine Berberich

The idea of genre, as Christopher Pittard has shown in the preceding chapter, started to evolve in the second half of the nineteenth century. Today, it has become second nature for us to talk about 'different genres': university syllabi offer modules specifically dedicated to 'Crime Fiction' or 'Horror Writing', and bookshops, apart from their general classification into 'Fiction A to Z', offer specialized shelves dedicated to 'Romance', 'Crime', 'Horror' or, more recently, 'Graphic Novels'. But while this differentiation into different genres has become so mundane for all of us as consumers, it is important to understand that this very division into different genres has a history of its own, a history that is intricately linked to the publishing industry, the idea of marketing and, ultimately, the notion of ideology and power. The twentieth century was the century that saw the further success of already existent genres as well as the birth of new ones, experienced the development of a mass market for fiction with its linked means of mass production and witnessed the power struggles between writers and publishers to secure their share of an increasingly cut-throat market. The following chapter will, briefly, outline the history of genre and look at developments in the publishing industry as well as the forces that dominate the market that has led to a veritable and potentially very problematic institutionalization of literature. The second half of the chapter will be given over to some of the more theoretical and often seemingly negative debates surrounding popular culture. No discussion of popular fiction can be complete without a brief mention of its 'other', 'high' fiction in the form and shape of canonical literature. F. R. Leavis' development of a canon of English literature and Q. D. Leavis' discussion of fiction and its markets contributed to the rather limiting division of literature into 'highbrow' and 'lowbrow', and this, in turn, led to discussions about power: who makes the decisions about what is deemed 'high' and what is deemed 'low', and what impact does that have on (a) the market and (b) the literature we buy and read? Critics, as will be shown, are divided when it comes to popular fiction: on the right, they lament the poor taste of popular narrative, the limiting and predictable scope of its formulae that appeal only to the senses and not the intellect; on the left, some celebrate it as a manifestation of the power of the people while others bemoan the fact that the reading public is manipulated by market forces (see, for example, Mukerji and Schudson 1991, 37ff). With so many critics, theorists and thinkers arguing over the relative merits of fiction and debating who holds the power over the 'popular' aspect of it, popular culture and, by extension, popular fiction has, indeed, in the words of Stuart Hall, turned into an ideological 'constant battlefield', a 'cultural struggle' that goes on 'continuously, in the complex lines of resistance and acceptance, refusal and capitulation' (1981, 233). As David Glover and Scott McCracken point out: 'For anyone trying to make sense of the "popular", this tension between what is genuinely a manifestation of popular taste or will and what is imposed upon people by those for whom culture is a business constitutes the central historical dynamic of modern popular culture . . .' (2012, 3). Economic and, by extension, political power is consequently an issue that, as will be seen, cannot be left out of any discussion of popular fiction.

Of Adventurers, Damsels and Space Travellers: Developments in Genre

Genre, as Jerry Palmer points out, is 'the French term commonly used to indicate that texts can be sorted into groups which have common characteristics' (1991, 112). These characteristics – the best known of them all probably the formulaic characteristics of the romance genre: boy meets girl, they overcome an obstacle, they live happily ever after – contribute, according to Palmer, to the readers' 'horizon of expectations' (113) when approaching certain texts: just as romance readers might expect a 'happy' ending, so readers of crime novels will demand a solution to the murder mystery, and readers of science fiction will eagerly scan the pages for tales of future worlds or incredible technological advances. Frederic Jameson points out that 'genres are essentially contracts between a writer and his readers; or rather, to use the term which Claudio Guillen has so usefully revived, they are literary *institutions*, which like no other institutions of social life are based on tacit agreements or contracts' (1975, 135). Clive Bloom asserts that these expectations for certain genres, in particular the romance, the adventure story and detective whodunits, solidified 'between the late 1880s and the 1930s' and that it corresponded to the 'fifty years of modern class consolidation' (2002, 13). Despite this solidification – Bloom points out that 'at the end of the twentieth century the two leading popular genres were the same as at its beginning . . . : detective fiction and women's romance' (13) – and its associated political connotations, there has always been room for development, as, Glover and McCracken assert, 'the reception of . . . genres is in a state of continuous evolution' (2012, 1). While detective fiction and romance have reigned supreme, they have, nevertheless, developed a number of ever-changing and evolving sub-genres, ranging, in the case of detective fiction, from cosy crime to hard-boiled detection or the particular contemporary obsession with Scandic Noir (see also Chapters 6 and 14) and, in the case of romance, evolving from the wishful-thinking pure romance to the edgier chick lit, or the formerly much more marginalized lesbian romance (see also Chapters 3 and 13). Other genres, for example the western, extremely popular in the first half of the twentieth century, have all but vanished in textual narrative, to be replaced by popular film and TV (see also Bloom 2002, 13ff).[1] At the same time, new genres, most prominently the graphic novel (see also Chapter 9), have emerged. The Introduction to this volume has already pointed out the potentially limited shelf-life of popular fiction and the same holds true for individual genres: contemporary Anglophone literature in the 2010s, for example, has seen a proliferation of Vampire writing (see also Chapter 16), whereas the preceding decade had experienced a craze for narratives about wizards and witches (which is also discussed in Chapter 8). What unites both these recent (sub)genres is their ability to transcend age boundaries in that texts initially aimed at child or young adult readers are now also marketed specifically for an adult readership. They also seem to be products very much of and within their time, linked to TV and film adaptations, marketing and a variety of 'spin offs' – until their novelty has worn off, the public's interest in them has been exhausted and they have been replaced by the next trend. Importantly, as Bloom points out, 'whilst different genres have flourished at different times, almost all have the capacity to be recycled, providing they are sufficiently modernised' (2002, 13). This is an important point that highlights the adaptability of individual genres (and, maybe, the inability of others) to reinvent themselves to provide something simultaneously familiar yet also fresh and titillating to new audiences.

While, on a positive note, it could be said that genres are mainly there to aid the reader in the potentially daunting and overwhelming selection process of new reading matter, they also have a different *raison d'être*, and one that is already hinted at by terms such as Palmer's 'horizon of expectations' or Jameson's 'institutionalization' above – for who shapes reader expectations and who benefits from the institutionalization of fiction?

Of Book Clubs, Paperbacks and Richard & Judy: The (Mass) Market and Popular Fiction

While the nineteenth century, as the preceding chapter has shown, was dominated by popular writing in serialized form and saw the meteoric rise of the lending library to facilitate mass *reading* of books, the twentieth century was, in turn, dominated by the idea of mass *ownership* of books. Lending libraries like Mudie's had, towards the end of the nineteenth century, already started to influence the *shape* of published books. The traditional three-decker novel was not practical for lending libraries or the newly emerging train station book stalls pioneered by W. H. Smith; novels became shorter so they could be picked up more easily, to be taken along and read on the new commuter trains, for example (see Bloom 1996, 51ff), a trend continued by today's increasing move towards e-readers. A number of developments went hand in hand in order to accelerate the growth of the publishing industry: by the end of the nineteenth century, for example, British society was almost universally literate. As John Carey has shown, 'a huge literate public had come into being, and consequently every aspect of the production and dissemination of the printed text became subject to revolution' (1992, 5). More readers demanded more, and more diverse, reading matter. David Glover, for example, has illustrated that the number of new novel publications rose from 380 in 1880 to 896 in 1886 and even further to 1,315 in 1895 (2012, 18). New technological advances – for instance the invention of carbon paper or the advent of the typewriter or, later on, the dictation machine – allowed writers to produce new material more quickly (see Bloom 1996, 65ff). But there were also advances in the actual printing process: the increasing popularity of magazines of all kiln had seen the advent of a faster rotary press and quicker drying glue, and these two inventions led, in the 1930s, to the publication of the first mass paperback books (see, for example, Smith 2012, 152) which led to the, in John Sutherland's words, 'paperback revolution of the late 1950s and 1960s' (1978, 20). Through paperback publishing, as Palmer has shown, books became a lot more affordable to readers and 'reading and ownership were easily linked' (1991, 38). In Britain, the paperback revolution is best exemplified with the arrival of Allan Lane's first Penguin Books on the literary scene in 1935. In an interview, Lane himself presented Penguin books as 'the means of converting book-borrowers into book buyers' (http://www.penguin.co.uk/static/cs/uk/0/aboutus/aboutpenguin_companyhistory.html). Lane's initiative, as Ken Worpole has stated, was driven by 'educational zeal' (1984, 87) and Lane biographer W. E. Williams highlights his 'devotion to the concept of Penguin's as the Popular Educator' (in Worpole 1984, 88). But, obviously, this educational premise was also closely linked to the idea of making money.

Printing presses could now manufacture paperback books more easily and more rapidly, but the publishing process still cost money – so the requirement for paperback publications was high sales, not only to established libraries or in traditional bookshops but also in newsagents, supermarkets, at petrol stations or railway termini. The advertising and marketing of books, and raising general awareness of new titles, consequently became more and more important. And this links back to the earlier discussion of genre: publishers released, and marketed, what had previously sold well. Existing formulae were thus pushed further and further and marketed with increasingly familiar terminology (see also Palmer 1991, 39ff; McCracken 1998, 20ff). Once a book had become a bestseller, it found many imitators, as readers, in Walter Nash's previously cited comment, did 'not want [the same book] *again*, though [they] may want *more*' (1990, 2). In publishing and marketing terms this meant identifying likely candidates to emulate the bestseller status of another text. An author's name, for example, became an important marketing tool. Adding the line 'by the bestselling author of . . .' to a new publication increased its market value. Even the early Penguins, for example, deployed an easily distinguishable marketing strategy: blocks of colour to indicate individual genres, for example 'orange for fiction, green for thrillers, blue for travel and adventure, red for biographies and yellow for miscellaneous' (Worpole 1984, 7). These newly emerging paratexts of novels – their cover design, the fonts used in the title, the blurbs on the back cover, potential excerpts from reviews or snippets from author interviews – made and still make it easier for consumers to identify new titles in previously tried and trusted categories. In a more negative assessment, though, it also made it easier for publishers to 'guide' their readers and thus push the consumption of some titles or genres over others.

It does, however, not only fall to the publishers to market and advertise books. Nicola Humble has convincingly outlined that, in the twentieth century, 'reading begins to be organised by a series of institutions, which create their own reading communities with their own sets of expectations about books and their relationships to them' (2012, 88), and it can consequently be argued that the idea that popular culture and, by extension, popular fiction, is manipulated and, in turn, manipulates its consumers, has to do with those early twentieth-century attempts to 'direct' readers through a number of institutions. Whereas the lending library and railway bookstall had, initially, helped change and shape the very *format* of fiction, new institutions sprang up that capitalized on this new format and helped change the *content* of fiction, too. The year 1926 saw the foundation of the American Book-of-the-Month Club that was, in Britain, swiftly followed by the formation of the Book Society in 1927 and the Book Guild in 1930 (see Humble 2012, 88). These clubs, like the lending libraries before them, carefully *selected* individual titles for their readers, and, through the sheer volume of their members, began to have a decisive influence on what was published and what wasn't. For publishers, it was of the utmost importance to produce what these influential clubs *liked*. Genres that were no longer taken up extensively by the big clubs were no longer commissioned by the publishers either. So what was being offered to the reading public increasingly became the choice of fewer and fewer people, and this trend has continued, with various institutions and societies, throughout the twentieth and into the twenty-first century.

A more recent phenomenon of consumer guidance is the Book Group. Traditionally, this might mean a small group of friends or acquaintances choosing to read a certain text at the same time and meeting up, over a cup of coffee or glass of wine, to discuss it in a friendly atmosphere, away from academic jargon or the environment of a classroom. Readers would take turns suggesting new titles, thus democratically ensuring that each member would have a say in the group's reading matter, and allowing for diverse authors and genres being covered. In the last decade of the twentieth century, however, the reading club, in the true fashion of the media age, went global: it was adopted by television. In 1996, the successful and influential American chat-show host Oprah Winfrey started up 'Oprah's Book Club' (see http://www.oprah.com/book_club.html). The books she reviewed and discussed in her programmes were immediately picked up and discussed by private book groups across the country and, soon, the world, and, more often than not, reached bestseller status. In Britain, chat-show hosts Richard and Judy started their very own book club in 2010 in association with, interestingly, W. H. Smith. Their website (http://www.richardandjudy.co.uk/home) now offers not only lists of each season's must-reads but also guidelines and discussion questions for private book clubs, podcasts with the authors and other book-world-related news, as well as a link to a specific 'Richard and Judy's Children's Book Club' (http://www.richardandjudy.co.uk/childrens-current-reads/Autumn-2012/229). Both show hosts have now also released their very own debut novels, Judy Finnegan's *Eloise* (2012) and Richard Madeley's *Some Day I'll Find You* (2013) that, thanks to their respective authors' public profiles, immediately made it on to the bestseller lists too. Interestingly, Richard & Judy's Book Club does not just stop at promoting already-published work but has now decided to uncover new and previously unpublished talent. A statement from 29 August 2013 on their website states that 'Together with Quercus (Stieg Larsson's publishers), WHSmith, and leading literary agency Furniss Lawton, we're actively searching for talented new writers. When we find our favourite, we're going to put them firmly on the road to success – with a £50,000 publishing deal' (http://www.richardandjudy.co.uk/book-club-news/Richard-and-Judys-Search-for-a-Bestseller/329). While their zeal to find new authors and help them on their way in a notoriously tough and competitive market is certainly laudable, their mission statement could also be seen to be problematic. How, for instance, is 'favourite' defined? Will this be the manuscript that most captures Richard's and Judy's *personal* imaginations? That will best satisfy their readers? That will generate most hype on the show? Against which *criteria* will the manuscripts that, undoubtedly, will cover many very diverse genres, be judged? Their call to new authors is also intrinsically linked to business: the lure to prospective authors is not literary merit and longevity but fast-selling profit; the project is supported by W. H. Smith and, as the website reveals, the chocolate manufacturer Thorntons. Thus the message is clear: hear about the book on the show; go into Smith's to buy your copy – and pick up some chocolates on your way home to increase your reading pleasure. TV Book Groups thus do not only influence their viewers' reading choices but also extend to other advertising and merchandise in an increasingly problematic merger of 'culture' and 'business'.

Similarly, literary prizes have also always helped to promote some titles over others. Although they *claim* to be awarded for literary merit, for innovation or daring experimentation, many prizes are now sponsored by business companies (the most prominent British examples are the annual Man Booker Prize [http://www.themanbookerprize.com] and the Costa Award [https://www.costa.co.uk/costa-book-awards/welcome]) and thus linked to big business. These companies, professionals where marketing is concerned, are very effective in 'pushing' not only their winners but all the other authors on their shortlist. Indeed, the fact that shortlists and, in some cases, longlists of nominees are announced weeks and months before the actual prize is awarded shows the close connection between prize and profit; many booksellers now dedicate a separate shelf, prominently displayed inside the shop, to the annual Booker longlist, and offer their customers posters with all preceding winners, no doubt as an enticement to purchase those books, too; the Booker website features blogs and podcasts from the judging panel or shortlisted authors; and bookmakers release the odds on individual titles to stir up a betting frenzy. The award ceremony is also broadcast live on TV. From its inception in 1969, the Booker Prize has thus aimed to combine business acumen and public awareness with cultural interests, and winning the prize almost always secures drastically increased sales and 'popularity' for the author and publishers. Richard Todd has pointed out that the annual Booker shortlist now acts as a 'consumer guide' that is, effectively, a 'commercial canon' (Todd 1996, 71). This annually changing, award-driven 'commercial canon' thus seems to be in direct competition with that other creation of the 1930s, the literary canon, that body of literature hailed to contain more merit and longevity than other works of fiction, taught to generations of pupils and students of literature and repeatedly set apart from the great body of *popular* fiction.

Of Canonicity and Various 'Brows'

Clive Bloom has lamented that whereas nineteenth-century literature had been a success story, characterized by much experimentation and testing of the literary waters to establish early genres and popular favourites, it soon became 'the tragedy of . . . literature that the authors, publishers, academics and critics who were made by this new world also sought to hierarchize it, restrict it, stabilize it and divide it: in a word, to tame the very forces that made . . . literature come to life' (1996, 51). This hierarchization of literature is inevitably linked to two names that were prominent in the British literary scene of the 1930s and 1940s: F. R. and Q. D. Leavis.

Q. D. Leavis first published her soon-to-be influential *Fiction and the Reading Public* in 1932. John Sutherland, in his 'Introduction', points out that Leavis undertook the 'first serious work of literary sociology to be published in English' though it resulted, in his words, in a book both 'so wrong, and yet so important' (2000, xi, xxiv). *Fiction and the Reading Public* sets out to anthropologically assess the reading habits of the British population, but descends into lamenting the, in Leavis' opinion, inexorable decline in 'quality' literature in favour of a simplified mass or popular fiction that is characterized by a 'thinness and surface liveliness of the writing, . . . crude, elementary prose, carefully constructed in phrases and simple sentences so as to read with the maximum ease' (Leavis 2000, 185). This value statement about the alleged shortcomings of popular fiction shows that, for Leavis, there is no demarcation line between popular novelists and journalists who both cater for the masses in small-scale, bite-sized and entirely unchallenging prose, a trend she blames on the nineteenth-century popularity of magazines that also serialized fiction (185). For Leavis, the 'modern bestseller and magazine story' do not provide intellectual enlightenment but, instead, nothing but 'wish fulfilment' in various forms (51). Rather than merely lamenting this decline, though, Q. D. Leavis saw it as an active threat to 'good' literature, predicting that the majority of readers would no longer appreciate and even understand quality literature and that the increasingly small minority that could would be more and more marginalized. In her opinion, novels should 'deepen, extend, and refine experience by allowing the reader to live at the expense of an unusually intelligent and sensitive mind, by giving him access to a finer code than his own'; popular novels, however, 'do not do' that, instead 'substitut[ing] an emotional code which . . . is actually inferior to the traditional code of the illiterate and which helps to make a social atmosphere unfavourable to the aspirations of the minority' (74). For Leavis, literature should help readers to 'deal less inadequately with [life]', not to act as a 'refuge' from it [74]. In her opinion, moral edification must *always* come before enjoyment or, heaven forbid, sheer entertainment.

In a similar vein, her husband F. R. Leavis' *The Great Tradition* of 1948 starts with the bold statement that 'the great English novelists are Jane Austen, George Eliot, Henry James and Joseph Conrad to stop for the moment at that comparatively safe point in history' and that the only poets worth reading since Donne are Hopkins and Eliot (2008, 9). Leavis was aware that his book would court controversy. What he was trying to establish was a 'tradition' of authors and literary works that new literature ought to be measured against. In Bloom's words, this has led to 'endless and fruitless debate among academics' about what measured up to the few *greats* of literature (1996, 107). Palmer, for instance, laments the, in his words, 'false universality' (1991, 3) of the literary canon that has remained largely unchanged and is up to this day predominantly male, white and very middle-class. Yet this so-called 'canon' of literature is still disseminated and taught in schools and represented – though increasingly alongside 'non-canonical writing' – on university syllabi, despite the fact that it is, in Christopher Pawling's words, a 'historical construct, rather than a fixed entity', and that it ought to be 'open to revision' (1984, 9). But while the controversy about the Leavises' position of unashamed cultural élitism rages on, their opinions and writings have, effectively, led to the division of literature into 'highbrow' and 'lowbrow': literature appreciated and understood by only the few, a distinction often related to the level of education (and, by extension, inevitably to class background) versus the writing enjoyed, uncritically, by the (unenlightened) many. It could, however, also be argued that the Leavises' critique of popular fiction and culture simultaneously, and seemingly incongruously, *elevated* its status to a subject suddenly worthy of consideration and debate. Without Q. D. and F. R. Leavis, a book specifically on 'popular' literature (as compared to other literatures) might never even have seen the light of day.

Q. D. Leavis herself used terminology such as 'highbrow' and 'middlebrow' as well as 'bestseller' which, for her, clearly meant 'lowbrow'. As part of her study she interviewed 60 authors to find out whether or not they had an awareness of their target audience. Her questions ranged from 'have you any views about the bestseller?' to 'What kinds of people do you imagine the bulk of your readers to be?' to 'Have any novels or novelists in particular influenced your work . . . ?' (2000, 43–4). The majority of her respondents considered themselves as authors of 'absolute bestsellers', as having 'no illusions about their work' and that they wrote merely 'as a comfortable way of getting a good living "with the minimum of exertion"' (45). For Leavis, this – undoubtedly very limited author survey – only confirmed suspicions that authors, too, had sold out wholesale to the new god of the popular and the mass media during the first decades of the twentieth century. But Leavis' survey also shows that authors were acutely aware of their market and fashioned their writing accordingly.

As Humble shows, this 'identification of particular classes of reader' only increased during the 1930s and had increasingly to do with educational background and, inevitably, social class (2012, 91). The 'highbrows' saw themselves as the self-appointed guardians of worthwhile art and literature that was under constant siege from 'low' literature and the relatively new media of radio and cinema. In between were the 'middlebrow', those readers with social aspirations who, probably, enjoyed 'lowbrow' art considerably more but felt they should orientate themselves upwards (see Humble 2012, 91). It is, in particular, these associations of 'what is read' with social class that have troubled critics throughout the twentieth century. But the boundaries between what is 'high', 'middle' and 'low' are, inevitably, fluid. Palmer points out that '"high" art defines itself as such by refusing the forms of ready comprehensibility and accessibility that characterize "low" art [that] is usually made available in the form of commodities and produced primarily for profit' but that 'high' art's 'refusal of easy access and . . . commodification . . . becomes both familiar and commodified'. 'High' and 'low' thus constantly shift, merge, interact and, ultimately, push their boundaries (1991, 110). Rather than referring to 'high', 'middle' or 'low', Roland Barthes, in *S/Z* (1975), differentiates between 'readerly', 'writerly' and 'producerly' texts that target different groups of readers. A 'readerly' text aims at a passive reader, who does not want to engage with a text beyond a general enjoyment level whereas a 'writerly' text engages and challenges its readers and is open to a variety of interpretations. A producerly text, by contrast, has the easy accessibility of the readerly text but also allows for differing engagements and interpretations as the writerly text (see Barthes 1975), and this is where boundaries become blurred and shifts between 'high' and 'low' can occur. Formerly experimental and even controversial authors – one such example could be Ian McEwan – can become so well known (for example as recipients of highly publicized and marketed literary prizes, or after the successful adaptation of one or other of their texts for film or TV) that they, effectively, become their own 'brand', cleverly managed and marketed in order to become accessible to an entirely new reader demographic who might formerly have considered them too 'highbrow'.

But despite this acknowledged fluidity between these different classifications, despite the recognition that literature has merit regardless of which value label is attached to it, critics are still at loggerheads over popular fiction, and this ongoing battle is largely due to the politicization of the term 'popular'. Is popular fiction a tool to manipulate the masses? Or is it a powerful weapon in the fight against élitism that playfully undermines class snobbery?

Wrangling for Position: The Theorists

The Leavises' conservative and élitist approach to literature courted controversy upon publication and has continued to elicit strong responses from many critics, jumping to the defence of 'the popular' and condemning the Leavises for their exclusionary stance on culture. Among the earliest cautious defenders of the popular was Walter Benjamin, writing before the Leavises, and commenting on the *liberating* effect of popular culture. In his reading, early twentieth-century mass production of cultural products (literature in paperback form, for instance, but also new and increasingly popular media such as film) serves to liberate and even democratize a society simply because it widens access to art and literature and, as such, allows the 'masses' to participate in a hitherto unknown way. In literature, for example, Benjamin felt that increased production linked to improved literacy led to a much wider and more receptive audience that, in turn, then began to increasingly participate in the actual production of literature (1978, 232). In his words, 'the greatly increased mass of participants has produced a change in the mode of participation' (1978, 239). In a similar vein, Clive Bloom argues that mass consumerism of literature does not 'turn us into mindless slaves of consumerism' but that it 'always includes imagination, negotiation and *refusal* and allows minority groups (with differing degrees of success) to negotiate their space in contradiction to the *vox populi*: a voice within a voice' (2002, 28). Both early and contemporary defenders of popular culture thus focus on the 'popular' as indicating a 'participatory' part of the people in what they consume as culture.

On the other side of this, though, are those critics who, though supportive of the idea of a 'popular' culture *per se*, are wary of what they consider the abuse of popular culture by those few in power in order to manipulate the many. Prominent among the latter was the so-called Frankfurt School. As Jenkins, McPherson and Shattuc have outlined, 'the Frankfurt School is usually cited as the Marxist group that described popular culture as a mechanism of modern capitalism's repressive ideology' (2002, 31). So while for F. R. and Q. D. Leavis, popular literature and, by extension, popular culture, was a manifestation of poor taste and lack of education, for the members of the Frankfurt School, most prominently among them Theodor Adorno (a disciple of Benjamin) and Max Horkheimer, it was a product of an increasingly ideological manipulation of the many by the few.[2] Both Adorno and Horkheimer disliked the term 'popular culture' because, in their eyes, it had lost its real association with 'popular' as an expression of the interest and wishes of 'the people'. Instead, they referred to 'culture industry' to show that the mass population had very little (if any) influence on cultural production that was 'manufactured more or less according to plan' (Adorno 2001b, 98). In his essay 'Art and Mass Culture', Horkheimer highlights the power of the 'amusement industry' and outlines the fact that 'popularity consists of the unrestricted accommodation of the people to *what the amusement industry thinks they like*' (1941, 303; emphasis mine). Similarly, Adorno, in 'The Schema of Mass Culture' (1981) lamented that, in popular culture, 'imagination is replaced' (Adorno 2001a, 64) and, instead, 'advertising becomes information when there is no longer anything to choose from, when the recognition of brand names has taken the place of choice' (85). For Adorno and Horkheimer mass culture had become standardized, an endless repetition of the same formulae, with the mass consumer manipulated by the media and entertainment industry into consuming the same distillation of 'culture' over and over again – and for them this clearly had ideological and thus political implications, as, effectively, the individual is disenfranchised. In 'The Culture Industry Reconsidered' (1975) Adorno points out that 'the culture industry intentionally integrates its consumers from above' in a 'system almost without a gap' where 'the customer is not king, . . . , not its subject but its object' (Adorno 2001b, 98–9). And this, as the quote suggests, came at the expense of individualism, creativity and subjectivity. Witkin points out that 'at the heart of Adorno's critique . . . is what he . . . perceived as a crisis of the "subject" and of "subjectivity" in the modern world; the sense . . . of a subjectivity increasingly overwhelmed and absorbed by the all-powerful machinery of the "totally administered" society' (2003, 6). At the heart of this 'totally administered society' is the aim to both control the population and stifle individual thought *and* to create profit. In order to create that profit, it could be argued, the culture industry needs to produce what the consumer wants. Ironically, and as Adorno does not fail to point out, it perverts this seemingly simple 'provider/consumer' relation by manipulating the consumer into only wanting what it produces. In the process, art loses its value as art in itself, but, instead, becomes a simple commodity. As Adorno points out, 'the autonomy of works of art . . . is tendentially eliminated by the culture industry . . .' (2001b, 99). A truly 'popular' culture in the sense of 'made by the people for the people' can give voice to the content, but also the *dis*content of the population, express hopes and fears and, potentially, also raise its voice in anger and protest. Under the auspices of the 'culture industry', however, it loses that capacity in Adorno's eyes. Instead, it only pursues its own ideological and profit-driven agendas and, in the process, debases the very 'people' it claims to represent.

Critics have often turned on Adorno's allegedly snobbish stance towards popular culture and the culture industry, especially condemning his fears about popular culture's attempts to merge high and low culture. In 'The Culture Industry Reconsidered', Adorno writes that the culture industry destroys 'the seriousness of high art . . . in speculation about its efficacy' as well as 'the seriousness of the lower' because of the 'civilizational constraints imposed on the rebellious resistance inherent within it' (2001b, 98–9). This has often been misread to represent Adorno's typically 'modernist' stance that favours canonical art over popular art as well as over postmodern attempts to merge the two, a stance that, seemingly, aligns him with the Leavises as an arbiter of taste. However, this is not what Adorno's critique of the culture industry was about. It was to highlight the dangers of institution-alizing all art; of depriving it of creativity, inventiveness and the potential to shock, outrage and shake up; of taking away, through constant manipulation and indoctrination, the individual's own interpretation of art and literature by replacing it with sanitized and streamlined products that had become standardized and predictable, and, for that, all the poorer.

Adorno's take on the culture industry is an indictment of its ideological corruption and a decrying of its manipulation and standardization at the expense of individualism, subjectivity and creative freedom. The French sociologist and philosopher Pierre Bourdieu, by contrast, returns to the Leavisite question of 'taste' – but considers it from a Marxist and class-based angle. Unlike the Leavises, whose stance is that taste in 'high' art is an expression of an individual's superiority, Bourdieu sees it as a by-product of a class-ridden and indoctrinated society. Like Adorno, Bourdieu believes that consumers are being 'produced'; but, unlike Adorno, he does not blame this production process on the manipulations of the culture industry but, rather, on the individual's environment. For him, the 'habitus' of each individual is formative in the development of taste. By 'habitus' Bourdieu understands 'the internalized form of class condition and the conditioning it entails' (2009, 101); and this conditioning forms the basis of a person's cultural capital. It is evident for Bourdieu that a person from an economically privileged position will always have more leisure time to develop his appreciation of arts and culture. This 'cultural capital' can be furthered and extended through 'educational capital' (12ff), but here it is similarly clear to Bourdieu that education differs from class to class. A person's life-style, accordingly, is consequently not a matter of choice but one of indoctrination from the cradle: 'life styles are thus the systematic products of habitus' (172). For Bourdieu, 'taste' is the 'propensity and capacity to appropriate (materially or symbolically) a given class of classified, classifying objects or practices' and becomes the 'generative formula of life-style, a unitary set of distinctive preferences' that 'only partially become[s] conscious' (173–4). This leads, inevitably, to a hegemonic stance on culture. The 'traditional definition of "hegemony"', Raymond Williams explains, 'is political rule or domination, especially in relation between states' but that 'Marxism extended the definition to rule or domination to relations between social classes, and especially to definitions of a *ruling class*' (1977, 108). For Bourdieu, cultural hegemony is expressed by the acknowledged 'taste' of the higher, more educated classes as the *only* taste to aspire to.

Unlike the Leavises, Bourdieu does not condemn popular culture as inferior; unlike Adorno he does not attack the culture industry. Rather the opposite – he sees the potential that popular culture offers: popular culture, with its multiplicity of products and choices and its associated advertising *could*, he argues, potentially have a liberating effect on the individual: '[it] transforms necessity into virtue by inducing "choices"' (175). However, Bourdieu's rather pessimistic conclusion is that the individual will almost always make choices based on 'taste', and that this taste, inevitably, has been 'assigned to him in the classifications' (175) of the class system or is, in turn, an aspiring taste that hopes to emulate that of the upper classes.[3] In that way, popular culture appears to be condemned forever to a lower position as, according to Bourdieu, the class system, that has introduced a hegemonic attitude to taste, has simultaneously resulted in a 'fundamental refusal of the *facile*'. He explains that 'the refusal of what is easy in the sense of simple, and therefore shallow, and "cheap", because it is easily decoded and culturally "undemanding", naturally leads to the refusal of what is facile in the ethical or aesthetic sense, of everything which offers pleasures that are too immediately accessible and so discredited as "childish" or "primitive" . . .' (486). So although he starts from a different point as Adorno in that he focuses solely on class, Bourdieu effectively comes to the same pessimistic conclusion: popular culture, as a representation of the will of the people, is manipulated by those in power.

For many cultural commentators, there are thus anxieties surrounding popular fiction that manifest themselves in negative theories either about those who read it or, more often, about those who produce and market it: its original premise, art for the people by the people, they say, is good; but it cannot succeed because it is manipulated; because it is controlled by a few; because it has become 'big business'; and its main aim is therefore to generate profit rather than to represent the 'people' and to serve as a fertile debating and sounding ground for public opinion. But there are also those critics that warn of the 'limitations' of 'negative theories of mass culture' (McCracken 1998, 27). John Fiske, for example, says that 'there is always an element of popular culture that lies outside of social control, that escapes or opposes hegemonic forces' (2004, 2). There are, for instance, the success stories of authors and texts that reached a mass audience purely by word of mouth, without the manipulative machinations of the marketing industry: Louis de Bernières' *Captain Corelli's Mandolin* of 1994 that became a huge, worldwide word-of-mouth success is a pertinent example here. And there is, of course, that Cinderella story of publishing, the case of J. K. Rowling and her Harry Potter series that was years in the making and turned into a global phenomenon almost overnight.

It is, then, probably best to conclude on the warning words of Fredric Jameson who, in 'Reification and Utopia in Mass Culture' points out that 'the works of mass culture cannot be ideological without at the same time being implicitly or explicitly Utopian as well: they cannot manipulate unless they offer some genuine shred of content as a fantasy bribe to the public about to be manipulated' (1979, 144). So while Jameson acknowledges the negative, hegemonic power aspect inherent in contemporary popular culture, its abuses to manipulate its consumers into acquiescence, he also sees its gratifying or almost conciliatory aspects: he refers to this as the coexistence of 'Utopian gratification and ideological manipulation' (1981, 288). Popular Culture, for Jameson, *does* represent genuine feelings and emotions, flights of fancy or escapism. But ultimately it is the reader who holds the power to interpret the text and, importantly, to reconcile the escapist utopia of the text s/he has just indulged in with the realities of everyday life (148ff). Ideally, Jameson writes that 'a Marxist negative hermeneutics, a Marxist practice of ideological analysis proper, must in the practical work of reading and interpretation be exercised *simultaneously* with a Marxist positive herme-neutics, or a decipherment of the Utopian impulses of these same still ideological cultural texts' (296). Jameson thus warns that a purely ideology- and hegemony-based critique of popular culture is too one-sided and ought to be tempered with something that, maybe, should simply be referred to as 'common sense' – an expression used by an earlier Marxist critic, the Italian Antonio Gramsci. In his *Prison Notebooks* (1929–35), Gramsci asserted that 'all men are "philosophers"' capable of applying a spontaneous philosophy based on, among other things, '"common sense" and "good sense"' (1988, 325). Common sense is thus not the prerogative of the privileged few in power; nor is it 'a single unique conception, identical in time and space' but, instead, something that 'takes countless different forms' (343). What it does is to, effectively, override the dictates of a hegemonic society to reinstate individual thought and opinion. In the realm of popular culture, Gramsci's 'common sense' allows for *individual* and *critical* everyday engagement with what the culture industry offers.

The twentieth century has been the century of mass consumption and mass production of cultural commodities. With mass production and mass consumption comes the generating of profit. With the generating of profit come the ideological debates about who profits from it and who abuses their privileged position to (a) create more profit for themselves and (b) manipulate the many. And while these ideological discussions and debates surrounding popular culture and assessing it from a variety of angles, both 'right' and 'left', are important to alert us to the power struggles taking place at every stage of cultural production, they often overshadow the actual works of fiction and their relative merit as pieces of writing that simply ought to be judged by the people who read them. And so the following chapters will largely leave the ideological debates aside and return to the actual focus of this collection: popular fiction in its many shapes and manifestations, and its development throughout the twentieth and into the twenty-first century.

Notes

1. The presentation of 'westerns' in film and tv has undergone a metamorphosis in recent years, leaving the stereotypical presentation of 'Cowboys versus Indians' behind for more cutting-edge and challenging presentations, for example in Kevin Costner's 1990 film *Dances with Wolves* and, in particular, Ang Lee's award-winning film *Brokeback Mountain* of 2005 (based on a short story by acclaimed writer E. Annie Proulx) that challenges the homosocial male concept of the western with its presentations of a homosexual relationship between the two main protagonists.
2. This approach was reiterated by Raymond Williams who argued in his *Keywords* definition of 'Popular Culture' that it 'was not identified by *the people* but by others' (1976, 199). See also the introduction to this volume.
3. Clive Bloom shares this attitude, though in a less political manner, in his previously cited statement that genres solidified in the early twentieth century and that this corresponded to the period of class consolidation (2002, 13).

Works Cited

Adorno, Theodor (2001a [1981]), 'The Schema of Mass Culture', in T. Adorno (2001 [1991]), J. M. Bernstein (ed.), *The Culture Industry: Selected Essays on Mass Culture*. London: Routledge, pp. 61–7.

—(2001b [1975]), 'Culture Industry Reconsidered', in T. Adorno (2001 [1991]), J. M. Bernstein (ed.), *The Culture Industry: Selected Essays on Mass Culture*. London: Routledge, pp. 98–106.

Barthes, Roland (1975), *S/Z*, trans. Richard Miller. London: Jonathan Cape.

Benjamin, Walter (1978 [1936]), 'The Work of Art in the Age of Mechanical Reproduction', in W. Benjamin (1978), Hannah Arendt (ed.), *Illuminations*. New York: Schocken Books, pp. 217–51.

Bloom, Clive (1996), *Cult Fiction: Popular Reading and Pulp Theory*. Houndsmill, Basingstoke: Palgrave Macmillan.

—(2002), *Bestsellers: Popular Fiction since 1900*. Basingstoke: Palgrave Macmillan.

Bourdieu, Pierre (2009 [1984]), *Distinction: A Social Critique of the Judgement of Taste*, trans. Richard Nice. New York: Routledge.

Carey, John (1992), *The Intellectuals and the Masses*. London: Faber & Faber.

Fiske, John (2004 [1989]), *Reading the Popular*. London: Routledge.

Glover, David (2012), 'Publishing, History, Genre', in D. Glover and
S. McCracken (eds), *The Cambridge Companion to Popular Fiction*.
Cambridge: Cambridge University Press, pp. 15–32.

Glover, David and Scott McCracken (2012), 'Introduction', in D. Glover and
S. McCracken (eds), *The Cambridge Companion to Popular Fiction*.
Cambridge: Cambridge University Press, pp. 1–14.

Gramsci, Antonio (1988), *A Gramsci Reader*, ed. David Forgacs. London:
Lawrence and Wishart.

Hall, Stuart (1981), 'Notes on Deconstructing "the Popular"', in R. Samuel
(ed.), *People's History and Socialist Theory*. London: Routledge and Kegan
Paul, pp. 227–40.

Horkheimer, Max (1941), 'Art and Mass Culture'. *Studies in Philosophy and
Social Science* 9(1), 290–304.

Humble, Nicola (2012), 'The Reader of Popular Fiction', in D. Glover and
S. McCracken (eds), *The Cambridge Companion to Popular Fiction*.
Cambridge: Cambridge University Press, pp. 86–102.

Jameson, Fredric (1975), 'Magical Narrative: Romance as Genre'. *New Literary
History* 7, 135–63.

—(1979), 'Reification and Utopia in Mass Culture'. *Social Text* 1(Winter),
130–48.

—(1981), *The Political Unconscious: Narrative as a Socially Symbolic Act*.
London: Methuen & Co.

Jenkins, Henry, Tara McPherson and Jane Shattuc (2002), 'Defining Popular
Culture', in H. Jenkins, T. McPherson and J. Shattuc (eds), *Hop on Pop: The
Politics and Pleasures of Popular Culture*. Durham, NC: Duke University
Press, pp. 26–42.

Leavis, Q. D. (2000 [1932]), *Fiction and the Reading Public*. London: Pimlico.

McCracken, Scott (1998), *Pulp. Reading Popular Fiction*. Manchester:
Manchester University Press.

Mukerji, Chandra and Michael Schudson (1991), 'Introduction: Rethinking
Popular Culture', in C. Mukerji and M. Schudson (eds), *Rethinking Popular
Culture: Contemporary Perspectives in Cultural Studies*. Berkeley, CA:
University of California Press, pp. 1–61.

Nash, Walter (1990), *Language in Popular Fiction*. London: Routledge.

Palmer, Jerry (1991), *Potboilers: Methods, Concepts and Case Studies in Popular
Fiction*. London: Routledge.

Pawling, Christopher (1984), 'Introduction: Popular Fiction: Ideology or
Utopia', in C. Pawling (ed.), *Popular Fiction and Social Change*. Houndsmill,
Basingstoke: Macmillan, pp. 1–19.

Smith, Erin A. (2012), 'Pulp Sensations', in D. Glover and S. McCracken (eds),
The Cambridge Companion to Popular Fiction. Cambridge: Cambridge
University Press, pp. 141–58.

Sutherland, John (1978), *Fiction and the Fiction Industry*. London: Athlone Press.

—(2000), 'Introduction', in Q. D. Leavis, *Fiction and the Reading Public*. London: Pimlico, pp. v–xxvii.

Todd, Richard (1996), *Consuming Fictions: The Booker Prize and Fiction in Britain Today*. London: Bloomsbury.

Williams, Raymond (1976), *Keywords: A Vocabulary of Culture and Society*. London: Fontana/Croom Helm.

—(1977), *Marxism and Literature*. Oxford: Oxford University Press.

Witkin, Robert W. (2003), *Adorno on Popular Culture*. London: Routledge.

Worpole, Ken (1984), *Reading by Numbers: Contemporary Publishing & Popular Fiction*. London: Comedia Publishing Group.

Websites

https://www.costa.co.uk/costa-book-awards/welcome

http://www.oprah.com/book_club.html

http://www.penguin.co.uk/static/cs/uk/0/aboutus/aboutpenguin_companyhistory.html

http://www.richardandjudy.co.uk/home

http://www.themanbookerprize.com

Part II

Genres

3

More than a Love Story: The Complexities of the Popular Romance

Maryan Wherry

Introduction

The romance has always revolved around the development of a relationship (a central love story) and a positive resolution (happy ending). The presumed simplicity of the romance plot is deceptive. Like all literature, every element of the formula is infinitely adaptable, which both explains and provides for the continuing popularity of the romance genre. Because the narrative is character driven, there is an almost infinite variety of combinations and permutations of people, personalities, places, issues, conflicts and sensuality. It is really a rather foolish assumption of the uninformed critic to say that a 'new' romance is simply a matter of plugging in character or setting names. The mutability of the literary elements – setting, character, theme – woven in and around the immutability of the romance formula makes romance one of the most complex and versatile of popular genres.

A basic understanding of what qualifies as romance fiction and how those codes and conventions are transformed by writers, cultural requirements and time is manifold. The dominant plotline, the development of a love relationship between two people, is often dismissed as a simple boy-meets-girl-who-live-happily-ever-after. However, as with all genre fiction, the skeletal formula is filled out in a variety of ways. The romance structure is used to examine and explore tensions and debates about social values, cultural conditions and gender relations; the relationships between the primary characters are places to confront and engage with traditional notions about gender, perhaps even to transform them. The focus within that relationship is on human desires and emotions. Romance writers explore the psychological concepts of whether opposites attract, whether there is such a thing as love at first sight and how desire develops, as well as the philosophical debate between heart and mind.

Because of the focus on emotions, or perhaps due to its mythic heritage, the romance has always been considered a woman's genre only: written primarily by women, for women, about women. Popular romances celebrate women's competency and potential; they are full of allusions and resonances of a long legacy which celebrates female intuition, female power and female environment. The 'hero' may begin as both villain and hero; through the story, the heroine must discover how to vanquish the villain without damaging the hero, all the while convincing the hero to acknowledge her power as woman.

Roots

The romance has a long history that goes beyond that of the current perception of popular romance. The meeting and reconciliation of two lovers is a narrative archetype common to Ancient Greek tales. The term 'romance' originated as a label for tales told or written in the vernacular spoken Latin. Such tales evolved into medieval courtly love narratives where the Knight-Hero embarked on his quest and performed deeds to prove his love for his lady and to impress her with his courage and heroism. 'Courtly love' of obedience and loyalty to a liege lady was an ennobling force. The tales of love and submission were not exemplars of actual behaviour but were forums in which to explore the influence of *eros* and idealized love. As such, these tales became popular among the growing literary class; they were seen as narratives about the values of the aristocracy. The earliest, perhaps, are the Lais (narrative poems) of Marie de France, written in the late twelfth century; later tales like *Floire et Blancheflor* (c.1250) and *Sir Eglamour of Artois* (c.1350) involve star-crossed lovers who are separated and finally united.

Another archetype of the romance is the fairy or folk tale tradition. These tales are essentially morality tales, rewarding or punishing behaviour. Because the fairy tale tends to contain an element of fantasy, showing what *should* be (rather than what is), they are invariably optimistic. The use of fairy tale archetypes in popular romance is fairly common and obvious: 'Beauty and Beast' (restoring humanity) and 'Cinderella' (disguised worth) are the most frequent, followed closely by 'Sleeping Beauty' (awakening by recognition) and the 'Ugly Duckling' (maturation). As folk tales, the purpose (through plot, characters, theme and moral) is to reinforce the fixed social order of the lower classes, who were less educated, less literate, more conservative; the tales are to teach conformity to current social needs. Fairy tales have been, and continue to be, revised as social conventions and values shift. Modern romance novels offer several examples of how the contemporary tale subverts, adapts, revises, recasts the classic archetypes and tropes (palatial manors, betrayal, virtuous or vicious characters, hidden identities) directed at all levels of society. Loretta Chase's *Lord of Scoundrels* (1995; Beauty and the Beast), Eloisa James' *The Duke is Mine* (2011; Princess and the Pea) and Jane Green's *Jemima J* (2000; Ugly Duckling) all rework fairy tale archetypes.

A major shift in the romance novel occurred in the late eighteenth and early nineteenth century. In 1794, Ann Radcliffe's novel, *The Mysteries of Udolpho*, created a world filled with a sense of horror and impending doom. The heroine had to negotiate and survive in a threatening world imbued with mystery and unexplained phenomena. Radcliffe engendered the medieval quest and allowed female readers to confront their own sense of confinement and lack of control. She also paved the way for writers such as the Brontë sisters and many American writers. American dime novels (equivalent to the 'penny dreadful') involve kidnapping, disasters, wild animals, villains, mysterious accidents, murder attempts, secret societies, etc. This melodramatic action intensifies the danger of the American frontier environment and, proportionately, the courage of the heroine and hero, as in Ann S. Stephens' *Esther: A Story of the Oregon Trail* (1862), where adventure is the key but romance is the resolution. Perhaps the most revealing characteristic of traditional American romance is its narrative tone inspired by Gothic Melodrama.

Writing at almost the same time as Radcliffe was Jane Austen, whose novels lightened the tone of romance and turned it into what has become referred to as 'women's fiction'. *Pride and Prejudice* (1813), a social comedy of wit and manners, is generally considered to be the foundation text of the modern romance. Austen refocuses the dominant theme of the romance not on the physical perils confronting the heroine but on the social restrictions facing women; she wraps social commentary and her observations of human foibles in, through and around the basic romance formula. The significance of Austen's contributions to the genre is reinforced by the ubiquity of references to her in romance novels: the heroines in historical and contemporary romances are invariably reading Austen. Several romances employ the structure and themes of Austen's novels – Stephanie Meyer's *Twilight* (2005) and Helen Fielding's *Bridget Jones' Diary* (1996) adapt *Pride and Prejudice*; Debra Smith White's *Amanda* (2006), *Emma*; Melissa Nathan's *Persuading Annie* (2004), *Persuasion* – in addition to countless editions of fan fiction spin-offs, prequels and sequels.

The sexual revolution of the 1960s and 1970s stimulated the next significant adaptation in romance writing. By the late twentieth century, the inclusion of explicit sex scenes – not anticipated sex, not implied sex, not 'fade to black' – had become common. This overt sex shows a heightened awareness and concern about women's sexuality, evidenced by the 'publicness' and inclusion of sex in all its manifestations – violent, painful, abusive, sweet, passionate, erotic. Whereas nineteenth-century romances involved sentimental elements of crying and cleansing, or the neglect or abuse of runaway husbands, the late(r) twentieth century was more explicit. Kathleen Woodiwiss' *The Flame and the Flower* (1974) and Rosemary Rodgers' *Sweet Savage Love* (1976) marked a significant transformation. The controversy surrounding overt female sexuality and passion raged, over the next decade, from accusations of rape fantasies to pornography to the pejorative label 'bodice rippers', a term coined by the *New York Times*. These shifts in the popular romance reflect a shift in culture itself when the sexual revolution matured; the early novels reflect the normal frenzy and distortion that arise after the removal of long-term social repression.

During the 1990s and early 2000s, popular romance reflected the development of gay studies and queer theory in the increased availability and mainstreaming of same-sex romances. Same-sex romances have led the way in showing that romance, love and desire are not only heterosexual. Ann Herendeen's *Phyllida and the Brotherhood of Philander* (2008) involves an m/m/f ménage with two happy endings; Alex Beecroft's *False Colors* (2009) explores the challenges and rewards of gay love and romance; and Sarah Waters elevates lesbian romance to Literature in her neo-Victorian romance *Tipping the Velvet* (1999; see also Chapter 13).

By the twenty-first century, popular formula romance in its most traditional manifestation has developed into a complex international industry involving writers, publishers, readers and scholars. In Britain and Australia, romance publishing is dominated by Harlequin Mills & Boon; HM&B has offices in dozens of international cities and publishes translations in several languages. In the United States, it is a far wider publishing field, including Harlequin, Avon, Simon & Schuster. All over the blogosphere, bloggers and readers are discussing various definitions of the romance genre, debating whether Margaret Mitchell's *Gone with the Wind* (1936) or Emily Brontë's *Wuthering Heights* (1847) are romances. The genre itself has expanded to contain several major subgenres: chick lit, contemporary, erotica, historical, inspirational, paranormal, same sex, suspense, western. The sheer multiplicity of subgenres reflects the universality and adaptability of the romance formula into a boundless variety of stories.

Subgenres

Romances are published in two general formats: category or single title/ mass market. Harlequin Mills & Boon is the largest publisher of category romances. These romances are published under a common imprint or series name, released at standard intervals and frequently identified by sequential numbers of a particular line. Category romances tend to be shorter than single-title novels. HM&B features several series, including Historical, Nocturne, Love Inspired, Superromance, Special Edition, Blaze. Margaret Jensen's *Love's $weet Return* (1984) is an early study focusing on the conventions that propel and account for the success and appeal of Harlequin romances. In *The Romance Fiction of Mills & Boon* (1999), jay Dixon has traced the evolution of plotlines, characters and issues within the HM&B, while Laura Vivanco, in *For Love and Money* (2011), provides a literary analysis of language, mimesis and metaphor in Mills & Boon category romances.

Single-title romances are longer novels released individually. The production and popularity of single-title releases exploded in the 1980s, as did sales of HM&B, due to massive expansion of world markets, a rise in prosperity and consumption, and shifts in marketing strategies (Pearce 2007). Each volume stands alone and because single-title romances are longer, they allow for multiple subplots and greater character development. As with category romances, they are not exclusionary and vary in subplots, motifs, locations and levels of sensuality. One of the fallacious assumptions about popular romance is that because it resolves in marriage, it cannot be serialized, but several writers have produced trilogies and multi-volume linked novels. Louise Allen wrote The Transformation of the Shelley Sisters series (August–October 2011), a trilogy which follows three sisters; Julia Quinn's Bridgerton family series includes eight volumes and several novellas (2000–13) chronicling a group of siblings.

Popular romance fiction, whether category or single title, may be classified into various subgenres which depend upon setting, plot and narrative elements. Most of the subgenres hybridize, incorporating characteristics from other genres like historical fiction, mystery, science fiction, action/adventure, and all have their own conventions. In 2003, Harlequin launched Flipside, an imprint specifically for Chick Lit, in addition to Red Dress Ink (2001). Harlequin also has imprints for paranormal (Luna), suspense (Rogue Angel), multicultural (Kimani) and Erotic (Spice).

The *contemporary* romance, broadly speaking, features stories which have post-World War II settings. Heroines, responsive to shifting cultural values, may be professionals, older, divorced, with teenage children. They may feature outright 'adventures' involving martial arts, daredevil rescues, etc. The emotional journey of the characters drives the story. Harlequin Mills & Boon features several categories, like Mills & Boon Modern or Harlequin Presents, devoted to contemporaries.

Contemporary romance, with its clear links to present-day challenges facing women on a daily basis, has been so successful that it has spawned its own subgenre: *Chick Lit*. Its primary features are the lives of single women in the big city, first-person narration, a preoccupation with material goods, weight, dating, etc., all presented with self-deprecating humour. These novels differ from traditional contemporary romance in that rather than focusing on the one female/one male relationship, Chick Lit includes relationships with friends, co-workers and family as equally important as developing a relationship with a man who might be Mr Right. Chick Lit romances focus on several issues of cultural importance to contemporary women: identity and self-image, insecurities bordering on neuroses, sex and sexuality, feminism and consumerism. The heroine must balance personal relationships with professional careers. Frequently, the ending is not so much a happily-ever-after as much as a happily-for-now resolution, revealing the dissolution of romantic ideals and reflecting shifting contemporary values.

Helen Fielding's *Bridget Jones' Diary* (1996) is widely credited as the first of the subgenre, even though Austen's *Pride and Prejudice* also fulfils the criteria and could be considered a very early example of Chick Lit (Ferris and Young 2006). Chick Lit is a much more popular phenomenon in Britain than it is in the United States where it is more often shunted into the generic 'women's fiction'. The initial concentration on shopping and fashion that garnered the label 'chick lit' has evolved into a broader treatment of the coming-of-age of the contemporary single urban female. It has become almost anti-romance, in which romance has been dislodged by sex and comedy (Pearce 2007). These novels reflect a greater degree of cynicism and irony about love than in traditional mainstream romance, which, again, reflects changes in cultural values towards relationships, romance and marriage.

By contrast, *historical* romances are set in the past, usually prior to the twentieth century in any of a multitude of locations. Historical fiction – especially historical romance – provides writers and readers with a created world in which to critique or resolve or reinforce 'reality'. The historical details must be accurate even as the past world is one sanitized by imagination; the emotions, hopes and fears are real. There must be enough 'fact' to create the sense of 'reality' of the period, and there will also be elements of the current writer's concerns, issues and place. Historical romance fiction mingles 'reality' and distance.

Regency England is so popular as a historical era that it is given its own subgenre. Technically only 1810–20 but often stretched to 1830, the Regency was a period of social and economic upheaval; with a rising new middle class, its threat to the aristocracy and continued war with France, the era provides a setting with plenty of conflict. The formal code of etiquette was to distance the upper classes – aristocracy and gentry – from any vulgarity of the lower classes and enforced a hierarchal structure of social, political or economic ranking. Georgette Heyer (1902–74), writing from the 1920s to the 1960s, is often credited as founder of the Regency with *Regency Buck* (1935), an Austen-esque romance but equally reflective of contemporary mores. Heyer remains, perhaps, the most influential Regency romance writer.

The *Gothic* tradition includes a threatening world imbued with mystery and unexplained phenomena. Heroines are the target of some danger or peril, both physical and psychological, the threat of violence coming from complete strangers or domestic partners. The style was popular in the nineteenth century and became re-vitalized with Daphne du Maurier's *Rebecca* (1938) into a new wave of modern Gothic. The Gothic tradition aided the development of romantic suspense and the paranormal. *Romantic suspense* incorporates a blend of love and danger. The action/adventure plotline parallels the development of the love relationship. Novels such as Mary Stewart's *Nine Coaches Waiting* (1958) and Victoria Holt's *Mistress of Mellyn* (1960) weave together romance and suspense: as the suspense heightens and expands, so too does the romance between the protagonists. Romantic suspense plotlines, such as Catherine Coulter's contemporary FBI thrillers, beginning with *False Pretenses* (1988), are driven by the tension of the danger and threat, even as the romantic relationship develops around and through the action.

The *paranormal*, by contrast, contains elements of a fantasy world, futuristic settings, time-travel, paranormal happenings or science fiction. Most frequently, human women become enamoured with shape-shifters, werewolves, vampires and sorcerers – heroes who are quite literally untamed. The tone, setting and sophistication within paranormals vary widely, from dark and intense to light and humorous, from historical to futuristic, from mild and sweet to erotic. Otherworldly or out-of-body experiences and ghosts are common. The Gothic threat appears usually in supernatural dangers. For the most part, paranormal romances are classic romances set in other worlds. Jayne Ann Krentz's *Amaryllis* (1986) is generally considered the first paranormal romance. One of the most popular recent series to incorporate vampires and romance is Stephanie Meyers' Twilight Trilogy (see also Chapter 16). In *Midnight Bayou* (2001), Nora Roberts weaves spirits, ghosts and genders across two centuries and multiple generations of legends.

Fantasy/paranormal elements allow for a greater suspension of realism, but the plot and characters must still be believable. The fantasy element of paranormal romance ought not be confused with the fantasy of the fairy/folk tale heritage, which also relies on elements of the supernatural. Like the historical subgenre, futuristic paranormals allow writers to build whole new worlds with conventional 'human' values and social constructs of 'reality'. Nalini Singh has two current series: one featuring winged archangels; the other, changelings. The fastest growing permutation of romance and fantasy is the steampunk romance, such as Meljean Brook's *Riveted* (2012), which exists in a sort of retro-futuristic world of robotics, cybernetics and steam power.

An increasingly popular subgenre is the *multicultural romance*, involving black, Asian, Hispanic, Indian or interracial couples. Romance writers have long incorporated non-white ethnicities and characters, usually as an 'exotic' Other; however, the sensibility and orientation remained essentially white. Harlequin's first African-American romance was Sandra Kitt's *Adam and Eva* (1984). Romances like Beverly Jenkins' *Indigo* (1996) speak to gender and race issues, conflicts, restrictions and experience. In 2011, Mills & Boon published a limited special edition of *The Love Asana* (2011), by Milan Vohra, HM&B's first Indian writer.

A particular form of the multicultural romance is the *Sheikh romance*, dating from E. M. Hull's *The Sheikh* (1920). These romances are set in an imaginary Middle Eastern country that acts as the site of desire and reconciliation. The Sheikh romance inverts Edward Said's Orientalism in that it contains masculinized Others; the female is the agent of and participant in imperialist discourse. In the case of the Sheikh (or the African American or the American Indian), the non-whites must reject their 'Otherness' and adopt white loyalties for the happily-ever-after resolution of the romance. The Sheikh trope and motifs of a still potent Orientalism serve to explore female sexuality against a rather long literary heritage between western Europe (and US) and the Muslim world (Teo 2013).

Erotic romances feature a much stronger sexual content. Cover and review taglines usually refer to them as 'hot, Hot, HOT!'. The relationship journey is linked to sexual interaction. The love relationship is the paramount cause of sexual pleasure, so the primary emphasis is on the romantic relationship; sexual activity is secondary, though explicit. This subgenre has ballooned in recent years, paralleling the growth of and attention to women's desire and sexuality. Writers like Pam Rosenthal in *The Edge of Impropriety* (2008) explore erotic sexual fantasies. This subgenre is further expanded by the growing number of writers in LGBT (lesbian, gay, bisexual, transgendered) and BDSM (bondage, dominant, sado-masochism) communities. Romances like Emma Holly's *Velvet Glove* (2004) allow readers to experience BDSM and alternative sexualities within a safe environment.

Finally, *inspirational romances* are those in which religious or spiritual beliefs form a major part of the romantic relationship. Most tend to incorporate a rather conservative Christian faith and are generally less sexually explicit. The resolution comes when the protagonists have not only discovered love for each other but have achieved their individual spiritual growth, developing a relationship with each other and with God. *Redeeming Love* (1997), Francine Rivers' retelling of the Biblical book of Hosea, is the story of the heroine's journey towards God and the power of unconditional love.

Formula

In *A Natural History of the Romance Novel* (2003), Pamela Regis identifies eight structural elements which must occur within any romance novel: Society Defined, the Meeting, the Barrier, the Attraction, the Declaration, Ritual Death, Recognition, Betrothal. Every romance will contain these elements but not necessarily in linear or temporal order. In, around and through this structure are woven a variety of social issues: sexual abuse, race, death, alcoholism, Alzheimer's, ageing, date rape, disabilities, body size, etc.

Society Defined is the physical location and social world of the novel; it is also when the readers meet the heroine and hero. Because the popular romance is based on emotional appeal, it must contain compelling characters whose emotional development must be believable and authentic. As social constructs have evolved, so too have the characteristics and personalities of the protagonists. Heroines can be a bluestocking governess, a fashionista or a single mother. Heroes can be anything from a medieval knight to a Navy SEAL to a sexy werewolf. Their personalities can be as varied and unique as the multitude of individuals in the world.

The most obvious shift in characterization is in the evolution of the heroine. In the 1950s, romance heroines had professions like teachers and nurses; when they married or had children, they quit their job. Since the sexual revolution of the 1970s, heroines have increasingly been allowed to have and keep their careers. Heroines have become more active; they are no longer 'required' to be mousy, orphaned, naïve or sexually innocent as their agency has increased. The contemporary romance heroine is a fully realized, self-sufficient female who is quirky enough to be beyond statistically average. In Jennifer Crusie's *Bet Me* (2004), the defined society is the yuppie world of several single professional females and males. Min Dobbs, a well-employed, slightly conservative actuary, is not particularly interested in any kind of relationship; Cal Morrissey, a reputed ladies' man, is coerced into a bet that he can't get Min into bed within a month. There are Little League ballgames, Italian restaurants, Elvis movies and family dinners in small city environment.

The heroine and hero first encounter each other in *The Meeting*. It can be accidental or intentional, begin with or without conflict. Some romances combine this meeting with an awareness of an attraction between the characters. Even if the heroine and hero are not physically perfect, their beauty will be in the eye of the beholder. She may consider herself fat, but the hero will see her as curvy and voluptuous. The hero's scars, which allow him to fend off dangerous intimacy, will be attractive to her. In *Bet Me*, the initial meeting between Min and Cal in a bar is rather prickly; she knows about the bet but has underestimated the amount, whereas Cal is simply trying to maintain his reputation.

The Barrier is the obstacle or conflict that must be overcome or removed for the hero and heroine to finally come together. It can be external or internal, physical or psychological, a physical threat or a moral dilemma; it is the problem which keeps the heroine and hero from acting on their mutual attraction the minute they set eyes on one another. Sometimes it is not one thing or one solution; like attraction, conflict can have an endless range of sources: mistrust, lack of self-esteem, opposing goals, fear of intimacy, etc. For Min and Cal, the primary barrier is the bet. However, both individuals also face internal barriers involving self-esteem, image and trust.

The Attraction is the developing awareness of the importance of the other. The basis for that attraction can be as varied as the heroines and heroes, ranging from shared goals to economic interests to some level of sexual chemistry. It is more than just physical attraction: qualities like honour, humour, courage and kindness generate admiration and love. It might be a quality the characters share; it could be something one lacks and the other supplies. The growing attraction occurs during a series of scenes. Critical points of development in Min and Cal's relationship revolve around Krispy Kreme donuts and chicken marsala.

The Declaration is the public revelation of love. Both the heroine and hero not only realize their love but publicly verbalize it. This announcement tends to follow the *Ritual Death*, in which 'the hoped-for resolution seems absolutely impossible' (Regis 2003, 35). Everything has gone astray and all hope seems lost until *The Recognition* of that which will resolve or overcome the barrier. The characters – usually the heroine – realize their sense of identity or accept their sense of Self. The hero's scars are healed. For Min and Cal, the ritual death comes when Cal learns that Min knows about the bet and thinks she's been playing him along. As the deadline for the bet nears, Cal and Min finally act on their recognition of love for each other; the declaration – private and public – follows in the ensuing chaotic scene.

The Betrothal, finally, is the promise of the future and leads to a resolution towards a companionate marriage. This promise of 'Happily Ever After', reaffirming values of commitment and self-esteem, is what makes romances satisfying. Things may go horribly wrong in real life; bad things happen to good people while villains prosper. But in the romance novel, the world is ultimately fair and forgiving, a place where love and poetic justice prevail. Despite Min's worries about what comes after the 'Happily Ever After', *Bet Me* ends with optimistic promise.

Sex

Much of the criticism surrounding the popular romance revolves around sex: popular romance novels are maligned as trashy lurid sex books, pornography for women. But romance is more than just writing about sex. The romance has always been about female desire and sexuality. As such, sex is an integral part of the romantic relationship. Sex includes intimacy, desire, eroticism, seduction, passion and love. The level of explicitness depends upon the writer. In a romance, though, it can never be simply gratuitous sex; the sex scene must move the story along. The use of sex scenes must be carefully incorporated into the plot structure in a meaningful way to build desire and reflect the romance. The point of development in the relationship complements the intensity of the scene and vocabulary used. A typical progression may go from touching and kissing to necking to foreplay to oral sex to intercourse.

A point of debate, particularly among romance writers, revolves around how to construct love scenes, how many to include and how much to explain. A good sex scene is so intimate that readers become privy to the characters' most private experience. Through the developing relationship, the sex scene is paradoxical: that which is intimate and private becomes profoundly public. In romance writing, though, it functions to further the relationship between the characters, to develop their courtship rites in a coherently integrated narrative. The explicitness of the scenes depends on the level of sensuality of the novel, running from sweet to erotica.

Prose: Purple and Otherwise

One of first items casual critics respond to is the use of language in romance, usually pulling quotations out of the context of the narrative voice of woman and female desire. Phrases like 'I'm hungry . . . but not for food' or 'throbbing shaft of manhood' or 'slid into the weeping furnace of her sheath' sound cheap and lurid when taken out of context. As writers struggle to capture the intensity of the emotions – whether anger or desire – they are often accused of 'purple prose', language that is excessively ornate or extravagant to surpass the context of the novel.

Women's sexuality had been repressed and disregarded for so long that the word choices appear maudlin, mawkish, purple, corny or scientific. Romance writers can be challenged to describe sex scenes because linguistically, the words or lexicon for adequate description don't exist. Without the vocabulary, women are unable to even think about the act. Furthermore, in US culture, sex as an acceptable public topic is still officially taboo, spoken of only in euphemistic terms. In the public sphere, at least, there is a linguistic deficit of intimate language which may well be responsible for the unease, dis-ease, with popular romance especially in the US which values action over emotions, where language about emotions makes people uncomfortable. Euphemisms are comfort words that soften and smooth harsh and rough discourse. So the lexicon remaining ranges from the very scientific Latin (penis, areola, testes, coitus) – used to create distance and objectivity and to avoid embarrassment – or the dreaded Purple Prose.

Language allows the expression of experience, but language is limited. Writers of popular romance use the same patriarchal language other writers have used before them. If a good sex scene should reach *beyond* language, then it is not surprising that many sex scenes simply fade-to-black – literally beyond language. The theorist Hélène Cixous (1976) demanded that a 'new' female language was necessary because 'the symbolic discourse of language is another means through which man objectifies the world, reduces it to his terms, speaks in place of everything and everyone else – including women' (Jones 1997, 371). Cixous promoted the development of a *l'écriture féminine* for women to establish subjectivity; to stop Others – predominantly men – telling them how to feel sexually and to bring to the surface their own sexuality. There is no place better to explore *l'écriture féminine* than in popular romance. When Loretta Chase, in *Lord of Scoundrels* (1995), writes about 'sizzling ripples of sensation over her skin' or a 'wanton tangle of curls' or that 'I'm clay in your hands' (154, 213, 349), she is constructing the heroine's woman's body and her sexual pleasure.

Conclusion

The critique and analysis of romance writing is as complex as the genre itself. First-wave feminist critiques like Germaine Greer (*The Female Eunuch*, 1971) and Tania Modeleski (*Loving with a Vengeance*, 1985) dismissed romance fiction as complicit to patriarchal hegemony, that romantic love and marriage were only traps for women. Scholars like Janice Radway (1984) and Carol Thurston (1987) inspired succeeding generations to examine the romance for its cultural significance, sociological and economic impact and literary qualities. Jayne Ann Krentz has argued that romances allow for female empowerment, that the romance is ultimately subversive because heroines are 'imbued with the qualities normally reserved for the heroes in other genres: honor, courage, and determination' (1992, 5). Second-wave feminists similarly began to read romance more closely, finding it subversive and empowering. Nevertheless, any contemporary discussion or study of popular romance still begins with a defence of the genre or an argument asserting the value of studying the genre, calling for recognition and respect.

More recent studies of popular romance, such as those included in Sally Goade's *Empowerment versus Oppression* (2007) or Selinger and Frantz's *New Approaches to Popular Romance Fiction* (2012), examine the tropes, motifs and innovations, and how they are continuously evolving. These works and others, including the *Journal of Popular Romance Studies*, reflect the growing academic studies of popular romance and continued critical analysis of how women characters, women readers and women writers are gaining and acting on their empowerment through the genre. As a forum which allows for the expression of female ideology, the popular romance is a repository for the evolution of cultural ideals, gender issues and writing conventions.

Ultimately, the romance is always about relationships, either about traditional boy-meets-girl relationships or, more recently, homosexual relationships. They generally focus on a lead couple but can also expand to take in friends and family – as in Chick Lit – or to trace how a couple settles down to start a family, as seen in Sheryl Woods' *The Unclaimed Baby* (1999) that discusses issues of family planning and adoption. The romance is always designed to engage the emotions; readers are supposed to laugh, cry and become aroused. Each subgenre of romance, each element of the formula allows for almost infinite iterations.

Romance, to put it simply, is more than a mere formula; rather, it is a set of principles, tropes and conventions. It is similar to other popular genres in which evil people are punished and good people are rewarded with emotional justice and unconditional love. Ultimately, the popular romance reveals how a powerless undervalued section of the population finds empowerment and copes with the hegemonic patriarchy to establish a sense of value and worth. It is a genre where women win.

Works Cited

Austen, Jane (1813; 1995), *Pride and Prejudice*. London : Dover.
—(1815; 1998), *Emma*. London: Dover.
—(1818; 1997), *Persuasion*. London: Dover.
Beecroft, Alex (2009), *False Colors*. Philadelphia, PA: Running Press.
Brontë, Emily (1847; 2002), *Wuthering Heights*. London: Penguin Classics.
Brook, Meljean (2012), *Riveted*. New York: Berkeley Sensation.
Chase, Loretta (1995), *Lord of Scoundrels*. New York: Avon.
Cixous, Hélène (Summer 1976), 'The Laugh of the Medusa', trans. Keith Cohen and Paula Cohen. *Signs: Journal of Women in Culture and Society* 1(4), 875–93.
Coulter, Catherine (1988; 2004), *False Pretenses*. New York: Signet.
Crusie, Jennifer (2004), *Bet Me*. New York: St Martin's.
Dixon, jay (1999), *The Romance Fiction of Mills & Boon, 1909-1990s*. London: Routledge.
du Maurier, Daphne (1938; 2002), *Rebecca*. New York: Avon.
Ferris, Suzanne and Mallory Young (eds) (2006), *Chick Lit: The New Woman's Fiction*. New York: Routledge.
Fielding, Helen (1996), *Bridget Jones' Diary*. New York: Penguin.
Frantz, Sarah S. G. and Eric Murphy Selinger (eds) (2012), *New Approaches to Popular Romance Fiction: Critical Essays*. Jefferson, NC: McFarland.
Goade, Sally (ed.) (2007), *Empowerment versus Oppression: Twenty-First Century Views of Popular Romance Novels*. Newcastle: Cambridge Scholars Publishing.

Green, Jane (2000), *Jemima J*. New York: Broadway.

Greer, Germaine (1970), *The Female Eunuch*. New York: Farrar, Straus and Giroux.

Herendeen, Ann (2008), *Phyllida and the Brotherhood of Philander*. New York: Harper Perennial.

Heyer, Georgette (1935), *Regency Buck*. London: Heinemann.

Holly, Emma (2004), *Velvet Glove*. London: Cheek.

Holt, Victoria (1960; 2008), *Mistress of Mellyn*, 2nd edn. New York: St Martin's.

Hull, E. M. (1920; 2001), *The Sheikh*. Philadelphia: University of Pennsylvania Press.

James, Eloisa (2011), *The Duke is Mine*. New York: Avon.

Jenkins, Beverly (1996), *Indigo*. New York: Avon.

Jensen, Margaret Ann (1984), *Love's $weet Return: The Harlequin Story*. Bowling Green, OH: Bowling Green University Popular Press.

Jones, Rosalind Ann (1981; 1997), 'Writing the Body: Toward an Understanding of *l'écriture féminine*', in Robyn R. Warhol, Robyn Varhol-Down and Diane Price Hendl (eds), *Feminisms: An Anthology of Literary Theory and Criticism*, rev. edn. New Brunswick, NJ: Rutgers University Press, pp. 370–83.

Kitt, Sandra (1984), *Adam and Eva*. New York: Harlequin.

Krentz, Jayne Ann (ed.) (1992), *Dangerous Men and Adventurous Women: Romance Writers on the Appeal of the Romance*. Philadelphia: University of Pennsylvania Press.

—(1996), *Amaryllis*. New York: Pocket.

Meyer, Stephanie (2005), *Twilight*. Boston: Little, Brown.

Mitchell, Margaret (1936), *Gone With the Wind*. New York: Macmillan.

Modeleski, Tania (1985), *Loving with a Vengeance*. New York: Methuen.

Nathan, Melissa (2004), *Persuading Annie*. New York: William Morrow.

Pearce, Lynne (2007), *Romance Writing*. Cambridge: Polity.

Radcliffe, Ann (1794; 2001), *The Mysteries of Udolpho*. London: Penguin Classics.

Radway, Janice (1984), *Reading the Romance: Women, Patriarchy, and Popular Literature*. Durham: University of North Carolina Press.

Regis, Pamela (2003), *A Natural History of the Romance*. Philadelphia: University of Pennsylvania Press.

Rivers, Francine (1997), *Redeeming Love*. Colorado Springs, CO: Multnomah.

Roberts, Nora (2002), *Midnight Bayou*. New York: Jove.

Rodgers, Rosemary (1974), *Sweet Savage Love*. New York: Avon.

Rosenthal, Pam (2008), *The Edge of Impropriety*. New York: Signet.

Stephens, Ann Sophia (1862; 2009), *Esther: A Story of the Oregon Trail*. New York: Beadle.

Stewart, Mary (1958; 2006), *Nine Coaches Waiting*. Chicago: Chicago Review Press.

Teo, Hsu-Ming (2013), *Desert Passions: Orientalism and Romance Novels*. Austin: University of Texas Press.

Thurston, Carol (1987), *The Romance Revolution: Erotic Novels for Women and the Quest for a New Sexual Identity*. Urbana: University of Illinois Press.

Vivanco, Laura (2011), *For Love and Money: The Literary Art of the Harlequin Mills & Boon Romance*. Penrith: Humanities-Ebooks.

Vohra, Milan (December 2012), *The Love Asana*. Mills & Boon Modern.

Waters, Sarah (1998), *Tipping the Velvet*. London: Virago.

White, Debra Smith (2006), *Amanda*. Eugene, OR: Harvest House.

Woodiwiss, Kathleen (1972), *The Flame and the Flower*. New York: Avon.

Woods, Sheryl (1999), *The Unclaimed Baby*. New York: Silhouette.

4

'The Lads' Own Paper': Male Confessional Literature and the Legacy of Adventure

Alice Ferrebe

In 2002, prominent American feminist writer Elaine Showalter made an unusual critical detour to consider the fictional genre of Ladlit, a 'romantic, comic, popular male confessional literature . . . stretching from 1950 to 1999 . . . , from Kingsley to Martin Amis' (2002, 60). Kingsley Amis's *Lucky Jim*, published in 1954, had helped to initiate the much vaunted, much derided literary label of the 'Angry Young Men', and like all noisily promoted, popular literary phenomena, Ladlit is a similarly contested category. Showalter, however, remains on a limb with her date for its genesis – most critics cite Nick Hornby's autobiographical *Fever Pitch* (1992) as a starting point, and though the genre was at its most culturally prominent through the 1990s, it continued well into the new century. Tony Parsons's *Man and Boy*, the genre's greatest success story in terms of sales, was only published in 1999, the first volume of a trilogy. Though the term 'Ladlit' has been (over)used to include everything from Andy McNab's action thrillers, so-called 'hoolie books' (accounts of gang violence between football supporters) and the self-consciously taboo-breaking early literary writing of Ian McEwan and Martin Amis, its most meaningful designation pertains to the confessional fiction of a group of male authors including Hornby, Parsons, Mark Barrowcliffe, Mike Gayle and John O'Farrell.

Ladlit began in part as a cultural riposte to (and commercial spin-off from) its 'sister genre', Chick Lit, eschewing that genre's pastel book covers for primary colours dotted with puff quotes. 'Brilliant', opined comedian Harry Enfield on the cover of Hornby's novel *High Fidelity*, 'A very funny and concise explanation of why we men are as we are. If you are male, you should read it and then make your partner read it, so they will no longer hate you but pity you instead' (Hornby 1996). The prospective reader is thus assured of observational accuracy and humour based upon a process of mutual, and male, recognition. This promise of masculine bonding was upheld in Ladlit's paratexts (the advertising material, reviews and authorial comment surrounding the genre) to be something distinctively new, at least in the experience of the contemporary young male reader. 'Women', claimed Hornby in 1995, 'are accustomed to reading fiction, then thinking, like Sybil Fawlty, "I *know*, I *know*." Men's fiction, over the last 20 or 30 years hasn't been like that' (Bennett 1995, A2). The genre self-consciously seeks to represent a personal, domestic experience that has long been the terrain of women writers, this time from a male point of view. That inclusivity, however, has clearly defined limits. Ladlit is a distinctly British genre. It is class-, age- and race-specific (middle-ish, young-ish and white), and it is heterosexual and metropolitan (or rather, Londoncentric). We might then assume that it represents 'hegemonic' British masculinity, defined as 'the currently most honoured way of being a man' (Connell 2005, 832). Yet the genre's representation of the male gender and the demands it places on men is considerably less stable than the hegemonic ideal allows.

Ladlit's context is a mix of economic and cultural conditions that pose particular challenges for traditional models of masculinity. The 1990s saw the culminating influence of decades of economic change and decline upon male dominance of the paid labour market, and a violent disruption of the traditional employment patterns of British men. Dominic Head has claimed of Hornby's novels that they 'have afforded a revealing insight into the social moment' (2002, 249). This is certainly one reward for careful critical consideration of Hornby's work and of Ladlit more generally: a better appreciation of the troubled position of men within British society around the turn of the millennium. But novels are not purely sociological documents, and we can and should attend to their textual stylistics as equally revealing. In identifying Ladlit as 'romantic', Showalter suggests its tendency to conform to a happy ending of heterosexual union (2002, 60). Yet the genre of romance has long roots, reaching through the popular (and feminized) sentimental fiction of the twentieth, to medieval narratives of heroic chivalry and adventure. Martin Green claims that 'Adventure is a concept ... signally linked to manliness': the discussions in this volume of the work of John Buchan and the character of James Bond certainly bear this out (1993, 15; see also Chapters 11 and 12). This chapter will offer a reading of Ladlit as a negotiation of traditional models of manliness amidst cultural conditions that seem to deny their continued possibility. As we shall see, Ladlit was determinedly sold by publishers as something new in fiction, but it is a consideration of the genre's legacy to much older fictional forms that will allow us better to understand its sensationalized sway as a popular genre at the turn of the twenty-first century.

New Men, New Lads

In 1990, Antony Easthope began *What a Man's Gotta Do* with a claim that, 'despite all that has been written over the past twenty years on femininity and feminism, masculinity has stayed pretty well concealed. This has always been its ruse to hold on to its power' (1990, 1). Ladlit's ruse is very different. Its narratives make masculinity into a spectacle, ostentatiously confessing all the practical and emotional difficulties of acting like a man in contemporary British society. Whether this gambit is symptomatic of a contextually specific crisis in the definition of the male gender or is simply another attempt to address masculinity's inherent conceptual instability is open to debate (see Ferrebe 2005). It is indisputably a response to the ongoing cultural prominence of the feminist debate in the West during the second half of the twentieth century. In 1949 Simone de Beauvoir opened *The Second Sex* with the provocative question, 'what is a woman?', asserting with justified conviction that, although a woman's experience was inevitably considered to be particular to her sex, 'A man would never set out to write a book on the peculiar situation of the human male' (1988, 15). The genre of Ladlit is founded upon precisely this peculiarity. It has been characterized by some critics as part of an anti-feminist backlash (Gill 2003); a reaction against political progress towards a more equitable society achieved since de Beauvoir's prescient analysis of Western culture as enduringly patriarchal. At the beginning of the 1990s in the United States, Susan Faludi identified an aggressive and widespread cultural response to the increased possibility of full gender equality; 'a pre-emptive strike that stops women long before they reach the finish line' (1992, 12). Any British backlash manifested in Ladlit is altogether milder mannered, but the genre's relationship with feminism is certainly complex and frequently contradictory. Its representation of contemporary gender roles is heavily inflected by two prominent popular cultural figures, both mediated through men's magazines, and both, in different ways, a response to feminism.

The 'New Man', the ideal reader of magazines like *GQ* and *Esquire* during the late 1980s, was contrived as a progressive character, respectful to (and successful with) liberated women, and as comfortable browsing grooming products as he was cars. The so-called 'New Lad' came a little later, in *loaded* magazine in the early 1990s. He rejected the New Man's self-conscious gentility for a studied boorishness, glorifying football and drinking, and gleefully objectifying women in a professed spirit of fun. The magazine was a place, contributor Irvine Welsh noted wryly, 'where middle class men play at being working class' (Kelly 2004, 12). 'So, is *loaded* sexist?' asked Tim Southwell, one of the magazine's founding editors, in his autobiography. 'If being sexist means that you enjoy looking at pictures of attractive women then take me to court and have Mary Whitehouse flay me alive. Men like looking at pictures of attractive women. Big deal. Get over it' (1998, 213). The New Lad did not replace the New Man, but coexisted antagonistically with him, mocking his aspiration and his perceived effeminacy and intellectualism. Yet the rivals did have something in common, as Tim Edwards pointed out: '"new lads" are just as much a phoney marketing phenomenon as "new men"' (1997, 249).

Within the literary genre of Ladlit, both these media figures are routinely reproduced and often amalgamated within the protagonist-narrators them-selves. Perhaps the most schematic representation of these competing roles occurs in John O'Farrell's *The Best A Man Can Get* (2000), which conducts its ironic examination of the demands of contemporary fatherhood through the character of Michael Adams. He is a writer of advertising jingles (and thus no stranger to the niggling lure of commercialized symbolism), and shares a flat with three other lads in their late twenties, as well as a family home with his wife and soon-to-be three children. The narrative charts the consequences of his wife's discovery of his second home. This schema of a dual masculine life is fairly common within Ladlit: in Mark Barrowcliffe's *Infidelity for First-time Fathers*, for example, Stewart Dagman has to choose between his fiancée and his lover, both of whom are pregnant. Yet another duality is apparent within the voice of the protagonist himself. Stewart tells us:

> With sex, it is the whole woman that the mature and rounded man makes love to. Her personality and her body are one, you cannot separate them. This said, I really can't go any further without mentioning Cat's tits, which are spectacular. Also – in a non-sexist way – I'd like to compare them to Andrea's as a way of showing how I relate to each of the women. Feminists will be glad I have resisted the overwhelming impulse to give them marks out of 10. (2001, 44)

The affective tone struck here is in many ways exemplary of Ladlit, with its ironized pre-emption of criticism and its exaggeration of what Michael Kimmel has called a 'deeply shallow' emotional response (2006, n.p.). It indicates the coexistence of compliance with and rebellion against feminist demands for mutual respect and equality. It manages to be both self-deprecating and self-justifying. It pays lip service to the New Man script, while also allowing the New Lad to speak his 'truths': that men instinctively objectify women, and we as readers should, in Southwell's words, 'Get over it'. Of course, this dichotomy of honesty is a false one – the Lad is as much a constructed category as the New Man – but the promise of a return to supposedly 'natural' gender roles is nonetheless a crucial element of laddish discourse in magazines and novels alike. The narrative voice of Ladlit signals its knowingness of the terms of feminist political and critique, while simultaneously rebelling against them in its nostalgia for an imaginary time 'when men could be men'.

Womanism

Ladlit's complicated relationship with feminism, then, is far from an unmitigated backlash: it signals a nuanced, if confused, response to numerous feminist demands, not least that of a social need for enhanced male emotional expression. Yet Ladlit protagonists are occasionally required to take up arms against the feminist cause. In Hornby's *High Fidelity*, Rob Fleming remarks of his girlfriend's best friend, 'She's OK but, you know, she's one of those paranoid feminists who see evil in everything you say' (1996, 156). In Parsons's *Man and Boy*, paranoia about feminism is embodied in Harry Silver's lawyer, a bitterly divorced divorce-specialist:

> 'Men die younger than women,' said my new solicitor. 'We catch cancer more often than women. We commit suicide with greater frequency than women. We are more likely to be unemployed than women. . . . But for some reason I have never been able to fathom, Mr Silver, women are considered the victims'. (2000, 282)

From the 1970s onwards, Second Wave feminism directed its critical focus upon the particular experiences of women, to redress a patriarchal insistence upon men as the norm. Yet when men's economic power faltered, debate around the male gender as particular rather than normative strengthened both in the academies and the media. As Anthony Clare put it in his 2000 study *On Men: Masculinity in Crisis*, 'Now, the whole issue of men – the point of them, their purpose, their value, their justification – is a matter for public debate. . . . At the beginning of the twenty-first century it is difficult to avoid the conclusion that men are in serious trouble' (2001, n.p.) A prominent strand of this debate might best be characterized by discourse not feminist, but *womanist*. Journalist Rosalind Coward has styled 'womanism' as

> a sort of popularized version of feminism which acclaims everything women do and disparages men. . . . Womanism is feminism's vulgate. It . . . is by no means confined to a tiny, politically motivated bunch of man-hating feminists, but is a regular feature of mainstream culture. . . . Womanism is a convenient response to many of the uglier aspects of the great convulsions shaking modern society; the very convulsions that are, in other aspects, delivering what feminism demanded. (1999, 11–12)

Contemporary conditions, Coward continues, demand a considerably finer drawn picture of the relations between social groups than the cartoonish figures of gender war. Sure enough, soldiers from this outdated battle do appear in Ladlit, but they are peripheral figures only, suggesting that the debate has moved on. Silver's solicitor is dismissed as (comically) unhinged, and in *High Fidelity* Rob finally stands up for himself and his gender against the 'paranoid feminist', asserting that men 'can't go on apologizing all our lives, you know' (Hornby 1996, 195). Ultimately, womanism's reflex disparagement of men is as unsatisfactory as patriarchy's compulsive concealment of women's cultural and social contributions: Ladlit heroes know that contemporary gender roles are much more complicated than simple divisions of good and bad.

However, a sense of contemporary male victimhood can still skew certain elements of the genre's representation of society. In marked contrast to the world of work represented by Chicklit, in which the female protagonists typically languish in undemanding, unrewarding jobs, professional women in Ladlit are flying high. In *High Fidelity*, the female romantic lead is a City lawyer; in Gayle's *Mr Commitment* (1999), an advertising executive. Their men/lads, however, work in peripheral jobs – writing jingles, owning record shops, standing up as comedians – they are low-, or at least sporadically paid, and dependent on their partners for financial stability. In *About a Boy* (1998), Hornby takes a further step into economic irresponsibility with his hero: Will Freeman lives solely, selfishly and supremely comfortably on the income from a nauseatingly jaunty Christmas song written in 1938 by his father. There is a marked difference here from the tenets of contemporary masculinity offered by other popular genres. As Gill puts it:

> In traditional romances the heroes are invariably strong, powerful and successful; in spy fiction and military genres they are presented as intelligent, valiant, purposeful; in lad lit, by contrast, readers are offered a distinctly unheroic masculinity – one that is fallible, self-deprecating and liable to fail at any moment. In relation to work, for example, lad lit heroes are portrayed as unsuccessful, struggling, or as clinging on by a thread to their tenuous 'careers'. (2009, n.p.)

Ladlit's lack of male professionals can also be read as a means of rebellion against the Lad's arch cultural rival, the New Man. Ladlit rejects professional fulfilment as a primary means of proving the male self. Within the prevailing economic climate that produces the genre, this is perhaps as much realistic as it is idealistic.

Acts of Bravery

Yet Ladlit's motley cast of protagonists have a more complex relationship with the masculinity of traditional popular literary narratives than Gill suggests. The clearest origins of the genre lie in a number of 1990s autobiographical works by men that were characterized by a fearlessness of confession and well publicized as a result (see, for example, Morrison 1993). Hornby claimed of *Fever Pitch*, the first and most famous of these male confessionals, that 'I wanted part of the thrill of the book, for the reader, being "My God, how can he say this in print?"' (Bennett 1995, A2). Bill Buford, editor of *Granta* magazine, likened this new brand of male writing to travel writing, 'Because the best travel writing is actually going to a place and coming back with the story of an experience that we haven't had', and it was he who coined a name for this adventurous mode: 'lad literature' (A2). Unlike the memoirs that predate it, Ladlit is not autobiographical (or at least not fully), but the popular success of this brand of fiction does rely upon its readership's perception that its protagonist's self-revelatory tone represents a daring breach of conventional masculine emotional repression. As we have seen, the environment of the late twentieth-century man provides him with few opportunities for more traditional, professional or physical means of demonstrating heroism. In Parsons's *Man and Boy*, the war-won medals of Harry Silver's father are insistently and nostalgically invoked as a symbol of past professional masculine bravery and prowess. Harry's workplace rings with phoney military banter, 'as though working in television was a lot like running an undercover SAS unit in South Armagh' (2000, 59). Though he can win no medals for it, Harry's determination to confess his failings is proffered as an authentically heroic alternative to this empty macho posturing. Ladlit recasts confession as a new action-adventure in male self-expression: travelling to the depths of a hidden self and returning with stories to tell.

Do Real Men Read?

The contemporary turn in linguistic analysis has had more influence upon Ladlit as a literary genre and marketing category than its devotedly anti-intellectual narrative voice would care to admit. As selfhood (and so gender) has become something routinely understood as performed within discourse, Ladlit's allegiance to those models of an authentic and masculine inner self and is tellingly anachronistic. Martin Amis emphasized the performance aspect of laddishness: 'A lad is not a lad by himself, he's only a lad when he's with the lads. You can't walk around in your own house being a lad, can you? It's a communal activity' (2000, 2). Judith Butler's seminal academic study *Gender Trouble* (1990) cast gender – traditional conceptions of masculinity, femininity and all identity points in between – as 'performative' – something we *do*, rather than something we intrinsically *are*. Laddishness therefore needs to be examined within the context of its performance, and this requires consideration not just of the tone of Ladlit's narrative voice, but also of the assumptions and demands relating to the 'listener' or ideal reader.

Ladlit texts might initially appear to have an uncomplicated relationship with their readership. Like all popular fiction, they are perceived as pleasurably easy to consume. Yet the relationship between the consumer and genre fiction – and the identity of the consumer him/herself – is a complex one, and revealing of the cultural context in which the textual and commercial transactions are taking place. As we have considered, the New Man and the New Lad function within late twentieth-century popular culture as part of the ongoing renegotiation of the links between masculinity and consumption, as male consumerism has been progressively legitimized within our culture. Yet linguistic research has routinely discovered gaps between the adept male consumer of advertising and the self-image of 'ordinary' men. Ladlit's narrative address, and the ease of its consumption, relies upon the sense of an unforced, immediate identification between narrator and reader.

One particular stylistic dedicated to achieving this identification is crucial to Ladlit texts: the address to a second person – 'you'. In *High Fidelity*, Rob speaks directly to an ideal co-conspirator: 'I never remember their birthdays – you don't do you, unless you are of the female persuasion?' (Hornby 1996, 170). The forgetful trait is presented as an inevitable, and biological, characteristic, and the narrator assumes instant recognition that laddish masculinity involves the admirably careless rejection of social niceties. This concurrence of ideas is presented as uncomplicated communication between the male narrator and male reader. Yet the assured dynamic of this address is actually undermined throughout Hornby's novel. The object of Rob's frequent second-person address soon shifts from the ideal reader to Laura, Rob's ex-partner. He begins the novel by attempting to humiliate her, listing his top five 'memorable split-ups', and claiming that 'those places are reserved for the kind of humiliations and heartbreaks that you're just not capable of delivering' (9). But elsewhere Laura is also appealed to directly as the representative of moral authority, as when Rob invokes a New Mannish appreciation of female wisdom: 'You'd say that this was childish, Laura. You'd say that it is stupid of me to compare Rob and Jackie with Rob and Laura who are in their mid-thirties, established, living together' (20). In fact, the referent of that 'you' shifts so frequently, and appeals to such increasingly esoteric fragments of supposedly shared knowledge (the rarity of certain Otis Redding singles, for example [69]), that the relationship between the narrator and his ideal reader becomes increasingly unstable.

One of the most important shifts in mass media reporting and advertising in recent years has been the way in which genres of communication associated with the private domain have increasingly been appropriated to the public sphere. This is a phenomenon which Norman Fairclough refers to a 'synthetic personalization' (2001, 62). In *Language and Gender*, Mary M. Talbot identifies three facets of synthetic personalization: the contrived impression of two-way interaction; a style relying upon informality and a particular pattern of pronominal usage (the frequent use of 'you' and 'we'); and the presupposition of common knowledge, often used to create classifications in the minds of the readership, rather than to reinforce pre-existing categories (2010, 151). In this way, media texts attempt to generate commercial success by constructing a consumer base, rather than discovering a pre-existent one. Compliancy with a particular point of view is demanded and enforced, rather than elicited and endowed.

We have seen these linguistic facets to be routine features of the mode of address of the Ladlit literary text too. Hornby's title *High Fidelity* puns, of course, on the novel's themes of long-playing records and potentially long-lasting relationships, but also trades upon the promise of the authentic reproduction of a contemporary male voice, received without distortion by his male peers. This ideal of direct communication has been a crucial part of the marketing of Ladlit. Of course, as Pierre Bourdieu has pointed out, all books exist within a 'two-faced reality', as commodities as well as cultural objects (1992, 26), and in the realm of popular fiction, the duality of commerce and culture is especially apparent. Yet the textual ambiguity over who exactly the Ladlit text is speaking to can be considered as both responding to and productive of an unusually pronounced conflict between its proffered ideal reader and the realities of its market. Does the confusion over the addressee of Ladlit's narrative voice extend to the identity of those who actually buy these books?

Critical writing from the Second Wave of feminism frequently addressed a sisterhood of readers. As we have seen, the branch of gender studies dedicated to the study of masculinity in particular did not develop until the 1990s. Michael Kimmel's definitive analysis of the homosocial dynamics of male gender construction makes striking use of synthetic personalization through the first-person plural ('we') precisely to emphasize the cultural unfamiliarity of a textual appeal to men *as* men, rather than gender-neutral (and thus ideal) readers: 'Other men: We are under the constant careful scrutiny of other men. Other men watch us, rank us, grant our acceptance into the realm of manhood' (2004, 186). For all its purportedly direct appeal to a shared masculine experience, Ladlit's register is distinctly anthropological, and anthropology is a discipline that wrangles with the presence, identity and position of an observer relative to the experiences being recorded. Ladlit narratives consist of the exposition of the male protagonists' justificatory motives for their (often despicable) behaviour and usually invoke a (humorous) plea for diminished responsibility on the grounds of their gender. To many, this reads not as an appeal to fellow lads, but to someone witnessing that laddishness. Gill summarizes a common critical response: 'The specificities of the confessions, and particularly their focus upon what all men are like, raises questions about the assumed readership of lad lit: is it really designed for women and not men at all?' (2009, n.p.).

Nick Hornby certainly thinks so, pronouncing the genre to be 'old-man writing for a feminine sensibility' (Bennett 1995, A2). We have already seen how its typical narrative voice can distort itself in anticipation of feminist expectations and in rebellion against them. Rather than 'other men', then, we might think of Ladlit's masculine performance as taking place before a female audience/readership and thus understand its ambiguities as the result of a peculiarly unstable mix of enforcing empathy and wheedling for sympathy. Kimmel explains the commercial failure of the US version of Ladlit by the fact that its cynical tone, greatly enhanced in comparison to the British genre, made it unlikely to appeal to women, who, he claims 'won't read these books unless there is some hope of redemption, some effort these guys make to change. And men won't read them because, well, real men don't read' (2006, n.p.).

On both sides of the Atlantic there is a long-established problem when it comes to fiction aimed at young men. As Kati Irons puts it, 'Men aged 18 to 30 are like the Holy Grail to booksellers. The industry waffles between shrugging them off with "eh, they don't read" to desperate attempts to woo them. This is how we end up with such unfortunate marketing attempts as "Lad Lit"' (2007, n.p.). Unfortunate from the point of view of the industry, that is, because, leaving aside whether the novels were bought and read by men or by women, they never sold in significant numbers. Natalie Danford underlines this point in relation to one of Ladlit's biggest sellers. Helen Fielding's *Bridget Jones's Diary* launched Chicklit in 1998 by selling over two million copies in hard- and paperbacks, while it took Nick Hornby six titles to hit a similar level of sales. Danford quotes a fiction buyer's damning verdict on the genre as literary commodity: 'the only place lad lit exists as a viable genre is in the imaginations of publishers' (2004, n.p.).

The global conglomerations that now produce the vast majority of books require popular genres with a clearly distinguishable target market and guaranteed volumes of sales. For the publishing industry then, Ladlit was soon finished as a commercial proposition, if it ever began. Showalter's liberalism in designating a starting date of 1950 is not matched by her abrupt truncation of Ladlit's era in 1999, by which point, she claims, the 'traditional distinctions of maturity and coming-of-age collapsed' (2002, 76). She is vague as to why this collapse occurred, but her sense of a post-millennial cultural turn is echoed in Harry Ritchie's review of Parsons's final instalment to the *Man and Boy* sequence. Ritchie lightly applauds the enhanced realism of *Men from the Boys* (2010), manifested in a 'welcome new uncertainty of its hero' (2010, n.p.). As the new century came in, it seems, so some old certainties went out, and the publishing industry's confidence in Ladlit as a genre speaking directly to an eager and untapped readership of young men went too.

Boy's Own Adventure Time

Yet in another, stylistic, sense, Ladlit was always out of time. As Gill has noted, much of the critical interest surrounding the genre was generated by a temporal logic that understood it to chronicle a new masculinity (that of the New Lad) that chronologically displaced all older models (2009, n.p.). As we have seen, that logic was false: New Men and New Lads coexisted as marketing phenomena throughout the 1990s, and the alleged newness of Ladlit as a mode of male self-expression was always undermined by its frequent appeals to older stereotypes of manliness – what Hornby called 'old-man writing' (Bennett 1995, A2). We might add to this temporal confusion the fact that the male narrators, be they men or lads, are often depicted as acting like boys.

Benwell notes the 'widely observed regressive and adolescent tendencies acted out by New Lad magazines in which there is a nostalgic retreat to infantile forms of behaviour' (2003, 14). *Man and Boy* works to valorize childish tendencies as indicative of a 'child within' – drawn in by Harry Silver's confessional tone, the reader is required to grant him licence for his petulance and fallibility. S/he should accept and even cherish the realization that the titular role of leading boy applies not to Harry's young son Pat but, to Harry, the man himself. A similar pun is apparent in Hornby's *About a*

Boy, in which the fatherless boy Marcus recognizes that, in Will Freeman, he has found a man who can teach him how to act like a 'real' teenager. Nancy Lesko has claimed that 'Adolescence is usually understood to end when a person finishes school, gets a full time job, marries, and has children' (2001, 132). The central male characters of Ladlit have commonly accrued all these markers, without having attained maturity itself. Harry Silver admits of his marriage that 'In my heart, I believed that Gina was only pretending to be a housewife, while I pretended to be my father' (Parsons 2000, 21). He is unfaithful to Gina and loses custody of Pat. The true marker of Harry's maturity at the end of the first novel in Parsons's trilogy is that he relinquishes the custody battle for his son's sake and lets him go to live with his mother in Japan.

Lesko claims, 'Like many novels, adolescent discourse is set in *abstract adventure time*; that is, time appears to have chronology, but the characters do not age and remain unaffected by time and events' (2001, 131). Ian Fleming's James Bond series would be a notable example of abstract adventure time, for example, with Fleming's vaunted 'reality effect' – his unwavering narrative eye for material detail – producing no more than the *effect* of reality, within an otherwise unreal narrative chronology. Like Romance novels, Ladlit texts almost inevitably end with a heterosexual union, and like the traditional 'novel of education', or *Bildungsroman*, they conclude with their heroes locating a more personally satisfactory place in the world. In his study of the *Bildungsroman*, Franco Moretti suggests that a 'successful initiation leads to group solidarity and a warm sense of belonging; a successful adolescence adds to these a profound sense of self – of one's personality' (2000, 106). Ultimately, then, we might think of Ladlit novels as the accounts of suspended periods of adolescence. As such, narrative time within the genre is notably out of joint. This places the protagonists at odds with that human role that most heightens the sensibility of the progression of time – parenthood.

In *Man and Boy*, Harry Silver has a son, but he is yet to leave adolescence and become a 'real' father. Pat is returned to London and his father in *Man and Wife* (2002), but in *Men from the Boys* (2010), now aged 15, his character is considerably less effective in generating emotional conflict, as the boy attains an increasing measure of emotional independence. Parsons uses him less and less frequently. Pat is a problem across the Silver trilogy: his growing up compromises the static sanctity of abstract adventure time and highlights Harry's own failure to progress, hence the child's repeated removal from the story. In Barrowcliffe's *Infidelity for First-Time Fathers*, the narrative climax is constructed around the almost simultaneous birth of three children: one to Stewart's fiancée Andrea, and twins to his girlfriend Cat. Stewart's first glance mercifully reveals Andrea's baby to have been fathered by his best friend, so the narrative's 9-month gestation of Stewart's dilemma – Andrea or Cat? – is immediately, and perfunctorily, at an end. The story closes before Stewart has to confront parenting with its relentless chronological progression of milestones: adventure time ends just as the clock starts ticking.

Alert to the pitfalls of relying upon reader empathy towards a boy-man with children of his own, as well as to the inevitable confrontation with chronological progression that fatherhood demands, Hornby cannily avoided it as narrative device beyond the clever feint of the pseudo-father in *About a Boy*. His Ladlit novels thus maintain the 'abstract adventure time' we have seen to be characteristic of these tales of arrested adolescence. It was in his novel for (genuinely) adolescent readers, *Slam* (2007), that Hornby eventually chose to confront fatherhood with the tale of Sam Jones, whose girlfriend gets pregnant when they are both 16. As Lesko has expressed, adolescence is a period with a peculiar relationship with time – supposedly a cherished stage of self-discovery and surging growth, but also one of stasis: a waiting for 'real life' to begin. While Alicia is expecting their baby, Sam twice time-travels into his future as a father. There he must confront realities (a weepy postpartum partner, the horror of nappies), negotiate obstacles and learn to believe in his own ability to offer love, compromise and commitment. Even within the novel's 'real time' diegesis Sam expresses his experience of fatherhood in terms of time's dynamic relativity: 'the boy who was talking to Alicia that afternoon . . . he wasn't sixteen. He wasn't just two years younger than the person who's talking to you now. It feels now, and it even felt then, as though that boy was eight or nine years old' (Hornby 2007, 140). On one level, this narrative device can be read as a sly mimicry of the 'I just don't know how I got here' sensibility of the careless Lad Dad, implying that while a confusion of roles and responsibility might be reasonable for a time-travelling 16-year-old boy, a thirty-something man deserves no such licence. Hornby's adolescent novel provides a humorous exaggeration of the disorientation of moving through a life-stage in which time is paradoxically both stalled and fleeting. Yet Sam's mature first-person account of himself, with its careful calibrations of time passing and emotions changing, contrasts revealingly with Ladlit. The genre's realist aspirations – the cultivated illusion of a man speaking directly to other men about his experience – exclude the possibility of Sam's spectacular chronological leaps. Yet, as we have seen, the integrity and immediacy of these 'real time' narratives is compromised further by their reliance upon an '*abstract adventure time*' that allows their men narrators to act like boys in a period of prolonged adolescence (Lesko 2001, 131).

Ladlit's impulse to cast male confession as heroic complicates its observational acuity with the legacies of an older fictional model, more at home in *The Boy's Own Paper* than *loaded*. Green named adventure writing as an 'alternative to moral realism, which is the aesthetic mode appropriate to England, the home country' (1993, 4). Ladlit seeks to play both home and away in this regard: the stylistics (and covers) of its novels blandish their honesty, while the protagonists' accounts of themselves rely upon an arrested chronology that suspends their moral progress to elicit the reader's sanction of their shortcomings. The identity of the ideal reader who will grant such acceptance is also a confused issue: the genre was initially marketed for a new readership of young men, yet its mode of textual address skews towards another gender altogether. Nor does Ladlit's woman trouble end there. Contemporary culture and economic reality force its lads to confront the expectation of equal maturity and responsibility in their relationships with inevitably female partners. They can balk at such demands, finding refuge in nostalgia for a time when male dominance was uncompromised and glorified. Yet ultimately the sensibilities of the narrators tend towards Coward's belief that 'the only convincing contemporary representation of heroism is that of an inner struggle towards greater awareness and deeper relationships; that is, a struggle towards a more "feminine" position. This', she adds with satisfaction, 'is one of feminism's most important legacies' (1999, 110). Ladlit's characteristic narrative voice, its structure and its readership is far more complex that might be first assumed. And though the genre might now be at an end (at least as a marketable commodity), the issues it raised in regard to the conflict of gendered roles in contemporary Britain remain all too current.

Works Cited

Amis, K. (1954), *Lucky Jim*. London: Victor Gollancz.
Amis, M. (2000), 'All about my father'. *Guardian*, 8 May, 2.
Barrowcliffe, M. (2001), *Infidelity for First-time Fathers*. London: Headline.
De Beauvoir, S. (1988), *The Second Sex*. London: Picador.
Bennett, C. (1995), 'True Confessions'. *Guardian*, 7 July, A2.

Bourdieu, P. (1992), *The Field of Cultural Production: Essays on Art and Literature*, ed. Randal Johnson. Cambridge, MA: Polity.

Butler, J. (1990), *Gender Trouble: Feminism and the Subversion of Identity*. London: Routledge.

Clare, A. (2001), *On Men: Masculinity in Crisis*. London: HarperCollins e-book.

Connell, R. W. and Messerschmidt, J. W. (2005), 'Hegemonic Masculinity: Rethinking the Concept'. *Gender and Society* 19(6), 829–59.

Coward, R. (1999), *Sacred Cows: Is Feminism Relevant to the New Millenium?*. London: HarperCollins.

Danford, N. (2004), 'Ladlit Hits the Skids'. *Publishers' Weekly* 251(13), 29 March, http://www.publishersweekly.com/pw/print/20040329/30116-lad-lit-hits-the-skids.html, accessed 5 January 2013.

Easthope, A. (1990), *What a Man's Gotta Do: The Masculine Myth in Popular Culture*. Boston: Unwin Hyman.

Edwards, T. (1997), *Men in the Mirror: Men's Fashions, Masculinity and Consumer Society*. London: Cassell.

Fairclough, N. (2001), *Language and Power*. London: Longman.

Faludi, S. (1991), *Backlash: The Undeclared War Against American Women*. London: Chatto & Windus.

Ferrebe, A. (2005), *Masculinity in Male-Authored Fiction 1950-2000*. Houndmills: Palgrave Macmillan.

Fielding, H. (1996), *Bridget Jones's Diary*. London: Picador.

Gayle, M. (1999), *Mr Commitment*. London: Flame.

Gill, R. (2003), 'Power and the Production of Subjects: A Genealogy of the New Man and the New Lad', in B. Benwell (ed.), *Masculinity and Men's Lifestyle Magazines*. Oxford: Blackwell, pp. 34–56.

—(2009), 'Lad Lit as Mediated Intimacy: A Postfeminist Tale of Female Power, Male Vulnerability and Toast'. *Working Papers on the Web*, 13(September), http://extra.shu.ac.uk/wpw/chicklit/index.html, accessed 25 October 2012.

Green, M. (1993), *The Adventurous Male: Chapters in the History of the White Male Mind*. Pennsylvania: Pennsylvania State University Press.

Head, D. (2002), *The Cambridge Introduction to Modern British Fiction 1950-2000*. Cambridge: Cambridge University Press.

Hornby, N. (1992), *Fever Pitch*. London: Victor Gollancz Ltd.

—(1996), *High Fidelity*. London: Indigo.

—(1998), *About a Boy*. London: Victor Gollancz Ltd.

—(2007), *Slam*. London: Penguin.

Irons, K. (2007), 'Harry Potter and the end'. *Blogcritics*, 1 August, http://blogcritics.org/books/article/harry-potter-and-the-end/, accessed 5 January 2013.

Kelly, A. (2004), 'Irvine Welsh in Conversation with Aaron Kelly'. *Edinburgh Review* 113, 7–17.

Kimmel, M. (2006), 'Guy Lit – Whatever'. *Chronicle of Higher Education*, 26 May, 52(38), n.p.

Kimmel, M. S. (2004), 'Masculinity as Homophobia: Fear, Shame and Silence in the Construction of Gender Identity', in P. F. Murphy (ed.), *Feminism and Masculinities*. Oxford: Oxford University Press, pp. 182–99.

Lesko, N. (2001), *Act Your Age! A Cultural Construction of Adolescence*. New York and London: Routledge Falmer.

Moretti, F. (2000), *The Way of the World: The Bildungsroman in European Culture*, London: Verso.

Morrison, B. (1993) *And When Did You Last See Your Father?*. London: Granta.

O'Farrell, J. (2000), *The Best a Man Can Get*. London: Doubleday.

Parsons, T. (2000), *Man and Boy*. London: HarperCollins.

—(2002), *Man and Wife*. London: HarperCollins.

—(2010), *Men from the Boys*. London: HarperCollins.

Ritchie, H. (2010), '*Men from the Boys* by Tony Parsons'. *Guardian*, 29 May, http://www.guardian.co.uk/books/2010/may/29/men-from-boys-tony-parsons, accessed 6 January 2013.

Showalter, E. (2002), 'Ladlit', in Zachary Leader (ed.), *On Modern British Fiction*. Oxford: Oxford University Press, pp. 60–76.

Southwell, T. (1998), *Getting Away With It: The Inside Story of Loaded*. London: Ebury.

Talbot, M. M. (2010), *Language and Gender*, 2nd edn. Cambridge: Polity.

5

Science Fiction: The Sense of Wonder

Andy Sawyer

What Gary Wolfe calls the 'icons' of science fiction – the robot, the alien, the spaceship; the futuristic city and the ruined wasteland (1979, xiv) – are familiar to many who never read it, through popular television series, computer games and the media-chatter of everyday life. Committed fans may pick up a novel by Ursula K. Le Guin or a 'Star Trek' spin-off novel, or Aldous Huxley's *Brave New World* (1932), and know that they are sf. But there are also readers who are barely, if at all, aware that the book they have begun by, say Jeanette Winterson or Audrey Niffenegger, can be so described: some would indignantly *deny* that these books are science fiction. There is, in fact, almost certainly 'no such thing as science fiction' (Bould and Vint 2008). There *are* many histories of science fiction, and there are many arguments about what it is.

There is certainly a body of literature which we – as sf readers – draw upon to suggest that writers such as Iain M. Banks and Margaret Atwood in the late twentieth and early twenty-first centuries, Mary Shelley and H. G. Wells in the nineteenth century and Margaret Cavendish and Jonathan Swift in the seventeenth and eighteenth centuries were and are engaged in similar arguments with the world. Drawing upon contemporary speculative science and philosophy – often within the traditions of the adventure story – they create imaginative fiction which appeals to what science fiction fans call the 'sense of wonder'. There is certainly what Hugo Gernsback called 'the Jules Verne, H. G. Wells and Edgar Allan Poe type of story – a charming romance intermingled with scientific fact and prophetic vision . . .' (1926, 3) which, first in magazines and then also in paperback form became what most people know as 'science fiction': the area where Wellsian 'scientific romance' collided with the literary utopia, the technological 'gadget story' and the 'dime novel' of the late nineteenth century. It is these subsections of a much greater historical and global whole that I am going to address, first considering *why* people read this literature and then briefly considering how it developed into what we, today, call science fiction.

'Worshipping at the Church of Wonder'

When the prominent editor David Hartwell used the phrases 'Worshipping at the Church of Wonder' and 'The Golden Age of Science Fiction is Twelve' as chapter-titles for his book *Age of Wonders* (1996), he was partly echoing readers' affectionately ironic reaction to vast spaceships, huge planet-busting weapons and 'big dumb objects' (Langford and Nicholls 2011). From the space opera novels of E. E. Smith, serialized in *Amazing* and *Astounding* from 1928–48, to George Lucas's 'Star Wars' series (1977–2005), sf has revelled in such delights. 'A sense of wonder, awe at the vastness of space and time, is at the root of the excitement of science fiction' (Hartwell 1996, 66). Hartwell here notes that the science fictional sense of wonder is more than simple admiration of super-technology. Farah Mendlesohn calls the sense of wonder sf's 'emotional heart' (2003, 3). She links it to the way that the *idea* or setting, rather than human character, can be hero; it is achieved by the mode's particular dissonances, the language-games and the sudden inversion of viewpoints we receive when we consider, for instance, that the characters whose viewpoints we have been empathizing with are in fact *not like us* but are aliens, or consciousnesses uploaded into software systems. The novelist and critic Samuel R. Delany encourages us to consider that science fiction is where clichés like 'her world exploded' have meanings as literal as they are metaphorical, and invites us to examine the first sentence of Frederik Pohl and Cyril M. Kornbluth's *The Space Merchants* (1953), set in a future New York: 'I rubbed depilatory soap over my face and rinsed it with the trickle from the fresh water tap' (quoted Delany 1979, 66–7). Radical differences between our world and the narrator's are suggested by the author's word-choice. A 'fresh-water' tap which 'trickles', argues Delany, implies volumes about the story's setting and invites us to read on to see if what we have deduced is confirmed: 'With each sentence [of a science fiction text] we have to ask what in the world of the tale would have to be different from our world in order for the sentence to be uttered' (67). Reading a story of this sort is like exploring a new world. At every stage, familiarity and difference combine against us. The novice science fiction reader enters into an imaginative space in which familiar understandings of how the world works cannot be relied upon.

This is a very different sense of wonder from mere amazement at scale. It is more akin to the sense of conceptual breakthrough which underlies many sf novels. During H. G. Wells' *The Time Machine* (1895) and Philip K. Dick's *Time Out of Joint* (1959), for instance, the emotional centre is the protagonists' realization that their understanding of the world in which they find themselves is *wrong*. Wells' time-traveller develops hypotheses about the future-world of Eloi and Morlocks which fit the evidence as he understands it, but in keeping with the scientific method new facts challenge each hypothesis: this is not a simple decayed utopia, but something more directly connected to the social anxieties of late-Victorian England. In *Time Out of Joint*, through apparently off-hand references to an unknown starlet named Marilyn Monroe or a model of car that never saw mass production, Dick allows the attentive reader to understand well before his protagonist does that the novel's 1959 is not the 'real' 1959 which Dick and his readers experience. As Nicholls and Robu put it, 'The "sense of wonder" comes not from brilliant writing nor even from brilliant conceptualizing; it comes from a sudden opening of a closed door in the reader's mind' (2012, n.p.). This is perhaps another reason why sf appeals to the young reader, for such sudden openings and understandings are an especial delight to the willing but inexperienced mind.

Brian Aldiss, in *Billion Year Spree*, points to what he calls the 'thinking' and 'dreaming' poles of science fiction, and suggests that some of its roots lie in Romantic and Gothic fascination with the uncanny and the marvellous (1973, 180). The sense of wonder here is darker, more numinous. Cornel Robu sees a source of what we might call the 'science fiction effect' in the eighteenth-century location of the 'Sublime' in the Infinite. He quotes Edmund Burke's *Philosophical Enquiry into the Origin of our Ideas of the Sublime and Beautiful*: 'Infinity has a tendency to fill the mind with that sort of delightful horror, which is the most genuine effect and truest test of the sublime' (1757; in Robu 1988, 22). Here, both the vast scale of the artificial world encircling a star in Larry Niven's *Ringworld* (1970) and the estranging sense of difference in Frederik Pohl and C. M. Kornboth's *The Space Merchants* may sit *in embryo*. Drawing also on Kant (who formulated major theories of cosmology), as well as the suggestions from Aldiss cited above, Robu suggests that our aesthetic and rational responses to the infinitely great (and small) scale of the universe combine in a form of fiction in which the potentiality of human understanding of this universe (science) is key: 'what makes us *think the infinite* in sf is science. In science fiction *science enforces the sublime*' (23). The science fiction writer (and reader) is *attracted* by Otherness, *seduced* by strangeness. The *Oxford English Dictionary* defines the noun 'wonder' as 'Something that causes astonishment' and the verb as 'To feel or be affected with wonder; to be struck with surprise or astonishment, to marvel.' But the verb 'wonder' also takes the secondary meaning 'be desirous to know or learn'. It is this combination of 'desire' and 'knowledge' (or 'dreaming' and 'thinking') that informs the science fiction 'wonder' even though the ambiguity of Burke's 'delightful horror' suffuses the genre. The Gothic uncertainties of Mary Shelley's Victor Frankenstein, who dares to go beyond the boundaries of known science, are never far from the surface of even the most optimistic sf.

The 'True Histories' of Science Fiction

Science fiction is therefore a mode of considerable complexity. Histories may begin in the second century AD with Lucian of Samosata's description of a journey to the moon in his *True History*; in 1666 with Margaret Cavendish's *The Blazing World*, which features an invasion from another world and is possibly the first English-language feminist utopia; in 1818 with Mary Shelley's *Frankenstein*, the first novel unmistakably about 'the two-faced triumphs of scientific progress' (Aldiss 1973, 29); or in 1926 with the first issue of Hugo Gernsback's *Amazing Stories*. In contrast, the theorist Darko Suvin defines sf ('the literature of cognitive estrangement' [1979, 4]) not by where it came from but by what it *does*: the 'cognitive estrangement' whereby the experience of a (fictional) imaginative environment alternative to the actual environment of author or reader causes readers to reflect *critically* upon their world. Tom Shippey contrasts the 'pastoral' mode – rural, nostalgic, conservative – and what might be called 'fabril' literature – urban, disruptive, future-oriented (1993, ix). John Clute (2013) and Adam Roberts (2005) place the genesis of modern sf in the scientific developments and speculations of the eighteenth-century Enlightenment. Paul Kincaid draws upon Ludwig Wittgenstein's ideas of 'family resemblances' between all those things that we consider as 'sport' to consider that science fiction is not a single genre but a *braided set* of genres, all of which are in constant flux and some examples of which will have virtually nothing in common with others. Just as, Kincaid argues, Wittgenstein says that we all know what sport is, but cannot necessarily agree on just what diving, a hundred-metre race, football, cricket or boxing have in common, so none of the histories or definitions of science fiction quite work (2008, 3–11). Using Kincaid's argument, we may consider that Isaac Asimov's *The Caves of Steel* (1954) and Jeanette Winterson's *The Stone Gods* (2007) are stories that involve robots and futuristic worlds, and that H. G. Wells' *The Time Machine* and Audrey Niffenegger's *The Time Traveler's Wife* (2003) share time travel as central motifs. But while the Asimov novel has clear roots in the sf tradition (Asimov was one of the authors nurtured by John W. Campbell in *Astounding* during the 1940s), most of Winterson's novels are removed from this tradition and she herself (from remarks on her website) seems uncomfortable with it. Similarly, while Wells was writing before the term 'science fiction' was in common use, his novel is in part a response to current scientific speculations on the nature of time, several of which are discussed in its first chapter. Niffenegger, in contrast, uses the random time-jumps of her protagonist's husband as more of a literary device without the pseudo-scientific explanations of many time travel novels; there is no time *machine*. Nevertheless, all four novels can be – and are – read as science fiction. Perhaps it is safer to assume that sf is a mongrel field made up of a collision of genres, read by different readers at different times for different experiences, but sharing Wittgensteinian 'family resemblances'. It is the nature of this collision which is, to many readers and scholars of the field, its most interesting attraction.

A Fiction of the Future

Through much of the nineteenth century, fiction dealing with scientific marvels was written in increasingly intricate braids with anticipations of the future. Louis-Sebastien Mercier's *L'an 2440* (1771) translated (1772) as *Memoirs of the Year Two Thousand Five Hundred* foreshadowed numerous novels of transformation through new political and technological ideas. The 'realistic' story set in a future, told entirely from the viewpoint of characters in that future, is a late development (see, for example, Clarke 1961): '[T]he future was reserved as a topic for prophets, astrologers, and practitioners of deliberative rhetoric' (Alkon 1987, 3).

Galileo's observations that the moon and the planets seemed to be worlds like our own certainly inspired speculative and satirical fictions such as Francis Godwin's *The Man in the Moone* (1638) and Cyrano de Bergerac's *Histoire comique contenant les etats et empires de la lune* (1657), which took us out of the *physical* world we 'know' into a realm extrapolated from post-Copernican theory about the universe. Godwin, inspired perhaps by his fellow-bishop John Wilkins's speculation in the third edition (1640) of his *The Discovery of a New World* that the moon could hold beings similar to us, takes his hero there in a craft drawn by geese: De Bergerac, anticipating rocket power, by fireworks. But these were not future-fictions. When space travel returned in the last decades of the nineteenth century, it was *time* which propelled the conceptual breakthroughs that would result in an identifiable, named genre. The melancholy meditations upon the effect of time on great civilizations found in poems like Percy Shelley's 'Ozymandias' (1818) and the personal apocalypses of Byron's 'Darkness' (1816) or Campbell's 'The Last Man' (1823) became the collective, *historical* apocalypse of Mary Shelley's novel *The Last Man* (1826). Shelley's future is technologically little different from her own time. What difference there is, though, was significant. Her characters travel regularly by balloon. Hot-air ballooning, begun in 1783 by the Montgolfier brothers, sparked anxieties about military invasion during the Napoleonic wars and became a symbol of progress and spectacle. Jane Webb's *The Mummy! A Tale of the Twenty-Second Century*

(1827) significantly added to the tool-kit of speculative fiction. Drawing upon both the 'futuristic' ballooning of Shelley's *The Last Man* and the experiments with electricity implied in her *Frankenstein*, and set in a future politically and technologically different from Webb's present, the novel's introduction argued the case for the largely untried setting of the future: 'you fear to sketch the scenes of which you are to write, because you imagine they must be different from those with which you are acquainted. This is a natural distrust . . . new governments will have arisen; strange discoveries will be made, and stranger modes of life adapted' (1827, vii).

Webb's satirical future – with intercontinental balloon transport, and steam-and electrical-powered agricultural machinery – was an important step forward. But it was not until political, scientific and technological developments later in the century that the futures of science fiction coalesce. Of the four great names of nineteenth-century sf – Mary Shelley, Edgar Allan Poe, Jules Verne and H. G. Wells – only Wells really explored the future.

Poe's influence lies more in the combination of weird fantasy and intellectual rigour in his stories, although his cosmological essay 'Eureka' (1848) approaches speculative sublimity. He manipulated a sense of wonder in stories like 'The Unparalleled Adventures of One Hans Pfaall' (1835), which satirizes the 'imaginary voyages' of Godwin and de Bergerac but through the language of technology, fact and detail rather than whimsical devices. Incongruous events are made plausible. The heavy-handed clowning of characters named 'Mynheer Superbus von Underduk' or 'Professor Rubadub' is supplemented (or undermined) by descriptive verisimilitude. Once Hans Pfaall is in transit to the moon, Poe plays a different game. The language of scientific investigation, fact and authority creates a sense of realism. 'The Facts in the Case of M. Valdemar' (1845) is usually discussed as gothic-horror but its focus upon the rational investigation of the then-fashionable 'science' of mesmerism makes it an influence upon later sf. As with *Frankenstein*, it is the use of scientific methods and theories to probe beyond the limits of human understanding into the regions commonly understood as 'supernatural' which is important.

Jules Verne's only major exploration of the future, *Paris in the Twentieth Century* (*Paris au XXe siècle*), written in 1863, stayed unpublished until 1994. His speculation includes ballooning, the unknown realm of the earth's interior, and the submarine *Nautilus*: one of sf's great 'inventions'. Verne's *20,000 Leagues Under the Sea* (Vingt Mille Lieues Sous les Mers) (1871) was by no means the first speculation about submarines, but his vivid and detailed descriptions of the alien undersea world through which *Nautilus* travelled fuelled the desire for fact and knowledge which many later readers were to find in pulp magazine sf. His 'extraordinary voyages' went beyond the atmosphere. Although the members of the Baltimore Gun Club never land on the moon, *From the Earth to the Moon* (*De la Terre à la Lune: Trajet direct en 97 heures 20 minutes*) (1865) and *Around The Moon* (*Autour de la Lune: Seconde partie de: De la Terre à la Lune*) (1870) are both the first great novels of space travel and the first modern satires of it. His fellow-countryman Albert Robida became famous for illustrations of flying-machines and weapons of warfare, anticipating the future in books like *Le vingtième siècle* (1883): it was his engraving of Verne's tombstone at Amiens which adorned the contents-page of *Amazing Stories*, signifying the 'prophetic vision' of this new kind of literature.

A Better World?

Increasingly, these tales of technological transformation became infused with utopian braids. Thomas More's *Utopia* (1516) and Bacon's 'New Atlantis' (1626) were set on islands, as was Jonathan Swift's *Travels into Several Remote Nations of the World (Gulliver's Travels)* [1726], in which the scientific aspirations of the Royal Society were satirized by the ludicrous savants of Laputa in a way similar to mockery of the hubris of 'mad scientists' in later sf. However, the hopes and fears of the *explored* modern globe needed different locations. Underground worlds sufficed in Mary E. Bradley Lane's *Mizora: A World of Women* (1890), or Bulwer-Lytton's enormously popular *The Coming Race* (1871), but while 'lost valley' utopias such as Charlotte Perkins Gilman's *Herland* (1915) and James Hilton's *Lost Horizons* (1933) remained useful settings, a transformed *future* became the favoured locale. Mary Griffith's pastoral utopia *Three Hundred Years Hence* (1836) and William Deslisle Hay's identically titled but more imperialistic vision published in 1881 were among numerous utopian or semi-utopian visions of the future which, as a sub-genre, exploded into mass popularity with Edward Bellamy's *Looking Backward 2000-1887* (1888).

Hailed for its political ideas, *Looking Backward* inspired the formation of discussion clubs and was answered by William Morris's critical response, *News From Nowhere* (1890). Organized technology is part of the utopian future Bellamy's Julian West awakens in. Goods are centrally manufactured, purchased by credit card and delivered by pneumatic tube from central stores. The labour force is enlisted in an 'industrial army' until the age of 45. By contrast, Morris imagined a much more pastoral array of mock-medieval handicrafts. A revolutionary socialist, Morris understood the need to *create* the future: his narrator has to return from his dream – 'Nowhere' – and try and recreate it. Later, Aldous Huxley's *Brave New World* (1932) cast doubt upon the very nature of a realizable utopia.

Threats and Invasions

For others, the future offered more pragmatic warnings. George Chesney's 'The Battle of Dorking' (1871) was originally published in *Blackwood's* magazine to awaken the public to the complacency of the British military machine. Within 2 months, the sixpenny pamphlet edition of the story sold 110,000 copies (Clarke 1995, 14–15). Such warnings were swiftly imitated in France, Germany and elsewhere. Reaching a crescendo in the years leading up to World War I, these fictions often exploited racial fears. Kenneth Mackay's *The Yellow Wave* (1895) and M. P. Shiel's *The Yellow Danger* (1898) looked anxiously to China in a scenario echoed in Philip Nowlan's melodrama *Armageddon 2419 A.D.*, published in *Amazing Stories* in 1928, which pitched one of pulp science fiction's first adventure heroes, 'Buck' Rogers (the nickname appears in later comic strip and film serial adaptations) against the invading Han.

By the end of the century, the fevered speculation about the possibility of powered flight, anticipating the Wright Brothers' great achievement in 1903, had extrapolated into space travel. Percy Greg's *Across the Zodiac* (1880) and George Griffith's *A Honeymoon in Space* (1901) took adventurers through the solar system. The Russian pioneer theorist of space flight and rocketry Konstantin Tsiolkovsky (1857–1935) promoted his ideas through fiction (for example 'On the Moon' [1893]), while the suggestions of the American astronomer Percival Lowell that the 'canali' (channels) on the surface of Mars observed by Schiaparelli in 1877 were constructed by a dying civilization inspired numerous anxious fictions, most notably Kurd Lasswitz's *Auf Zwei Planeten* (1897) in which a utopian Martian civilization invades Earth. For an English-reading audience the culmination of such speculations was H. G. Wells' *The War of the Worlds* (1898) which shattered the façade of British Imperial destiny as a Martian invasion did to London what British armies had done in Africa and India.

The Scientific Romance and 'Scientifiction': A Genre Forms

Wells is the figure through whom these various strands become channelled into what looked like a unified 'genre'. While by no means the only contemporary exponent of the art – his aerial apocalypses were exceeded in bloodthirstiness by George Griffith's novels of airborne terrorist outrages like *The Angel of the Revolution* (1893), and M. P. Shiel's *The Purple Cloud* (1901) rivalled Shelley's *The Last Man* as an apocalypse – Wells' short stories and the series of novels beginning with *The Time Machine* helped define the tone and subject matter of what became known as the 'scientific romance'.

Early in 1894, Lewis Hind, editor of the *Pall Mall Budget*, proposed that Wells submit stories that exploited his knowledge of science. In June, the *Budget* published 'The Stolen Bacillus', the first of over 30 stories published over the next 18 months. In 1895 Wells published his first novel. The eponymous 'time machine' itself may simply be a device to take his protagonist into a future where he may formulate several hypotheses about the eventual destiny of the human race. Its significance, though, is that it *is* a machine; a plausible impossibility described in the language of science. Most previous examples (the exception is the Spanish writer Enrique Gaspar's time ship in *El Anacronópete* [1887], published the year before Wells' prototype of *The Time Machine*, a story called 'The Chronic Argonauts') used dream, suspended animation or inexplicably charged clocks to manipulate time. With the scientific romances that followed – *The Island of Doctor Moreau* (1896), *The Invisible Man* (1897), *The War of the Worlds* (1898), *When the Sleeper Wakes* (1899), *The First Men in the Moon* (1901) – Wells shaped the taste of an audience for what we now recognize as the major themes of sf: the invention that goes wrong, space travel, invasion, the manipulation of the body, the first puzzling and dazzling glimpses of the future.

As an *identifiable* popular fiction genre, then, the 'H. G. Wells, Jules Verne, Edgar Allan Poe' story may have crystallized either in the 1890s with Wellsian scientific romance or in 1926 with Gernsback's 'new sort of magazine' devoted to what he dubbed 'scientifiction'. *Amazing* published fiction drawing upon modern scientific discovery, hailing the future. Gernsback, who had emigrated to the USA from Luxembourg to establish himself as an entrepreneur in radio technology, filled early issues of *Amazing* with Poe, Verne and Wells, but also drew upon contacts in France and Germany.

He encouraged women writers such as Clare Winger Harris and Leslie F. Stone. Lively letter-columns allowed readers to express their opinions; and his later championing of a 'Science Fiction League' allowed fans to correspond with each other and form local groups, trading 'fanzines' and nurturing new generations of writers. With the expansion of markets and a proliferation of titles, the somewhat crude stories of the early years achieved greater sophistication, thanks to editors like John W. Campbell, who led *Astounding* from 1937 until his death in 1971.

Despite later championing L. Ron Hubbard's 'Dianetics', encouraging pseudo-scientific propulsion machines and racist opinions, Campbell's editorial influence was immense. A writer himself – 'Twilight' (1934) and 'Night' (1935) are Wellsian meditations on a decadent future – he threw out controversial ideas and published the results. Isaac Asimov's robot stories presented moral and ethical paradoxes based around the three 'laws' with which robots are programmed to ensure compliance with instructions and self-preservation. Robert A. Heinlein's fiction, especially the novels for young people published between 1947 and 1955, stressed competency and family, though his interpretation of 'family' in his later novels for adults extended to a championing of sexual liberality which resounded with the youth culture of the 1960s, who overlooked the way Heinlein had championed military values as a touchstone for a 'good' society in *Starship Troopers* (1959). *Stranger in a Strange Land* (1961) introduced a Messiah-figure from Mars who 'discorporated' enemies without any sense of moral guilt. Heinlein's gift was to present, especially in his children's books and short stories, a realistically plausible future-history. More liberal versions of Heinlein's characters' conceptual breakthroughs into understanding worlds were the novels of Andre Norton: her books similarly introduced young readers to a consensus world of sf in which the development of space travel opened up a universe rich with possibilities.

Campbell also published E. E. Smith's 'Lensman' space opera series between 1937 and 1948, and Canadian writer A. E. Van Vogt's first sf. Both writers, in different ways, expressed the power of the naive 'sublime'. Smith's epic escalates through greater and more destructive weaponry exploding first planets, then stars, and leads to the gradual revelation that the history of the universe is a cosmic conflict between two opposed civilizations. Van Vogt intrigued his readers by overturning their expectations every few pages with new complications and reversals. *The World of Null-A* (serialized August–October 1945) claims a higher (Null-Aristotelian) logic for its dream-like complexities. Van Vogt's 'driven hauntedness' (Clute 2013) suggests science fiction's appeal to generations of bright but thwarted adolescents for whom fiction became a symbol of their alienation.

Many of these 'Golden Age' writers and their successors started as fans. Asimov was one. Arthur C. Clarke was another, discovering sf through magazines and attending the first science fiction convention held in Leeds in 1937. As for many of his peers, the wonder of science fiction was inextricably linked to the wonder of the natural universe revealed by science. Clarke became an official of the British Interplanetary Society, formed to promote the idea of space travel as a realizable enterprise, and invited the author Olaf Stapledon to address the society in 1948. Stapledon, a philosopher and social activist, had no knowledge of science fiction magazines when he wrote *Last and First Men* (1930), an epic 'history' of the human race charting 18 separate species of humanity. While considering human history on a sublime scale, through ever-increasing leaps of time (two chapters from the end we are only half-way through the story), Stapledon also saw it as embodying a dynamic between the intellectual and spiritual wills. His inventiveness (his human species include the artificially created 'Fifth Men' and the 'Flying Men' evolving on Venus), his ethical dilemmas (humanity establishes itself on Venus after wiping out its indigenous inhabitants) and his poignant 'cosmic' viewpoint (several near-utopias fail to reach their potential through almost random accident) influenced generations of succeeding writers.

New Waves

The establishment of magazines such as *Galaxy* (1950–80) and *Fantasy and Science Fiction* (1949–present) in the USA and *Nebula* (1952–9) and *New Worlds* (1946–70) in the UK offered greater range and opportunities for exploring both styles and subject-matter (especially social criticism). Philip K. Dick's stories, for instance, reflected the paranoia of living in a world in which the outbreak of nuclear war seemed to be simply a matter of time, as well as the interior confusions and obsessions with the nature of reality which marked his novels in following decades. Post-war nuclear anxieties inspired fictional explorations of possible futures. George Orwell's *Nineteen Eighty-Four* (1949) is the novel against which all modern dystopias are measured. Following the success of *Fahrenheit 451* (1953), Ray Bradbury became a favourite of the more up-market 'slick' magazines like the *Saturday*

Evening Post. In Britain, a writer who had achieved moderate success in the pre-war American magazines as 'John Beynon' or 'John Beynon Harris' adopted another name for an attempt to move beyond the limited range of the specialist readership. The scenario of John Wyndham's *The Day of the Triffids* (1951) – the collapse of civilization following a natural disaster – was standard enough, but his subtle unease (was this disaster, in a sky filled with orbiting satellite weapons, a 'natural' one?), his 'double-whammy' technique (the 'triffids', mobile carnivorous plants farmed for their valuable oil, are no real threat until humanity is blinded by the 'comet') and the moral dilemmas faced by his characters gave *Triffids* mass appeal. John Christopher's more pessimistic *The Death of Grass* (1956), which tapped into fears of food shortages and overpopulation, and Nevil Shute's apocalyptic *On the Beach* (1957) were similar best-selling stories of catastrophe. While Wyndham suggested the possibility of rebuilding, Shute's story of humanity's last days, when the fallout from the nuclear bombs which have obliterated the northern hemisphere drifts inexorably southward, offered no hope and dramatized the implications of the nuclear arms race for an audience of general readers no sf magazine or novel could have reached.

Also in Britain, encouraged by a young Michael Moorcock, John Carnell began publishing stories by J. G. Ballard in *New Worlds*. Ballard's May 1962 'guest editorial' in the magazine proclaimed a psychological 'inner space' as the new, true subject of science fiction. Adventure-stories of 'outer space', he declared, were outmoded and juvenile (1962, 2–3). On taking over *New Worlds* in 1964, Moorcock proclaimed William Burroughs, who had drawn upon the work of sf writers for his cut-up techniques, as the model for 'A New Literature of the Space Age' (1964, 2) and radically transformed the magazine to include the iconoclastic fiction of a 'new wave' of sf. Ballard overturned the conventions of what Brian Aldiss named the 'cosy catastrophe' (1973, 293–4) of Wyndham and his followers, while Aldiss, whose greater sympathies with conventional sf perhaps made him all the more critical of its literary limitations, drew upon the French anti-novel for *Report on Probability A* (1968) and pop-psychedelia (and James Joyce) for the stories collected as *Barefoot in the Head* (1969).

As with most 'movements' the differences between these writers were as important as what they had in common. While Moorcock published American writers such as Thomas M. Disch and Pamela Zoline and American writer/editor Judith Merril championed the 'New Wave' in an anthology entitled *England Swings SF* (1968), British and American 'versions' of the movement were different. Philip K. Dick, for example, was strongly rooted in the culture of the 50s magazines where many of his stories first appeared, but his dislocations of reality in *The Three Stigmata of Palmer Eldritch* (1964) and *Ubik* (1969) appealed to both 1960s drug culture and postmodern literary theorists.[1] The increasingly wide range of possible subject matter offered 'New Wave' labels to Dick, to writers strongly influenced by American feminism, such as Joanna Russ (*The Female Man*, 1975) and Ursula K. Le Guin (*The Left Hand of Darkness*, 1969), and Samuel R. Delany, the first major African-American figure in the field and probably the first openly gay sf writer. All these were published by Harlan Ellison in his 'new wave' anthologies *Dangerous Visions* (1967) and *Again, Dangerous Visions* (1972). If some of these visions no longer seem particularly 'dangerous', it is perhaps because expectations have so radically changed.

Even Newer Waves

A younger and much larger audience was also being created by television programmes like *Star Trek*, which first aired 1966–9 and resulted in an industry of films, sequels, tie-in novels and comic books. These unashamed adventures of outer rather than inner space were followed in the late 1970s by George Lucas's 'Star Wars' sequence. Newer technologies were addressed in the wake of William Gibson's *Neuromancer* (1984); the first major 'cyberpunk' novel, which fused the literary sensibility of new wave sf with a *noir*-influenced future in which alienated young people 'jacked in' to a 'matrix' similar to today's internet. Cyberpunk and post-cyberpunk fictions explored potential human futures in greater detail, with Australian writer Greg Egan a particular trailblazer during the 1990s in developing the literalized metaphor of the 'consensual hallucination' (Gibson 1984, 51) of cyberspace to explore more fully the moral and philosophical questions of the cyberpunk fantasy of downloading or manipulating human consciousness. This, or something like it, had been part of sf for decades (Moore's 'No Woman Born' [1944] questioned the nature of 'femininity' when a severely injured actress's brain is encased in a robot outer body). During this period, however, Gibson, Egan and other writers such as Pat Cadigan adapted these thought-experiments to the coming world of information overload.

While sf as a *popular* written form has been overtaken by television and film – very few sf writers reach bestsellerdom – no other form of literature has expressed so unsettlingly what it is *like* to live in the past 150 years of rapid technological change. Its vocabulary has been enriched by writers who may have rejected or not understood the label of 'science fiction writer' but whose work has both attracted a readership beyond the core sf readership and been acclaimed by readers as core texts in the field. Perhaps the most solid example is the way Karel Capek's play *R. U. R.: (Rossum's Universal Robots)* (first performed 1921) introduced a word to our everyday vocabulary. While the idea of 'artificial humans' was central to *Frankenstein*, Capek's *word* 'robot' (in the original Czech a word for forced labour) filled the need for a word to express industrial alienation. It appeared in British and American newspapers within 6 months of the first English-language performance of the play (1922).[2] From Capek, science fiction concepts become part of our thought process, a concept wittily explored in Gwyneth Jones's *White Queen* (1991), where human reaction to the alien 'Aleutians' is shaped by 'what we know' about aliens; for example, their ability to communicate through a complex mechanism of pheromones and 'wandering cells' is interpreted as 'telepathy'; they are, of course, here to invade because that is what aliens in science fiction *do*.

The claim that science fiction as a category is dissolving into the literary mainstream appears every decade or so – Judith Merril was arguing it in the early 1960s (1964, 391) – but it has never really come to pass, partly because we seem to need the easily recognizable icons of science fiction to describe our collision with change. Just as quickly as conventions and images fossilize through over-familiarity, writers discover that they are appropriate to a newer context; the space opera, once the lowest form of adventure sf, has been revitalized in the past few decades by writers such as Iain M. Banks, whose 'Culture' series explores utopian and moral dilemmas. The robot becomes an image available for Jeanette Winterson's *The Stone Gods*. One of the most interesting aspects of the initial response to Kazuo Ishiguro's *Never Let Me Go* (2005) was the way the author's delayed spelling out of the nature of its protagonists was seen as a revelation or a twist, even though (for those familiar with science fiction tropes) the implications within the text were perfectly clear and knowledge of them enhanced, rather than spoiled, the story. It is perhaps here that science fiction becomes a truly 'popular' (rather than 'cult') literature.

What is perhaps new in the story of sf as a 'popular' form is the current challenge to the way that the story of science fiction – largely the story as presented here – has predominantly been written by those for whom it is self-evident that it is an Anglo-American form. While the influence of

Western figures, such as H. G. Wells and Jules Verne, is important to the development of sf elsewhere (Wells was published throughout Europe and in India, influencing other writers; translations of Verne in Japan and India very soon resulted in similar stories being published), it is certainly not the whole story. Kurd Lasswitz's *Auf Zwei Planeten*, for instance, was published in 1897, the year *before* Wells' *The War of the Worlds*. Russian writers such as Yvgeney Zamyatin, (whose novel *We* [1924] also influenced Orwell), Alexander Bogdanov (*Red Star*, 1908), Alexei Tolstoy (*Aelita*, 1923), Ivan Yefremov (*Andromeda*, 1957) and Arkady and Boris Strugatsky, who flourished from the late 1950s to the 1980s with novels such as *Hard to Be a God* (1973) and *Roadside Picnic* (1977), are as central to any 'history' of science fiction as any British or American author mentioned above. The Polish writer Stanislaw Lem, author of *Solaris* (1961) (like *Roadside Picnic* filmed by Andrei Tarkovsky), is 'widely considered to be the sf writer who was most successful in bridging the gap between the popular genre and literature' (Csicsery-Ronay 2010, 151). Sf is now a popular form in China, while an entire essay may be written on the influence of Japanese sf on Western popular culture. If we consider sf's roots as coming from a reaction to global ideas – the influence of technology, scientific theory, new ways of looking at the world – we cannot confine it to the Capitalist West.

Science fiction is more and more a way of looking at things than a specific literary genre. Its defenders point to the 'Sense of Wonder' and call it a literature of ideas; its detractors point to the triviality of some of those ideas and poor expression of even the most wondrous concepts. True, some sf writers have neglected character because they cannot write it. But others have not considered it to be part of the necessary tool-kit. Is it necessarily a criticism of a novel to have its most sympathetic character a robot or an alien or Artificial Intelligence rather than a human being? Much effort may be expended in an sf novel in developing a *plausible* world, whether an alien world as such or an extrapolated future of our world. There is a sense that *The Left Hand of Darkness* is a travel tale, in which we gradually learn more and more about this imagined world, but it also uses this understanding to help us question the assumptions of *our* world. The 'Sense of Wonder' is also linked to the *speculative*, extrapolative undercurrents of sf: the 'what if?', the thought-experiment and the way the 'icons' of sf can be used to drive considerably different worlds of story. It is the scientific enquiry at its most basic ('What happens if I do *this*?') and its most urgent ('How do I *understand* the universe and my place in it?').

Notes

1. Jean Baudrillard's meditations upon reality and 'simulacra' draw heavily upon J. G. Ballard and also Philip K. Dick whose *The Simulacra* was published in 1964. See 'Simulacra and Science Fiction'. *Science Fiction Studies* 18(3) (November 1991), 309–13.
2. The *Oxford English Dictionary* gives 1922 as the first written instance of the 'artificial human' meaning and 1923 (quoting George Bernard Shaw) as meaning a person who acts mechanically or without emotion.

Works Cited

Aldiss, B. W. (1968), *Report on Probability A*. London : Faber.
—(1969), *Barefoot in the Head*. London: Faber.
—(1973), *Billion Year Spree* (rev. 1986 as *Trillion Year Spree*). London: Weidenfeld & Nicholson.
Alkon, P. (1987), *Origins of Futuristic Fiction*. Athens, GA: University of Georgia Press.
Asimov, I. (1954), *The Caves of Steel*. Garden City, NY: Doubleday.
Bacon, F. (1626), *The New Atlantis*. London: John Haviland for William Lee.
Ballard, J. G. (1962), 'Which Way to Inner Space?'. *New Worlds* 118(May), 2–3, 116–18.
Bellamy, E. (1888), *Looking Backward 2000-1887*. Boston, MA: Ticknor & Company.
Bogdanov, A. (1908), *Krasnaia Zvezda* (repr. 1984 as *Red Star: The First Bolshevik Utopia*), trans. Charles Rougle. Bloomington, IN: Indiana University Press.
Bould, M. and Vint, S. (2008), 'There is No Such Thing as Science Fiction', in J. Gunn, M. Barr and M. Candelaria (eds), *Reading Science Fiction*. Basingstoke: Palgrave Macmillan, pp. 43–51.
Bradbury, Ray (1953), *Fahrenheit 451*. New York: Ballantine.
Bulwer-Lytton, E. (1871), *The Coming Race*. Edinburgh: Blackwood.
Byron, Lord (1816), 'Darkness', in *The Prisoner of Chillon and Other Poems*. London: John Murray, pp. 17–19.
Campbell, J. W. (as Don A. Stuart) (1934), 'Twilight'. *Astounding* 14(3) (November), 44–58.
—(1935), 'Night'. *Astounding* 16(2) (October), 8–22.
Campbell, T. (1823), 'The Last Man'. *New Monthly Magazine* 8, 272–3.

Capek, K. (1923), *R. U. R.* (*Rossum's Universal Robots*), trans. Paul Selver. London: Humphrey Milford.

Cavendish, M. (1666), 'The Description of a New Blazing World', in *Observations Upon Experimental Philosophy*. London: A. Maxwell.

Chesney, G. T. (1871), *The Battle of Dorking*. Edinburgh: Blackwood's.

Christopher, J. (1956), *The Death of Grass*. London: Michael Joseph.

Church, A. J. (trans.) (1879), *A Traveller's True Tale After the Greek of Lucian of Samosata*. London: Seeley, Jackson and Halliday.

Clarke, I. F. (1961), *The Tale of the Future*. London: Library Association.

—(1995), *The Tale of the Next Great War, 1871-1914*. Liverpool: Liverpool University Press.

Clute, J. (2013), 'A.E. Van Vogt'. *The Encyclopedia of Science Fiction*, 3rd edn, http://www.sf-encyclopedia.com/entry/van_vogt_a_e, accessed 28 March 2013.

Csicsery-Ronay Jr, I. (2010), 'Stanlislaw Lem', in M. Bould, A. M. Butler, A. Roberts and S. Vint (eds). *Fifty Key Figures in Science Fiction*. Abingdon: Routledge, pp. 147–52.

De Bergerac, C. (1657), *Histoire comique contenant les etats et empires de la lune*. Paris: Chez Charles de Sercy.

Delany, S. R. (1979), 'Science Fiction and "Literature" or, Conscience of the King'. *Analog* 99(5) (May), 59–78.

Dick, P. K. (1959), *Time Out of Joint*. Philadelphia: Lippincott.

—(1964), *The Three Stigmata of Palmer Eldritch*. Garden City, NY: Doubleday.

—(1969), *Ubik*. Garden City, NY: Doubleday.

Ellison, H. (ed.) (1967), *Dangerous Visions*. Garden City, NY: Doubleday.

—(1972), *Again, Dangerous Visions*. Garden City, New York: Doubleday.

Gaspar, E. (1887), 'El Anacronópete', in *Novelas*. Barcelona: Biblioteca Arte y Letras, pp. 7–218.

Gernsback, H. (1926), 'Editorial'. *Amazing Stories* 1(1), 3.

Gibson, W. (1984), *Neuromancer*. New York: Ace.

Gilman, C. P. (1979 [1915]), *Herland*. New York: Pantheon Books.

Godwin, F. (1638), *The Man in the Moone*. London: J. Norton.

Greg, P. (1880), *Across the Zodiac: The Story of a Wrecked Record*. London: Trübner and Co.

Griffith, G. (1893), *The Angel of the Revolution*. London: Tower Publishing.

—(1901), *A Honeymoon in Space*. London: Pearson.

Griffith, M. (1836), 'Three Hundred Years Hence', in *Camperdown: Or, News From Our Neighbourhood*. Philadelphia: Carey, Lea & Blanchard, pp. 9–92.

Hartwell, D. (1996), *Age of Wonders*. New York: Tor.

Hay, W. D. (1881), *Three Hundred Years Hence*. London: Newman & Co.

Heinlein, R. A. (1959), *Starship Troopers*. New York: Putnam's.

—(1961), *Stranger in a Strange Land*. New York: Putnam's.

Hilton, J. (1933), *Lost Horizon*. London: Macmillan.

Huxley, A. (1932), *Brave New World*. London: Chatto & Windus.

Ishiguro, K. (2005), *Never Let Me Go*. London: Faber.

Jones, G. (1991), *White Queen*. London: Gollancz.

Kincaid, P. (2008), *What It Is We Do When We Read Science Fiction*. Harold Wood, Essex: Beccon Publications.

Lane, M. E. B. (1890), *Mizora: A World of Women*. New York: GW Dillingham.

Langford, D. and Nicholls, P. (2011), 'Big Dumb Objects', in J. Clute (ed.), *The Encyclopedia of Science Fiction*, 3rd edn, http://www.sf-encyclopedia.com/entry/big_dumb_objects, accessed 28 March 2013.

Lasswitz, K. (1897), *Auf zwei Planeten*. Weimar: Emil Felber.

Le Guin, U. K. (1969), *The Left Hand of Darkness*. New York: Ace.

Lem, S. (1970 [1961]), *Solaris*, trans. J. Kilmartin and S. Cox. New York: Walker and Co.

Mackay, K. (1895), *The Yellow Wave*. London: Richard Bentley.

Mendlesohn, F. (2003), 'Introduction: Reading Science Fiction', in E. James and F. Mendlesohn (eds), *The Cambridge Companion to Science Fiction*. Cambridge: Cambridge University Press, pp. 1–12.

Mercier, L. S. (1772), *Memoirs of the Year Two Thousand Five Hundred*, trans. William Hooper. London: George G. Robinson.

Merril, J. (1964), 'Summation: S-F, 1961', in *The Best of Sci-Fi* 2. London: Mayflower, pp. 391–6.

—(ed.) (1968), *England Swings SF*. Garden City, NY: Doubleday.

Moorcock, M. (1964), 'A New Literature of the Space Age'. *New Worlds* 142 (May/June), 2–3.

Moore, C. L. (1944), 'No Woman Born', in *The Best of C. L. Moore*. New York: Ballantine Books, pp. 236–88.

More, T. (1516), *Utopia*. Louvain, NL: Thierry Martin.

Morris, W. (1890), *News From Nowhere*. Boston, MA: Roberts Brothers.

Nicholls, P. and Robu, C. (2012), 'Sense of Wonder', in J. Clute (ed.), *The Encyclopedia of Science Fiction*, 3rd edn, http://www.sf-encyclopedia.com/entry/sense_of_wonder, accessed 28 March 2013.

Niffenegger, A. (2003), *The Time Traveler's Wife*. San Francisco, CA: MacAdam/Cage Publishing.

Niven, L. (1970), *Ringworld*. New York: Ballantine.

Nowlan, P. F. (1928), 'Armageddon – 2419 AD'. *Amazing Stories* 3(5) (August), 422–49.

Orwell, G. (1949), *Nineteen Eighty-Four*. London: Secker and Warburg.

Poe, E. A. (1976 [1835]), 'The Unparalleled Adventures of One Hans Pfaall', in H. Beaver (ed.), *The Science Fiction of Edgar Allan Poe*. Harmondsworth: Penguin, pp. 12–64.

—(1976 [1845]), 'The Facts in the Case of M. Valdemar', in H. Beaver (ed.), *The Science Fiction of Edgar Allan Poe*. Harmondsworth: Penguin, pp. 194–203.

—(1848), 'Eureka. A Prose Poem', in H. Beaver (ed.), *The Science Fiction of Edgar Allan Poe*. Harmondsworth: Penguin, pp. 205–309.

Pohl, F. and Kornbluth, C. M. (1953), *The Space Merchants*. New York: Ballantine.

Roberts, A. (2005), *The History of Science Fiction*. London: Palgrave Macmillan.

Robida, A. (1882), *Le vingtième siècle*. Paris: G. Decaus.

Robu, C. (1988), 'A Key to Science Fiction: the Sublime'. *Foundation* 42 (Spring), 21–36.

Russ, J. (1975), *The Female Man*. New York: Bantam.

Shelley, M. (1818), *Frankenstein, or, the Modern Prometheus*. London: Lackington, Hughes, Harding, Mavor & Jones.

—(1826), *The Last Man*. London: Henry Colburn.

Shelley, P. B. (1818), 'Ozymandias'. *The Examiner* (11 January), 24.

Shiel, M. P. (1898), *The Yellow Danger*. London: Grant Richards.

—(1901), *The Purple Cloud*. London: Chatto & Windus.

Shippey, T. (ed.) (1993), *The Oxford Book of Science Fiction Stories*. Oxford: Oxford University Press.

Shute, N. (1957), *On the Beach*. London: Heinemann.

Stapledon, O. (1930), *Last and First Men*. London: Methuen.

Strugatski, A. and Strugatski, B. (1973 [1964]), *Hard to Be a God*, trans. Wendayne Ackerman. New York: Seabury.

—(1977 [1972]), *Roadside Picnic/Troika*, trans. Antonia W. Bouis. New York: Macmillan.

Suvin, D. (1979), *Metamorphoses of Science Fiction*. New Haven, CT: Yale University Press.

Swift, J. (1726), *Travels into Several Remote Nations of the World . . . (Gulliver's Travels)*. London: Printed for Benj Motte.

Tolstoy, A. (1980 [1923]), *Aelita*, trans. Lucy Flaxman. Moscow: Foreign Languages Publishing House.

Tsiolkovsky, K. (1963 [1893]), 'On the Moon', trans. A. Shkarovsky, in V. Dutt (ed.), *The Call of the Cosmos*. Moscow: Foreign Languages Publishing House, pp. 10–51.

Van Vogt, A. E. (1948), *The World of Null-A*. New York: Simon & Schuster.

Verne, J. (1865), *De la Terre à la Lune: Trajet direct en 97 heures 20 minutes*. Paris: Hetzel.

—(1870), *Autour de la Lune: Seconde partie de: De la Terre à la Lune*. Paris: Hetzel.

—(1871), *Vingt Mille Lieues Sous les Mers*. Paris: Hetzel.

—(1994), *Paris au XXe siècle*. Paris: Hachette.

Webb, J. (1827), *The Mummy! A Tale of the Twenty-Second Century*. London: Henry Colburn.

Wells, H. G. (1895), *The Time Machine*. London: Heinemann.

—(1896), *The Island of Doctor Moreau*. London: Heinemann.

—(1897), *The Invisible Man*. London: Pearson.

—(1898), *The War of the Worlds*. London: Heinemann.

—(1899), *When the Sleeper Wakes*. London: Harper & Brothers.

—(1901), *The First Men in the Moon*. Indianapolis: Bowen-Merrill.

Wilkins, J. (1640), *The Discovery of a New World*, 3rd edn. London: Printed for John Maynard.

Winterson, J. (2007), *The Stone Gods*. London: Hamish Hamilton.

Wolfe, G. K. (1979), *The Known and the Unknown: The Iconography of Science Fiction*. Kent, OH: Kent State University Press.

Wyndham, J. (1951), *The Day of the Triffids*. London: Methuen.

Yefremov. I. (1959 [1958]), *Andromeda: A Space-Age Tale*, trans. George Hanna. Moscow: Foreign Languages Publishing House.

Zamyatin, Y. (1924), *We*. New York: Dutton.

6

Rules are Meant to be Broken: Twentieth- and Twenty-First-Century Crime Writing

Stefania Ciocia

The Rules of the Game

It is all too appropriate that crime writing – a type of fiction which, by definition, is concerned with transgressions and misdemeanours – should be very aware of its own generic conventions, and of the subsequent scope for creative reinterpretations and surprising disruptions of its formulas. Particularly in its incarnation as classic detective fiction, that is in those (series of) novels where a clever investigative figure unravels a seemingly insoluble mystery, crime writing is a highly codified genre, as witnessed by the various manifestos and critical pieces drafted by some of the best-known practitioners of this popular literary form.

Especially outside the boundaries of genre fiction, however, it is hard to take altogether seriously the prescriptiveness of such lists as S. S. Van Dine's 'Twenty Rules for Writing Detective Stories' (1928), whose first article of faith maintains that '[t]he reader must have equal opportunity with the detective for solving the mystery' (1946, 189). The fervour in Van Dine's self-declared 'sort of Credo' is echoed by the 1928 'Decalogue' for The Detection Club, an association of fellow authors of mystery fiction founded a year earlier in London by Anthony Berkeley, and counting among its members best-selling writers of the calibre of G. K. Chesterton, Dorothy L. Sayers and Agatha Christie. The mandatory oath to be taken upon admission to the Club is more tongue-in-cheek than the 'commandments', with which it shares the desire to emphasize the most basic requirement of the genre: the need to stay firmly within the realm of the rational and of the possible, avoiding 'Divine Revelation, Feminine Intuition, Mumbo Jumbo, Jiggery-Pokery, Coincidence, or the Act of God' (reprinted in Haycraft 1946, 198). Underscored by The Detection Club's allusions to legal rituals and religious obligations[1] is the investment in the notion of Fair Play, also present in Van Dine's characterization of the genre as a 'kind of intellectual game' – indeed, more than that, 'a sporting event' (1946, 189) where writers are challenged to design ingenious plots, peppered with red-herrings as well as genuine clues, so that the key to the solution, while theoretically accessible to those resourceful enough, will retain at least an element of surprise and command the readers' satisfied admiration.

By contrast, even if devoid of any apparent programmatic intent, Raymond Chandler's own barbed, candid and unapologetically subjective account of the genre in 'The Simple Art of Murder' (1944) has been generally received as a landmark evaluation of the state of the field. It is difficult to overestimate the influence of Chandler's passionate apology of the 'tough guy' school of detective fiction; his often-quoted identification of Dashiell Hammett as a pioneer of this grittier approach to writing about crime – 'Hammett gave murder back to the kind of people that commit it for reasons, not just to provide a corpse' (1950, 330) – belongs to one of the most memorable summations of the opposition between the English and American treatment of the subject. This dichotomy has since become a staple in taxonomies of detective fiction; as we will see, it is only relatively recently that critics have started to focus on its oversimplifications and blind spots.

Classic or Hardboiled?

The stark opposition between the classic English formula of the clue-puzzle/whodunit and the later, less genteel and (supposedly) less contrived American hardboiled tradition, with its claim to a focus on 'real' crime, is reiterated in another canonical short piece on the genre: in 'The Guilty Vicarage: Notes on the Detective Story, by an Addict' (1948), W. H. Auden declares his reluctance to read mystery novels 'not set in rural England' (1962, 146). Auden thus draws attention to the provincial, tight-knit society that is the customary, ostensibly idyllic setting for clue-puzzle mysteries, whose select cast of characters offers a limited choice of suspects and is sketched against a suitably circumscribed background: a small village community, a professional or family gathering, an isolated manor house, or an even more self-contained location, such as a train or a cruise-ship, bound on a fatal journey.

Nothing could be further away from the illusion of order conveyed by these environments than the anonymity, the chaos and the endemic corruption associated with the sprawling metropolis whose 'mean streets' (Chandler 1950, 333) are roamed by the cynical private eye in the hardboiled formula. In fact, Auden goes so far as to suggest that 'whatever he may say, . . . Chandler is interested in writing, not detective stories, but serious studies of a criminal milieu' and therefore that 'his powerful but extremely depressing books should be read and judged, not as escape literature, but as works of art' (1962, 151). This conclusion about the relative literary merits of the two sub-genres, with the light-hearted intellectualism of the classic formula pitted, and found lacking, against the high-brow aspirations of its hardboiled variation has also become something of a critical orthodoxy – a misleading one not merely in overlooking the wide range of abilities of writers from both traditions, but also because it underplays the significant potential for aesthetic experimentation and political subversion inherent in a narrative form so rigidly codified, and so deeply implicated with ethical issues.[2]

Leaving aside, for the time being, further considerations about the political charge of the genre, and returning to the question of its definition, we ought to mention Tzvetan Todorov's 'The Typology of Detective Fiction' (1966), a seminal formalist study of the distinction between the classic whodunit, 'which reached its peak between the two World Wars', and the later hardboiled school 'created in the United States just before and particularly after World War II' (1977, 44, 47). Besides perpetuating the divide between the English and American traditions, Todorov grounds his taxonomy on a lucid analysis of narrative patterns: the whodunit contains two stories, 'the story of the crime and the story of the investigation' (44); the former is 'what really happened' (45) and it must necessarily remain absent in order to trigger the narrative proper, that is, the account of how the detective retrospectively pieces together the chain of events leading to the crime, thus reaching its solution. In the hardboiled formula instead – or in 'the thriller', to use Todorov's words – '[w]e are no longer told about a crime anterior to the moment of the narrative; the narrative coincides with the action' (47). The first story is suppressed altogether, whereas the second typically unfolds in 'real' time, often through the first-person narration of the private eye. This second type of detective fiction underplays the element of mystery in favour of suspense: at no point does the narrator 'comprehend all past events, we do not even know if he will reach the end of story alive' (47). In this way, the figure of the investigator is firmly placed centre-stage and duly fleshed out, becoming much more than a stylized function of the plot: Hammett's Sam Spade – or even his unnamed Continental Op – and Chandler's Philip Marlowe are a different breed from the rather mono-dimensional sleuths of the so-called Golden Age era of detective fiction.

These earlier creations are memorable because they are painted in broad strokes, as the eccentric, impartial observers who approach the investigation with emotional detachment and relish for its intellectual challenge. They are often represented as slightly outside or above – socially, as well as morally – the world they investigate, and their quirks can be perceived as caricatural, rather than endearing: even Dorothy L. Sayers's Peter Wimsey – a member of the House of Lords, an accomplished piano player and a collector of incunabula – begins to look positively commonplace against the pompousness of Van Dine's dandyish, monocle-wearing Philo Vance, or of Ellery Queen's eponymous hero, who somewhat anachronistically sports a pince-nez, and calls his father 'pater' (educated at Harvard, he is clearly part of the American intellectual aristocracy).[3] At least the affectations of Agatha Christie's Hercule Poirot – a former refugee from Belgium to London – can be ascribed to his foreignness, as can the idiosyncrasies of Rex Stout's Nero Wolfe, a Montenegrin living in New York, whose expensive tastes and reluctance to leave his luxury brownstone – he is the exemplary 'armchair detective' – are compensated by the more active, down-to-earth and masculine pursuits of his assistant, Archie Goodwin.

Interestingly, in their privileged refinement and foppish fastidiousness, these classic detectives are all somewhat feminized, as if to emphasize their key role as moral guardians of an endangered social order, their ability to deal with crimes pertaining to a private, domestic sphere, their familiarity with – and aptitude for infiltrating – its undercurrent of shameful secrets, petty jealousies and strong emotions. Her naturally unobtrusive access to this feminine dimension is a major asset for Christie's other famous creation, the amateur detective Miss Marple: as a respectable, elderly spinster, she can count on her great knowledge of human nature and on the freedom to move inconspicuously in relatively different social circles, while enjoying the instinctive trust both of her community and of casual acquaintances. Her age, gender and social status also mean that she is generally underestimated as a threat by the criminal – and as a help by the police – who fail to see in her anything other than a meddling, but ultimately harmless, old gossip.

Conversely, there is not even a semblance of order and domesticity in the uncertain world inhabited by the tough guy of the hardboiled tradition (and it is always a guy, in the early days), whose own life is riddled with existential doubts and haunted by the impossibility of making truly ethical choices. A troubled figure, the private eye is the compromised protagonist of his investigations, which expose his flaws and weaknesses together with the moral murkiness and the treacherousness of the modern urban environment. In this, as in the focalization through the detective's subjective perspective, the genre partakes of the epistemological insecurity and the aesthetic sensitivity of modernist writing, with which it also shares a doomed yearning for redemption and meaning: Marlowe is poignantly referred to as a 'shop-soiled Galahad' (Chandler 2001, 149), a hint to his worn-out mythical lineage as a hero on a difficult and solitary quest. Still, the heroic stature of the private eye never fully obscures his failings, most notably the inability to remain detached from the case and immune to the fascination of the *femme fatale*, whose irresistible sexual allure, histrionic disguises and knack for manipulation make her a dubiously empowered figure. Her dangerous seductiveness throws into relief the ambiguous gender politics of the entire sub-genre: is the *femme fatale* simply a misogynist stereotype or is she rather an (admittedly larger-than-life) embodiment of the female determination to pursue independence and exercise authority – in any way possible – in a world clearly dominated by men? On the other hand, the male protagonist's all too human susceptibility to follow his instincts, take calculated risks and overrate his ability to get out of scrapes unscathed allows scope for self-reflection and growth, especially if compared with the functional presence of a large cast of supporting roles, including various gangsters and lowlifes, good cops and corrupt ones, wealthy but morally bankrupt tycoons and clients with ulterior motives.

In hardboiled novels, characterization, setting and narrative mood take precedence over the careful plotting and the tightening of loose ends of the classic clue-puzzles. Indeed, the conclusion of the tough guy's investigation does not even approximate the sense of closure generally provided by the neatly staged revelation of the solution to the whodunit, and is instead often undercut by the knowledge that the detective himself has been tainted by the surrounding corruption: 'Me, I was part of the nastiness now' (Chandler 1970, 220), says Marlowe at the end of *The Big Sleep* (1939).

Golden Age versus Tough Guy: A Spurious Distinction

In spite of the striking differences that we have just outlined between the Golden Age whodunit – notice the deliberately idyllic connotations of the modifier – and the hardboiled tradition, with its upfront display of roughness, the two share more common ground than it appears, even in areas of great, superficial contrast. For example, classic clue-puzzles are not as politically conservative, nor are tough guy novels as ideologically innovative as they seem. In classic detective fiction, the murderer usually turns out to be a member of the very élite society that projects its fears of disorder onto alien threats. Short of having to fend off the sudden intrusion of a violent outsider, the ostensibly peaceful, rigorously hierarchical 'Golden Age' world must come to terms with the realization that evil lurks among its own ranks: as John Scaggs quips, 'the butler rarely did it' (2005, 46). However, for all of Chandler's contention – supported by Auden – that hardboiled detective fiction has restored murder to its natural environment of gangsters and small-time crooks, more often than not these unsavoury characters do not drive the plot, but are mere accessories to the creation of the dark atmosphere that has given the name *noir* to the sub-genre (especially in its cinematic incarnation). Mobsters, unscrupulous social climbers, show-business hopefuls and chancers in search of their lucky break all cluster around gambling joints, drinking establishments and other unwholesome hangouts. Yet, against this scenario of endemic decay, rife with institutionalized corruption and organized crime, the private detective usually finds himself investigating offences triggered by very personal motives – motives, that is, not significantly different from those in the classic repertoire.

By the same token, the claim to greater realism of the hardboiled tradition is also a matter for debate: much like its clue-puzzle counterpart, this sub-genre too has its fair share of improbable twists and turns, double bluffs and mistaken identities, not to mention the recurrence of surprise endings, where an earlier, and seemingly conclusive, deduction is shown to be only a link in the logical chain that leads to the actual solution. Besides, the tough-talk of the private eye is no less an act – especially in the constant wisecracking and verbal sparring – than the mannerisms of the Golden Age detectives, whose milieu demands more polite foibles. Across the range of crime writing in the first half of the twentieth century, realism is a question of perceptions, rather than facts, with the hardboiled tradition appearing to be more 'true to life' because of its less self-contained, exclusive setting, and because its looser narrative architecture gives the impression of a less codified formula.

Similarly, the distinction between English and American variations of the genre – respectively synonymous with classic/Golden Age/clue-puzzle detective story (focused on the mystery) and thriller/tough guy/hardboiled fiction (focused on the private eye) – is more indicative of longstanding (mis)*perceptions* than of actual trends. Most comprehensive studies of crime writing – John G. Cawelti's (1976), Martin Priestman's (1998), Stephen Knight's (2004), John Scagg's (2005), to name but a few – do acknowledge this geographical classification, if only implicitly or with a nod to the history of the reception of the genre, but they are careful to problematize it. Like most generalizations, this taxonomy along geographical lines does contain a nugget of truth: the logical investigative method so crucial to the classic detective formula was made popular by British writers of truly global renown like Sir Arthur Conan Doyle and Agatha Christie, while the birth of hardboiled fiction is uncontroversially linked to *Black Mask*, an American pulp magazine founded in 1920, and to Hammett and Chandler, its two most famous contributors. Notwithstanding Christie's long reign as the 'Queen of Crime', and the large number of early practitioners of the clue-puzzle in Britain, the Golden Age style of detective fiction flourished just as easily in the U.S., in the novels of S. S. Van Dine, Ellery Queen and Rex Stout.[4] On the other hand, the hardboiled formula – at least in its early offshoots between the late 1920s and 1950s – is clearly indigenous to the U.S. (see also Chapter 14);[5] however, its water-tight distinction from contemporary British offerings begins to crack upon closer scrutiny of its catalogue of narrative tricks and of the limitations of its scope for social critique.

(Postmodern) Subversions

Another persistent truism currently under revision is the centrality of 'ratiocination'– to quote Edgar Allan Poe (see 'Review' 1845), the alleged inventor of modern detective fiction – in the conception of the genre. The investigator's talent for logical reasoning and his/her reliance on scientific knowledge and technological advances are a great part of the intellectual appeal of classic detective fiction. They heavily underscore the characterization of two very influential early literary sleuths: Poe's Auguste Dupin and, more famously, Sir Arthur Conan Doyle's Sherlock Holmes.[6] These detectives' extraordinary analytical skills and command of various learnt disciplines have been traditionally played up at the expense of another aspect of their personality: their artistic flair, which allows them to draw on imagination as a complementary resource to mere reason. In time, this early combination of 'the creative and the resolvent' (Poe 2003, 146) has given way to a fetishization of rationality alone, while the sleuth's bohemian tendencies and imaginative talents have receded to the level of the idiosyncratic mannerisms outlined in our discussion of Golden Age detectives above.

Nonetheless, the characterization of Dupin (or Holmes) as an artistic, as well as an intellectual, genius is a reminder that the genre does not stem entirely from a fascination with cold logic and scientific methods. Recent studies, such as Maurizio Ascari's *A Counter-history of Crime Fiction* (2007), outline how the genre is partly steeped in irrational, sensationalistic literary traditions, and can count among its predecessors and sources of inspiration texts with a penchant for the excessive, both in their themes and in their narrative development: the eighteenth-century Newgate Calendar, with its vivid accounts of crimes and punishments, and Gothic fiction, riddled with mysterious occurrences and intricate plots, and geared to the creation of fear and suspense (see Ciocia 2012).

These uncontainable, eccentric drives have been revisited to great effect by postmodern writers, whose critique of traditional Western philosophical systems and celebration of randomness and indeterminacy find fertile ground in the disruption of the rational side of detective fiction, and particularly in the parody of its rules. This is proof of the fruitfulness with which well-known conventions can be exploited by authors determined to push literary boundaries: the quotation and/or reversal of familiar formulas in more 'intellectually ambitious' projects is an exemplary case of so-called popular fiction seeping into the avant-garde and making it mainstream. The astonishing success – in terms both of critical reception and of sales figures – of a number of postmodern classics is due to their skilful marriage of detective clichés and more challenging material: consider Umberto Eco's medieval *tour de force* in *The Name of the Rose* (1980), where the Franciscan friar William of Baskerville investigates a series of deaths – deaths which turn out to be connected to a controversy over Aristotle's teachings on comedy – against the backdrop of the theological and political diatribe about the doctrine of Apostolic poverty. Paul Auster's *The New York Trilogy* (1987) similarly plays with the norms of detective fiction in order to tackle wider philosophical issues, such as the nature and limitations of language. This theme is also explored in Mark Haddon's *The Curious Incident of the Dog in the Night-time* (2003), alongside the moving first-person account of the amateur sleuth, a 15-year-old boy with learning disabilities and a difficult family background.

Common traits in postmodern subversions of the detective formula are the prominent function played by chance in the unfolding of the plot, the deliberate confusion of the roles of the investigator, the criminal and the victim, and the inconclusiveness or the absence of a solution. These novels also flaunt a high degree of intertextuality and often revolve around the investigation of linguistic crimes, and epistemological and ontological questions. Their developed philosophical concerns have earned them the collective label of 'metaphysical' detective fiction (see Tani 1984; Merivale and Sweeney 1999). Given their cerebral nature, postmodern takes on the genre tend to revisit the rules of classic clue-puzzles – as intimated by the title of the third instalment of Auster's trilogy, *The Locked Room* – of which they represent the most innovative, modern variation. That said, they are equally at ease wreaking havoc with hardboiled conventions: see, again, Auster's work, Thomas Pynchon's *The Crying of Lot 49* (1966) or William Hjortsberg's *Falling Angel* (1978).

Towards a Greater 'Realism'

Hardboiled fiction has lent itself to a multiplicity of (re)appropriations, especially on the part of writers with a social or political agenda. Such versatility is related to the key assets – and to the obvious weaknesses – of the original formula. For example, its claim to realism has driven it to delve into noticeably darker situations, depicted in ever more graphic terms, and to branch out into the sub-genre of the 'police procedural' (pioneered by Ed McBain's 87th Precinct series in 1956), where various crimes are tackled by a team of professionals, rather than a lone investigator. More recently, this same drive for greater realism has led to a shift in focus on main characters who aid the police in their investigations, partly – one suspects – as a way of reflecting the growing importance that science and technology play in the fight against crime, and the ensuing rise of increasingly more specialized professions in the field.

Patricia Cornwell is generally credited with starting the forensic boom with *Postmortem* (1990) and the creation of Dr Kay Scarpetta, a medical examiner as capable and level-headed in the morgue, and in catching criminals, as she is comfortable and skilled in her large kitchen, cooking Italian food. This prolific series does not recoil from the treatment of heinous crimes, including violence against children and the bloodthirsty actions of serial killers, and of gruesome forensic procedures: the key location of the fifth Scarpetta novel, *The Body Farm* (1994), is the Decay Research Facility of the University of Tennessee, also known by the macabre nickname of the title, where pathologists observe the effect of different surroundings on the stages of decomposition of various corpses. On the other side of the Atlantic, Val McDermid's most recent crime series, starting with *The Mermaids Singing* (1995), features Dr Tony Hill, a psychological profiler who, in close professional relationship with police detective Carol Jordan, brings to justice the perpetrators of particularly cruel murders. Protagonists well versed in any of the areas of forensic science naturally come into play alongside the exploration of cases of extreme degeneracy and violence – a fact which at times has led to an implausible over-reliance on the presence of serial killers as the hero/ine's antagonist.

A gloomy outlook on human nature and a keen interest in the roots of moral deviancy are also said to be the key ingredients of the 'Tartan noir', an expression first coined by James Ellroy with reference to Ian Rankin, whose short-tempered detective John Rebus has risen through police ranks and aged in real time, recently coming back from retirement in *Standing in Another Man's Grave* (2012), 25 years after his first appearance in print. Together with McDermid, Rankin is the leading figure of a talented group of Scottish crime writers, whose national literary pedigree numbers such studies of perversity and evil as James Hogg's *The Private Memoirs and Confessions of a Justified Sinner* (1824) and Robert Louis Stevenson's canonical *Strange Case of Dr Jekyll and Mr Hyde* (1886), with its disclosure of the troubling co-existence of wickedness and respectability in each individual. Tartan noir's dour, northern setting and Calvinistic sense of morality are a far cry from the reputation for cosiness of Golden Age English detective fiction, although – of course – the change in sensibility cannot be ascribed to mere geographical or meteorological matters.

In temperate California, miles away from the inclement northern weather, James Ellroy knows himself a thing or two about humanity's worst instincts: in his 'L. A. Quartet', set in the 1940s and 1950s, Chandler's mean streets become almost unrecognizably meaner, providing the stage for scenes of utter degradation and explicit ferocity, often at the hands of representatives of the law. This choice is configured by Ellroy, with typical sharpness, as a *departure* from, rather than a continuation of, Chandler's formula: 'I consciously abandoned the private-eye tradition that formally jazzed me. Evan Hunter [Ed McBain's real name] wrote "the last time a private eye investigated a homicide was never". The private eye is an iconic totem spawned by pure fiction' (in Scaggs 2005, 31). In the Quartet, as in the rest of Ellroy's output, the mood of abject corruption and squalor is compounded by the presence of deeply flawed, even unsympathetic heroes, and by the distinctive style of the narratives, courtesy of the author's great ear for language. His terseness is well suited to capture the frenzied, dog-eat-dog world of his characters, and it makes no concessions to political correctness. It would be an understatement to point out that his books are not for the faint-hearted, nor for those easily offended by foul-mouthed, racist, misogynist and homophobic language.

The Challenge to Misogyny, Homophobia and Racism

In a sense, Ellroy's provocative approach goes against another major trend – perhaps *the* main trend – in post-World War II adaptations of the hardboiled tradition: the attempt to modernize it by deliberately taking on, and subverting, its white, masculinist foundations. P. D. James addresses this issue from the very title of her *An Unsuitable Job for a Woman* (1972), whose heroine Cordelia Gray inherits her detective agency after the death of her working partner/boss, and decides to continue to run it on her own, instead of going back to her previous employment as a secretary.[7] Sarah Paretsky's V. I. Warshawsky and Sue Grafton's Kinsey Millhone – first featured respectively in *Indemnity Only* (1982) and *A is for Alibi* (1986) – have followed on in Gray's footsteps, and are conspicuously more at ease with the need to resort to, as well as handle, physical violence, and with the antisocial hours that are the lot of the private investigator. By and large, these female detectives, and their authors, have been perceived as aiming to promote a feminist agenda, and their success continues to be measured in terms of how closely they are to having brought on a real change in the ideological premises of the hardboiled formula. The problem with such a response is that it can put these writers in a no-win position: they are liable to be charged either with being ambivalent in the characterization of their protagonists (see Cordelia Gray's 'feminine' reluctance to fire a gun), or with being too heavy-handed, thus ending up with heroines who are more masculine than their male predecessors (see V. I. Warshawsky's wish to be known by her androgynous initials, or Kinsey Millhone's violent show-down with her very own *homme fatale*). In a 2008 interview for the BBC World Book Club, Patricia Cornwell remembers the angry reaction of many of her readers who complained about the gender politics of *Postmortem*: in the novel's tense conclusion, Scarpetta is rescued by the providential intervention of police detective Pete Marino, whose unreconstructed patriarchal values add insult to injury. One wonders how many of these readers have stopped to think about whether Marino's macho posturing might not be interpreted as (over)compensation for his own fragility, and for the insecurity about behavioural norms experienced by both men and women at a time when – thankfully – gender roles are becoming more and more fluid.

A few decades on, it is easy to forget the resistance encountered by these women writers from the publishing industry, and hence to belittle the pioneering nature of their work. Val McDermid has spoken of her encounter with V. I. Warshawsky as a 'defining moment' in her creative career, because it made real the possibility to focus on 'contemporary women's lives' in a form of crime writing 'that didn't shy away from engaging with the politics of the society it reflected' (Onatade 2002). Inspired by Paretsky's example, McDermid's first novel, *Report for Murder* (1987), introduces the investigative journalist Lindsay Gordon whose adventures, by the author's own admission, 'operate within the classic English whodunit tradition, although having a lesbian protagonist means there is a bit of a twist' (Onatade 2002). With her subsequent series, instead, McDermid has ventured into hardboiled territory, creating the Manchester-based private detective Kate Brannigan who, since her first appearance in *Dead Beat* (1992), has starred in five more novels to date.

A much more playful attack on the masculinist ethos of the tough guy tradition is provided by Barbara Wilson's *Gaudí Afternoon* (1990), whose title – a cheeky parody of Dorothy Sayer's *Gaudy Night* (1935), as well as a reference to the great Catalan architect – betokens the flamboyant nature of its plot and of its colourful cast. Showcasing a multifaceted Barcelona with its labyrinthine gothic core and expansive Modernista creations, the novel follows the free-spirited lesbian translator-turned-amateur-detective Cassandra Reilly and offers an unashamed, thoroughly enjoyable celebration of the GLBT community and of the fluidity of gender and sexual identity. Interestingly, the questioning of patriarchal and heteronormative values effected by the presence of lesbian protagonists in mainstream crime fiction – and by 'mainstream' I mean best-selling writing like McDermid's, where the narrative focus is on the investigation rather than on the sexual orientation of the sleuth, as in Wilson's case – has yet to find a counterpart in the creation of equally successful male homosexual detectives. In *A Queer Kind of Death* (1966), George Baxt brings to life Pharoah [sic] Love, a gay, black detective, whose 'aggressively confident and yet vaguely flirtatious manner affirms both his queerness and ability to "kick ass" as a police officer' (Pepper 2000, 97). Love's adventures, though, are clearly engineered so as to foreground the homophobic and racist prejudices that surround him, and to challenge the common stereotypical association of black masculinity with a rigorously straight sexual prowess. In trying to find an explanation for the dearth of notable male gay detectives, compared to the relative abundance of lesbian appropriations of the genre, Knight points out that the macho detective of hardboiled fiction might be an image that 'the male gay community is reluctant to identify' with (2004, 181). This would seem to suggest that the very same 'tough guy' figure does appeal to lesbian rewritings, presumably because in a female context 'macho' would lose its misogynist connotations and some of its belligerent edge, and roughly translate as 'powerful and assertive'. Of course, the inability and/or the unwillingness to sustain deep and long-lasting attachments – romantic or otherwise – and to have a stable domestic life is another common trait to hardboiled detectives, and one that does not really reflect the campaigns for gay rights to civil partnership and parenting of recent decades.

A further 'militant' turn in detective fiction, used as a convincing vehicle to challenge gender, racial and class stereotype, is represented by the work of BarbaraNeely – no space between first and last name – whose heroine Blanche White is an African American maid in both senses of the word: she is in service and not at all interested in marriage. As intimated by the overdetermined name of her amateur sleuth, BarbaraNeely addresses racial tensions head on: for example, the second novel in the series – *Blanche and the Talented Ten* (1994), whose title is a reference to an essay by W. E. B. DuBois – explores the relationship between colour and class divisions *within* the African American community, pitting Blanche against episodes of racism and (self-)hatred which hurt twice as much because they come from fellow black people.

Walter Mosley is another writer who has revisited the genre from an African American perspective, determined to make use of the hardboiled formula as a vehicle for social critique. His protagonist Easy Rawlins makes a memorable first appearance in a telling homage to the opening scene of Chandler's *Farewell, My Lovely* (1940). There, Marlowe had found himself in a nightclub for black patrons only, following an ex-con in search of his woman; in *Devil in a Blue Dress* (1990), Easy Rawlins is approached, in a bar frequented by African Americans, by DeWitt Albright, a shifty white man who is looking for a missing girl. The girl's real identity is tied in to Mosley's focus on racial tensions, while the Chandleresque echo is an apt beginning for a story set in the segregated L. A. of the post-World War II period where Marlowe plied his trade. Unlike Marlowe, though, Easy is a war veteran, caught up between middle-class aspirations and very real economic difficulties: he reluctantly gets involved in an investigation, because he is desperate for money to pay his mortgage. If Mosley chooses to go back a few decades to fill in the gaps in Chandler's representation of L. A., where blacks and Hispanics are conspicuous in their absence, other authors use the genre as a way of chronicling their own times. Chester Himes does so with his novels about NYPD detectives 'Grave Digger' Jones and 'Coffin' Ed Johnson, published in the late 1950s and through the 1960s: their fictionalized New York captures the mood of the black struggle for civil rights and of the 1965 Watts riots, most famously in *Cotton Comes to Harlem* (1965). In the UK, anticipating by two decades the practitioners of 'Tartan noir', Ruth Rendell has charted recent British history with her Inspector Wexford series. Spanning over 50 years since *From Doon with Death* (1964), the 23 novels featuring this Sussex-based liberal policeman have taken the cosiness out of crime writing set in the English countryside. Deliberately seeking to eschew the limitations of traditional representations of the rural idyll, Rendell admits that her novels are conceived 'to have a very strong social theme' (Lawson 2012). She has written about domestic violence, racism, homelessness and environmental concerns, often drawing inspiration from subjects at the forefront of the public consciousness because of their presence in the news.

Spotlight on the Villains

Whether focused primarily on the investigation, on the investigator(s) or on a particular social milieu, the novels mentioned so far typically offer at best an intermittent glimpse of the criminal frame of mind. This is not the case in another distinctive permutation of this protean category of popular fiction: in what Priestman defines as the *noir* thriller, and what Knight simply calls the crime thriller, the spotlight is on the figure of the criminal himself (or, much less frequently, herself). In the most famous examples of this sub-genre, the protagonists are no arch-villains or criminal masterminds in the mould of Professor Moriarty, Sherlock Holmes's infamous nemesis. Instead, these novels dwell on the ordinariness of evil, and on how easy it is to be seduced by crime. The first-person narration in James M. Cain's *The Postman Always Rings Twice* (1934) and *Double Indemnity* (1936) makes these novels 'whydunits' rather than 'whodunits', while the careful study of the characters' social environment, and the seeming inexorability of their degeneration, has led critics to remark on this sub-genre's affinity with naturalism and with a Puritan belief in predetermination. Patricia Highsmith has also repeatedly explored the banal temptation of crime: in her standalone novel *Strangers on a Train* (1950), two men hatch a double homicidal plot – each will kill the other's intended victim – banking on the tenuousness of their relationship as accidental fellow passengers. The success of this novel has been followed by five books, starting with *The Talented Mr Ripley* (1955), featuring an ambitious, charming young man of poor means, determined to con his way up the social ladder. Mesmerized by the care-free, sophisticated and hedonistic life-style of a rich acquaintance, Ripley murders and then impersonates him, spinning a fantastic web of lies and displaying extraordinary resources in ruthless pursuit of his own perverted American dream. Sharing the interest in psychology of the thriller, and capitalizing on our fascination for charismatic, deviant characters, in *Darkly Dreaming Dexter* (2004) Jeff Lindsay has come up with a bold twist on the serial killer formula: the protagonist of his Dexter Morgan series, a blood-spatter analyst for the Miami police, is himself a serial killer who preys on fellow criminals, thus channelling his sociopathic tendencies – the result of a horrific childhood trauma – for a 'good' cause.

'Exotic' Crime

At the opposite end of the spectrum from this gory delight in the aberrant lies a further, recent trend in crime writing – one that mingles its potential for social commentary with an interest in foreign locations. Michael Dibdin and Donna Leon are just two of the English-speaking writers to have set their detective series abroad: their respective creations, Aurelio Zen (first featured in *Ratking*, 1988) and Guido Brunetti (*Death at La Fenice*, 1992), are both based in Italy, whose Mediterranean charm and touristy familiarity have been grafted onto its darker exotic image dating back to its days as the privileged setting for Gothic narratives of debauchery and terror. The translation into English of Andrea Camilleri's Commissario Montalbano series (see *The Shape of Water*, 2002, first published in Italian in 1994) has provided Anglophone readers with a fresh way to combine a love for Italian culture with a passion for crime writing. Montalbano's adventures – hugely successful in Italy, where they have been further popularized by Camilleri's own TV adaptations (broadcast by the BBC in 2012) – rely less on tightly structured investigative plots but more on the characterization of the mercurial, principled (and, predictably, food-loving) protagonist and his team of faithful collaborators, who at times resemble figures from the *commedia dell'arte*. Readers less keen on the presence of strong comic and/ or melodramatic elements, and looking for greater psychological and social realism, have embraced instead the stern tradition of Scandinavian noir. Pioneered by Maj Sjöwall and Per Wahlöö's Martin Beck series (1965–75) and turned into a global phenomenon by Stieg Larsson's posthumous, multi-million selling 'Millennium Trilogy' (2005–7), this tradition is unforgiving in its exposure of the cracks in the political system and the societal tissue of northern European countries, otherwise typically perceived as models of progressive, egalitarian, community-minded liberalism. An altogether gentler take on the exotic, and on crime in general, is provided by Alexander McCall Smith, in whose *The No 1 Ladies' Detective Agency* (1999) and its sequels, the thin mystery element is just an excuse for the exploration of the endearing idiosyncrasies of Mma Ramotswe, its commonsensical, 'traditionally-built' heroine, and the beauty of Botswana, her beloved country. Such a – dare we say it? – soft-boiled approach to the genre has been so successful that McCall Smith has transplanted it back to Scotland in his Isabel Dalhousie mysteries, whose compassionate lament for the decline of civility in contemporary Edinburgh is miles away from the harsh grittiness of the Tartan noir.

This is further proof of the extraordinary variety available within crime writing, a literary category of such suppleness as to warrant being called an 'unclassifiable genre' (Scaggs 2005, 1). The perfect detective novel is not the one that best follows the generic rules, as Todorov has claimed (1977, 43): rather, crime writing keeps its hold on readers for its ability to adapt to changing social and cultural conditions, all the while flaunting its contradictions, as it continues to surprise us.

Notes

1. The connection between detective fiction and a spiritual dimension is reiterated by Nicholas Blake who suggests that the rise of the genre compensates for the 'decline in religion at the end of the Victorian era' (1946, 400). Blake is the pseudonym under which Cecil Day-Lewis wrote detective fiction and criticism.

2. Unsurprisingly, both W. H. Auden and Nicholas Blake think of the genre as the escapist literature of choice for intellectuals. On his part, Todorov also subscribes to the elitist prejudice against genre writing by arguing that mystery stories which do not conform to the formula become 'literature' and not 'detective fiction' (1977, 43).

3. Ellery Queen is the pseudonym adopted by Frederic Dannay and Manfred Lee, who published their first detective novel, *The Roman Hat Mystery*, in 1929.

4. Often mentioned as Christie's fellow queens are Margery Allingham (the creator of Albert Campion in 1929), the New Zealand-born Ngaio Marsh (with her London-based Inspector Roderick Alleyn, first featured in 1934) and Dorothy L. Sayers, whose Peter Wimsey makes his earliest appearance in *Whose Body?* (1923). G. K. Chesterton's Father Brown's stories date back to 1910. Philo Vance made his debut in *The Benson Murder Case* (1926), followed shortly afterwards by Ellery Queen (1929 – see above) and

Nero Wolfe in *Fer de Lance* (1934). Christie introduces Poirot and Miss Marple respectively in *The Mysterious Affair at Styles* (1920) and *Murder at the Vicarage* (1930).

5. Dashiell Hammett's *Red Harvest* and *The Maltese Falcon*, featuring the Continental Op and Sam Spade, were published in 1929 and 1930 respectively, having been previously serialized in *Black Mask*. Philip Marlowe's career spans eight novels from *The Big Sleep* (1939) to *Poodle Springs*, left unfinished by Chandler on his death in 1959, and completed by Robert B. Parker in 1989.

6. Dupin makes his debut in 'The Murders in the Rue Morgue' (1841), and returns in 'The Mystery of Marie Rogêt' (1842) and 'The Purloined Letter' (1844). Holmes is the protagonist of 56 stories and four novels, published between 1887 and 1927.

7. Cordelia Gray comes back only in another novel, *The Skull Beneath the Skin* (1982). P. D. James' most famous creation, and the protagonist of 14 books to date, is Scotland Yard detective Adam Dalgliesh, first featured in *Cover Her Face* (1962). Knight describes him as 'the most internationally successful' of 'reconfigured heroic detectives' (2004, 136): although a policeman, and not a private investigator, Dalgliesh comes from the same mould as the amateur gentlemen-detectives of the Golden Age, with whom he shares a certain conservativism, as well as an aura of superiority. His love of poetry – a shorthand for his education and refined sensibility – functions as a modern-day equivalent of upper-class markers.

Works Cited

Ascari, M. (2007), *A Counter-History of Crime Fiction: Supernatural, Gothic, Sensational*. Basingstoke: Palgrave Macmillan.

Auden, W. H. (1962), 'The Guilty Vicarage: Notes on the Detective Story, by an Addict' [1948], in *The Dyer's Hand and Other Essays*. New York: Random House, pp. 146–58.

Auster, P. (1992), *The New York Trilogy* [1987]. London: Faber and Faber.

Baxt, G. (1998), *A Queer Kind of Death* [1966]. Los Angeles and New York: Alyson.

BBC (2008), 'Patricia Cornwell'. BBC World Book Club. [podcast] 28 February 2008, http://downloads.bbc.co.uk/podcasts/worldservice/wbc/wbc_20080228-1710.mp3, accessed 20 November 2012.

Blake, N. (1946), 'The Detective Story – Why?' [1942], in H. Haycraft (ed.), *The Art of the Mystery Story: A Collection of Critical Essays*. New York: Grosset & Dunlap, pp. 398–405.

Cain, J. M. (1934), *The Postman Only Rings Twice*. New York: Knopf.

—(2005), *Double Indemnity* [1936]. London: Orion.

Camilleri, A. (2002), *The Shape of Water* [1994], trans. S. Sartarelli. London: Penguin.

Cawelti, J. G. (1976), *Adventure, Mystery, and Romance. Formula Stories as Art and Popular Culture*. Chicago and London: The University of Chicago Press.

Chandler, R. (1940), *Farewell, My Lovely*. New York: Knopf.

—(1950), 'The Simple Art of Murder' [1944], in *The Simple Art of Murder*. London: Hamish Hamilton, pp. 318–33.

—(1970), *The Big Sleep* [1939]. London: Penguin.

—(2001), 'The High Window' [1943], in *The Lady in the Lake and Other Novels*. London: Penguin, pp. 1–188.

Chandler, R. and Parker, R. B. (2010), *Poodle Springs* [1989]. New York: Berkley Books.

Christie, A. (1920), *The Mysterious Affair at Styles*. London: Lane.

—(1930), *Murder at the Vicarage*. London: Collins.

Ciocia, S. (2012), 'The Last of the Romantics? The Accidental Investigator in Postmodern Detective Fiction', in C. Casaliggi and P. March-Russell (eds), *Legacies of Romanticism: Literature, Culture, Aesthetics*. London and New York: Routledge, pp. 198–210.

Cornwell, P. (1990), *Postmortem*. New York: Scribner.

—(1995), *The Body Farm* [1994]. London: Warner Books.

'The Detection Club Oath' (1946) [1928], in H. Haycraft (ed.), *The Art of the Mystery Story: A Collection of Critical Essays*. New York: Grosset & Dunlap, pp. 197–9.

Dibdin, M. (1988), *Ratking*. London: Faber and Faber.

Eco, U. (1983), *The Name of the Rose* [1980], trans. William Weaver. London: Picador.

Grafton, S. (1993), *A is for Alibi* [1986]. London: Pan Books.

Haddon, M. (2004), *The Curious Incident of the Dog in the Night-Time* [2003]. London: Vintage.

Hammett, D. (1929), *Red Harvest*. New York: Knopf.

—(2003), *The Maltese Falcon* [1930]. London: Orion.

Highsmith, P. (1950), *Strangers on a Train*. New York: Harper and Row.

—(1999), *The Talented Mr Ripley* [1955]. London: Vintage.

Himes, C. (1965), *Cotton Comes to Harlem*. New York: Putnam.

Hjortsberg, W. (1978), *Falling Angel*. New York: Harcourt Brace Jovanovich.

Hogg, J. (2010), *The Private Memoirs and Confessions of a Justified Sinner* [1824]. Oxford: Oxford World Classics.

James, P. D. (1962), *Cover Her Face*. London: Faber.

—(1974), *An Unsuitable Job for a Woman* [1972]. London: Sphere.

—(1982), *The Skull Beneath the Skin*. London: Faber.

Knight, S. (2004), *Crime Fiction 1800–2000: Death, Detection, Diversity.* Basingstoke and New York: Palgrave Macmillan.

Lawson, M. (2012), 'Commander Dalgliesh and Chief Inspector Wexford'. *Foreign Bodies.* [podcast] 29 October 2012, http://www.bbc.co.uk/podcasts/series/foreignbodies/all, accessed 20 November 2012.

Leon, D. (2004), *Death at La Fenice* [1992]. London: Arrow.

Lindsay, J. (2005), *Darkly Dreaming Dexter* [2004]. London: Orion.

McBain, E. (1956), *Cop Hater.* New York: Simon and Schuster.

McCall Smith, A. (2003), *The No.1 Ladies' Detective Agency* [1998]. London: Abacus.

McDermid, V. (1987), *Report for Murder.* London: Women's Press.

—(1992), *Dead Beat.* London: Gollancz.

—(1995), *The Mermaid Singing.* London: HarperCollins.

Merivale, P. and Sweeney, S. (eds) (1999), *Detecting Texts: The Metaphysical Detective Story from Poe to Postmodernism.* Philadelphia: University of Pennsylvania Press.

Mosley, W. (1990), *Devil in a Blue Dress.* New York: Norton.

Neely, B. (1995), *Blanche Among the Talented Ten* [1994]. London: Penguin.

Onatade, A. (2002), 'Val McDermid's Last Temptation' [online], *Shots: Crime and Thrillers Ezine,* http://www.shotsmag.co.uk/interview_view. aspx?interview_id=97, accessed 20 November 2012.

Paretsky, S. (1982), *Indemnity Only.* New York: Dial.

Pepper, A. (2000), *The Contemporary American Crime Novel: Race, Ethnicity, Gender, Class.* Edinburgh: Edinburgh University Press.

Poe, E. A. (1845), 'Review of *Tales* by Edgar A. Poe' [online], http://people. virginia.edu/~sfr/enam315/texts2/eappoe.html, accessed 10 December 2012.

—(2003), *The Fall of the House of Usher and Other Writings.* London: Penguin.

Priestman, M. (1998), *Crime Fiction from Poe to the Present.* Plymouth: Northcote House.

Pynchon, T. (2006), *The Crying of Lot 49* [1966], New York: HarperCollins.

Queen, E. (1929), *The Roman Hat Mystery.* New York: Stokes.

Rankin, I. (2012), *Standing in Another Man's Grave.* London: Orion.

Rendell, R. (1964), *From Doon with Death.* London: Hutchinson.

Sayers, D. L. (1923), *Whose Body?.* London: Unwin.

—(1935), *Gaudy Night.* London: Gollancz.

Scaggs, J. (2005), *Crime Fiction.* London and New York: Routledge.

Stevenson, R. L. (2006), *Strange Case of Dr Jekyll and Mr Hyde and Other Tales* [1886]. Oxford: Oxford World Classics.

Stout, R. (1934), *Fer de Lance.* New York: Farrar and Rinehart.

Tani, S. (1984), *The Doomed Detective: The Contribution of the Detective Novel to Postmodern American and Italian Fiction.* Carbondale and Edwardsville: Southern Illinois University Press.

Todorov, T. (1977), 'The Typology of Detective Fiction' [1966], in *The Poetics of Prose*, trans. R. Howard. Ithaca, NY: Cornell University Press, pp. 42–52.

Van Dine, S. S. (1926), *The Benson Murder Case*. New York: Scribner.

—(1946), 'Twenty Rules for Writing Detective Stories' [1928], in H. Haycraft (ed.), *The Art of the Mystery Story: A Collection of Critical Essays*. New York: Grosset & Dunlap, pp. 189–93.

Wilson, B. (1991), *Gaudí Afternoon* [1990]. London: Virago.

7

Disturbance, Disorder, Destruction, Disease: Horror Fiction Today

Gina Wisker

Horror constitutes the limit of reason, sense, consciousness and speech, the very emotion in which the human reaches its limit. Horror is thus ambivalently human.

(Botting 1995, 131)

No amount of rationalism, reform, or Freudian analysis can quite annul the thrill of the chimney-corner whisper or the lonely wood.

(Barker 1997, 12)

What is the fascination of horror in popular fiction? In the twenty-first century, horror seems to be mainstreamed. It is the genre, the language through which we write and read our everyday as well as our most hidden desires and fears. The familiar figures and formulae of horror appear on TV adverts and in soaps. Cultural explorations of neighbourliness, social tolerance of difference, family cohesion and fidelity, as well as love and death, are now expressed through the familiar figures of horror, vampires and shapeshifters (Charlaine Harris' *True Blood* series), vampires and werewolves (Stephanie Meyer's *Twilight* series). Early and recent critics emphasize horror's ubiquitous presence in everything we think and do, its unavoidable lurking undertones destabilizing our certainties and undercutting our security of identity, wholeness of self, time and place, family, relationships, reality, the familiar. Horror exposes, undermines and feeds on our need for coherence and hope. In recruiting the twin responses of desire and fear, it permeates everything. Horror deploys many Gothic formulae, such as the return of the repressed, haunting, the monstrous Other, doubling and unsafe haunted spaces and places, but it is more likely to use violence, terror and bodily harm than the more traditional Gothic.

This chapter first looks at some relatively recent history of horror fictions, its ubiquitous presence today and its intents upon us. It explores physical and psychological bases to and uses of horror, and its engagement with ethics, learning, social and self-awareness and change. In exploring three stories in depth, issues such as disturbance, disorder, destruction and disease are explored to show how horror fictions engage with our terrors, complacencies, fears and desires.

Background and History

Horror in one form or other is at least as old as storytelling itself and appears in a wide range of oral, written, filmic and other forms. It is an essential, troubling accompaniment to the complacencies of the everyday, reminding us that behind artifices of comfort and rules, order and stability, wholeness and righteousness, lie the flip sides of these: discomfort, terror, violence, disgust. Freud's use of the term 'unheimlich' (1919) theorized this disturbance as the unfamiliar, building on the German Romantic writer E. T. A. Hoffman's short story 'The Sandman' (1885). The destabilizing energies of horror offer a thrill of disorder and of radicalism, which is why the horror comics of the

1950s were seen as so dangerous, so politically and morally questionable (see M. Barker 1984), their dark scenarios aligned with the undercutting of political as well as personal security. Horror also offers a disquieting peek behind the curtains of the everyday, the familiar and the complacently secure, revealing that this is an artifice, a front. Horror fiction upsets and challenges us at a psychological and personal level, troubling identity, relationships, domestic security, the body and the mind. Simultaneously, it derives from and troubles the body politic, broader contexts and values. It is culturally, temporally and spatially constructed from specific contexts, disturbing any simple alignment with dominant beliefs – and its disturbances are embodied spatially, physically and psychogeographically (ways in which locations effect, embody, resonate with events and so affect our visions and versions of them [see Debord 1955]) in terms of those contexts: Gothic castles, brutal urban environments, swamps.

We can also recognize horror's trappings, characters and themes as well as its settings, as Linda Holland-Toll suggests:

> the reader of horror fictions expects at least some of the following elements to surface: an aspect of the supernatural – an actual physical monster embodied in the vampire, werewolf, ghost, or aliens; fantastic or inexplicable events which may or may not have a non-fantastic cause, or which . . . may or may not be explicable; characters with super/paranormal powers; extreme emotions, melodramatic situations and sensational plots; emotional engagements of terror, horror, or revulsion; and, of course, the paradoxical feeling of enjoyable terror. (2009, 6)

We can expect body horror, body swaps and body destruction, contagion and deadly science, the return of the repressed in the form of vampires, zombies, the beast in man rising as werewolf or other shapeshifter, and the ultimate taboo, cannibalism. One of the earliest theorists, the great horror author H. P. Lovecraft, identified a history to weird tales and horror in the United States, and noted the ways the 'weird' tale (his term) dismays and disturbs, unites psychological and physical fears, removing the smirk of complacency. He notes:

> the genuineness and dignity of the weirdly horrible tale as a literary form. Against it are discharged all the shafts of a materialistic sophistication which clings to frequently felt emotions and external events, and of a naively inspired idealism which deprecates the aesthetic motive and calls for a didactic literature to 'uplift' the reader toward a suitable degree of smirking optimism. (1973, 12)

Lovecraft's own legacy is palpable in much contemporary horror fiction (as is that of the other earlier great master, Edgar Allen Poe). Bleiler sees a movement involving writers and readers as insiders, and some horror writing developing into science fiction:

> *Supernatural Horror in Literature* is in a sense the collective of a movement in the history of popular literature in the United States. The field of weird fiction, as exemplified in the magazine *Weird Tales* (and its less successful rivals, *Ghost Stories, Tales of Magic and Mystery*), paralleled and even slightly preceded the development of its mechanistic sister, science-fiction. The readers of *Weird Tales* had a feeling of fraternity and community, a feeling of participating in a development. (1973, vii)

I would argue that horror writing has also led to graphic novels, and the rich plethora of popular fictions and horror films with which we are surrounded.

While Lovecraft finds horror present in our histories, in the darkness of the forests and in the great unknown surrounding the safety of familial and cultural gatherings, Clive Barker locates it in the everyday, in the monstrous qualities of terror, violence, murder, rape, and in the politics of Fascism. It is also disturbingly located in the seemingly safest places so it is a worldview, a perspective, either an unbalanced response or one which is helpfully insightful, exposing contradictions and enabling us to cope above and beyond the narratives in which we invest. Horror is everyday, everywhere, real and fantastic:

> As soon as we begin to delve into the nature of horror, or attempt to list its manifestations in our culture, the sheer scale of the beast becomes apparent. Horror is everywhere. It's in fairy tales and the evening headlines, it's in street corner gossip and the incontrovertible facts of history. It's in playground ditties (*Ring-a ring o' roses* is a sweet little plague song), it's on the altar, bleeding for our sins ('Forgive them, Father, for they know not what they do'). (1997, 15)

It takes over our imaginations and reasserts its presence in our personal and community narratives. It is historical, supernatural, both fantastic and ever present in reality and in our imaginations, histories.

How does everyday horror differ from that of horror fiction? As with art and fiction more broadly, horror *fiction* implements, enacts representation, emphasizes constructedness, metaphor, symbol and so encourages an engagement at the level of the imagination, the conscience, enabling irony, critique, comment and decisions to act above and beyond mere depiction.

Nowadays, comfortably in front of our TV, we see genocide, everyday mutations, college kids gunning down their classmates, nail bombs targeting marathon runners, serial killers and parents who murder their own infants, or children who murder their parents. We see epidemics, Ebola and AIDS, and we hear lies and the uncovering of genocide based on deceit and oppression. This is the news, the documentary programmes, and it is our everyday reality. Such everyday real horrors are replayed with irony, with elements of the supernatural, and with critical insight in horror fiction and films. Indeed, horror is more than entertainment, it is dangerous, as is all Gothic, of which it is a major strain, because it disturbs, it explicitly demonstrates the dark side, enacts the fears and twitches the net curtains of the suburban compliance and conformity which keep the night outside. The strategies of horror fiction expose the night inside our minds, our secret fears of the unusual or the mundane, and it exposes the disturbed minds of serial killers, evil politicians, rapists, murderers, of uncanny or everyday monsters. These are all embodied in the horror fictions we read and watch, and our critical engagement can lead to actions to manage, prevent and overcome some of what horror depicts and acts out (or not . . .).

Role and Effect of Horror

Those who teach horror are very aware of its power to engage the critical, insightful reading practices which lead to citizenship, an ethical awareness of the need to expose the undersides of conformity, enabling clarity and an imaginative capacity to see beyond what is presented as everyday and comforting, and in so doing perhaps forestall, ward off, uncover, expose, confront the darker elements of our lives, our societies and the things we fear individually and culturally. On teaching horror, Mike Arnzen, an American horror author and academic notes:

> Horror provides an excellent context for learning. It raises the serious questions that allow critical inquiry to transpire. This is, perhaps, patently true of all literary texts, but the omnipresent mode of 'uncertainty' that underpins most works in the horror genre inherently moulds the reading experience into the shape of a question mark. (2009)

The horror 'turn' is not merely to titillate, disgust or shock, although much schlock (visceral, brutal, deliberately offensive) horror does only that. It is cathartic. It exposes falsity, reveals alternatives, enables an imaginative embodiment and working through of the worst terrors and fears, facing or avoiding the most destructive. Horror fictions, whether written or film text, enable this embodiment, since much horror is about the real, about the body, and through the deployment of imagery and symbol, catharsis results.

Horror comes in several forms – psychological, supernatural, physical and a mix of these. The great texts which established the genre appeared in the nineteenth century. Mary Shelley's *Frankenstein* (1818) is frequently seen as the first horror fiction. The physical construction of a Monster by the first mad scientist, Dr Victor Frankenstein, is a tragic example of hubris which still influences android and robot films including *Blade Runner* (1982) and *I, Robot* (2004), and questions the nature of what it means to be human. The monster's lack of social development leads it to internalize a sense of its own Otherness, to abject itself. A key theory of psychoanalytic theory argues that in the 'mirror' stage (Lacan 1977) identity development is accompanied by construction and then abjection (rejection with disgust) of the 'Other'. The feminist theorist Julia Kristeva (1982) and critic Barbara Creed (1993) recognize this Otherizing as gendered. The non-self, that is, women, aliens, the culturally different, monsters, is abjected. With a psychological turn, we construct and reject the strange, terrifying potential, all that we fear and desire. As Kristeva points out, the Other is a construct of our own minds (1994).

But horror can also be realistic, even historically verifiable and it can be psychological, supernatural, riddled with imagery and symbols, or a disturbing mix of both. Historical accounts of cannibalism and serial killing inform horror. Serial killer Ed Geins is the basis for Thomas Harris's *The Silence of the Lambs* (1988) and Robert Bloch's *Psycho* (1959). Horror is also spliced with speculative fiction, the fantastic, science fiction, the supernatural with alien invasions (*Alien* trilogy, 1979, 1986, 1992), the scourge of flesh-eating zombies (*Dawn of the Dead*, 1968), vampires transcending time, space, death and the fixity of bodily shape (*Dracula*, 1897; *Interview with the Vampire*, 1994; Poppy Z. Brite's *Lost Souls*, 1992).

Horror Fictions – Three Stories

Three stories are explored here to illustrate a variety of ways in which contemporary (twentieth- and twenty-first-century) horror fiction entertains, disturbs and challenges. H. P. Lovecraft's 'The Shadow over Innsmouth' (1936) builds on the identity, heredity and body horror we find in the great master Edgar Allen Poe (1809–49), especially in 'The Fall of the House of Usher' (1839) and in Robert Louis Stevenson's *Dr Jekyll and Mr Hyde* (1886); on the Monstrous Other, established in Shelley's *Frankenstein*, and the destabilizing terrors of the unfamiliar emerging from the ostensibly ordinary, the unheimlich (Hoffmann's 'Sandman') rendered more threatening when revealed as disgustingly familiar. Lovecraft is known for his use of the supernatural, the threats of Cthulhu, a fearful abhorrent octopus-like Otherworldly being, and of the Elder Gods undersea, and/or from beyond the stars, awaiting their return to take over the world. At the other end of the twentieth century, in 'The Sixth Sentinel' (1981), Poppy Z. Brite, known for her vampire novels and stories, employs Gothic horror locations, the swamps of Louisiana, family betrayals, romantic love as death, destruction and lingering bondage, body horror and dissolution, death and damned returns. In a postcolonial context, Nalo Hopkinson's 'The Glass Bottle Trick' (2000) rewrites the Bluebeard tale from a contemporary, Caribbean/Canadian perspective, uniting postcolonial and feminist lenses to expose the horror latent in racism, which leads to self-loathing, and in patriarchal power, which leads to brutality and death.

H. P. Lovecraft

H. P. Lovecraft creates terrifying scenes and scenarios utilizing the full range of nightmare horrors. Many of his images and strategies have become absorbed into public discourse through films such as *Van Helsing* (2004) (in the harpies), *Underworld* (2003) and, for tentacled octopus monsters, even the comic-originated *Hellboy* (2004) and *Spiderman 2* (2004).

His 'The Shadow over Innsmouth' is a travel tale, which adds cultural difference to the already complex misinterpretations possible for Lovecraft's warned-off lone wanderer figure. The tale reminds us of the more recent *An American Werewolf in London* (1981), where Jack and his friend stumble wearily into 'The Slaughtered Lamb' on the Yorkshire Moors and are met with similar covert warnings and hints. The tale also harks back to that other familiar travel horror, *Dracula* (1897), where Jonathan Harker travels to Transylvania and encounters the vampire Count. Locals always know secrets, keep them, warn the traveller a little, watch him or her fall straight into the trap and sometimes, as in 'Innsmouth', are *part* of the trap. The films *Wrong Turn* (2003) and *A Texas Chainsaw Massacre* (1974) operate a similar trajectory

– as does Ian McEwan's *The Comfort of Strangers* (1981). Travellers are always a little gauche, confused, liable to fear, miss hints about the truly dangerous, mistake the strange and excitingly different for the deadly and vice versa. Horror's ability to nudge us out of our comfort zone is located in the context of the de-familiarization of people and places, the misreading of signs.

Lovecraft's protagonist is on a research trip visit to Innsmouth, a place shrouded in mystery where figures in priests' robes and tall tiaras dodge in and out of houses turned into temples. There is a secret society, a society hiding a secret. Staying a night in Innsmouth, while interviewing old inhabitants, against advice and good sense, he not only uncovers the story of a pact with the fishy folk to provide rich catches in exchange for interbreeding, but also discovers that, although hidden from family and local history, his own grandparents were right at the heart of the Marsh family, and so he is himself a descendant of a monstrous fish person. The revelation comes gradually after his escape from being hunted down by strange, inhuman fishy folk, cult members wearing ancient ornaments and jewellery:

> They were the blasphemous fish-frogs of the nameless design – living and horrible – and as I saw them I knew also of what that humped, tiaraed priest in the black church basement had so fearsomely reminded me. Their number was past guessing. It seemed to me that there were limitless swarms of them. (1936, 26)

Their strangeness is disgusting, blasphemous, unthinkable, and the huge numbers of them, the swarms, are one of the things he fears most: 'the figures I glimpsed were in voluminous robes, and one wore a peaked diadem which glistened whitely in the moonlight. The gait of this figure was so odd that it sent a chill through me – for it seemed to me the creature was almost hopping' (23–4, 29). The creatures from the sea are an invading horde, utterly alien. Their number, the interrelating and the nebulousness all disgust.

Later he feels similar 'repulsion and alienation' upon his return to his wider family. He also both builds on his latent memories and suspicions and adds family tales and strange heirlooms into the mix. Through its focus on miscegenation, the tale exposes terrors concerning identity and heredity. The grandmother's eyes, like his, were 'true' Marsh eyes, and the worst of all, some of the strange ancient jewellery is a family heirloom, so 'I began to acquire a kind of terror of my own ancestry' when 'gradually a horrible sort of *comparison* began to obtrude itself on my unconscious' (28–9). The dreams he has following his visit introduce his ancient, living fishy Grandmother and her grandmother, indicating his future as an immortal. The archaic language suggests sickness, decay, something threatening because a mixture of unpleasantly familiar and indefinable:

> One night I had a frightful dream in which I met my grandmother under the sea. She lived in a phosphorescent palace of many terraces, with gardens of strange leprous corals and grotesque brachiate efflorescences, and welcomed me with a warmth that may have been sardonic. (29)

Abjection is a key feature of Lovecraft's work as are disturbance, disorder, destruction and disease. He is known for his problematic views on racial difference, his disgust at the Other seen as alien and his representation of women as witchlike hags and dangerous sources of miscegenation.

The work of Kristeva provides useful inroads into use of the abject, engaging on a feminist and psychoanalytical level with the ways in which horror represents how the West imagines and treats foreign Others, initially based on an examination of racism in France. In her exposure of the boundaries, rejections and repressions of Western patriarchal-based horror, Kristeva reveals its sources, stressing the need for equality, both racially and politically:

> Our disturbing otherness . . . is what bursts in to confront the 'demons', or the threat that apprehension generated by the protective apparition of the other at the heart of what we persist in maintaining as a proper, solid 'us'. By recognising *our* uncanny strangeness we shall neither suffer from it nor enjoy it from the outside. The foreigner is within me, hence we are all foreigners. If I am a foreigner, then there are no foreigners. (1982, 192)

This aligns itself with David Punter's explorations (2000) of ways in which postcolonial Gothic criticism identifies strategies of horror engaging at the level of abjection in colonial and imperial texts to render colonized, foreign subjects as objects, as Other. Identity construction and representation and psychoanalytically based theories explain the abjection of women and foreigners and their representation as victims or monsters. This casts a light on Lovecraft's work, showing how anything and anyone conceived as Other is represented as both strange and disgusting, and any coupling with this Other is terrifying.

Poppy Z. Brite

Poppy Z. Brite's vampire and American Gothic horror fictions undermine values and narratives which play out on our TV screens, in magazines and in theatres and films – eternal love coupledom, friendships, family values. Her families reject their young, and groups of travelling post-war Vietnam generation vampire youth pick them up. Nothing has value and the chief character, adopted by the group in her novel *Lost Souls* (1992), is tellingly called Nothing.

Brite's collection *Swamp Foetus* (1981) offers several horror scenarios. Though mostly situated in the United States and the South, one culturally inflected tale explores the dangerous fascination of Kali, Indian goddess of death, while more locally adolescents are turned into sideshow freaks, companionship leads to binding beyond death and true love lovers each become vampires, one in thrall to another. Her signatures are betrayals, dissolution, graveyards, a tortured life after death. In 'The Sixth Sentinel' Brite undercuts true romance, offering it up to devouring decay: a Louisiana couple seeking eternal commitment of mind and body end up with companionship through enthralment and death. Rosalie is rescued from her terrible dreams by her new lover and social inferior, Cajun Theophile. She escapes her mundane home to be with him, but Rosalie's parents refuse the romance, and when their sexual consummation leads to pregnancy, Theophile is murdered by Rosalie's father. The father is hunted down by dogs in the swamp. Two families are destroyed by their small-minded response to inappropriate relationships. Rosalie and Theophile are star-crossed lovers, but their tale does not end simply in death. Rosalie's mother brews up a homespun bayou remedy of evil-tasting herbs, her daughter convulses and aborts her shapeless child, but the ill-fated love continues to haunt Rosalie's dreams. The graveyard scenes of Southern Gothic, with the overblown and the creeping, floating dead are liminal spaces where Rosalie's dreams wander. She seeks Theophile out, and when she finds him in his grave, a union awaits her of decay, worms, dissolution of her body into his rotting, bloated corpse. This is disturbance and dark theatre:

> Some of the things that have floated to the surface are little more than bone, others are swollen to three or four times their size, grassy mounds of decomposed flesh rising like islands from the mud; women of these have silk flower petals stuck on them like obscene decorations, flies rise lazily, then descend again in glittering, circling clouds, yarning eyeless faces thrust out of stagnant pools. (1981, 102)

The artificial plaster saints' silk petals float together, recombining with the fungal, the putrefying and the parasitic. In the middle of this, Rosalie dreams she falls into her lover's rotting corpse: 'his eyes have fallen back into their sockets and his mouth is open; his tongue has gone, she sees thin white worms teeming in the passage of his throat, his nostrils are widening black holes beginning to encroach upon the greenish flesh of his cheeks' (103). Nothing is as it should be – flesh is green, tongues and bodies once used in love are rotted. His body starts to suck hers in to join him in death, dissolving barriers between life and death, corpse, worms, the enveloping water and body fluids.

The story is relentless in its dismemberment of romance. When Rosalie's new suitor rescues her from her dreams, obliterating them by reaching inside her mind, his intention is devious. She is tricked into becoming both the victim guard of his ghostly wealth and his companion, able to fulfil his desires for their eternal unity, wandering hand in ethereal hand over the misty swamps. Brite mixes the heat of illicit passion and family revenge with death, punishment and eternity.

This is Gothic horror, which dwells 'on the connections between violence and sexuality', 'closely interlocked with the rather belated spread of Freudian theory' (Punter 1980, 348, 361). It exposes contraries and punishes the fatally attractive, while leaving the attraction lingering on as potential, and threat. Desire and fear are intertwined – proffered and problematic. Both Lovecraft and Brite deal with desire and disgust, the unmentionable and destabilizing brought into the family, romance, and into one's bodily self. As Botting notes:

> Horror is evoked by encounters with objects and actions that are not so much threatening as taboo: what is least avowable in oneself, what is symbolically least palatable or recognizable, may be the most horrible. Horror appears when fear comes a little too close to home. (1995, 124)

Secret desires and fears are close to home and often unacknowledged. The link between the untrustworthy familiar and the unfamiliar is theorized by Freud's notion of the uncanny or unheimlich, which influences psychoanalytic readings of fantastic and horror fiction, unlocking our understanding of how such writing destabilizes and threatens by offering the safe and comfortable and then utterly undercutting it. Those we know are not those we know, no safe space is safe, and seemingly fixed boundaries – life and death, male and female – are all threatened with dread and apprehension, defamiliarization, then undermined, leaving the reader insecure if alert. Horror explodes or implodes the familiar suburban location, family and relationships, projecting something repressed, embodied in a demon spirit, ghost, monster or disruptive energy. So houses implode and explode (*Poltergeist*, 1982) because they are built over desecrated graves, children are possessed by demons (*The Exorcist*, 1973; *The Omen*, 1976) and in Toni Morrison's *Beloved* (1987), a returned now adult baby ghost embodies the lived haunting of the horrific legacy of slavery.

Perhaps it is not so surprising that horror so frequently dwells on issues of ethnicity, family, relationships and children, threats to the wholeness of the body and mind, to security and identity since these are some of the assumed stabilities on which we build our lives. Lovecraft's disturbing histories undermine security of family and identity where racial intermixing is seen as a threat of equal enormity as that of the supernatural intruding on the seemingly dependable. In Brite's story Rosalie's parents are afraid of intermingling across ethnic and class differences. The results of these phobias acted out is doubly threatening and disturbing.

Nalo Hopkinson

the good horror tale will dance its way to the center of your life and find the secret door to the room you believed no one but you knew of.

(King 1981, 149)

Stephen King emphasizes the domesticity of horror and its ability to probe the hidden areas of our minds, like Bluebeard's fatal inner rooms where his series of unsuspecting wives were murdered for their inquisitiveness and desire for knowledge. Nalo Hopkinson's take on this tale combines domestic horror with abjection from a postcolonial, feminist perspective. David Punter, who in *The Literature of Terror* (1980) intertwined Gothic and horror, defines the postcolonial condition as one of haunting, a natural location to be explored, expressed and sometimes imaginatively overcome through the tropes, images, scenarios of horror, arguing that 'the process of mutual postcolonial abjection is, I suppose, one that confronts us everyday in the ambiguous form of a series of uncanny returns' (2000, vi). In these liminal, haunted spaces the undead stalking the living to feed on them, a damaging history and the damaged present intermingle, draining all concerned.

Hopkinson's 'The Glass Bottle Trick' (2000) is a Caribbean-Canadian rewrite of the Bluebeard tale, spliced with the Brothers Grimm's variant 'Fitcher's bird', mixed in with Caribbean myth and post feminism's doubts about sisterhood, providing a radical challenge to gendered and racialized constructions of the abject. Like Morrison's *Beloved* and Jamaican Erna Brodber's tale of internalized negative teachings and zombified existence in *Myal* (1989), Hopkinson's tale addresses destructive racial and gendered ideology in practice. The story focuses on Beatrice, the feisty, less-than-innocent wife of successful Samuel. Samuel might be financially successful but he has internalized a racialized self-loathing of his own black skin, and in order to avoid their producing (his own) black children, he murders a series of wives when they each become pregnant. Glass bottles, hidden rooms and secrets indicate the hidden internalized abjection of self. Eggs, with their potential for new life and change, are vulnerable to snakes, and a threat to the preservation of a certain performance of self. 'The Glass Bottle Trick' replays and rewrites the Bluebeard story with duppies trapped in glass bottles, egg-swallowing snakes, semi-dead semi-alive wives preserved and controlled in air-conditioned stasis, questionable sisterhood and the empowered self-preservation of Beatrice.

Hopkinson uses the Bluebeard tale, the tale of 'Fitcher's bird' and Caribbean folklore to offer a postcolonial, gender-inflected Gothic horror rewrite which undercuts myths and power in the traditional tales and subsequent versions. She uses Gothic and Caribbean images and narratives, challenging, on the one hand, the damage done by internalizing racialized self-loathing, and on the other hand, the traditional tale's underlying warning to women to comply and not ask questions.

Taunted by her ex-friends, 'Leggo beast . . . Loose woman', Beatrice escapes into marriage with the respectable, 'cultured, punctual', 'courteous, self deprecating' but 'stocious, starchy' (Hopkinson 2000, 87, 90–1) bookseller, BMW-driving Samuel, who differs from the fun-loving sensuality of her gold-chain-wearing boyfriend Clifton. His flattering comments help her overlook his morose, meticulous, bad tempered and controlling behaviour and her original views of him as 'so boring' (86). The attraction here is not just the wealth but the social conformity Samuel offers, a chance to settle down and so reclaim her respectability. When he asks her mother for her hand, her heart's entrapment in a bottle resembles that of the two blue glass bottles jammed into the branches of the guava tree in his garden (containing the spirits of his duppy wives). Similar to Angela Carter's version of the Bluebeard tale, 'The Bloody Chamber' (1979), where the new bride recognizes her own eroticism, so too Beatrice develops a sexual relationship with the ostensibly calmer Samuel.

What might in one culture be traditionally just a way of identifying a freeing of self-awareness and passion through marriage is read through a variant of the Bluebeard tale spliced with 'Fitcher's bird' and Caribbean folk lore where the folktale of entrapping riotous duppies in bottles ominously equates her *rescue* into marriage with the superstition, the management, under Caribbean custom, of the previous dead wives.

> 'Is just my superstitiousness, darling,' he'd told her. 'You never heard the old people say that if someone dies, you must put a bottle in a tree to hide their spirit, otherwise it will come back as a duppy and haunt you? A blue bottle. To keep the duppy cool, so it won't come at you in hot anger for being dead'. (86)

If Beatrice knew her Caribbean superstitions and legends, she would know that this imprisonment is that of the earthly soul rather than the heavenly one – but can also indicate a malevolent spirit. The duppy usually stays with the body for 3 days after death – so separating the duppy from the body is an unusual activity, and probably should indicate to Beatrice that Samuel fears their wrath. Such containment is only for control of the dangerous, those whose anger is pent up, who would like to wreak revenge. Noting the originality of Caribbean folklore, Donald Hill says:

> Caribbean folklore is fresh and lacks an ancient history, it is wider than indigenous cultures of the continents from where it came. It holds pieces from all those areas, like a kaleidoscope with bits of glass (but not the entire glass), in ever shifting patterns. It is combinations of ancestral lore, remembered in fragments, and fit and refit to new. (2007, 6)

Original also is Hopkinson's splicing of West African and Canadian speculative fiction, Gothic scenarios and settings, European, African and Caribbean folklore – with something new – fusing the tales, settings and the problems into a new hybridity, exhibiting the chance fusion of different traits into a new lore. Samuel's internalized self-loathing, his distaste at his own black skin derived from a legacy of racism, leads him to not just kill his pregnant wives but to rip the foetus and placenta, the whole womb from their bodies, leaving each inside on their beds in the air-conditioned icebox room. His sealing of his house from the warmth outside reflects his sealing of his emotions, his refusal to procreate from internalized abjection articulated in his extreme anger when Beatrice calls him 'Black Beauty'. When she discovers the frozen bodies, Beatrice suddenly realizes that her pregnancy will not produce the normal married response of celebration, but her own death. The cry of the bird losing its eggs, the Caribbean keskidee replayed round the garden throughout the story, questions the word of patriarchy, of the law and the meaning of events, 'dit, dit, qu'est-ce qu'il dit!" (say, say, what's he saying!) (Hopkinson 2000, 87). The snake in the tree eating the indignant birds' eggs, one by one, is replayed in Samuel's destruction of his wives and unborn children, eggs which are not preserved but destroyed.

Beatrice, angrily trying to hit the snake, accidentally smashes the glass bottles. She's wrong when she feels Samuel will not be as cross as her father used to be with her mother. She is, in fact, under threat. It is only when she finds the duppy wives waking up in the warming house, feeding from their own blood to gain strength, that she realizes Samuel is like the snake, eating the eggs, denying life, in his case a culturally inflected response afflicted with the desire to prevent his own reproduction. She remembers him joking that 'no woman should have to give birth to his ugly black babies' (97) and understands his reason to keep her out of the sun as she darkened up, no longer 'Beauty. Pale beauty to my Beast' (94).

Bringing the wives back to life is Hopkinson's own invention, merging the Caribbean tales of duppies with the Bluebeard myth. Like the girl in 'Fitcher's bird', Beatrice takes the initiative, but it is not so simple to save these wives – who are not the sisters of the heroine in the tale 'Fitcher's bird'. Hopkinson supplies no easy feminist ending – of feminist sisterhood – since Beatrice is not sure whether when fully restored, the wives will treat her as fellow victim or as rival: 'The duppy wives held their bellies and glared at her, anger flaring hot behind their eyes. Beatrice backed away from the beds. "I didn't know", she said to the wives, "don't vex with me. I didn't know what it is Samuel do to you"' (100). The mixed Caribbean creolized English and received pronunciation mirrors the newly remixed culturally inflected tales with her own tale. Whether she can preserve her own egg, like the song 'Eggie Law, what a pretty basket' (101), which her father used to sing to her while hurling her in the air, is to be seen.

Hopkinson is playing on versions of guilt, evil, power and gender, rewriting more than the Bluebeard myth, indicating its origins in Biblical and international folktales which impress and perpetuate patriarchal power, women's guilt and obedience. The horror in this tale engages issues of gender and culture, exposing the usually tragic ending of patriarchal power games on the one hand, and the self-destruction arising from internalizing negative self-images based on racism, the legacy of colonial power games and the postcolonial Gothic horror which Punter emphasizes (2000) on the other hand. Hopkinson's postcolonial Gothic horror rewrite with Caribbean and post-feminist inflections undermines the disempowerment embedded in the Bluebeard tale, while avoiding an investment in dubious sisterhood.

Conclusion: The Power, Attraction and Warning of Horror

Mark Jancovich defines the role of conventional horror and its pleasures based on

> narrative closure in which the horrifying or monstrous is destroyed or contained. The structures of horror narratives are said to set out from a situation of order, move through a period of disorder caused by the eruption of horrifying or monstrous forces, and finally reach a point of closure and completion in which disruptive, monstrous elements are contained or destroyed and the original order is re-established. (1992, 9)

Part of the attraction of horror is its trajectory from dismay and displacement to resolution, but the resolution in each of the three tales discussed is an uneasy one: coming to terms with a dubious mixed heritage, eternal thraldom at the hands of a ghostly lover and the threat of vengeful duppy wives on the new acquisition, the new wife.

If it merely reinforced our complacencies after some disruption, horror would be essentially conservative. However, much of it is more deeply disturbing, more radical than that, offering a deeper critique of beliefs, behaviours and certainties. It must generate a

> degree of unresolved dis/ease or conflict significant enough that the reader who inhabits the society cannot simply gloss it over and return to business as usual. Spreading glossy white frosting over the burned and lumpy cake is not enough; people know that the frosting only hides the ghouls, whatever those ghouls may be, without destroying them. It is the knowledge that horror fiction, rather than reflecting unreal horror, is metaphorically or allegorically discussing everyday horror that causes dis/ease. (Holland-Toll 2009, 9)

Horror is more than entertainment, more than fantasy. We are aware we can, if only temporarily, think our ways out of, or face up to, the worst that horror embodies, the disturbance, disorder, destruction and disease. It uses the representational strategies of fiction to problematize the taken for granted and posit, embody the very worst. Through that trajectory it enables our engagement and offers us imaginative agency.

Works Cited

Arnzen, M. A. (2009), 'Horror and the Responsibilities of the Liberal Educator'. *Dissections*, http://www.simegen.com/writers/dissections/May%202009/ dissections_page3.html, accessed 8 July 2013.

Barker, C. (1997), *Clive Barker's A—Z of Horror*. Compiled by Stephen Jones. New York: HarperCollins.

Barker, M. (1984), *A Haunt of Fears*. London: Pluto.

Bleiler, E. F. (ed.) (1973), 'Introduction to the Dover Edition', in H. P. Lovecraft (ed.), *Supernatural Horror in Literature*. Mineola, NY: Dover Publications, pp. 12–16.

Bloch, R. (1959), *Psycho*. New York: Simon & Schuster.

Botting, F. (1995), *The Gothic*. Oxford: Routledge.

Brite, P. Z. (1981), 'The Sixth Sentinel', in *Swamp Foetus*. Republished in 1995, *Wormwood*, etc. Harmondsworth: Penguin Books.

—(1992), *Lost Souls*. Harmondsworth: Penguin.

Brodber, E. (1989), *Myal*. London: New Beacon Books.

Carter, A. (1979), *The Bloody Chamber and Other Stories*. London: Gollancz.

Creed, B. (1993), *The Monstrous Feminine: Film, Feminism, Psychoanalysis*. London: Routledge.

Debord, G. (1955), 'Introduction to a Critique of Urban Geography', in *Le Levres Nues*, available at http://library.nothingness.org/articles/SI/en/ display/2, accessed 6 June 2013.

Freud, S. (1919), 'The Uncanny', in James Strachey (ed. and trans.) (1953), *The Standard Edition of the Complete Psychological Works of Sigmund Freud*, vol. XVII. London: Hogarth, pp. 219–56.

Harris, C. (2008–11), *True Blood* series. New York: Ace Books.

Harris, T. (1988), *The Silence of the Lambs*. New York: St Martin's Press.

Hill, D. (2007), *Caribbean Folklore: A Handbook*. Westport, CT: Greenwood Press.

Hoffman, E. T. A. (1885), 'The Sandman', in *Weird Tales of E. T. A. Hoffmann* [1885], 2 vols. New York: Scribner.

Holland-Toll, L. J. (2009), 'Unleashing the Gremlins in the Crypt: Teaching Horror Fiction'. *Dissections*, http://www.simegen.com/writers/dissections/ May%202009/dissections_page_08.html, accessed 8 July 2013.

Hopkinson, N. (ed.) (2000), 'The Glass Bottle Trick', in *Whispers from the Cotton Tree Root*. Montpelier, VT: Invisible Cities Press, pp. 252–72.

Jancovich, M. (1992), *Horror*. London: Batsford.

King, S. (1981), *Danse Macabre*. New York: Everest House.

Kristeva, J. (1982), *The Powers of Horror: An Essay on Abjection*, trans. Leon S. Roudiez. New York: Columbia University Press.

—(1994), *Strangers to Ourselves*, trans. Leon S. Roudiez. New York: Columbia University Press.

Lacan, J. (1977), *Ecrits*. New York: W.W. Norton.

Lovecraft, H. P. (1936), 'The Shadow over Innsmouth', in *'The Lurking Fear' and Other Stories* [1970]. London: Panther, pp. 7–22.

—(1973), *Supernatural Horror in Literature*, ed. E. F. Bleiler. New York: Dover.

McEwan, I. (1981), *The Comfort of Strangers*. London: Vintage.

Meyer, S. (2005–8), *Twilight* series. New York: Little, Brown.

Morrison, T. (1987), *Beloved*. New York: Alfred Knopf.

Poe, E. A. (1966), *Complete Stories and Poems of Edgar Allan Poe*. New York: Doubleday.

Punter, D. (1980), *The Literature of Terror: A History of Gothic Fictions from 1765 to the Present Day, Vol. I, Modern Gothic*. London and New York: Longman.

—(2000), *Postcolonial Imaginings Fictions of a New World Order*. Edinburgh: Edinburgh University Press.

Shelley, M. (1818), *Frankenstein*. London: Lackington Hughes, Harding, Mavor & Jones.

Stevenson, R. L. (1886), *Dr Jekyll and Mr Hyde* [2004]. Harmondsworth: Penguin Books.

Stoker, B. (1897), *Dracula* [1979]. Harmondsworth: Penguin.

8

Alternative Worlds: Popular Fiction (Not Only) for Children

Lena Steveker

Chapter Outline

Going Shakespeare: British Children's Literature and the London 2012 Opening Ceremony

On 27 July 2012, at 9 p.m., I settled down on my sofa, switched on my TV set and joined an estimated one billion people around the globe watching the opening ceremony of London 2012, the XXX Olympiad. Following the by now well-established tradition that an opening ceremony serves not only to herald the beginning of the games, but also to present the host nation to a global public, the ensuing show represented contemporary Britain as a multicultural and tolerant society that is, at the same time, firmly rooted in history. Taking his cue from Shakespeare's *The Tempest* (1610–11), artistic director Danny Boyle entitled his show 'Isles of Wonder', and although it was small wonder that Shakespeare, as *the* British cultural heavyweight, would play a prominent role in the ceremony, it was indeed with wondrous excitement that I watched how Boyle's presentation of British identity encompassed children's fiction, too. Shakespeare, even though he was affirmed as a key figure of British cultural memory, was made to share his place of honour with the more popular literary realm of children's literature. Boyle introduced the segment of the show he dedicated to British children's literature with a camera panning across an open book with little paper houses and trees protruding from its pages along with letters forming the words that Peter Pan gives as his address the first time he meets Wendy in J. M. Barrie's novel *Peter and Wendy* (1911), nowadays known as *Peter Pan*: 'second to the right and straight on till morning' (2004, 24). Six hundred members of the NHS and staff of the Great Ormond Street Hospital dressed as nurses and doctors then wheeled iron bedsteads into the stadium atop of which sat children clad in pyjamas. After some dancing, the nurses put the children to bed; a young girl was seen reading *Peter and Wendy* under her bedcovers by the light of a torch; and J. K. Rowling appeared in the stadium, reading out a short description of Neverland, taken from the first chapter of Barrie's novel. After Rowling had announced the 'two minutes before you go to sleep' during which Peter Pan's imaginary island becomes real, the arena was invaded by villains from British children's fantasy fiction. Led by Roald Dahl's Child Catcher[1] and a mob of dancers dressed in black hooded costumes with acid green eye masks, gigantic puppets representing Lewis Carroll's Queen of Hearts, J. M. Barrie's Captain Hook and Dodie Smith's

Cruella de Vil rose from among the children's beds, while J. K. Rowling's Voldemort, largest of all, towered above them, threatening the children and putting the adults under the Imperius Curse. It was not until several women representing P. L. Travers's Mary Poppins floated from the sky on extended umbrellas that the villains and their followers were banished. Hospital staff and children alike celebrated their deliverance with another round of revelling, before the scene concluded with the nannies helping the nurses put the children back to bed.

All academic interest aside, it was good fun to watch this part of the show. However, its extended engagement with children's literature is also significant from a critic's point of view. Boyle's show is indicative of a time in which British children's literature, paradoxical as it may sound, has ceased to be regarded as belonging exclusively to the literary realm nor to the sphere of children. Texts from children's literature have migrated into fan fiction, film, TV and computer games, complete with large-scale merchandising, theme parks and film-studio tours; (former child) actors playing characters such as Harry Potter and Hermione Granger have become celebrities. However, the Olympic opening ceremony did not merely stress the current cross-cultural popularity of British children's literature. The show's references to both children's literature and Shakespeare undermined the cultural hierarchies between 'high' and 'popular' literature. Putting canonical Shakespeare on an equal footing with popular children's literature, Boyle's show not only followed the by now common cultural practice of popularizing Shakespeare (see Lanier 2002; Shaughnessy 2007); it also Shakespeareanized popular literature for children. It conceptualized children's literature as a significant element of the British collective imaginary, ascribing to it a formative role for contemporary British identity today. Thus, the London 2012 Opening Ceremony not only paid tribute to the current popularity of British children's literature, but also acknowledged the rich tradition of this genre.

Children's Literature and Crossover Fantasy Fiction

The history of children's literature spans several centuries. Some critics trace its origins back to the fifteenth century, but '[m]ost cultural historians agree that children's literature, as we recognize it today, began in the mid eighteenth century' (Grenby 2009, 4) when books written for children first became a market commodity. As a generic term, children's literature has been notoriously difficult to define, as it not only negotiates culturally and historically specific concepts of childhood, but also includes different forms of texts such as nursery rhymes, poems, plays, pantomimes, short stories, novels and comics. Children's literature is indebted to fairy tales, myths, ballads, fables and legends as well as to diverse literary genres such as the pastoral, the bildungsroman, the public-school story, the adventure story, the realist novel and fantasy fiction. What is more, the term 'children's literature' can easily be seen as a misnomer, because it erases the element of adult engagement which necessarily belongs to the genre. Children's literature is literature for children, but it is (in most cases) written by adults, published by adults, reviewed by adults as well as marketed by and, in fact, for adults as they are usually the ones who make books available to children both educationally and economically. Adults are also involved in children's literature as readers, either for children or in their own right. Indeed, many of the texts which are responsible for the success contemporary children's literature has had with readers both popular and critical belong into the category of crossover literature, which is commonly defined as 'children's novels which have crossed over to adult readers' (Falconer 2010, 158). As with children's literature, the crossover phenomenon is by no means exclusive to the late twentieth and early twenty-first centuries. Texts such as Charles Kingsley's *The Waterbabies* (1863), Lewis Carroll's *Alice's Adventures in Wonderland* (1865) and *Through the Looking-Glass and What Alice Found There* (1871), Kenneth Grahame's *The Wind in the Willows* (1908), J. R. R. Tolkien's *The Hobbit* (1937) and C. S. Lewis's *Chronicles of Narnia* (1950–4) make clear that 'there is a strong tradition of children's literature being adopted by adult readers in Britain' (Falconer 2009, 11; see also Beckett 2006 and 2009). Yet, the heyday of crossover fiction only began when both children and adults enthusiastically received novels such as Philip Pullman's His Dark Materials trilogy (1995–2000), Eoin Colfer's Artemis Fowl series (2001–12), G. P. Taylor's Shadowmancer books (2003–6) and above all, J. K. Rowling's Harry Potter series (1997–2007).

Much has been said as to the reasons why adults have found children's novels worth reading (Beckett 2006, 2009; Falconer 2009, 2010), and one of the answers to this question can be found in genre theory. Each of the novels listed above heavily draws on the genre of fantasy fiction. Since fantasy can be defined as 'a popular genre that straddles the boundary between children's and adults' literature' (Petzold 2006, 95), the novels' indebtedness to fantasy can be seen as one reason for their crossover appeal. Given '[t]he prominence of fantasy within children's literature' (Nikolajeva 2006, 58) in general, and within contemporary crossover texts in particular, I will devote the rest of this chapter to a discussion of J. R. R. Tolkien's *The Hobbit* and J. K. Rowling's Harry Potter heptalogy as the two 'flagship fantasies' (Coats 2010, 80) of the twentieth and twenty-first centuries. As one of the key texts of children's fantasy fiction, *The Hobbit* 'remains the forerunner of a great release of fantasy' (Hunt 2001, 175), including Rowling's series about the boy with the lightning scar which not only 'kick-started the millennial crossover phenomenon' (Falconer 2009, 15), but is also currently the most popular set of children's novels. In the following paragraphs, I will use *The Hobbit* and the Harry Potter series as two case studies in order to discuss characteristic elements of children's fantasy fiction before I will contextualize each of them within their specific moment of cultural history. I will show how both Tolkien's and Rowling's novels construct alternative worlds which confront their readers, children and adults alike, with the cultural discourses of the specific historical contexts these texts have emerged from.

Flagship Fantasies: J. R. R. Tolkien's *The Hobbit* and J. K. Rowling's Harry Potter Series

J. R. R. Tolkien is commonly regarded as 'the greatest influence within the fantasy genre' (Birch 2009, n.p.), and his novel *The Hobbit* is one of the founding texts of modern children's fantasy fiction. *The Hobbit* was an instant success in both the United Kingdom and the United States, where it was first published in 1937 and 1938, respectively. Many critics received it favourably, praising it as a future classic (Anderson 2003, 17–22); the *New York Herald Tribune* awarded it a prize of $250 as the best book published for children in 1938; and *The Times Literary Supplement* anticipated the crossover potential of *The Hobbit*, commending it as a book to which readers would repeatedly return during their lives (Anderson 2003, 18). By the beginning of the twenty-first century, '[s]ales of the book [have] long ago soared into the multimillion copy level' (Anderson 2003, 23), and the novel has been firmly inscribed into the canon of British children's literature. It is, however, difficult, if not downright impossible, to discuss *The Hobbit* without mentioning Tolkien's (adult fiction) trilogy *The Lord of the Rings*.

Tolkien began the latter as a sequel to *The Hobbit*, but when he completed the three novels in 1949, they had developed into a series which was published in three volumes between 1954 and 1955. Indeed, Tolkien rewrote parts of *The Hobbit* for its second edition in 1951, changing the earlier text so as to adjust it to the later novels instead of making the trilogy work as a sequel to *The Hobbit*. The first editions of the three volumes sold well, and the trilogy became a cult phenomenon among college students in the 1960s (see Becket 2009, 106; Petzold 2006, 97). Its runaway success rekindled interest in *The Hobbit*, too (see Anderson 2003, 22). When Peter Jackson's Oscar-winning film adaptations of *The Lord of the Rings* were released in 2001–3, sales of *The Hobbit* picked up once again (see Holden 2008). Probably spurred by the success of the films, Jackson decided to adapt *The Hobbit* to the screen in three instalments, and the release of the first part in December 2012 was flanked by a new 'film tie-in edition' of the novel.

The rise of J. K. Rowling's Harry Potter series to global popularity has been less drawn out. The first of the seven novels, *Harry Potter and the Philosopher's Stone* was published in 1997. In 2007, on the release of its concluding volume, *Harry Potter and the Deathly Hallows*, the series had been translated into more languages than the Bible (Blake 2002, 1). In less than 10 years, Rowling's novels 'had broken practically every sales record in publishing history' and 'ma[de] Rowling the richest author in literary history' (Falconer 2009, 15–16). Various instalments of the series won prestigious literary prizes (see Beckett 2009, 112–14; Falconer 2009, 15–16); the seven Potter novels have been adapted into eight blockbuster films; the series has triggered controversial debates among critics[2]; 'Potter Studies' have developed into a research discipline; and 'Pottermania' has become a global cultural phenomenon of the early twenty-first century.

Within the context of twentieth-century children's fantasy fiction, *The Hobbit* and the Potter heptalogy are positioned at two points in time which mark the beginning of the genre's rise to popularity and its heyday, respectively. Tolkien's and Rowling's novels differ in historical context as well as in plot, structure and narrative perspective. Nevertheless, they share a number of elements which make them typical representatives of British children's literature. First and foremost, Tolkien's book and Rowling's heptalogy are children's novels that draw on other texts for children, which in fact makes them less uniquely original than many an enthusiastic reviewer may have thought (Anderson 2003, 18; Nel 2001, 53). Some of the sources *The Hobbit* relies on are, for example, George MacDonald's *The Princess and the Goblin* (1872), its sequel *The Princess and Curdie* (1882) and E. A. Wyke-Smith's

The Marvellous Land of Snergs (1927) (Anderson 2003, 5–6). The Potter saga is, for instance, indebted to Thomas Hughes's *Tom Brown's School Days* (1857), modelling its contemporary wizard hero on the gentlemanly ideals propagated in the nineteenth-century public-school story (see Berberich 2011). Rowling's novels furthermore make use of a 'Blytonesque kids-plus-friendly-adult formula' (Blake 2002, 22); the Potter novels are also linked to the fiction of Roald Dahl, who was Britain's most popular (read bestselling) author of children's literature before J. K. Rowling arrived on the scene (see Hollindale 2008, 273). When the first Potter novel, *Philosopher's Stone*, was published, reviewers announced Rowling as Dahl's successor (see Eccleshare 2002, 10), and there are indeed 'moments of grotesquerie and doggerel [in the Potter novels] that echo Dahl' (Hunt 2001, 123). In *Philosopher's Stone*, for example, '[t]he origins of the loathsome Dursleys come directly from snobbish Dahlesque caricatures of limited culture and intelligence. Orphaned Harry comes with immediate Dahl appeal' (Eccleshare 2002, 36).

Generic Affiliations

Establishing intertextual references to other novels written for children is only one way in which *The Hobbit* and the Potter heptalogy inscribe themselves into the canon of British children's literature. They also refer to various genres which have been prominent in popular fiction for children such as fairy tales, myth, legend, the bildungsroman and, as I have already mentioned above, the public-school story and fantasy fiction. The latter is the strongest generic marker in both Tolkien's and Rowling's texts. To various degrees, the plot of *The Hobbit* and the Potter series, respectively, is set in what Tolkien, in his theoretical essay 'On Fairy Stories' (1947), defined as a 'Secondary World', that is, a magical or otherwise fantastic world which differs from the 'Primary World' representing the 'real' world (Tolkien 2001). In contrast to fairy tales, the Secondary Worlds of fantasy fiction are anchored in the Primary World. *The Hobbit* and the Potter novels represent different

> pattern[s] of . . . combining the Primary and the Secondary worlds, [which] can vary from a complete magical universe with its own geography, history, and magical laws to a little magical pill that enables a character in an otherwise realistic story to understand the language of animals. (Nikolajeva 2006, 58)

Set in Middle-earth, *The Hobbit* conjures up a fantastic world of its own populated by hobbits, humans, dwarves, wizards, elves, trolls, goblins, dragons and shape shifters, a world in which animals can speak and inanimate objects such as gems, swords and rings have magic properties. The only link between Middle-earth and the Primary World is provided by the text's narrator, whose direct addresses to the reader reach beyond the boundaries of the novel's otherwise self-contained Secondary World. By contrast, the Primary World of Rowling's Muggle England is much more directly linked to the Secondary World of the community of wizards. The reader witnesses Harry and his fellow wizards constantly crossing the boundary from one world into the other at sites of transition such as the Leaky Cauldron, Platform 9¾ at King's Cross and the telephone booth in Muggle London which serves as the visitors' entrance to the Ministry of Magic.

The Secondary Worlds in both *The Hobbit* and the Potter series owe much to literary genres originating in the oral tradition. Each novel's story follows the outline of what Joseph Campbell, in his analysis of important myths around the world, has termed the 'monomyth'. In short, the monomyth's archetypal pattern is as follows:

> A hero ventures forth from the world of common day into a region of supernatural wonder: fabulous forces are there encountered and a decisive victory is won: the hero comes back from this mysterious adventure with the power to bestow boons on his fellow man. (Campbell 1971, 30)

Both Tolkien's Bilbo and Rowling's Harry represent monomythical heroes: Bilbo leaves the comfortable security of the Shire, helps to rid the world of the dragon Smaug and returns home a rich man, while Harry leaves his childhood in the ordinary Muggle world behind, defeats Voldemort and brings lasting peace to the wizarding world (see Boll 2009). On a less general level than that of the Campbellian monomyth, '[m]any of [. . . Bilbo's] adventures are inspired by German myths, legends, and fairy tales' (Petzold 2006, 97). Bilbo's and Harry's stories refer to Arthurian legend, and Harry can also be seen as a male Cinderella (see Blake 2002, 17). The genre of the fairy tale, which serves as the 'wellspring of modern fantasy' (Coats 2010, 80) and which has also fed into children's literature (see Zipes 2006), is a prominent influence in both Tolkien's and Rowling's novels. According to Maria Nikolajeva's definition, 'fantasy has inherited superficial attributes of fairy tales: witches, genies, dragons, talking animals, flying horses and flying carpets, invisibility mantles, magic wands, swords and lanterns, magic food and drink' (2006, 61). Such attributes indeed abound in both *The Hobbit* and in the Potter heptalogy. There are wizards wielding magic wands in Tolkien's Middle-earth as well as in – *nomen est omen* – Rowling's wizarding world. The hobbit Bilbo Baggins joins a company of dwarves in their fight against the dragon Smaug. On his way to the dwarves' former homestead under the Lonely Mountain, now occupied by Smaug, Bilbo meets birds capable of communicating with humans, becomes the owner of the magic sword Sting and finds an invisibility ring. In *Philosopher's Stone*, Rowling's hero inherits his father's invisibility cloak; Harry faces dragons in *Goblet of Fire* as well as in *Deathly Hallows*; in *Order of the Phoenix*, he and his friends ride Thestrals, skeletal flying horses seen only by those who have witnessed somebody dying; and in several of the novels he drinks magic potions and, inverting the motif of the talking animal, talks to snakes.

Typical of children's literature, Tolkien's and Rowling's novels feature children or child-like characters as their protagonists. The Potter series begins with Harry discovering his identity as a wizard on his 11th birthday, and it concludes with Harry defeating his arch-enemy Voldemort, most evil of all dark wizards, at the age of 17 (when children come of age in the wizarding world). Although Bilbo is an adult hobbit in his fifties when he is introduced to the reader in the novel's first chapter, he shares many qualities typically found in child protagonists. A small and morally ambivalent person who loves food and drink, he embodies the child-like hero. It is through their heroes that the fantasy novels under discussion in this chapter draw on the bildungsroman, a genre of realistic fiction which is 'significant for children's literature because of its focus on a youthful person and his or her growing self-awareness and maturity' (Pettigrew 2006, 161). Not unlike the Campbellian hero, the protagonist of a bildungsroman typically leaves his or her home, completes a quest and returns home a person improved in mind and heart. *The Hobbit* slightly deviates from this formula, as Tolkien does not allot Bilbo a quest of his own, but has him adopt the dwarves' mission to reclaim their former kingdom. Yet, Bilbo returns home a changed and, indeed, more mature hobbit. The Potter heptalogy also confirms and, at the same time, departs from the pattern of the bildungsroman. On the one hand, Harry is a more traditionally generic hero than Bilbo in that he pursues his own quest. Ageing from an 11-year-old boy to a 17-year-old young adult, Harry develops from child to man during the series as well as from an ignorant novice to the wizarding world to its selfless, wise and mature hero who successfully fulfils his destiny of vanquishing Voldemort. On the other hand, Rowling's series inverts the common structure of a character leaving home, undergoing ordeals and returning a hero. Departing from his abusive

Muggle aunt and uncle's house in Privet Drive for magical Hogwarts, Harry leaves the site of his childhood misery for a fascinating if unknown place he comes to call home in the course of his quest (see Rowling 2010g, 558).

Bilbo and Harry define Tolkien's and Rowling's novels as children's literature not only because they represent this genre's stereotypical protagonists, but also because we read their stories through their eyes. Typical of children's novels, the child-like Bilbo and the boy/teenager Harry serve as their stories' focalizers. Both Tolkien's and Rowling's novels employ heterodiegetic narration, but their narrative voices are different. In Tolkien's novel, an overt narrator's voice repeatedly intrudes into the text, identifying him(?)self as 'I' and/or directly addressing the reader as 'you' (see Tolkien 2003, 31, 47, 64, 70 and *passim*). In these intrusions, the narrator reveals himself as being both omniscient and condescending towards the child-like Bilbo as well as towards the child readers the novel was initially aimed at. By contrast, 'Rowling's child protagonists are never patronized by an authoritative narrator's voice' (Petzold 2006, 97). Owing to the limited knowledge of the novels' covert narrator, readers only know as much as the protagonist; their knowledge and insight grow with Harry's. Rowling's narrative style 'emphasizes sympathetic engagement with Harry's character' and 'encourages readers to view the adult world with skepticism as well as sympathy' (Westman 2011, 97). Like Rowling's child protagonists, her child readers are spared the condescension of Tolkien's 'avuncular narrator' (Petzold 2006, 97). Owing to its different narrative voice, the Potter series displays a significantly different attitude towards children than *The Hobbit*. While *The Hobbit*'s narrator lays open the strict social hierarchies between adults and children of the 1930s, the Potter books are indicative of the more liberal society of the late 1990s and early noughties, which encourages children to develop self-confidence and autonomy. In Rowling's novels, child readers 'are prompted, along with Harry, to wonder at the values of adult society' (Westman 2011, 97).

Cultural Contexts

The Potter series does not only critically engage with the values of the adult world depicted in the novels. Like *The Hobbit*, and indeed any other literary text, Rowling's heptalogy negotiates the social, cultural and ideological discourses of its specific historical contexts. Fantasy fiction has often been wrongly accused of escapist tendencies, allowing readers to close their eyes to reality in the act of reading. In fact, '[t]he best fantasies are not escapist literature transporting us to another world, but rather show us our own world in a new guise' (Garner 2006, 369). Typical of modern fantasy fiction, Tolkien's *Hobbit* and Rowling's Potter novels 'reflect and give form to the concerns and assumptions of their own age, including responses to tragedy and trauma' (Hancock 2005, 46). *The Hobbit* was written during a period in which the trauma of World War I, the century's seminal catastrophe, still reverberated in British culture. The ruin and devastation which the dragon Smaug brings to the area surrounding the Lonely Mountain, turning it into a 'bleak and barren land' dotted with 'broken and blackened [tree] stumps' (Tolkien 2003, 257), as well as the bloodshed during the Battle of the Five Armies (see Tolkien 2003, 339–44) have been read as representations of the Western Front (see Croft 2002). Set against these are the pastoral Shire and its easy-going inhabitants, representing a nostalgic longing for a 'bucolic, peaceful, little England' untouched by war (Hunt 2001, 173). *The Hobbit* furthermore negotiates its period's ideologies of gender and race. Its all-male character set-up and the complete absence of female figures reflect the strongly patriarchal order of 1930s British society, while the novel's bio- and geo-politics are indicative of the racist tendencies that were part of British and other European cultures in the 1930s, though not as pronounced as in Germany (see Firchow 2008, 16). In Tolkien's novel, the races populating Middle-earth are clearly divided into 'good' ones (hobbits, elves, dwarves and humans) originating from the west and 'evil' ones (goblins, wargs and dragons) originating from the east. The members of the western races are shown as being morally superior by nature to those belonging to the eastern races. Scenes such as the shape shifter Beorn's unprovoked killing of a warg and a goblin (see Tolkien 2003, 181–2) and the ruthless extinction of the defeated goblins after the Battle of the Five Armies (see Tolkien 2003, 350) imply that '[t]o kill one or more or even all members of these despised, inferior races is to perform an act of valor and virtue, something that will be remembered to one's credit forever' (Firchow 2008, 24). Contrasting a 'good', 'superior' and 'valiant' western culture with an 'evil', 'inferior' and 'perfidious' eastern culture that needs to be controlled, *The Hobbit* taps into the Orientalist ideology of British colonialism which was still prevalent in British culture at the time of the novel's publication.

The Potter series also negotiates aspects of gender and race, but as the novels' historical context is different from that of Tolkien's book, their representation of these aspects is different, too. In contrast to *The Hobbit*,

Rowling's novels are not set in an exclusively male environment, but aim at a more balanced representation of gender. Harry himself undermines the binary difference of gender, since he, according to Susanne Gruss (2011), represents both hero and heroine of Gothic fiction. As Karley Adney demonstrates in her critical reading of the Potter series, 'throughout the seven novels, very masculine influences cultivate traditionally feminine traits in Harry', allowing him to acquire 'the ability to move between these classifications of gender' (2011, 178). Scholars have wrongly criticized Rowling's novels for allegedly clichéd female characters and purportedly misogynist undertones, since, as Katrin Berndt shows, the series represents Hermione 'as a female subject beyond the limits of alterity and fixed gender categories' (2011, 159). In short, the Potter novels question gender as a category of binary difference through the character of Harry, and they privilege female emancipation in their 'post-feminist heroine' Hermione (Berndt 2011, 169). As such, Rowling's Potter heptalogy is very much a product of British society of the late twentieth and early twenty-first centuries, in which the formative control of patriarchal gender roles has abated and the second-wave feminism of the 1960s/1970s has developed into third-wave or post-feminism.

The Potter novels also critically engage with questions of race. At the beginning of the saga, Hogwarts 'represents the multicultural contemporary England' (Blake 2002, 15) celebrated in the London 2012 Opening Ceremony. However, as becomes clear while the story develops, the wizarding world is by no means an ideal society. The Death Eaters' fixation with 'pure blood' is merely the strongest sign of the racist tendencies underlying wizarding culture. Harry and Hermione, who have both been raised by Muggles, draw the reader's attention to the prejudices prevalent in the magical community. Hermione's spirited fight for the welfare of House-elves starting in *Chamber of Secrets* and Harry's failure to grasp the full implication of Hagrid's status as a half giant in *Goblet of Fire* serve to lay open and criticize the racist stereotypes of the wizarding world and, by implication, those of British society of the late 1990s and early noughties. In the end, however, the racist and xenophobic ideology championed by Voldemort and his followers is defeated and, as the heptalogy's concludes, 'all was well' (Rowling 2010g, 607). With its happy ending and its reaffirmed certainties, the Potter series contains the cultural anxieties it negotiates, thus conforming to the scripts of contemporary children's fantasy fiction which 'hold subjectivities together with a promise of unified reality when present realities seem in danger of disintegrating' (Coats 2010, 85).

The Hobbit in the Twenty-First Century

In 2000, Harold Bloom, self-proclaimed defender of the Western Canon, announced that '[t]he Harry Potter phenomenon will go on, doubtless for some time, as J. R. R. Tolkien did, and then wane' (Bloom 2000). However, two recent films have proven Bloom wrong. *Harry Potter and the Deathly Hallows – Part Two* (2011) is a clear sign that the Harry Potter phenomenon has not yet waned, while *The Hobbit: An Unexpected Journey* (2012) shows that Bilbo's story has never lost its popular appeal in the first place. Like other film adaptations of children's fiction such as *The Narnia Chronicles* (2005, 2008, 2010) and *The Adventurer: The Curse of the Midas Box* (2014, based on G. P. Taylor's novel *Mariah Mundi – The Midas Box*), these films demonstrate that the crossover potential of contemporary children's literature has an intergenerational as well as an intermedial dimension. However, a literary text's appeal for the film industry does not necessarily indicate its popularity with a mixed-age readership, as the recent adaptation of *The Hobbit* shows. Unlike Tolkien's novel, Jackson's film represents Bilbo as depending on Gandalf as his adult guardian, thus playing down the hobbit's autonomy as a child-hero. While the novel has Bilbo choose the sword Sting for himself, thus ascribing to him responsibility for his own fate, the film shows Gandalf selecting the sword for Bilbo and negotiating the hobbit's contract with the dwarves. In short, Jackson's film belittles children by unnecessarily infantilizing its child-hero. In migrating Bilbo's story from the page to the screen, Jackson has lost the novel's child readership. As a classic of British children's literature, *The Hobbit* would have deserved a better fate.

Notes

1. Strictly speaking, the Child Catcher is not a literary character since Roald Dahl invented it for the screen adaptation of Ian Fleming's three-volume children's story entitled *Chitty-Chitty-Bang-Bang* (1964–5). This blurring of boundaries between novel and film is repeated in the representations of the other villains whose designs are also modelled on the screen adaptations of the novels in questions.

2. While some critics such as Harold Bloom and A. S. Byatt have whole-heartedly dismissed Rowling's novels, others such as Jack Zipes have looked into the Potter phenomenon in more detail, even if they have expressed doubt as to their literary quality (2001, 170–88). Again others have admitted to having been 'hooked' (Falconer 2009, 1) by Rowling's story of the wizard boy.

Works Cited

Adney, K. (2011), 'The Influence of Gender on Harry Potter's Heroic (Trans)formation', in K. Berndt and L. Steveker (eds), *Heroism in the Harry Potter Series*. Farnham: Ashgate, pp. 177–91.

Anderson, D. A. (ed.) (2003), *The Annotated Hobbit,* rev. and expanded edn. London: HarperCollins.

Barrie, P. (2004), *Peter Pan: Peter and Wendy and Peter in Kensington Gardens*, ed. J. Zipes. London: Penguin.

Beckett, S. L. (2006), 'Crossover Books', in J. Zipes (ed.), *The Oxford Encyclopedia of Children's Literature*, vol. 1. Oxford: Oxford University Press, pp. 369–70.

—(2009), *Crossover Fiction: Global and Historical Perspectives*. New York: Routledge.

Berberich, C. (2011), 'Harry Potter and the Idea of the Gentleman as Hero', in K. Berndt and L. Steveker (eds), *Heroism in the Harry Potter Series*. Farnham: Ashgate, pp. 141–57.

Birch, D. (2009), 'Fantasy Fiction', in D. Birch (ed.), *The Oxford Companion to English Literature*. Oxford: Oxford University Press, 2009. Oxford Reference, http://www.oxfordreference.com/view/10.1093/acref/9780192806871.001.0001/ acref 9780192806871-e-2688, accessed 8 March 2013.

Blake, A. (2002), *The Irresistible Rise of Harry Potter*. London: Verso.

Bloom, H. (2000), 'Can 35 Book Buyers be Wrong? Yes'. *Wall Street Journal*, 11 July, http://online.wsj.com/article/SB963270836801555352.html#article Tabs%3Darticle, accessed 19 December 2012.

Boll, J. (2011), 'Harry Potter's Archetypal Journey', in K. Berndt and L. Steveker (eds), *Heroism in the Harry Potter Series*. Farnham: Ashgate, pp. 85–104.

Byatt, A. S. (2003), 'Harry Potter and the Childish Adult', *New York Times*, 7 July, http://www.nytimes.com/2003/07/07/opinion/harry-potter-and-the-childish-adult.html, accessed 19 December 2012.

Campbell, J. (1971), *The Hero with the Thousand Faces*, 2nd edn. Princeton: Princeton University Press.

Coats, K. (2010), 'Fantasy', in D. Rudd (ed.), *The Routledge Companion to Children's Literature*. London: Routledge, pp. 75–86.

Croft, J. B. (2002), 'The Great War and Tolkien's Memory: An Examination of World War I Themes in *The Hobbit* and *The Lord of the Rings*'. *Mythlore* 90, 4–21.

Eccleshare, J. (2002), *A Guide to the Harry Potter Novels*. London: Continuum.

Falconer, R. (2009), *The Crossover Novel: Contemporary Children's Literature and Its Adult Readership*. London: Routledge.

—(2010), 'Crossover Literature', in D. Rudd (ed.), *The Routledge Companion to Children's Literature*. London: Routledge, pp. 158–60.

Firchow, P. E. (2008), 'The Politics of Fantasy: *The Hobbit* and Fascism'. *The Midwest Quarterly* 50(1), 15–31.

Garner, B. C. (2006), 'J. K. Rowling', in J. Zipes (ed.), *The Oxford Encyclopedia of Children's Literature* (vol. 3). Oxford: Oxford University Press, pp. 368–9.

Grenby, M. O. (2009), 'The Origins of Children's Literature', in M. O. Grenby and A. Immel (eds), *The Cambridge Companion to Children's Literature*. Cambridge: Cambridge University Press, pp. 3–18.

Gruss, S. (2011), 'The Diffusion of Gothic Conventions in *Harry Potter and the Order of the Phoenix* (2003/2007)', in K. Berndt and L. Steveker (eds), *Heroism in the Harry Potter Series*. Farnham: Ashgate, pp. 39–53.

Hancock, S. (2005), 'Fantasy, Psychology, Feminism: Jungian Readings of Classic British Fantasy Fiction', in K. Reynolds (ed.), *Modern Children's Literature: An Introduction*. Basingstoke: Palgrave Macmillan, pp. 42–56.

Holden, J. (2008), 'The 12 Books You Must Stock'. *The Bookseller*, 31 July, http://www.thebookseller.com/feature/12-books-you-must-stock.html, accessed 21 December 2012.

Hollindale, P. (2008), '"And Children Swarmed to Him like Settlers. He Became Land". The Outrageous Success of Roald Dahl', in J. Briggs, D. Butt and M. O. Grenby (eds), *Popular Children's Literature in Britain*. Aldershot: Ashgate, pp. 271–86.

Hunt, P. (2001), *Children's Literature*. Oxford: Blackwell.

Lanier, D. (2002), *Shakespeare and Modern Popular Culture*. Oxford: Oxford University Press.

Nel, P. (2001), *J. K. Rowling's Harry Potter Novels: A Reader's Guide*. London: Continuum.

Nikolajeva, M. (2006), 'Fantasy', in J. Zipes (ed.), *The Oxford Encyclopedia of Children's Literature*, vol. 2. Oxford: Oxford University Press, pp. 58–63.

Pettigrew, D. (2006), 'Bildungsroman or Novel of Education', in J. Zipes (ed.), *The Oxford Encyclopedia of Children's Literature*, vol. 1. Oxford: Oxford University Press, p. 161.

Petzold, D. (2006), 'Tolkien, J. R. R.', in J. Zipes (ed.), *The Oxford Encyclopedia of Children's Literature*, vol. 4. Oxford: Oxford University Press, pp. 95–8.

Rowling, J. K. (2010 [2007]), *Harry Potter and the Deathly Hallows*. London: Bloomsbury.

Shaughnessy, R. (2007), *The Shakespeare Companion to Shakespeare and Popular Culture*. Cambridge: Cambridge University Press.

Tolkien, J. R. R. (2001), 'On Fairy Stories', in J. R. R. Tolkien (ed.), *Tree and Leaf: Including Mythopoeia and The Homecoming of Beorhtnoth*. London: HarperCollins, pp. 1–82.

—(2003 [1937]), *The Annotated Hobbit: The Hobbit, or There and Back again* (rev. and expanded edn), ed. D. A. Anderson. London: HarperCollins.

Westman, K. (2011), 'Blending Genres and Crossing Audiences: *Harry Potter* and the Future of Literary Fiction', in J. Mickenberg and L. Vallone (eds), *The Oxford Handbook of Children's Literature*. Oxford: Oxford University Press, pp. 93–113.

Zipes, J. (2001), *Sticks and Stones: The Troublesome Success of Children's Literature from Slovenly Peter to Harry Potter*. London: Routledge.

—(2006), 'Fairy Tales and Folk Tales', in J. Zipes (ed.), *The Oxford Encyclopedia of Children's Literature*, vol. 2. Oxford: Oxford University Press, pp. 58–63.

9

The Coming of Age of Graphic Narratives

Monica Germanà

It's fashionable to say that articles promoting the graphic novel as an art are redundant because this is now a truth universally acknowledged. It's not. There's still a tremendous amount of prejudice against the comics medium that's in dire need to redress.

(Talbot 2012, n.p.)

Introduction

Although, as Bryan Talbot suggests, 'there's still a tremendous amount of prejudice against the comics medium' among publishers, writers and critics, over the last three decades, the rise in popularity – and move towards the mainstream – of graphic narratives also appears to be undeniable. The year 1986 has been pinpointed as the medium's '*annus mirabilis*' (Wolk 2007, 8) with three important publications: Frank Miller's *The Dark Knight Returns*, Alan Moore and David Gibbons's *Watchmen* and Art Spiegelman's *Maus*. In terms of content, what these works share is the distinctly serious – though not, by all means, humourless – approach to their storylines, which would characterize much of the subsequent output in comic art. In terms of form, the three publications also present a model which would prove popular: rather than serialized, as was the case with earlier comic strips, these were self-contained narratives, demanding the same level of reader attention and commitment as textual novels. It is significant of the shift in the reception of graphic narratives and comics that *Watchmen* was awarded the Hugo Award in 1988 and, following the publication of the second volume of Spiegelman's work in 1991, *Maus* was awarded the Pulitzer Prize in 1992. While these works are still hailed as landmarks of modern comic writing, the number and breadth of comic publications and studies of comic art has risen exponentially since the end of the twentieth century and has continued to grow steadily into the new millennium. The twenty-first century has also consolidated the reputation of graphic narratives, which continue to receive prestigious accolades: in 2012, *Days of the Bagnold Summer* by Joff Winterhart became the first graphic novel to be shortlisted for the prestigious Costa Novel of the Year Award, while *Dotter of Her Father's Eyes*, a dual graphic biography written by Mary and Bryan Talbot, was awarded the Costa Award for Biography.

Narrative art is not a contemporary phenomenon. The use of pictorial systems of representation for narrative purposes has been traced back to the earliest stages of human civilization as seen, for instance, in the Lascaux cave paintings (France) and San rock art (South Africa); both examples display the use of stylized images which tell stories through the pictorial short-hand of specific symbols. Rock paintings in pre-Colombian America and Aboriginal 'dream world' art in Australia share similar characteristics. Throughout millennia of artistic development, the variety of materials and graphic techniques deployed to illustrate stories includes artefacts as diverse as Trajan's Column in Rome and the eleventh-century Bayoux tapestry. What these – and many other – manifestations of narrative art share with modern comics is the fact that they can be loosely categorized both as 'graphic narratives' – pictorial texts that use stylized images to tell a story – and 'sequential art', defined by Will Eisner as 'the arrangement of image elements and the construction of the sequence of the narration' (Eisner 1985, 127).

While systems of pictorial narrative representations have been in use for millennia, factors such as increased levels of literacy, the invention of the press and, subsequently, the wider distribution of print materials have contributed to the development of graphic narratives in modern times (Petersen 2011, xx). Significantly, the use of caricature and political satire soon became associated with the earliest manifestations of sequential graphic art. The works of eighteenth-century British illustrator William Hogarth (1697–1764), such as *A Harlot's Progress* (1730), can be considered precursors of the sequential modern illustrations that began to appear in British popular publications such as *Punch* and *Police News* the following century (see, for example, Petersen 2011, xxi). It is, however, Rodolphe Töpffer (1799–1846) who is frequently hailed as the 'inventor of "stories in etchings"' (Groensten 2007, 1): his early nineteenth-century satirical picture stories used 'the first independent combination of words and pictures seen in Europe' (McCloud 1993, 17.iii).

The history of the medium reveals the contentious reception and subversive uses that comics have been associated with from the start. In Britain, the roots of modern comics strips can be traced to the 1880s' campaign against another form of popular literature, the Penny Dreadfuls (See also Chapter 1), that were, by many, considered unsuitable reading material for the young. It was then that British publisher Alfred Harmsworth started to produce alternative literature for children: his *Comic Cuts* only cost half a penny, and specifically attempted to provide 'non-serious, "harmless" but attractive material for youngsters' (Barker 1989, 8). Simultaneously, The Religious Tract Society started producing similar material – *Girl's Own Paper* (1880–1956) and *Boy's Own Paper* (1879–1967) – for older children. These were followed by what is often referred to as the comics' Golden Age: in Britain the first decades of the twentieth century saw the rise of long-lasting comic strips such as *The Dandy* (1937–2012) and *The Beano* (1938–); in America it was the superhero genre that dominated the scene, with the birth of archetypal characters such as Superman, Batman, Wonder Woman and Captain Marvel.

While the origin of comic writing in Britain appears steeped in political and moral conservativism and intellectual control, the evolution of the medium in and outside Britain has frequently transgressed the boundaries of mainstream culture to embrace taboo subject matter, radical ideas and subversive ideologies, often attracting criticism and censorship from the most conservative corners of society. In the 1950s, for instance, the crusade against American crime and horror comics led by Dr Fredric Wertham almost killed the medium. At the time, comics were only banned in a few states, but the message behind the campaign was loud and clear: comics were dangerous, and could have a detrimental effect on children's minds. In Britain the publication and circulation of horror comics was banned. Other European countries, Canada, Australia and New Zealand, also attempted to regulate and censor the material published in comics books. Such attempts at control and censorship led to 'Underground Comix', a late 1960s, countercultural phenomenon, which saw the publication of cheaply produced, highly popular comics in Britain and America. The popularity of 'Underground Comix' rested not only on their inclusion of taboo subject matters such as sex and drugs, but also, significantly, on their subversive use of the 'innocent' comics as a medium to spread controversial ideas (Kannenberg 2008, 7). In the following decades, publishers DC and Marvel gradually began to publish more horror graphic narratives, which eventually lead to the emergence of pioneering works by Alan Moore, Neil Gaiman and Garth Ennis among others.

Looking at the contemporary context of globalized cultural production, comics appear to have retained their political function and effective use for the spread of ideological messages. While distinctive traits of national and cultural traditions can be identified in the stylistic choices made by individual cartoon artists, it can also be argued that one of the reasons behind comics' success and their popular use in political discourse is that 'the vocabulary and grammar of comics are widely accessible and adaptable' (Whitlock 2006, 969). The political – and controversial – value of comic art is demonstrated by the endemic use of comics by the satirical press both in the West and in the East. Commenting on his early experience of reading comics, Edward Said observed that 'comics . . . seemed to say what couldn't otherwise be said, perhaps what wasn't permitted to be said or imagined, defying the ordinary processes of thought, which are policed, shaped and re-shaped by all sorts of pedagogical as well as ideological pressures' (2003, ii). It is then not surprising that political messages deemed to be too subversive by certain regimes have also been the focus of controversial comics: Marjane Satrapi's *Persepolis* (2008) is still banned in Iran, although unofficial copies circulate in the black market (Chute 2008, 94). Similarly, in September 2005, cartoon depictions of the prophet Mohammed in the Danish newspaper *Jyllands-Posten* instigated an outraged response and violent outbreaks in some Islamic communities. Graphic narratives may have become a globalized phenomenon, but their reception – and the ideological manipulation of their meaning – can be a powerful reminder of cultural differences (Whitlock 2006, 970).[1] Significantly, the internet has become the ideal platform for cartoon strips such as *Zahra's Paradise* (2010–13), an anonymous 'online serial webcomic' (zahrasparadise. com), telling the story of Mehdi, an Iranian political protester, set against the 2009 political elections in Iran. Collected in a volume and translated into 12 languages, the strips were eventually published under the pseudonyms of Amir and Khalil in 2011.

Cultural Contexts and Terminology

Geopolitical factors of change including colonialism and globalization have, inevitably, led to processes of cross-fertilization whereby Eastern and Western traditions have frequently influenced each other. In the late nineteenth and early twentieth centuries, the problematic politics of British and American colonialism were reflected in the developments of popular cultural forms, such as comics, in Asia: 'On the one hand comics came to represent the advances of Western-style democracy and a free press, but on the other hand, they represented the oppressive wrongs of colonialism that threatened traditional values and social autonomy' (Petersen 2011, 113). The porousness of political boundaries also applied to aesthetic cross-fertilization: 'In the last **century** or two, as **Western** cultural influences swept the East, so too have **Eastern** and **African** ideas of **fragmentation** and **rhythm** swept the **West**' (McCloud 1993, 82). In particular, McCloud argues, the input of other cultural influences on Western visual and performative arts has led to a more economic way of representing action, relying on a '**less is more**' approach and 'a new awareness of the picture plane' (83).

The numerous traditions and canons converging into the medium have produced a varied – and sometimes inconsistent – terminology. *Manga* refers to the prolific canon of popular graphic literature in Japan; *bandes desinées* ('illustrated strips') define the comic production of France: in both cases, the terms identify specific cultural contexts, which include aesthetic paradigms and techniques, as well as status and distribution. *Fumetti*, meaning 'small smoke puffs', a visual metaphor for the speech balloons, refers to the Italian tradition. The medium's problematic reception, however, is still reflected in the question of categorization in English-speaking contexts: the term '"graphic novel" . . . is used to create distance and construct difference between more "serious" adult texts and the simple juvenile narratives and styles generally associated with comic books' (Naghibi and O' Malley 2005, 227). Nevertheless, the term 'graphic novel', which was coined by Will Eisner to 'label' his own serious comic book *A Contract with God* (1978), has been frequently criticized for its generic reductiveness and, in some cases, suspect elitism. Justifying her preference for the more open 'graphic narrative' in place of 'graphic novel', Hilary Chute notes that 'the most gripping works coming out now . . . claim their own historicity – even as they work to destabilize standard narratives of history' (2008, 92). The same choice – and that appearing in the title of this chapter – is behind Petersen's important study of the medium: 'As more content neutral than "comics" because it is not historically or culturally linked to a specific era', Petersen notes, the phrase 'graphic narratives', first coined by David Kunzle in his *History of the Comic Strip* (1990), 'allows our focus to rest on two essential ideas: *graphic*, a composed and nonanimated visual form, and *narrative*, a crafted story' (2011, xv).

Form

As well as terminology, it is not easy to find a comprehensive definition of graphic narratives that accounts for the medium's formal variations. For instance, relying, for the purposes of definition, on the most universally acknowledged features of comic art – 'the insertion, in the image, of verbal enunciation' (Groensten 2007, 14) – would exclude all 'mute comics', which do not use any kind of verbal enunciation, but solely rely on images to convey a story. Rather than attempting to find a singular definition that might apply to this wide-ranging medium, it might be more productive to identify the formal techniques of comic art, bearing in mind these might not always apply to all instances.

The use of a particular style and choice of images constitutes the distinctive vocabulary of a specific form of narrative art, a system of conventional signs, to be decoded by the recipients of the artefact: thus, the intended viewer of an Aboriginal dreamworld painting would be able to identify the maps and itineraries depicted in the abstract art of the paintwork. Similarly, modern comics rely on semiotic interpretation, the decoding of a language of signs shared by illustrators and readers: 'Reading a graphic narrative, such as a modern comic, requires some translation of coded images into real experience' (Petersen 2011, xvii). What is distinctive about comic art is the 'universal' language that the medium's employment of icons has achieved by a process of simplification that has led from the detailed mimetic strategies used in visual realism to the streamlined use of simplified lines and symbols in comic art. McCloud explains: 'By **stripping down** an image to its essential "**meaning**" an artist can **amplify** that meaning in a way that realist art can't. . . . The more cartoony a face is, the more people it could be said to **describe**' (1993, 30–1). In other words, 'cartooning isn't just a way of drawing, it's a way of seeing' (31).

Comics use a specific – though not unchangeable – code of visual conventions to support the basic elements of storytelling: point of view, setting, time, action and dialogue appear on the page with or without the use of actual writing. Framing, typically, each scene of a graphic narrative, is the *panel*, the basic narrative unit of comic writing. As a form of narrative demarcation, the panel frame traces the borderlines of subject matter, pointing to what claims the centre and what remains on the margins: as a device that encapsulates the reader's viewpoint (Eisner 1985, 90), the panel frame can also, as is the case with Satrapi's *Persepolis*, draw attention to the contentious nature of all borderlines and frameworks (Elahi 2007). The layout of a panel, its size and shape also carry information about the prominence of a moment in time and, occasionally, action duration: the transition between panels may indicate a change of subject matter, scene, point of view and, most importantly, time: 'in the world of comics, **time and space** are **one and the same**' (McCloud 1993, 100). Frequently, comic art can break its own conventions by juxtaposing apparently unrelated panels or deliberately disrupting linear chronology: the coalescence of different chronologies in Alison Bechdel's *Fun Home* (2006) does precisely this. What separates one panel from the next, the *gutter*, may also be an important source of information: in Spiegelman's *Maus*, for instance, the untold and unrepresented – because unrepresentable – is exactly what belongs to the liminal space of the interframe.

The most recognizable feature in comic writing is the *speech balloon*, which, in its usage as a visual device to express speech, goes back to medieval art (Petersen 2011, xix). The balloon visualizes the invisible, attempting 'to capture and make visible an ethereal element: sound' (Eisner 1985, 24). Like other stylized marks and symbols used to indicate all *emanata* – 'invisible elements as music, noise, thought, and motion' (Petersen 2011, xix) – the balloon embodies the semiotic essence of graphic narratives, and their reliance on a system of recognized pictorial codes to convey meaning. The deployment – or lack of – speech balloons, the self-conscious use of panels and gutters along with colour and pictorial style create 'the "grammar" of sequential art' (Eisner 1985, 2). The apparent structure of comics, however, should not lead to the assumption that the act of comicreading is in any way simple. On the contrary, as a semiotic process, reading comics establishes a complex – and complicit – set of interactions between reader and writer/illustrator (Morris 2012, 6).

Complementing this overview of the key concepts, aesthetic, historical and cultural trajectories running through the medium of comic writing, is a set of two case studies offering detailed analyses of Spiegelman's *Maus* and Satrapi's *Persepolis*. Graphic narratives can now be recognized as a distinctive canon in popular literature, with its own traditions, history and medium-specific formal concerns. As the following sections highlight, what the coming of age of graphic narratives demonstrates is the sophisticated development of a long-standing form of aesthetic expression, simultaneously driven by serious political questions and not afraid of taking risks with its own conventions.

Case Study I: Art Spiegelman's *Maus* (1986–91)

Originally published in two volumes (*Maus Part I: A Survivor's Tale: My Father Bleeds History*, 1986 and *Maus Part II: A Survivor's Tale: And Here My troubles Began*, 1991), *Maus* is a historiographic memoir recounting the author's father's experience as a Holocaust survivor, his captivity in Auschwitz and his life as a Jewish immigrant in America. Largely shaped by the biographical framework and the relationship between Art Spiegelman and his father, Vladek, the narrative provides a compelling commentary on one of the most sensitive chapters in twentieth-century history. This is made considerably more poignant by the choice of medium – Whitlock coins, in this instance, the term 'autographics' (2006, 966) – and the specific graphic and visual choices employed by Spiegelman to represent both story and history. The self-conscious aspect of Spiegelman's narrative emerges strongly in the first chapter of the second volume, 'Mauschwitz'. The chapter starts off with a frameless scene, which, by way of displaying some sketches from Art's notebook, reflects on the graphic technique used throughout the book: 'What kind of **animal** should I make you?' (2003, 171.iii). Put to Françoise, Art's French wife, the question points to the animal metaphor which underpins the graphic style of Spiegelman's work: Jews are the mice of the eponymous title, Germans are – predictably – cats, Poles are pigs, Americans are dogs, Frenchmen are frogs. As Philip Pullman suggests, the use of such anthropomorphic animal metaphors is problematic: 'it implies a form of essentialism that many readers will find suspect. Cats kill mice because they are cats, and that's what cats do. But is it in the nature of Germans, as Germans, to kill Jews?' (2003, n.p.). To an extent, the question remains uncomfortably unanswered throughout the narrative, and, admittedly, the nucleus of the 'mouse' metaphor has its roots in Nazi propaganda. As Spiegelman explains in *Metamaus*:

> The most shockingly relevant anti-Semitic work I found was The Eternal Jew, a 1940 German 'documentary' that portrayed Jews in a ghetto swarming in tight quarters, bearded caftaned creatures, and then a cut to Jews as mice – or rather rats – swarming in a sewer, with a title card that said 'Jews are the rats' or the 'vermin of mankind.' This made it clear to me that this dehumanization was at the very heart of the killing project. (2011, 114)

In more than one way, *Maus* subversively engages with the politics and ethos of Nazi iconography used in anti-Semitic propaganda. As Thomas Doherty explains, 'To the Nazis, art was more than just an expression of totalitarian ethos; it was the rationale for it. The Nazi aesthetic celebrated perfection in form just as Nazi ideology demanded purity of bloodlines' (1996, 72). As ideology increasingly controlled artistic expression, it did so not just in terms of content, but also, and perhaps, more disturbingly, in terms of style and subject matter (72). In their disregard for aesthetic perfection and – frequently, though not always, as Doherty would seem to claim – devoid of the erotic pleasure more easily found in other visual representations of the human body, cartoons become the antithesis of idealized physical perfection and eroticized bodies of Nazi visual arts. Furthermore, resisting the mimetic principles of photographic realism, cartoon drawings also defy the aesthetics of 'pure' lines embedded in Nazi art: 'Relying mainly on sparse black lines and the shadings of the monochromatic scale, the cartoonist conjures the survivor's landscape with rough sketches, black silhouettes, and white space' (77). In doing so, the drawings become more evocative and, simultaneously, challenge prescriptive ways of seeing, and representing, authentic subject matter.

While the use of animal metaphors is central to many serious narratives – and particularly satire – including, for instance, Jonathan Swift's *Gulliver's Travels* (1726) and George Orwell's *Animal Farm* (1945), to Spiegelman it is the use of the cartoon as a narrative medium for serious subject matter that becomes inherently problematic:

> I feel so inadequate trying to reconstruct a reality that was worse than my darkest dreams.
>
> And trying to do it as a comic strip! I guess I bit off more than I can chew. Maybe I ought to forget the whole thing.
>
> There's so much I'll never be able to understand or visualize. I mean, reality is too complex for comics. . . . So much has to be left out or distorted. (Spiegelman 2003, 176.v–vii)

Continuing on from these questions, which open *Maus II*, the narrator returns to these issues at the beginning of Chapter 2, 'Auschwitz: Time Flies', where he reflects on the successful reception of *Maus I*. In these pages, both 'Art' and other characters – unidentified, but clearly related to Spiegelman's professional life – wear the masks representative of their nationalities, following the technique deployed throughout the Holocaust narrative. In this section of *Maus* the masks function as a metafictional device, drawing the reader into the world of the graphic narrative, laying bare its artifice and interrogating its own methodologies. In the same chapter, commenting on his psychiatrist's house – 'His place is overrun with stray dogs and cats'– the narrator is prompted to question his technique: 'Can I mention this, or does it completely louse up my metaphor?' (203.v).

In *Maus* the reader is confronted with three narrative levels, corresponding to three narrative times: (1) Vladek's Holocaust experience, (2) Vladek and Artie's conversations about Vladek's memories and (3) Art's reflections on his work after the publication of the first volume of *Maus* and the death of his father. The boundaries between past and present remain ideologically ambiguous, as cross references – both visual and textual – blur the lines of neat chronological divides. This is particularly evident at the beginning of 'Auschwitz (Time Flies)', where the epigraph foreshadows one of the most disturbing images to come: the single panel depicts two mouse heads in the foreground, agape and surrounded by flames; sitting on and outside the panel frame, are six flies, a self-conscious reference to the double-meaning of 'flies', and, according to McGlothlin, one of the strategies deployed in *Maus* to confound narrative and chronological levels:

> The flies seem to emerge from this stark and disquieting image into the non-circumscribed space of the text, from the Auschwitz past contained in the frame in the present in which this past is embedded. They are *time* flies (the substantive phrase rather than the verbal phrase), buzzing reminders of time passed and a past time that carry the trace of the past into the present. Thus, with the trope of the fly, time itself becomes, in a sense, a character in Spiegelman's book. (2003, 187)

McGlothlin's argument is supported by the fact that the image of buzzing flies serves as a thematic thread running through the chapter. Thus such conflagration of narrative and chronological levels continues to exist beyond the chapter threshold into the opening pages, which, as already noted, present 'Art' the author affected by dilemmas about his own work. The last panel of the first page shows Art sitting at his desk, on what would, at first glance, appear to be a heap of waste paper, but which, on closer inspection, is a morbid pile of dead mice: more than a reconstruction of the Holocaust survivor's past, and in a classic demonstration of the workings of postmemory, Vladek's memories increasingly bleed into the present life of both survivor and descendants.

The expressionist aspect of Spiegelman's style serves a dual purpose. In stripping all characters of their human connotations, it creates more narrative distance, so that the story becomes a less personal – and less sentimental – account of an individual survivor's tale; in doing so, as Whitlock notes, Spiegelman's 'autographic' tale of survival succeeds in defamiliarizing the 'familiar' narrative of a Holocaust survivor (2006, 977). Paradoxically, the simplicity of the stylized, streamlined drawings, while removing the possibility for any easily empathic response from the reader, prompts a more reflective response to the story. Rather than in the foreground, the horror is mostly found in the elliptic gaps in Vladek's narrative, whose simple, factual tone, makes no concession to sentimentalism, aligning itself with the medium's characteristic concise exposition: in comic art, images, rather than words, convey meaning (Doherty 1996, 80). Thus, it is the prisoners' daily circumstances, the lack of adequate food, clothing and sanitation, and the subterfuges, tricks and strategies of survival that progressively build up the trauma of the Holocaust survivor's tale. For instance, in order to gain the favours of the Polish Kapo, Vladek applies his resourcefulness to shoemaking: the detailed shoe-mending instructions included in a large panel design

(Spiegelman 1996, 220.iv), and its meaning for Vladek's survival, acquires a chilling significance when juxtaposed to the panels depicting the violence and squalor of life in the camps. That is not to say that *Maus* offers a 'soft' view of the events. Conversely, the violence, both physical and psychological, gradually seeps into the character's world, slowly unveiling the anxiety, the fears and the despair of the victims of Nazi persecution campaigns. The panel depicting a prisoner's legs trampling over the heads of other prisoners fully displays the horror of concentration captivity; humanity loses any value, and individuality is reduced to a discontinuous narrative of faceless bodies. Identities are replaced by numbers, both figuratively and literally: in the concentration camps, identification is by numbers rather than names (255, iv).[2]

Case Study II: Marjane Satrapi's *Persepolis* (2000–3)

Persepolis (2000–3), Satrapi's historiographic memoir, combines a personal story with a strong political commentary on the events that shaped modern Iran. The first part of the book, *The Story of a Childhood*, outlines the events leading up to and following the Islamic Revolution alongside Marji's childhood. The second part of the book, *The Story of a Return*, reflects on Marjane's immigrant experience, the process of negotiating her identity in a different country, Austria, and her difficult adjustment after her return to Iran. Published several years after *Maus*, which Satrapi acknowledges as a strong influence in her work (Hattenstone 2008, n.p.), *Persepolis* presents a less anxious attitude to the adoption of comic art for the purposes of serious narrative, while displaying, as in Spiegelman's work, a self-conscious awareness of the medium, its position in the cultural canon and formal preoccupations. As with Sacco and Spiegelman, and also, Alison Bechdel and Phoebe Gloeckner, Satrapi's graphic memoir employs the conventions of graphic narratives to create an account of personal trauma interwoven with wider political questions (Chute 2008, 92–3).

Persepolis, like *Maus*, has a multi-level narrative and chronological structure; the author is both the narrative subject and object of the story. Focussing on Satrapi's childhood and adolescence, the memoir also graphically draws attention to the physical changes Marji's body undergoes, thus highlighting – visually and textually – the instability of the autobiographical subject. This is particularly evident in chapter 5 of *Persepolis 2*, 'The Vegetable': the first page is entirely dedicated to a series of two-panel sequences displaying the physical changes occurring to Marjane's size, shape and features as she turns 16. Preceding the sequence is a stand-alone frame in which the depiction of Marjane's body bursting out of her own clothes is a self-reflective reference to Stan Lee and Jack Kirby's comic hero 'The Incredible Hulk'. Satrapi's use of such intertextual references points to the convergence of physical discourses in the textuality of graphic narratives and bodies.

Satrapi's deployment of the panel is revelatory of the permeability of form and content in the memoir. *Persepolis* opens with a chapter called 'The Veil'. Here Satrapi introduces her narrative, starting not with the birth of the author, but the introduction of the compulsory *hijab* in 1980, when Satrapi was 10 years old. In the chapter's second panel only a thin slice of Marji's body is visible on the left margin: 'her self-presentation as fragmented, cut, disembodied, and divided between frames indicates the psychological condition suggested by the chapter's title, "The Veil"' (Chute 2008, 96). The notion of Marji's inner split – and the links between her internal conflict and the civil conflict dividing the Iranian people – is exemplified, later in the same chapter, in a panel representing Marji as a body of two halves (Satrapi 2008, 6.i): on the left-hand side, Marji is unveiled, against a background of mechanical tools (cogs, a hammer, a ruler), signifying the rational, socialist, but also Western influences of her upbringing; on the right-hand side, Marji stands veiled against a background of Persian design, referencing her country's traditional art and culture. The positioning of the two halves allows for a double reading of the Western/Eastern binary opposition; if reading left to right, as in Western languages, Marji's Occidental self precedes her Oriental one, but the reverse is true if reading the image right to left as in Farsi and all Arabic languages. More than anything, however, the image captures the composite structure of hybrid subjectivity, visualized in the adjoining halves of Marji's body and psyche.

Persepolis attempts to interrogate Iranian history as well as Western stereotypes about Iran. Satrapi's employment of the frame motif as a visual device turns it into a narrative symbol used to focalize the graphic memoir's central theme – the problematic construction of Iranian identities – and political drive – a response to 'framings' of Iranian identity by the Western media (Elahi 2007, 313). An important moment of such 'reframing' strategies at work in *Persepolis* occurs at the end of *The Story of a Childhood*, when, having said good-bye to her grandmother before leaving for Austria, Marjane looks at herself in the mirror and promises 'I will always be true to myself'

(Satrapi 2008, 151.ii). As Elahi points out, although the panel may invite a Lacanian interpretation, viewed as a whole, the episode moves beyond the merely visual to accommodate a multi-sensory reading of the self exceeding the constrains of the (male) gaze. In the panels preceding the mirror frame, Marjane's moment of self-recognition is in fact linked to her grandmother and, in particular, to the scent of jasmine, which is, in turn, pictorially rendered in the pattern of her grandmother's nightgown: 'in Marji's matriarchal embrace is an imaginary formation of identity through senses other than the visual' (Elahi 2007, 319). Situated on multiple thresholds – between the two parts of the memoir, childhood and adulthood, Iran and Western Europe – the sequence offers a model of identity that challenges the politics of patriarchal genealogy and emphasizes alternative ways of seeing – and framing – the self.

The notion of an alternative point of view is supported, throughout the first part of the narrative, by the perspective of the child. From the beginning this creates a sense of distortion, whereby political oppression, torture and violence are defamiliarized through the child's point of view (Naghibi and O'Malley 2005, 224). In this way, Satrapi's narrative catalyses a process of 'estrangement' which simultaneously deconstructs certain Western clichés about Iranian history and culture, while, at the same time, exposing the ways in which Western culture is constructed in Iran (Leservot 2011). Using a medium widely found in Western popular culture, Satrapi's own style also imports aesthetic elements from her native Iran, creating a distinctively hybrid style (Chute 2008, 98). For instance, the recurrent pictorial use of tulips – as seen in the cover of the first edition of *The Story of a Childhood* – becomes an important reference to Iran, where the flowers are typical, but also to the specific symbolic connotations attached to them. The hybrid combination of Western and Eastern aesthetics at play in *Persepolis* is closely referenced in a large panel illustrating Marjane's drawing for her Art School entry test; here we have a transposition of Michelangelo's *Pietà* in which the female figure holding the body of a martyred soldier is clad in the traditional Iranian chador. Against the black background, four large stylized tulips stand out on either side of the human figures, a deliberate reference to the current political situation: 'I added two tulips, symbols of the martyrs, on either side so there would be no confusion' (Satrapi 2008, 283). The panel's mixed imagery highlights the subversive hybridity of Satrapi's blend of Occidental and Oriental aesthetic frameworks (Naghibi and O' Malley 2005, 231).

As Marji grows up, the notion of a split identity becomes a much more endemic, collective way of being. The negotiation of the female body in the public spaces of Teheran is interpreted in the strictest sense and is subject to the all-seeing gaze of the regime: in 1990, for instance, Marjiane gets into trouble for wearing visible red socks (Satrapi 2008, 304.vi). The rigid control over the appearance and dress code to be respected by all women, Satrapi explains, is a form a brainwashing that will eventually take root even in the most resistant mindsets. The speech balloons in the bottom sequence of the same page show how questions such as 'Are my trousers long enough?', 'Is my veil in place?', 'Can my make-up be seen?' and 'Are they going to whip me?' replace a deeper kind of enquiry: 'Where is my freedom of thought?', 'Where is my freedom of speech?', 'My life, is it livable?' and 'What's going on in the political prisons'? (2008, 304.vi–vii). Simultaneously, whereas women must adhere to a strict dress code in the public space, in private they may perform different identities, supported by more relaxed sartorial styles. As Satrapi observes: 'Our behaviour in public and our behaviour in private were polar opposites. . . . This disparity made us schizophrenic' (307.i–ii).

In documenting the impact that the Islamic Revolution had on public dress code, Satrapi also draws attention to the sartorial alterations deployed to express dissent and resistance to the regime. Earlier, in *The Story of a Childhood*, towards the beginning of the revolution, two sets of split panels display the 'Fundamentalist Woman', who is covered, head to toe, by the traditional chador, and the 'modern woman', who wears a looser scarf over her head and a long coat over trousers. In Marji's words: 'You showed your opposition to the regime by letting a few strands of hair show'. The sequence also points to similar kinds of sartorial variations among male Iranians: on the adjacent panel, the two drawings represent 'the fundamentalist man', with a beard and his 'shirt hanging out', and, on the other side, 'the progressive man', shaved and with his 'shirt tucked in' (75.i–ii).

Significantly, when *Persepolis* was published, France was going through one of the phases of the nation's 'veil controversies', which led, eventually, to the ban on the wearing of the *hijab* in all public places in France.[3] What Satrapi's memoir shows, pictorially, is the possibility for a different reading of the veiled woman, one that does not necessarily conform to the stereotype attached to it by the Western media. In accentuating the subversive strategies employed by Iranian women to resist the law, and in illustrating the range of responses – cultural, intellectual, sartorial – performed by them, Satrapi's memoir interrogates paradigms of reading, privileging the human, individual, heterogeneous experience in place of the dehumanized, collective, homogeneous cliché of the oppressed veiled women: 'In *Persepolis* drawings of veiled women refuse that stereotype of the nondescript archetypal Muslim woman. Rather, Satrapi's female figures are human, and full of character and individuality even with the veil' (Whitlock 2006, 974–5).

Conclusion

Narrative art has a long-standing history: since the dawn of civilization, prehistoric evidence suggests the endemic use of pictorial language and symbolic images to put places on maps, tell stories and record important historical events. On a formal level, it is the iconic use of images and their place in a sequence that paved the way for modern-day comic art. A favourite medium for satirical writing, and the object of political and cultural controversies both in the Western and in the Eastern traditions, comics have, nevertheless, occupied a relatively marginal position in relation to mainstream culture: 'Invariably, they have been there, however, as an aside, a digression, to demonstrate the inspiration for the "proper" art that constitutes the bulk of the book' (Sabin 1996, 7). Postmodernism's debunking of the high/low art distinctions and the late twentieth-century's increased interest in visual cultures can be seen as one of the drives behind the rise of graphic narratives. The works of pop-up artists such as Roy Lichtenstein, who explicitly referenced comic writing techniques in his canvases, are exemplary of the ways in which, throughout the twentieth century, comic art has gradually come of age. Although the peripheral positioning of graphic narratives may still be a debatable cause of concerns for some, the end of the twentieth century has seen a steady increase in the publication of 'serious' comics as well as studies that take comics seriously. Graphic narratives have been nominated and awarded prestigious literary prices. Collaborations such as those of David Mazzucchelli and Paul Karasic in the graphic adaptation of Paul Auster's *City of Glass* (1994) or Mattotti and Kramski's version of R. L. Stevenson's *Dr Jekyll and Mr Hyde* (2002) are but two examples of the ways in which popular comic art and the literary canon have intersected. The works of women writers and illustrators, such as Posy Simmonds, Alison Bechdel and Alisa Torres, and the cultural production beyond the British and American contexts are evidence not only of the universal appeal – and accessibility – of the medium but also of the diverse range of topics, genres and approaches it accommodates. Following the trajectory of non-realist fiction, such as Gothic, SF and fantasy, which struggled to be accepted within the canon until the last quarter of the twentieth century, the twenty-first century continues to see graphic narratives progress in a similarly promising fashion.

Notes

1. See also Malise Ruthven, 'Why Are the Muhammad Cartoons still Inciting Violence?'. *The New York Review of Books Blog*, 9 February 2011. Available at: http://www.nybooks.com/blogs/nyrblog/2011/feb/09/why-are-muhammad-cartoons-still-inciting-violence/.
2. The illustration may be compared to Menashe Kadishman's *Shalechet* ('Fallen Leaves') installation in The Jewish Museum, Berlin. This comprises 10,000 metal 'faces' carved in metal discs and placed in an area of the museum that visitors are invited to walk on.
3. Satrapi, who has been living in France since 1994, nevertheless does not endorse the country's legislation about the Islamic veil: 'I really believe in a society where if someone wants to walk in the street completely naked they will be able to, and if someone wants to wear a veil they will also be able to'. See Hattenstone 2008.

Works Cited

Amir and Khalil (2011), *Zahra's Paradise: Graphic Novel*. New York: First Second.

Barker, M. (1989), *Comics: Ideology, Power and the Critics*. Manchester: Manchester University Press.

Chute, H. (2008), 'The Texture of Retracing in Marjane Satrapi's *Persepolis*'. *Women's Studies Quarterly* 36(1 and 2), 92–110.

Doherty, T. (1996), 'Art Spiegelman's *Maus*: Graphic Art and the Holocaust'. *American Literature* 68(1), 69–84.

Eisner, W. (1985), *Comics and Sequential Art: Principles and Practices from the Legendary Cartoonist*. New York: W. W. Norton & Co. Reprinted 2008.

Elahi, B. (2007), 'Frames and Mirrors in Marjane Satrapi's *Persepolis*'. *Symploke* 15(1/2), 312–25.

Groensten, T. (2007), *The System of Comics*, trans. B. Beaty and N. Nguyen. Jackson: University Press of Mississippi. First published 1999.

Hattenstone, S. (2008), 'Confessions of Miss Mischief'. *The Guardian*, 29 March 2008, http://www.guardian.co.uk/film/2008/mar/29/biography, accessed 23 April 2013.

Kannenberg, Jr, G. (2008), *500 Essential Graphic Novels: The Ultimate Guide.* Lewes: Ilex.

Leservot, T. (2011), 'Occidentalism: Rewriting the West in Marjane Satrapi's *Persépolis*'. *French Forum* 36(1), 115–30.

McCloud, S. (1993), *Understanding Comics: The Invisible Art.* New York: HarperCollins. Reprinted 1994.

McGlothlin, E. (2003), 'No Time Like the Present: Narrative and Time in Art Spiegelman's *Maus*'. *Narrative* 11(2), 177–98.

Mattotti, L. and Kramski, J. (2002), *Dr Jekyll and Mr Hyde.* New York: NBM.

Mazzucchelli, D. and Karasic, P. (1994), *Paul Auster's City of Glass.* New York: Avon Books.

Miller, F. (1986), *The Dark Night Returns.* New York: DC Comics. Reprinted 2006.

Moore, A. and Gibbons, D. (1986), *Watchmen.* New York: DC Comics. Reprinted 2005.

Morris, J. (2012), 'Of Mice and Men: Collaboration, Postmemory and Working through in Art Spiegelman's *Maus: A Survivor's Tale*', in R. Iadonisi (ed.), *Graphic History: Essays on Graphic Novels And/As History.* Newcastle: Cambridge Scholars, pp. 6–36.

Naghibi, N. and O'Malley, A. (2005), 'Estranging the Familiar: "East" and "West" in Satrapi's *Persepolis*'. *ESC* 31(2–3) (June–September), 223–48.

Petersen, R. S. (2011), *Comics, Manga, and Graphic Novels: A History of Graphic Narratives.* Santa Barbara: Praeger.

Pullman, P. (2003), 'Behind the Masks'. *The Guardian*, 18 October, http://www.guardian.co.uk/books/2003/oct/18/fiction.art/, accessed 23 April 2013.

Ruthven, M. (2011), 'Why Are the Muhammad Cartoons still Inciting Violence?'. *The New York Review of Books Blog*, 9 February 2011, http://www.nybooks.com/blogs/nyrblog/2011/feb/09/why-are-muhammad-cartoons-still-inciting-violence/, accessed 23 April 2013.

Sabin, R. (1996), *Comics, Comix and Graphic Novels: A History of Comic Art.* London: Phaidon.

Sacco, J. (2003), *Palestine.* London: Jonathan Cape.

Said, E. (2003), 'Homage to Joe Sacco', in Joe Sacco (ed.), *Palestine.* London: Jonathan Cape, pp. i–v.

Satrapi, M. (2008), *Persepolis.* London: Vintage.

Spiegelman, A. (1996; 2003), *The Complete Maus.* London: Penguin.

—(2011), *Metamaus.* London: Viking.

Talbot, B. (2012), 'Book of a Lifetime: *Maus* by Art Spiegelman'. *The Independent*, 29 December, http://www.independent.co.uk/arts-entertainment/books/reviews/book-of-a-lifetime-maus-by-art-spiegelman-8432097.html, accessed 19 June 2014.

Talbot, M. and Talbot, B. (2012), *Dotter of Her Father's Eyes*. London: Jonathan Cape.

Whitlock, G. (2006), 'Autographics: The Seeing "I" of the Comics'. *Modern Fiction Studies* 52(4), 965–79.

Winterhart, J. (2012), *Days of the Bagnold Summer*. London: Jonathan Cape.

Wolk, D. (2007), *Reading Comics: How Graphic Novels Work and What they Mean*. Cambridge: Da Capo Press.

Part III

Case Studies

10

H. G. Wells, Élitism and Popular Fiction

Ben Clarke

From Literature into the Annals of History

H. G. Wells was one of the most influential and popular writers of the early twentieth century. Author of more than a hundred books, from scientific romances such as *The Time Machine* (1895) to educational works including *The Outline of History* (1920), he was a prominent public intellectual, actively involved in debates on subjects from sexual liberation to world government. Lance Sieveking recalls that when 'I was a boy in the reign of Edward the Seventh, a day seldom passed without the name of H. G. Wells cropping up' (1980, 60). He was an inspirational figure for many, particularly on the left. George Orwell argued that '[t]hinking people who were born about the beginning of the century are in some sense Wells' own creation' and that the 'minds of all of us, and therefore the physical world, would be perceptibly different if Wells had never existed' (1970a, 170–1). For his contemporaries, Wells was remarkable for the range of his intelligence, his willingness to confront entrenched interests and his engagement with a broad audience. Reflecting on his achievements in the *New York Times*, Waldemar Kaempffert described him as 'the greatest public teacher of his time' (1946, n.p.).

Despite this, Wells' critical standing declined rapidly after his death. Some of his early novels are still discussed as pioneering works of science fiction, but much of his writing is neglected and, as John Huntington argues, his 'accomplishment is always in question' (1991, 1). Wells recognized the decreasing interest in his work even during his lifetime. In a satirical essay on his own writing, first published in 1945 under the name Wilfred B. Betterave, he observed that it 'was no longer the thing to read him', and 'My Auto-Obituary' begins by noting that the 'name of H. G. Wells . . . will have few associations for the younger generation' (in Hammond 1980, 116–17). In part, this was due to the marginalization of his political ideas. Orwell famously claimed that he was 'too sane to understand the modern world', and that the belief in the emancipatory power of science and rationalism which 'made him seem like an inspired prophet in the Edwardian age, make him a shallow, inadequate thinker' (1970a, 171–2) in an era of nationalism, purges and concentration camps. The decline in his position is also frequently justified on artistic grounds. Wells was widely praised as a writer during his lifetime. Henry James insisted that 'I am compelled, utterly to *drivel*' (in Parrinder 1972, 126) about Kipps, and Joseph Conrad told Wells that 'I am always powerfully impressed by your work' (in Parrinder 1972, 60). Reviews could be just as complimentary. In 1906, W. D. Howells argued that there 'are few novels of the last three or four years . . . half or one-tenth as good as *Love and Mr. Lewisham*' (in Parrinder 1972, 128) while an anonymous piece on *Tono-Bungay* in the *Daily Telegraph* argued that '[u] nless we are greatly mistaken' it 'is one of the most significant novels of modern times' (in Parrinder 1972, 148). Post-war criticism, though, has often been less appreciative, and in 1948, only 2 years after Wells' death, Mark Schorer argued that his lack of 'respect for the techniques of his medium' meant that 'he escaped – he disappeared – from literature into the annals of an era' (1948, 73). For Schorer, Wells is significant only insofar as he illuminates the period that produced him; he makes no contribution to art.

The decline in Wells' standing raises broader questions about dominant accounts of twentieth-century literary history, which focus on the movement from modernism to postmodernism, obscuring the important traditions of realist, speculative and polemical writing to which he contributed. His marginalization is in part a result of this narrative, and the associated idea of literature as something consumed by a minority and defined by its concern with form and refusal of a distinct social function. Wells' texts rarely fit this model. They were extremely popular and were often loosely structured. He used, but rarely adhered to, familiar narrative models, moving freely between forms, genres and vocabularies which enjoyed different levels of cultural prestige. His writing was also didactic, using its broad appeal to promote specific ideas and causes. As Steven McLean argues, Wells addressed a 'newly created popular readership' produced by the 1870 Education Act and saw his writing as having a 'definite educational function' (2009, 5). Wells argued that this emerging audience had 'distinctive needs and curiosities' (Wells 1934, 426), and his work sought to communicate new ideas and scientific discoveries to them. For Wells, literature is not a specialist concern, but a public practice; it should intervene in political debates, rather than offer an escape from them.

Wells' work challenges the notion that popular fiction is characterized by a lack of critical thought and failure to consider its own methods. Despite their accessibility, his novels possess a radical openness. Their juxtaposition of multiple forms, voices and ideas enables them to function as discursive structures that generate questions they cannot answer. This counters Wells' own claims to authoritative judgement, and suggests a democratic politics founded upon the recognition of difference at odds with his declared conception of effective government, which emphasizes expert consensus. His texts insist on the importance of the particular, on what escapes the kinds of intellectual and political systems he insistently devised. They are also more complex and self-reflective than criticism of him as an artist often allows. His importance, as both a writer and a thinker, lies in his contradictions, the ways in which his work questions itself. This does not simply mean, as Kingsley Martin put it, that 'at least two people struggled inside him' (1980, 87) but describes a critical process in which an authoritative voice is destabilized, undermining the idea of narrative or political closure.

Art versus Propaganda

Any argument for the plurality of Wells' narratives must address the contrary claim that his sense of the urgency of his material led him to neglect aesthetic questions and impose ideas on his readers. As Patrick Parrinder observes, the 'problematic of "art versus propaganda"' emerged in Wells' criticism in the first decade of the twentieth century and 'has tended to dominate it ever since' (1972, 17). It is founded, in part, upon Wells' representation of his own work. As Huntington argues, his description of himself as 'a journalist as opposed to an artist' deliberately distinguishes him from those who argued that literature was an end in itself and emphasizes that he consistently 'wrote from a position involved in the debates of the moment' (1991, 10). This is true of his novels as well as his non-fiction. Wells recognized that his focus on contemporary problems meant that his texts did not always retain their force once the conditions of their production had passed. Maugham claims that Wells, confronted with a complete edition of his own books, commented '[t]hey're as dead as mutton, you know. They all deal with matters of topical interest and now that the matters aren't topical any more they're unreadable' (1998, 177). Maugham thought that there was 'a good deal of truth' in this, and that Wells' view that the 'function of the novelist was to deal with the pressing problems of the day' (177) prevented him from producing works of art. His novels failed because they were determined by his political commitments, which were enacted rather than explored in the plot and characters; '[t]he people he puts before you are not individuals, but lively and talkative marionettes whose function is to express the ideas he was out to attack or to defend' (178–9). Another friend, Arnold Bennett, told Wells bluntly that '[y]ou aren't an artist, except insofar as you disdainfully make use of art for your reforming ends; you are simply a reformer' (in Bennett 1960, 124). These judgements insist upon writing literature as a discursive practice, in which ideas are questioned rather than reproduced, but they also evoke the image of art as timeless, in contrast to both politics and popular fiction, which are represented as inherently ephemeral.

The notion that Wells' fiction is a vehicle for fixed ideas suggests a relation between his political and aesthetic failings. His subordination of his characters to a particular end parallels Wells' concept of a future state in which the interests of all would be met by an expert minority, in that it demands readers accept the positions advanced by a central narrative authority. His work locates itself within a tradition of what Stephen Ingle calls 'scientific socialism', which maintained that 'although government must be carried out in the interests of the many, it can only be managed *on their behalf* by their superiors' (1979, 10). Throughout his career Wells attacked existing social hierarchies, satirizing the institutions and discourses that legitimized the dominance of a minority, but his work nonetheless returns repeatedly to what John Carey describes as the 'idea of the superior individual' (1992, 140), and the notion that government is best conducted by an élite. Wells saw himself as 'being made of better stuff, intrinsically and inherently, than most other human beings' (1934, 68), and his arguments against the established order attack its inefficiency rather than inequality, advocating a meritocracy, rather than universal participation in decision-making. As he put it, '[w]e want the world ruled, not by everybody, but by a politically minded organization open, with proper safeguards, to everybody' (563). This idea is embodied in the 'samurai' of A Modern Utopia, the 'voluntary noblemen who have taken the world in hand' (2005a, 86). Membership of the samurai is not hereditary, and in fact the 'order is open to every physically and mentally healthy adult in the Utopian State', but it is a governing class. Its existence is predicated on failure of previous democratic systems, on the idea that the 'intricacy of Utopian organization demands a more powerful and efficient method of control than electoral methods can give' (174), a statement that constructs government as primarily a technical practice, a matter of meeting demands that are revealed rather than negotiated.

The élitism of A Modern Utopia is challenged by its form, though, a pattern that recurs in Wells' work. While the text insists on the necessary dominance of an expert minority, it addresses a popular audience. Indeed, the opening pages imagine the narrative being delivered to a public meeting by an anonymous 'Voice' who sits 'a little nervously, a little modestly, on a stage' (8), conscious that his arguments are a contribution to a debate rather than an alternative to it. Wells' open, accessible prose, with its debts to popular fiction, subverts the closed, ordered systems he often represents. The text is also complicated by its reflection on the tradition within which it operates. The 'Owner of the Voice' is initially pictured 'reading a manuscript about Utopias' (7) and displays a wide knowledge of preceding texts including 'the Republic and Laws of Plato, and More's Utopia, Howell's implicit Altruria, and Bellamy's future Boston, Comte's great Western Republic, Hertzka's Freeland, Cabet's Icaria, and Campanella's City of the Sun' (13). The concern with genre emphasizes that utopian literature is satirical as well as prescriptive, and that there is consequently always an ambiguity in its claims. This is realized partly in its insistence on its own fictiveness, the fact that, as the word itself emphasizes, utopias do not exist; at the end of

A Modern Utopia, the efficient, orderly society dissolves, leaving the protagonist in 'that grey and gawky waste of asphalt – Trafalgar Square' (237), confronted with news of a 'Massacre in Oddessa' and a 'Lynching Outrage in New York State' (239).

Despite this, Wells' utopian fiction is central to his political thought. It also demonstrates the ways in which he was a product of his time, of what Zygmunt Bauman calls 'solid' modernity, a historical stage characterized by the conviction that 'human needs' are '*finite*, steady and calculable' (2011, 36). This idea that it is possible to achieve a stable society 'in which all human needs are provided for and all problems afflicting humans and their cohabitation are resolved' (31) depended upon an instrumental rationalism. Social development could be analysed using techniques modelled on those employed in natural sciences, which revealed its underlying laws and enabled the construction of a stable society that was not subject to the uncertainty that had characterized previous human history. Bauman argues that the Communist tradition that produced the Soviet Union was 'a most (perhaps *the* most) faithful, devoted, loving child, as well as (at least in its intention) the most zealous pupil among solid modernity's offspring' (27), but its basic assumptions were held by a range of political organizations, including the Fabian Society, to which Wells belonged from 1903 to 1908.

A Badly Managed World

The ideas Bauman sees as characteristic of 'solid' modernity were productive because they insisted on the possibility of significant positive change. Material and social problems were neither an inevitable part of the human condition nor indissolubly complex but could be solved given sufficient technical knowledge and political will. Wells argued in his pamphlet *This Misery of Boots*, published by the Fabian Society, that those who suffered, along with their families, from the recurrent discomforts of early twentieth-century life, should not

> be humbugged for a moment into believing that this is the dingy lot of all mankind. Those people you love are living in a badly-managed world and on the wrong side of it; and such wretchednesses are the daily demonstration of that.

> Don't say for a moment: 'Such is life.' Don't think their miseries are part of some primordial curse there is no escaping. The disproof of that is for any one to see. There are people, people no more deserving than others, who suffer from none of these things. (1907, 17–18)

The bluntness of the passage does not demonstrate a failure to grasp the complexity of existing economic structures but insists upon simple moral obligation to change them and realize the 'essential idea of Socialism', which is too often buried beneath 'elaborations' (40). Wells' prose enacts his argument, which is partly a process of demystification, a stripping away of the insidious myths that represent the legitimacy of the established order as self-evident. His argument for socialism is radical in its appropriation of common sense, a term often controlled by conservatives, its claim that the need for change is there 'for any one to see', and is obscured only by poor management, apathy and a stubborn commitment to outdated ideas. The emphasis on the waste and confusion of early twentieth-century society, on the notion that real progress is prevented only by failures of education and will, undermines the image of revolutionary change as a break from a natural order embodied in existing institutions. Revolution is instead the product of rational thought, the attempt to realize a sanity that is currently denied.

The idea that human development obeys knowable laws could also, though, be used to justify the elimination of those who could not be integrated into new social structures. Bauman argues that in the Soviet Union the 'promise of a bliss guaranteed by a rationally designed and rationally run' state produced instead a 'society treated by its governing bodies in the way gardens are viewed and tackled by gardeners', which 'came to focus on an obsessive and in the end compulsive and coercive tracing, spotting, uprooting and extermination of the social equivalent of "weeds": that is, humans who did not fit the intended order' (2011, 35). Purges were not a deviation from the system, but part of its logic.

A similar tendency is evident in Wells' work, particularly in his writing on eugenics. As Carey argues, managing reproduction became for Wells an 'ethical duty' (1992, 123). While he recognized that the means might sometimes be distasteful, he saw them as justified by the end, the improvement of future generations. In *Men Like Gods*, 'Utopian science' has, for centuries, 'been able to discriminate among births', with the result that there 'are few dull and no really defective people' left (Wells 1902, 73–4). In *A Modern Utopia*, the state also confronts the problem of people who 'spoil the world for others', such as 'idiots and lunatics ... perverse and incompetent persons . . . people of weak character who become drunkards, drug takers, and the like', and 'persons tainted with certain foul and transmissible disease' (2005a, 99). Though Wells insists that the Utopian state will not be 'vindictive' (100), scientific certainty legitimizes the destruction of those regarded as biologically inferior. *A Modern Utopia* recognizes that the 'laws of hereditary are far too mysterious' (181) to enable a positive programme of selective breeding but insists that improvement can be achieved by preventing the unfit from reproducing or eliminating them altogether; the government would 'kill all deformed and monstrous and evilly diseased births' (100). In Utopia, individuals damage the community most by passing on inferior genetic material, and the worst offences are 'reckless begetting or the willful transmission of contagious disease' (102). Wells was not alone in his interest in eugenics, which remained prominent in discussions of social reform until World War II, when its association with Nazism led to its displacement or disguise. It not only informed the work of writers such as Wells and Aldous Huxley, but was also diffused through popular culture, in part as a consequence of the work of eugenics societies, who helped to shape individual attitudes to sex, procreation and personal worth; in *Caliban Shrieks*, Jack Hilton recalls that after encountering these 'cleaners of society' he 'accepted the fact of my inferiority', and that 'the only decent thing I could do was to see that I played no part in multiplying the vast hordes of flotsam and jetsam who annoyed, upset and tended to impoverish the super select race' (1935, 31–2). Wells' concern with managing reproduction was not an individual failing but demonstrates the extent to which a particular form of scientific rationalism shaped the political culture within which his ideas were formed.

The societies described in texts such as *Men Like Gods* and *A Modern Utopia* develop but only along a fixed trajectory. They aim at an increasing dominance over nature, including human beings, an imposed, rational order; as Urthred explains in *Men Like Gods*, '[e]very day we learn a little better how to master this little planet' (1902, 99). They are consequently both dynamic and static; they progress, but towards a known end. The problems of this are described in Wells' first novel, *The Time Machine*. The Eloi, whom the Time Traveler encounters in 802,701, are the product of a complete 'conquest of Nature' and have achieved a 'too-perfect security' (1992, 37). They are not, though, like the Utopians of *Men Like Gods*, idealized figures who have passed 'beyond man towards a nobler humanity' (1902, 87) but demonstrate 'a slow movement of degeneration' (1992, 57). The elimination of chance and difference has led to a regression into a 'mere beautiful futility' (66). This narrative is the product of a problematic interpretation of Darwinian thought that sees 'intellectual versatility' as 'the compensation for change, danger, and trouble' (89) but emphasizes the importance of the diversity and change that his utopian narratives often suppress.

Right but Absurd

Despite his reputation for a naïve faith in scientific progress, Wells' work is characterized by a scepticism of its own claims and methods. From the very start of his career, he provides a foundation for his critique. As Carey argues, he 'is nearly always in two minds, and this saves him from mere prescription'; even the 'utopias he invents seem to waver and change into dystopias as we watch, robbing us of certainty' (1992, 135). He not only provides alternatives to the ideas he advocates, but also disrupts the arguments on which they depend and satirizes the individuals who make them. His work is a product of solid modernity but also challenges its logic, insisting on what does not fit the pattern. It does this not only in its explicit statements, but also, more importantly, in its form. Its humour, ambiguities and digressions, its insistent concern with the particular and its constant transgression of generic boundaries all undermine the authority to which it lays claim. The deconstruction of apparently authoritative discourses by a subversive energy they cannot contain is Wells' dominant critical method, which does not mean it is a conscious strategy. As Carey argues, Wells 'seems anxious to put forward ideas but not to be held accountable for them', and '[s]ome part of him – his imagination? his story-telling gift? – does not trust the creeds his brain formulates' (140). This is demonstrated in his writing itself. The authoritarian tendencies of his thought are continually challenged by his accessible, anarchic prose, which suggests a scepticism of intellectual élites and a democratic impetus that resists attempts to constrain it.

Wells often attacks powerful institutions and individuals directly, but he also uses a humour that exposes them to a critical scrutiny from which their status normally protects them. In *The World Set Free*, Wells imagines a prosperous 'sober Englishman at the end of the nineteenth century' who, sitting down to breakfast, chooses whether to drink 'tea from Ceylon or coffee from Brazil, devour an egg from France with some Danish ham, or eat a New Zealand chop' and scrutinizes his 'investments in South Africa, Japan and Egypt', while telling 'the two children he had begotten (in the place of his father's eight) that he thought the world has changed very little' (1988, 16). The passage represents the conservative middle classes, integral to Victorian ideologies, as absurd despite their dominance, unable to grasp the changed historical circumstances which manifested themselves in even the apparently mundane details of their lives. Orwell argued that good comedy is inherently subversive, that a 'thing is funny when . . . it upsets the established order' (1970b, 325), and Wells consistently uses laughter to challenge social élites and élitism. He often focuses on the use of what Kipps perceives as that 'hidden thing called culture' (Wells 1998, 114) to maintain established hierarchies. Kipps' attempts to become 'if not a "gentleman", at least mistakably like one' (38), exposes the use of taste to legitimize inequality, as social structures are represented as the product of cultural rather than material distinctions. Released from Folkestone Drapery Bazaar by a legacy, Kipps squanders his time attempting to master texts such as '*Manners and Rules of Good Society*' (133) and follow the guidance of Chester Coote. Coote is ridiculous in part because he claims a sophistication and intelligence he does not possess, but his desire to use cultural knowledge to achieve social eminence is itself misguided, and the emphasis on his absurdity attacks the foundations of 'that great world "up there"' (114), to which he promises access, rather than his failings alone.

Wells satirizes not only the dominant classes, but also the kind of intellectual communities with which he himself was identified. In *Ann Veronica*, he represents the 'Children of Light' who dedicate themselves to 'Higher Thought, the Simple Life, Socialism, Humanitarianism' and attend the meetings of organizations such as the Fabians, as 'in many respects so right' but also 'somehow, and even in direct relation to that rightness, absurd' (2005b, 110–12). Their ideas are a symptom of 'a great discontent with and criticism of life as it is lived' (117), which also drives Ann Veronica's rebellion, but are complicated by their individual obsessions. This is demonstrated by the discussions of progressive thought hosted by the Goopes; Alderman Dunstable interrupts repeatedly to detail 'his personal impressions of quite a number of his fellow-councillors', while the unnamed 'roughish-looking young man' (113) attempts to give 'the whole discussion a daring and erotic flavour' (114). Wells is implicated in this satirical portrait in the figure of 'Wilkins the author' (111), one of the 'giant leaders of the Fabian Society', whose 'daring essays' (116) the group discusses. This does not suggest a simple equivalence between him and members of the Goopes' circle but implies that he may also be 'absurd' even if he is 'right'. The novel describes a complex and often confused struggle for emancipation, undertaken by flawed human beings under shifting historical conditions. This is a political process, a necessarily open-ended negotiation between diverse interests and ideas, rather than a narrative of steadily growing scientific dominance over nature and society.

A Capacity for Joy and Beauty

Wells' satire, which is rooted in popular comedy as well as the work of predecessors such as Swift, Sterne and Dickens, undermines the idea that certain people are exempt from criticism, insisting upon a shared fallibility that exposes everyone, including himself, to scrutiny. His work also emphasizes experiences and perspectives that cannot be successfully integrated into grand narratives. It traces the limitations of general social theories even as they recognize their importance to any effective project of emancipation. In *The History of Mr. Polly*, he describes a 'certain high-browed gentleman living in Highbury' who 'wrestles with what he calls "social problems" in a bloodless but at times . . . extremely illuminating manner' from 'the library of the Climax Club' (2005c, 121), much as Wells himself wrote from the Reform Club. This 'dome-headed monster of intellect' explores, among other things, the forces that have produced that 'vast mass of useless, uncomfortable, under-educated, under-trained, and altogether pitiable people we contemplate when we use that inaccurate and misleading term, the Lower Middle Class' (122). His analysis exposes the social and economic structures that shape people like Polly, a failing shopkeeper, but cannot provide a complete account of his experience. There are, as Wells recognizes, 'unbridged abysses between the general and particular'. The study of 'the big process that dooms millions of lives to thwarting and discomfort' (123) is necessary but not sufficient; one is still left with 'Mr Polly, sitting on his gate, untrained, unwarned, confused, distressed, angry, seeing nothing except that he is, as it were, netted in greyness and discomfort – with life dancing all about him; Mr Polly with a capacity for joy and beauty at least as keen and subtle as yours or mine' (123–4). Political theory provides an explanation for what Polly experiences as fate, and therefore a basis for changing his condition, but it also risks reducing him to an abstraction. The text's insistence that Polly exceeds the categories he inhabits, that his life is potentially 'at least' as rich and complex as that of the reader or Wells himself, emphasizes the problems of systematic analysis and the need for a dialectical movement between general and particular. It also suggests a democratic politics founded on difference rather than similitude, on the fact that everybody matters rather than the idea that everybody is the same.

The emphasis on Mr Polly's individual as well as representative qualities challenges the notion that Wells' characters are one-dimensional 'marionettes'. They often subvert the notion of fixed, general categories, insisting instead upon their irreducible complexity and contradictions. Polly, like Kipps, is defined by his attempts to escape the social roles assigned to him. This is demonstrated, not only in his escape from Fishbourne and respectability, but also in his day-to-day behaviour including, most famously, his speech. His linguistic improvisation is the result of a lack of education, but it also demonstrates his vivid, individual response to his environment, which cannot be expressed in the terms he has been given. American tourists in Canterbury are driven by a 'Cultured Rapacity' and seek a 'Voracious Return to the Heritage' (42), while his relationship with Miriam is an 'Unfortunate amoor' (91), and his marriage, drawing on *Much Ado About Nothing*, a 'Benedictine collapse' (98) celebrated with 'Convivial vociferations' (109). His speech is both an attempt to communicate more directly with others and the product of an idiosyncratic individual consciousness. It strains continually at the boundaries of meaning, gesturing towards a plenitude it cannot achieve. Its suggestion of an unrealized desire for fullness is paralleled in Polly's eventual flight from his failing shop and failed marriage. His reinvention of himself is not a steady progress towards a known end but is necessarily incomplete, and his reflections on his experience emphasize chance and contingency; it 'isn't what we try to get that we get', but '[y]ou got to work it out, and take the consequences' (208).

The novel does not embody solid modernity's conception of '*finite*, steady and calculable' needs that can be fulfilled, enabling narrative closure, but suggests a more open-ended quest. The text seems to culminate in a state of rest, as Polly declares he would return to the Potwell Inn to contemplate the sunset even after death ('[c]ome here always, when I'm a ghost'), but it also insists on the impossibility of stasis ('we can't sit here for ever') (209). His journey demonstrates an individuality that cannot realize itself within imposed structures, and which is always incomplete. Kipps also identifies the personal with the exception, declaring that 'I don't suppose there ever was chap quite like me before', though his self-awareness remains limited and ambiguous; his final statement in the novel is, significantly, 'I dunno' (302).

Polly and Kipps are both oppressed by the irrationality as well as the inequalities of the societies they inhabit. In *Kipps*, Wells imagines 'Stupidity' as the 'ruling power of this land', threatening his protagonist like a 'lumpish monster' (279). Kipps and Ann are the products of this environment and are at once absurd and tragic; Wells, like Conrad, writes 'in scorn as well as in pity' (Conrad 1990, 4). Wells declares that 'I have laughed, and I laugh at these two people; I have sought to make you laugh', but also represents them as 'little, ill-nourished, ailing, ignorant children – children who feel pain, who are naughty and muddled and suffer, and do not understand' (Wells 1998, 279), a description that is compassionate as well as patronizing.

For people like this, enduring 'clipped and limited lives', rationality, knowledge and order offer an opportunity to escape 'the claw of this Beast' (279), the restrictive and wasteful ideologies of the Victorians. However, Wells' work also demonstrates the ways in which this rationality itself tends towards the production of rigid systems, which are more efficient but which still cannot accommodate the unique lives of Polly, Kipps and Lewisham. Frank Swinnerton wrote that there would have been 'no room' for Wells' own 'energy . . . his jubilant sense of absurdity' in 'any of his utopias' and that if 'some dreadful chance were to land him in one of those sterilized communities' he risked being 'put to death by the mandarins for being intractable'. One of the signs of this 'energy' was the 'rich fecundity' of his 'talk' (1980, 43), the ways in which his language insistently overran conventional, accepted bounds. In the end, Wells is a significant thinker because of the artistry he disavows, because the humour, density and contradictions of his work provide a foundation for its own critique, preventing it from achieving the state of rest and closure it seeks.

Works Cited

Anonymous (1972), 'Unsigned Review, *Daily Telegraph*', in P. Parrinder (ed.), *H. G. Wells: The Critical Heritage*. London: Routledge & Kegan Paul, pp. 147–50.

Bauman, Zygmunt (2011), *Collateral Damage: Social Inequalities in a Global Age*. Cambridge: Polity.

Bennett, Arnold (1960), 'Bennett to Wells, 30 September 1905', in Harris Wilson (ed.), *Arnold Bennet and H. G. Wells: A Record of a Personal and a Literary Friendship*. Urbana: University of Illinois Press, pp. 122–5.

Carey, John (1992), *The Intellectuals and the Masses: Pride and Prejudice among the Literary Intelligentsia, 1880-1939*. London: Faber.

Conrad, Joseph (1972), 'Joseph Conrad's Impression', in P. Parrinder (ed.), *H. G. Wells: The Critical Heritage*. London: Routledge & Kegan Paul, p. 60.

—(1990 [1907]), *The Secret Agent*. Harmondsworth: Penguin.

Hilton, Jack (1935), *Caliban Shrieks*. London: Cobden-Sanderson.

Howells, W. D. (1972), 'William Dean Howells, review in *North American Review*', in P. Parrinder (ed.), *H. G. Wells: The Critical Heritage*. London: Routledge & Kegan Paul, pp. 128–31.

Huntington, J. (1991), 'Introduction', in John Huntington (ed.), *Critical Essays on H. G. Wells*. Boston: G. K. Hall, pp. 1–14.

Ingle, Stephen (1979), *Socialist Thought in Imaginative Literature*. London: Macmillan.

James, Henry (1972), 'Henry James's View', in P. Parrinder (ed.), *H. G. Wells: The Critical Heritage*. London: Routledge & Kegan Paul, pp. 126–7.

Kaempffert, W. (1946), 'Herbert George Wells: In Memoriam'. *New York Times* (25 August), n.p.

McLean, Steven (2009), *The Early Fiction of H. G. Wells: Fantasies of Science*. Basingstoke: Palgrave.

Martin, K. (1980), 'Shaw and Wells', in J. R. Hammond (ed.), *H. G. Wells: Interviews and Recollections*. Totowa, NJ: Barnes and Noble, pp. 84–97.

Maugham, W. S. (1998 [1958]), *The Vagrant Mood*. London: Mandarin.

Orwell, George (1970a [1968]), 'Wells, Hitler and the World State', in Sonia Orwell and Ian Angus (eds), *My Country Right or Left 1940-1943*. Harmondsworth: Penguin, pp. 166–72.

—(1970b [1968]), 'Funny, But Not Vulgar', in Sonia Orwell and Ian Angus (eds), *As I Please 1943-1945*. Harmondsworth: Penguin, pp. 324–9.

Parrinder, Patrick (1972), 'Introduction', in P. Parrinder (ed.), *H.G. Wells: The Critical Heritage*. London: Routledge & Kegan Paul, pp. 1–31.

Schorer, M. (1948), 'Technique as Discovery'. *Hudson Review* 1, 1(Spring), 67–87.

Sieveking, L. (1980), 'H.G. Wells', in J. R. Hammond (ed.), *H.G. Wells: Interviews and Recollections*. Totowa, NJ: Barnes and Noble, pp. 60–9.

Swinnerton, F. (1980), 'Wells as seen by his Friends', in J. R. Hammond (ed.), *H.G. Wells: Interviews and Recollections*. Totowa, NJ: Barnes and Noble, pp. 37–51.

Wells, H. G. (1902), *Men Like Gods*. London: Cassell.

—(1907), *This Misery of Boots*. London: The Fabian Society.

—(1934), *Experiment in Autobiography: Discoveries and Conclusions of a Very Ordinary Brain (Since 1866)*. New York: Macmillan.

—[as Wilfred B. Betterave] (1980), 'A Complete Exposé of this Notorious Literary Humbug', in J. R. Hammond (ed.), *H.G. Wells: Interviews and Recollections*. Totowa, NJ: Barnes and Noble, pp. 108–17.

—(1980), 'My Auto-Obituary', in J. R. Hammond (ed.), *H.G. Wells: Interviews and Recollections*. Totowa, NJ: Barnes and Noble, pp. 117–19.

—(1988 [1914]), *The World Set Free*. London: Hogarth.

—(1992 [1895]), *The Time Machine*. London: Everyman.

—(1998 [1905]), *Kipps*. London: Everyman.

—(2005a [1905]), *A Modern Utopia*. London: Penguin.

—(2005b [1909]), *Ann Veronica*. London: Penguin.

—(2005c [1910]), *The History of Mr. Polly*. London: Penguin.

11

John Buchan and the Spy Thriller

Patrick Parrinder

> He had a kind face despite a tough jaw; it was the jaw of a John Buchan hero.
>
> (Neville 1991, 108)

When Nancy, the protagonist of Jill Neville's short story 'Common Decency' (1991), speculates about an attractive fellow-guest at a London dinner party, she reveals that the life of popular fiction extends well beyond the pages of the books in which it appears. Nancy is not alone in fantasizing about the Buchan hero's good looks, and the historian Bill Schwarz is among those who regard the 'clean-cut jaw' as a 'prominent . . . feature of these stories' (2011, 259). At the risk of pedantry, it needs to be said that Buchan's best-known novels are the first-person narratives of a man, Richard Hannay, who is not given to looking at himself in the mirror and whose face therefore remains invisible. In the Hannay novels, a jaw that sticks out 'like a prize-fighter['s]' (1956b, 78) is the sign of a villain, though a minor one; the major villains, like the heroes, are masters of disguise. The kind of 'John Buchan hero' who would be instantly recognizable in the street is a film actor – such as Kenneth More in the 1959 movie *The 39 Steps* – rather than the protagonist of one of Buchan's novels.

A film actor must have a face that attracts attention, and if the plot requires him to go in disguise, that disguise is a secret shared with his audience. Disguise in a novel is very different, since if a narrator such as Hannay is taken in, so should the reader be. In Buchan this effect is so powerful that it often survives even a second or third reading of the novels. Disguise, then, is the first of a number of elements which convey the distinctive flavour of the five Hannay novels stretching from *The Thirty-Nine Steps* (1915) to *The Island of Sheep* (1936). The other elements that I shall discuss are riddles, the chase, allies and enemies, and the hero's progress from secret battlefield to a kind of Valhalla.

The Teller of Tales

John Buchan did not invent the spy thriller. The international arms race before World War I inspired many such novels, at least one of which, Erskine Childers's *The Riddle of the Sands* (1903), is still highly readable today. But *The Riddle of the Sands*, in which two amateur British yachtsmen stumble across the evidence of a German naval build-up, lacks the two 'staples' of the modern spy story that the critic Andrew Lownie has identified: the 'hunted man' and the 'mole within' (1995, 294). These are Buchan's territory. His characters are less stereotyped than Childers's, and his approach to the adventure novel is more deliberate and self-conscious even though Buchan, like Childers, was a political activist who would be remembered if he had never written a word of fiction. Childers, formerly a clerk in the House of Commons, became an extreme republican who was executed in 1922 by the Irish government; Buchan, who began his working life as an assistant to Lord Milner in South Africa, died in 1940 during his term of office as Governor-General of Canada.

Buchan published his first novel in 1895 while still an Oxford undergraduate. As a partner in the publishing firm of Thomas Nelson, he was moved to write his first memorable work, *Prester John* (1910) by his perception of the 'dullness of most boys' books' (Buchan 1940, 194). *The Thirty-Nine Steps* was meant to fill another gap in the market. The outbreak of war caused a slump in the publishing industry, and Buchan began a popular history of the war in monthly volumes in order to keep Nelson's presses running. His bestselling spy novel had much the same effect. As he explained in the dedicatory note to his partner Tommy Nelson, it was an example of 'that elementary type of tale which the Americans call the "dime novel," and which we know as the "shocker" – the romance where the incidents defy the probabilities, and march just inside the borders of the possible' (1922, 9). Buchan, who regarded himself as a natural storyteller, later described his novels as 'facile' (1940, 199), but clearly he knew exactly what he was doing even if he did not think it would stand up to literary criticism. Until very recently, most critics have been equally dismissive. John Gross, for instance, wrote in 1965 that 'one of the main reasons for enjoying Buchan is because he is so preposterous' (in Lownie 1995, 289).

Buchan *is* preposterous whenever he (or, his defenders would say, Hannay) repeats the Tory prejudices of his time: the racism, the anti-semitism, the imperial jingoism, the genteel misogyny. The British Empire and the white races are the centre of his world. His storytelling technique, however – with its reliance on coincidence, high melodrama, the thrill of danger, quick wits and the lucky escape – is no more preposterous than a Shakespearian romance or a Jane Austen comedy of manners. Or, at least, not much more preposterous. This is nowhere more evident than in his handling of the theme of disguise.

Cloak and Dagger

For most of *The Thirty-Nine Steps* Hannay is on the run, both from the sinister agents of the Black Stone and from the British police. He dodges pursuit in both London and Galloway thanks to his ability as a quick-change artist, posing successively as a milkman, a hill-farmer, a colonial mining magnate, a roadman, a metropolitan fop, a petty thief and a pack-shepherd. Even after making contact with the spymaster Sir Walter Bullivant he has to return to London disguised as Bullivant's chauffeur. These disguises usually succeed in concealing his identity from the police and from casual members of the public, but they do not fool the Black Stone, his real enemies – or only very briefly. In *Greenmantle* (1916) Hannay penetrates wartime Germany in the guise of an anti-British Boer, but in *Mr Standfast* (1919) his identity is known to the enemy agents from the moment of his entry into the pacifist community of Biggleswick in Chapter 2. Hannay often repeats the theories of disguise outlined by his South African comrade Peter Pienaar, and, in everyday life, his skill at acting a part – especially the part of a manual labourer such as 'Specky' the roadman or, in *Mr Standfast*, the Swiss porter Joseph Zimmer – is quite remarkable. But he is no match, in this respect, either for his best friend or for his worst enemy.

Although he appears in only two of the novels, Hannay's arch-enemy is the German agent finally unmasked at the end of *Mr Standfast* as the Graf von Schwabing. In *The Thirty-Nine Steps* he is the member of the Black Stone who, in one of Buchan's most audacious scenes, impersonates the First Sea Lord at a secret meeting of British and French defence chiefs. He goes unrecognized until he leaves the meeting and happens to walk past Hannay. Hannay, however, is not so quick to recognize him the next day, in the seaside house at the top of the 39 steps leading down to the unobtrusive jetty used by the German spies' getaway vessel. Nor does Hannay recognize the Graf von Schwabing in his next disguise as Moxon Ivery, the wealthy Biggleswick radical. It is only when, in a moment of crisis, the German count's mask-like features seem to 'dislimn' that he becomes known. As Hannay sums up in *The Thirty-Nine Steps*, 'He hadn't a face, only a hundred masks that he could assume when he pleased. That chap must have been a superb actor' (1922, 167). The fact that, for Buchan, disguise and acting are synonymous is just one indication that these novels were conceived and, mostly, written well before the great age of cinema. A successful film actor remains a well-known face in role after role, while a Buchan protagonist must merge into the background in order to survive.

Hannay, indeed, is not only deceived by his arch-enemy but also, time and again, by his friend and brother-officer Sandy Arbuthnot. Arbuthnot, not Hannay, is the British 'mole' who repeatedly penetrates a network of enemy agents, but when he does so he fools not only his enemies but the narrator as well. Thus Hannay (and nearly every reader) fails to recognize the leader of a band of whirling dervishes in *Greenmantle*, the Oriental sage in *The Three Hostages* (1924) and, most absurdly of all, the chief villain's scar-faced henchman in *The Island of Sheep*. 'God knows how he had managed it' (1956b, 229), Hannay reflects in the latter novel. Sandy Arbuthnot is to some extent modelled on T. E. Lawrence, the controversial war hero and proverbial 'Englishman who could pass as an Arab', but his cultural virtuosity far exceeds Lawrence's. He is shown as a guerrilla warfare expert in South

America, not Arabia, in a Buchan novel loosely related to the Hannay sequence, *The Courts of the Morning* (1929), and in *The Island of Sheep* he displays a knowledge of the Norland (Faroe) Islands' language and lore sufficient for the Norlander Anna Haraldsen to take him for a fellow-countryman. Sandy is the most gifted, the most magical figure in the Hannay novels. The part of the 'mole' suits him perfectly, since to maintain his credibility as a character it is necessary that his doings should remain mysterious and hidden from the reader for long periods.

The Puzzle and the Journey

Early on in nearly every Hannay novel we are introduced to Buchan's next characteristic narrative device, the riddle. When Hannay is on the run in *The Thirty-Nine Steps* he has with him the notebook of the dead agent Scudder, with its series of cryptic clues that Hannay has to unravel as if he were solving a crossword. The analogy is even closer in the next novel, with its three words on a torn sheet of notepaper left by the dying agent Harry Bullivant (Sir Walter's son) at a military outpost in Mesopotamia. Hannay and his associates puzzle over Bullivant's message from the outset of *Greenmantle*, but we are well into the narrative of *Mr Standfast* by the time the protagonist overhears three crucial names while spying on a secret U-boat rendezvous on the Isle of Skye. Buchan's technical self-consciousness is evident in Hannay's reflections on this occasion: 'Twice in the past three years I had had two such riddles to solve [*sic*] . . . I remembered how it had only been by constant chewing at them that I had got a sort of meaning, and I wondered if fate would some day expound this puzzle also' (1956c, 125). Needless to say, 'fate' does expound the puzzle. The device appears again in *The Three Hostages*, where a fragment of verse provides the key to the children's disappearance. Dr Greenslade, a minor character, holds forth on the use of the riddle in storytelling:

> 'Let us take three things a long way apart –' He paused for a second to consider – 'say, an old blind woman spinning in the Western Highlands, a barn in a Norwegian *saeter*, and a little curiosity shop in North London kept by a Jew with a dyed beard. Not much connexion between the three? You invent a connexion – simple enough if you have any imagination, and you weave all three into the yarn. The reader, who knows nothing about the three at the start, is puzzled and intrigued and, if the story is well arranged, finally

satisfied. He is pleased with the ingenuity of the solution, for he doesn't realize that the author fixed upon the solution first, and then invented a problem to suit it.' (1953, 12)

Hannay's response that '"You've gone and taken the gilt off my favourite light reading"' (12) suggests that he reads spy thrillers as well as starring in them; but, be that as it may, in the fifth novel, *The Island of Sheep*, Buchan introduced another riddle only to turn the joke back on his readers. A huge mystery surrounds the jade tablet purchased by Sandy Arbuthnot in a junk-shop in Peking, with an inscription in an unknown tongue. Supposedly it contains the location of the buried treasure sought by the international gang of criminals pursuing Valdemar Haraldsen, but, although Sandy has it translated, the meaning of the inscription is not revealed until the novel's final sentence.

Here Haraldsen is the hunted man, but in *The Thirty-Nine Steps* it is Hannay himself. In *Greenmantle* and *Mr Standfast* he is both hunter and hunted. Buchan was well aware of the importance to the thriller-writer of what he called the 'hurried journey' (1940, 194). These journeys often use what was then the new technology of aeroplanes and fast cars, but they also rely on the kindness of strangers, introducing a variety of mainly 'peasant' characters (crofters, boatmen, agricultural workers) who help Hannay on his way or give him shelter for the night. Buchan here draws on the tradition of Walter Scott, and he uses his own knowledge of the Scottish Borders and Highlands in all the novels except *Greenmantle*. In *Mr Standfast* Hannay travels in disguise from the 'red Clyde' to the Cuillins before escaping from Scotland thanks to a new character, the airman Sir Archie Roylance, who here makes his first appearance. Later in the novel Hannay drives a stolen car across the Alps from Switzerland to Italy only to be faced with the immediate necessity of returning on foot, in a forced march across the ice-fields led by Lancelot Wake, the pacifist who turns out to be both a staunch patriot and an experienced mountaineer. *The Island of Sheep* is the one novel to contain a classic car chase, from Northamptonshire up the Great North Road to the upper Tyne valley, though here it is not Hannay but his friend Lombard who is at the wheel of the Bentley pursued by a sinister yellow-and-black Stutz. Adding to the tension of most of these journeys is that the traveller, whether hunter or hunted, must arrive at a particular place by a particular time. In *Greenmantle*, for example, Hannay, a wanted man stricken with malaria, spends a wartime Christmas holed up in a snowbound cottage in the middle of the Bavarian forest. He has 3 weeks to get to his rendezvous in Constantinople. Buchan, as always, has fixed on the solution first (a train of barges sailing down the Danube with munitions for the Turkish government), and the reader is delighted with his ingenuity.

The journey is possibly the oldest device of fictional narrative, and Buchan must have encountered the hurried journey in the books he would have read as a boy: Robert Louis Stevenson's *Kidnapped* (1886) is a famous example. Buchan's particular ability lies in weaving what Bill Schwarz, mindful of the novelist's South African experience, calls the 'skills of *veld*-craft' into the journey narrative (2011, 268). Not only is the hero on the run in the position of a hunted wild animal, but also Buchan's 'chase' episodes tend to be set in open country such as a grouse moor or deer forest. At the end of *The Three Hostages* Hannay relies on his experience of stag-hunting for survival, while his 14-year-old son Peter John escapes his pursuers in *The Island of Sheep* thanks to an out-of-the-way piece of ornithological knowledge. Schwarz explains that Buchan's use of *veld*-craft in the novels reflects his preoccupation with the 'metaphysics of the frontier' – with the dangerous edge of experience unknown to the vast majority of his 'suburban-bound' readers (268). These readers – almost by definition sedentary, domestic and middle-class – have lost nearly all contact with the natural world and will never have to throw themselves on its resources. The spy novel and the chase-narrative offer a strictly vicarious experience of the lives of the fugitive and the outcast.

The White and the Dark

Hannay, the chance recipient of Scudder's confidences, is on his own for most of *The Thirty-Nine Steps* and thus truly an outcast. There are just three chapters to go when he has his first meeting with Sir Walter Bullivant, the Permanent Secretary at the Foreign Office. At the beginning of *Greenmantle*, however, he is recruited by Bullivant for a special mission and therefore becomes part of a worldwide network of secret agents: 'pedlars in South Russia, Afghan horse-dealers, Turcoman merchants, pilgrims on the road to Mecca, sheikhs in North Africa, sailors on the Black Sea coasters, sleek-skinned Mongols, Hindu fakirs, Greek traders in the Gulf', and the like (1956a, 18–19). Doubtless this romantic catalogue owes more to Kipling's *Kim* (1901) than it does to the realities of early twentieth-century British intelligence; and it has more relevance to the 'great game' of defending the Indian Empire than it does to war against Germany. As a recognized agent, however, Hannay is now a team player (and usually a team leader), and each of the subsequent novels shows him working together with a small band of allies. The choice of team-members suggests, above all, Buchan's desire to appeal to an ever-widening readership. Thus there are the Scottish laird Sandy Arbuthnot, the South African Peter Pienaar and the airman Archie Roylance. *Greenmantle* introduces John S. Blenkiron, a patriotic American who finds no difficulty in working for British intelligence even before the United States has entered World War I; one recent critic attributes Blenkiron's appearance to the fact that 'the allies badly desired U.S. support and . . . Buchan was becoming aware of the importance of wartime propaganda' (Macdonald 2009, 6). In *Mr Standfast* we meet Mary Lamington, who is not only Hannay's future bride but the first female British agent in Buchan's fiction, together with two demotic Glaswegians, the trade-unionist Andrew Amos and the fusilier Geordie Hamilton. All these characters reappear in subsequent novels. Finally, Buchan caters to the younger members of his audience with the youthful captives in *The Three Hostages* and the addition of two teenage recruits, Peter John Hannay and Anna Haraldsen, to the band of comrades in *The Island of Sheep*. That these groups of allies are heroes fighting a just cause is stressed in *Mr Standfast* by Buchan's pervasive analogy with John Bunyan's company of pilgrims.

The pilgrims, needless to say, are ranged against tightly knit groups of conspirators whose mutual loyalty and determination rivals their saintly opponents. The landscape of early twentieth-century war and criminality in the Hannay novels is one of an unremitting struggle between good and evil. This has two consequences. The evil characters present a reverse mirror-image of the good, and their defeat must take the form not of an efficient police round-up but of something closer to the one-to-one conflicts of ancient chivalry.

First of all, the arch-villains are either natural aristocrats (like Hannay) or hereditary aristocrats (like Sandy Arbuthnot), not common men. In *The Island of Sheep*, for example, Arbuthnot accepts a personal challenge from Jacques D'Ingraville, the lord of an Alpine château whose family goes back to the Crusades. Hannay is trapped and imprisoned by the 'Bald Archaeologist' in *The Thirty-Nine Steps*, and again by von Schwabing (one of the Archaeologist's co-conspirators) in *Mr Standfast*. He escapes each time but then insists, quite unnecessarily, on returning for a final single-handed confrontation with his enemies in their respective lairs. *The Three Hostages* ends likewise in one-to-one combat in a Scottish deer forest. This is the melodrama of spy fiction with which fans of James Bond and other more recent fictional special agents are familiar. In *Greenmantle*, Hannay, on his undercover travels through Germany, even secures a brief interview with the Kaiser himself. Buchan's band of saints and their evil opponents belong in a world of ruling-class privilege and power to which the ordinary citizen, and reader, can only have access in the pages of fiction.

How, then, are the good and the bad distinguished in these novels? It is here that Buchan's racial mythology comes into play. Hannay is not anti-German, since he recognizes that most Germans are good, honest people who play by the gentlemanly code. Nor, in this narrow sense, is he anti-semitic. Anti-semitism, however, is part of the atmosphere of the novels, as we see from Hannay's disingenuous comment about the banker Julius Victor: 'Blenkiron, who didn't like his race, had once described Victor to me as "the whitest Jew since the Apostle Paul"' (1953, 17; see also Macdonald 2009, 40–4). What others call the gentleman, Hannay, the former South African mining engineer, calls a 'white man'. Scudder identifies Hannay as a 'white man' at the beginning of their very short acquaintanceship in *The Thirty-Nine Steps* (1922, 23), and from then on Hannay finds his ideal of whiteness in the British secret service and the officer corps of the Army. When he is ordered by Bullivant to pose as a non-combatant and pacifist in Biggleswick, he moodily reflects that 'There are some things that no one has a right to ask of any white man' (1956c, 16) before buckling down to do his duty. He has no comparable objection to posing as a non-combatant in wartime Germany, since that is self-evidently highly dangerous. His chief embarrassment comes when he finds himself deceiving Germans who are themselves 'white men'; above all, the railway engineer Herr Gaudian, who will later join Hannay's company of saints as a result of a chance encounter by a Norwegian fjord in *The Three Hostages*. In *Greenmantle*, Gaudian is contrasted with the brutal homosexual Colonel Stumm: 'Gaudian was clearly a good fellow, a white man and a gentleman. I could have worked with him for he belonged to my own totem. But the other was an incarnation of all that made Germany detested' (1956a, 69). As the reference to his 'totem' suggests, 'whiteness' for Hannay is an expression of class as well as race. By the time of *The Island of Sheep* he has come to think of a country gentleman's existence as 'the only life for a white man' (1956b, 21).

As for the non-white races, their position in the human pecking-order is suggested when Sandy Arbuthnot speaks of the Arabs with the imperial condescension that Edward W. Said has taught us to call 'Orientalism': '"It's the humanity of one part of the human race. It isn't ours, it isn't as good as ours, but it's jolly good all the same"' (1956a, 184). And what about women, even 'white' women? In the first part of the sequence they are largely seen from a distance as, in Peter Pienaar's phrase, 'queer cattle' (1956c, 243). There are no significant women characters in *The Thirty-Nine Steps*. *Greenmantle* builds on the Mata Hari legend with the German spymistress Hilda von Einem, who frankly terrifies Hannay and finally dies a warrior's death. The women characters in the later novels of the sequence are excellent wives and mothers – appropriate partners, in fact, for a country gentleman who wishes to continue his line – but they are also essentially tomboys, as Lownie points out: 'Janet Roylance is a fine rifle shot while Mary Lamington talks like a member of a schoolboy sports team' (1995, 199). He might have added Anna Haraldsen, the pale-faced boarding-school girl who, once returned to her native islands, becomes not only an expert canoeist but the leader of a band of bloodstained whale-hunters intent on slaughtering the pirates who are threatening her father. By this time Buchan's racial mythology is clearly meant to appeal to girls as well as boys.

Homes Fit for Heroes

In *The Island of Sheep*, Buchan's interest in the mythological backgrounds to adventure fiction is also much more explicit than it had been earlier. Defenceless in the world of southern English domesticity, Haraldsen and his daughter come into their own when they take on the combative roles of ancient Norse heroes. But in the end a warrior must either get killed or retire from the fray, and in Norse mythology the home for dead heroes was Valhalla. Hannay, too, feels the need to make a home for himself and settle down after World War I. Although the phrase is never used by Buchan, his post-war novels remind us that the British prime minister, David Lloyd George, had promised in a famous parliamentary speech in November 1918 that he would 'make Britain a fit country for heroes to live in'.

Behind the frenzied journeys recounted in each Hannay novel there is a longer journey, the transformation of the colonial mining engineer Dick Hannay into his namesake Sir Richard Hannay, KCB. *The Three Hostages* and *The Island of Sheep* show the country gentleman and retired soldier brought back to life, as it were, as Sir Richard proves to be the old Dick Hannay in disguise. When Valdemar Haraldsen comes to England to seek out the South African engineer who swore a pact with his father, he meets

Sir Richard on a shooting holiday but does not dream that it is the same man. "'In you I saw only an English general and a grandee'", he later explains (1956b, 73). The transformation is from a hard-boiled colonial adventurer to the epitome of English respectability, but it is not just that. Hannay has fulfilled the imperial dream of retiring to the 'mother country' after a life on the frontiers, but he is also a confirmed bachelor and 'man's man' enjoying the comforts of marriage, and, still more significantly, a Scotsman who has become an Englishman. In this he is closest to Buchan himself. Buchan spent less than 2 years (from September 1901 to August 1903) in South Africa; but he had earlier begun the process of Anglicization by moving from Glasgow University to take his degree at Oxford.

Scotland and South Africa are the background of the young Hannay, and at first he is shown as chippy, disillusioned and ill at ease in London. 'I returned from the City about three o'clock on that May afternoon pretty well disgusted with life. I had been three months in the Old Country, and was fed up with it' (1922, 11). These are the opening words of The Thirty-Nine Steps, but it is remarkable how quickly the mood and personality that they reveal is discarded and forgotten. By the end of the novel he has begun lifelong friendships with Sir Walter Bullivant and the head of Scotland Yard, and is hobnobbing on equal terms with the French Minister of War. Eighteen months later, at the beginning of Greenmantle, he is an infantry officer already marked out as a future commander. The undisciplined loner of The Thirty-Nine Steps is now thoroughly at home in the British Army. Once recruited by Bullivant, however, he poses as a Dutch South African until Blenkiron gives him a new identity as an American mining expert. He joins up with Peter Pienaar, for whom "'There is only one white man's land, and that is South Africa'" (1956a, 134). Peter eventually becomes a fighter ace in the Royal Flying Corps but he will never be an Englishman or, indeed, a European. Hannay in his most imaginative moments is also deeply South African. The Galloway moors remind him of the *veld*, and a railway halt in the heart of a bog suggests 'one of those forgotten little stations in the Karroo' (1922, 41, 76). He compares the Cuillins in *Mr Standfast* to Damaraland and the Drakensberg (1956c, 101, 109). Travelling across Turkey in Greenmantle, he dreams of taking cover on 'a rum little hill with a rocky top: what we call in South Africa a *castrol*' (1956a, 195). He finds his *castrol*, and he and his friends stage a last-ditch defence there until saved by the Russian cavalry. Later in the sequence, however, these South African visions fade, and his imagination is dominated by the English landscape.

Buchan places the moment of conversion early in *Mr Standfast*, when Hannay first sets eyes on his future home in the Cotswolds, Fosse Manor: 'Before my country had been South Africa. . . . But now I realized that I had a new home. I understood what a precious thing this little England was, how old and kindly and comforting, how wholly worth striving for. The freedom of an acre of her soil was cheaply bought by the blood of the best of us' (1956c, 21). Hannay has found his Valhalla, and no sooner has he arrived there than he meets his future partner, Mary Lamington, who is upper-class Englishness personified. Fosse Manor belongs to her aunts.

After the war, Hannay's contentment with Mary at Fosse becomes a byword among his friends and, at least in *The Courts of the Morning*, something of a joke. In terms of the parable of *The Pilgrim's Progress*, he is the pilgrim who has reached the end of his journey and passed over to the other side. The country house is his Heavenly City. But from time to time he grows restless and discontented with this complacent domesticity, hence *The Three Hostages* and *The Island of Sheep*. Mary takes an active part in the former novel, and at one point Hannay sees 'my own wedded wife' transformed into an avenger out of Norse mythology, 'a stern goddess that wielded the lightnings' (1953, 248). We need such reminders that Fosse Manor is indeed a Valhalla, a home not for an ordinary upper-class family but for heroes and gods. This is made explicit in *The Island of Sheep*, where the island in the Norlands is Haraldsen's paradise, just as Fosse Manor is Hannay's and Laverlaw in the Scottish Borders is Arbuthnot's (1956a, 241–2). The heroes of romance do not die, but fade away like old soldiers into their country estates. For Sir Richard Hannay, unlike the Scots Sandy Arbuthnot and Archie Roylance and the Norlander Valdemar Haraldsen, Valhalla is rural southern England. It is a world that Hannay first entered in the chapter of *The Thirty-Nine Steps* called 'The Dry-Fly Fisherman' (1922, 111–26), the fisherman being Sir Walter Bullivant at his weekend retreat in the Kennet Valley. They return to London the next morning, suggesting the connection between the twentieth-century idealization of southern England and the invention of the motor car. (Buchan himself had left Glasgow and the Scottish Borders for a manor-house near Oxford which, once again, was highly convenient for a London publisher and Member of Parliament.)

'The freedom of an acre of [England's] soil was cheaply bought by the blood of the best of us': those words were first published in 1919, within a year of the Armistice, and they should be read in the light of that age's need to justify the First World War's sacrifices. But they also reveal a final aspect of the spy thriller. Buchan's inspiration, and that of his successors, owes everything to the emotional appeal of nationalism and national alliances. The Hannay novels will continue to exert their spell until we have entered a more peaceable world, a world freed at last of global warfare and deadly international rivalries. If that were to happen, we should have found our Valhalla and would no longer need the mythology of spy fiction, though we might miss its excitements.

Works Cited

Buchan, John (1922), *The Thirty-Nine Steps, in The Thirty-Nine Steps and The Power House*. London: Thomas Nelson & Sons.

—(1940), *Memory Hold-the-Door*. London: Hodder & Stoughton.

—(1953), *The Three Hostages*. Harmondsworth: Penguin.

—(1956a), *Greenmantle*. Harmondsworth: Penguin.

—(1956b), *The Island of Sheep*. Harmondsworth: Penguin.

—(1956c), *Mr Standfast*. Harmondsworth: Penguin.

Lownie, Andrew (1995), *John Buchan: The Presbyterian Cavalier*. Edinburgh: Canongate.

Macdonald, Kate (2009), *John Buchan: A Companion to the Mystery Fiction*. Jefferson, NC and London: McFarland.

Neville, Jill (1991), 'Common Decency', in Marsha Rowe (ed.), *So Very English*. London: Serpent's Tail, pp. 106–16.

Schwarz, Bill (2011), *Memories of Empire. Volume I: The White Man's World*. Oxford: Oxford University Press.

12

Manipulating Popularity: A Case Study of Ian Fleming's James Bond Series

Juan F. Elices[1]

Whenever we delve into the James Bond universe, there are questions that seem to be inextricably linked to this figure and which have defined both the literary and filmic character. Glamour, luxury, elegance and occasional extravagances have modelled Ian Fleming's creation in such a way that Bond emerges as one of the most recognizable icons in contemporary popular culture. The year 2012 saw the 50th anniversary of the first James Bond motion picture and, considering the commercial impact this series has generated, it is not surprising that the so-called James Bond industry continues to be one of the most fruitful and profitable. Paradoxically, and even though Bond's concerns no longer accord with the current political climate, he still draws the attention of academics, film critics and ordinary citizens alike, who see him as the incarnation of a thrilling lifestyle of adventures, money and endless pleasures (see Chapman 2005, 135).

Nonetheless, this external façade has quite often concealed a series of issues that scholars and critics have tried to decipher in an attempt to present a more humanized, down-to-earth and even critical vision of this character. From 1953, the year in which *Casino Royale* was first published, James Bond has been recurrently depicted as a womanizer and misogynist, a racist and an unbearable snob. Being such a global phenomenon, and although Bond has traditionally embodied the ethos of the typical British gentleman, his figure has been the object of profound scrutiny by both the reading public and the academic community. And it is precisely due to Bond's international repercussion that this character has been approached and interpreted from many divergent viewpoints and at very different historical moments. The purpose of this chapter is to analyse the reception of the James Bond series and, in particular, how censorship succeeded in coercing the popularity and circulation that these novels had in Spain. Via this case study, the chapter also aims to raise some general points about the relationship between the 'State', on the one hand, and 'popular culture', on the other.

The Role of Censorship in Franco's Spain

The establishment and consolidation of the Spanish censorship board finds its origins in the Civil War (1936–9) that devastated the country and which raised General Francisco Franco to power in 1939. Franco's victory marked a turning point not only in the history of the country, embarking on a dictatorship that was to last until his death in 1975, but also in the international liaisons the dictator managed to forge with other emergent fascist regimes, especially Hitler's Germany and Mussolini's Italy. It has been widely observed that the relation of these powers with culture was always characterized by a profound sense of distrust and suspicion. If we focus specifically on literature, the authorities took for granted that an exhaustive control of anything that was written and published was the most reliable means to cut down on the amount of 'menacing' information that citizens could have access to. The purpose underlying this policy was to manipulate and control the population and to do away with any hint of critical and/or liberal thinking. Although censorship has been an unavoidable part of the cultural ethos of most countries, it seems that its presence was prevailing in those that shared certain similarities in terms of their socio-political and religious make up. Broadly speaking, censorship is a mechanism of intellectual control, ideological surveillance and, on most occasions, threat and punishment, and it is inevitably, though not solely, associated with any expression of authoritarianism. As in most dictatorships, Francoist advocates nurtured an irrational atmosphere of hysteria in which the invention of false enemies and external threats was a recurrent strategy to propagate fear and, consequently, submission among citizens. Ordinary people were only allowed to read those documents that were sanctioned by the government and could only watch those programmes that celebrated the nation's past and present glories.

The Spanish censorship board that started to operate once Franco took over power was firmly sustained by the principles that governed the dictator's own strict vision of morality, and it primarily sought to filter all those publications – either fiction, poetry, journals, essays or plays – that could be considered 'pernicious' for the readers' minds. The limitations imposed upon particular authors were not based on their intrinsic literary qualities but were mostly grounded on the arbitrariness of the board that was appointed to read and evaluate this or that work. It is now widely known that the profile of most censors did not fully respond to this image of infallibility and rigour that was officially transmitted. According to Spanish journalist and writer Georgina Cisquella, most members of this board were selected not because they excelled in their intellectual capacities but mainly because they epitomized and protected the regime's one-dimensional moral, ideological and religious outlooks. Cisquella points out that censors were either civil servants, who worked directly or indirectly for the Ministry, or priests, as embodiments of the country's spiritual integrity (1977, 44–5). It is, therefore, easy to conclude that their approach to the complexities of a literary work was not very reliable and, worst of all, the reports that were issued after the reading of a particular book were sustained almost exclusively on arbitrary opinions and not on solid judgements and interpretations. However, and in spite of these obvious deficiencies, the social reputation of censors was unquestionable and the influence they exerted upon writers, editors and entire publishing houses was very effective. If 'popular culture' and 'popular literature' could generally, and perhaps rather naïvely, be taken to be expressions of the populace's unmediated cultural and literary predilections, then the heavy-handed presence of the Spanish censorship board seemed set to end any kind of popular engagement in the country's culture.

Literature, Censorship and the Popular: The James Bond Series

How, then, does this affect a popular *British* literary creation that had become a global phenomenon? Censorship of books in Spain did affect not only local anti-Franco activists, but also many foreign authors who were systematically accused of being politically oriented towards the former Republican government. Studies such as Douglas La Prade's *La censura de Hemingway en España (Hemingway's Censorship in Spain* (1991), Alberto Lazaro's various works on the reception of H. G. Wells, George Orwell or Sheridan LeFanu (2004), among others, or Marisol Morales' recent analysis on the reception of Kate O'Brien in Franco's Spain (2010) demonstrate that overseas literature was also rigidly controlled and regulated. The reactions among international writers were not uniform; some accepted that their books were manipulated (as in the case of Fleming) while others challenged the censors' decisions. The consequences of this are very significant and they can even be observed nowadays, as many of the books read in contemporary Spain are versions that were mutilated from the 1940s up to the 1970s. Jordi Cornellà-Detrell points out that some of *Dr No*'s current editions are still those that were heavily censored during Franco's times: 'The Catalan and the Spanish 1965 and 1974 texts . . . were reprinted again, in 1996 and 2003 respectively, which means that both the abridged [i.e. censored] and unabridged [i.e. uncensored] versions are currently on sale' (136). Although censorship in Spain was abolished after Franco's death, its damaging effects over literature are, as Cornellà-Detrell asserts, still present 40 years later.

Focusing particularly on Fleming and his James Bond series, it is easy to appreciate the incongruities and inconsistencies that marked the activities of the Spanish censorship board and that can be repeatedly noticed in the reports issued by its members. To better understand this case, it is important to provide a brief comparative overview of the historical situation of both Great Britain and Spain at the time Fleming's novels started to be imported and translated in the latter. As Christine Berberich (2012) has noted, Fleming's novels were a clear product of their time, representing a Britain that had started to witness great many social, political, religious and 'moral' changes. Berberich suggests that, for example, the novels' prolific use of erotic scenes and gratuitous sex is symptomatic of the increasing sexual liberation the country enjoyed throughout the 1950s and, particularly, the early 1960s (19).

If Great Britain represented the careless and optimistic spirit of the 'Swinging Sixties' after a sombre and turbulent post-war period, Spain, by contrast, was immersed in a period of profound economic shortages and political unpredictability. The differences among social classes were unbridgeable and power was almost exclusively circumscribed to a very limited oligarchy of aristocrats, military men and renowned church members who exemplified the most backward and obsolete values of a clearly decadent country and who displayed unreserved loyalty and devotion to the Franco regime. Spanish families replicated this hierarchical pattern, with women increasingly ostracized and relegated to a purely domestic environment and with men emerging as the uncontested patriarchal leaders. Contrary to the increasing emancipation that the female population started to enjoy in Britain, the role of women during Franco's dictatorship proves that Spanish society was moving in the opposite direction. The marginalization of women at a social level led many Spanish writers and censors to stigmatize them as inherently sinful creatures and, therefore, dangerous examples for the general readership.

Discussing the role of women under Franco's dictatorship seems to be a good starting point to deal with some of the elements that turned Fleming's novels into a remarkable target for Spanish censorship. The relationship of female characters with James Bond is surely one of the most polemical and debated issues. The presence of women in these works is preeminent, although the narrative space they occupy is, to say the least, rather subsidiary. In that respect, the Bond novels are also patriarchal and hierarchical. Kingsley Amis, for example, points out that 'Bond's attitude to women in the mass is not respectful. Masculine domination is the natural state of affairs between the sexes, he ruminates after one of his rare rebuffs' (1965, 47), summarizing quite accurately that, in spite of the gradual liberation experienced by British women, there were some remnants that still traced back to very conservative assumptions. Simply by reading a Bond novel or watching any of the film versions, it is easy to observe that women always respond to a set of very stereotypical paradigms that are solely constructed as a means to meet Bond's expectations and, with him, those of other males. As Tony Bennett and Janet Woollacott also suggest: 'Typically, in such contexts, the figure of Bond served as an ideological shorthand for the appropriate image of masculinity in relation to which feminine sexual identities were to be constructed' (2003, 24). For him, women come to represent simply another must-have accessory at his personal disposal, whose only end is to satisfy his most primary needs. As Robert Arp and Kevin Decker argue, Bond's attitude towards women falls into a clearly objectifying category that turns them into mere things (2006, 202), an attitude shared by Cynthia Baron who points out that the use of the word 'girls' for Bond's women 'objectif[ies] and infantalise[s]' them (2003b, 172). In all his adventures, most female characters are invariably seduced by 007's masculinity and attractive personality, which indirectly enable both Bond and Fleming himself to justify their respective position as regards women.

Interestingly, and despite increasing sexual liberation in the Western hemisphere and the popularity of the Bond novels, there was, even in Great Britain and the United States, some reluctance to publish a Bond novel without expurgating some passages, complete pages or even chapters that violated the norms of *decorum*. In the blog 'The Bondologist', which analyses the cultural impact of James Bond on contemporary society, we can find an illuminating review of the novels and films that were either edited, censored or banned in various countries around the world (see Anonymous n.d., n.p.). The common idea that the adventurous and popular spirit of the Bond stories made them harmless or innocuous turns out to clash with how they were actually received and catalogued. In Ireland, a nation with a long-standing and severe Catholic tradition, for example, most Bond novels that were published in the 1950s and 1960s were heavily censored for breach of religious (read: moral) standards. *Live and Let Die*, for instance, was banned outright in 1954 (see Anonymous, n.d., n.p.). Many of Fleming's works were categorized as indecent and overtly explicit in their treatment of sex and were subsequently banned by the Irish censorship board. In a similar vein, Amis argues that Bond's values were highly questionable, a fact that indirectly legitimized the censors to cut off all that was not permissible on sexual, religious or moral grounds: 'The moral content of Mr Fleming's work, the values expressed or implied, whether through Bond or directly by the author, have been denounced all over the place. . . . *The Spy who Loved Me* was banned in Australia and the Central African Federation' (1965, 84). Obviously, the growing popularity of the Bond novels was taken as a threat for the moral well-being of the population, a fact that explains why they became very habitual targets not only for the Spanish censorship board.

The removal of any veiled or open reference to sex and eroticism was thus a top priority for censors. In the case of the Bond novels, the reports submitted by the censorship board demonstrate that the only aim was to erase any word or passage that might contain a sexual implication. If we analyse these annotations, it is noteworthy that Franco's censorship merely focused on limiting and expurgating scenes in which any allusion to sex is contained. However, many episodes where women are openly humiliated or harassed remain uncensored. This points to widely taken-for-granted assumptions about the inherent inferiority of women and their unquestioned dependence on the male authority and guidance. Depicting women being manipulated by male characters implies that censors consciously legitimized the idea that women deserved to be punished.

Among the Bond novels, *Dr No* is by far the most thoroughly censored, as it includes many episodes in which Bond and Honeychile Rider express their passion in a more uninhibited way. Nonetheless, and it is here where the paradox about the Spanish censorship lies, there are many instances in which Bond abuses Honeychile both physically and psychologically; scenes that did not trouble the censors as they seemed to confirm that women are innately dangerous and provocative. In the following excerpt, borrowed from the 1965 Spanish edition of *Dr No*, we can very clearly see the extent to which the board aimed at enhancing the submission of women:

> Vacillating, Bond told her: 'Honey, if you don't get into the bathtub right now, I will slap you.' Smiling and not uttering a single word, she obeyed. Once she was in, she stretched her entire body. Her blond hair shone through the water like golden coins. Then she stared at him and told him provocatively: 'You have to bathe me. I don't know how to do it. Come on, show me how it's done!' Desperately, Bond replied: 'Shut up, at once, Honey, and stop tempting me, damn it! This is not the right moment to make love' [My translation]. (Report 976-65, file 21-15896, 1965)[2]

It is not only the patronizing stance Bond adopts with respect to Honeychile, who is addressed as though she were a baby that needs to be enlightened that is relevant. If we read the complete report, we can see that the only parts that are crossed out are those that contain references to Honey's 'firm breasts' or to her 'mound of Venus', something that, at the time, was simply scandalous. Bond's humiliating, patronizing attitude towards Honey, by contrast, so troubling to a present-day readership, simply confirms the Francoist regime's beliefs that women deserved this treatment and that their marginalization in Spanish society was completely justified.

Another example of the deliberate decision to keep passages that present an image of women as inferior creatures can be found in *On Her Majesty's Secret Service* (1963). In the file that can be consulted at the Administration's General Archive (Alcalá de Henares), we find the English version of the novel edited by Pan Books. One simple glance at its pages reveals that it also underwent severe mutilation through the censors, which once again focused on the same 'indecent' content. In an impeccable manifestation of moral rectitude, the censor eliminates all that might have an obscene implication but, curiously, 'forgets' that women are more than simple objects. The following extract appears completely mutilated in the book: '"Take off those clothes. Make love to me. . . . I remember what it can be like. Do anything you like. . . . Be rough with me. Treat me like the lowest whore in creation. . . . Take me"' (Report 4836-65, file 21-16388, 1965). In this same quote, the sentence 'And tell me what you like and what you would like from me' is maintained, which shows that Bond's male chauvinism seemed to accord with the regime's agenda on gender differences.

In certain novels, the censors' attitude towards Fleming's female characters is also applied to their treatment of racism, which is lamentably prominent in Fleming's work. His frequent stays in Jamaica, where he built his 'Goldeneye' estate, led Fleming to manifest a typically 'Orientalist' attitude towards the black population, which he considered inferior and backward. According to Paul Stock: 'Bond's presence on the margins of empire is an attempt to retain paternalistic and empowered positions in a 'post-colonial' era. But the resonance of that rendering of Britishness hints at a new age of colonialism. . . . The sun might just have set on the British Empire, but the ideologies are pervasive, and the traces maintain a resonance in the former colonies' (2003, 225). As an epitome of the most conservative Western values, Bond's racism stems from his attempt to restore a vanishing world order, in which the British empire would once again recuperate its former leadership. Therefore, the intersection of his abusive disposition regarding women and minority races can be perceived in many of his adventures. *Live and Let Die* (1954) exemplifies this, as it presents a black female character whom Bond dehumanizes in racial and sexual terms. Jeremy Black points out that 'the frequency of his references and his willingness to offer racial stereotypes, typical of many writers of his age, jars on the modern consciousness and are ignored or understated in the films' (2005, 12). Cynthia Baron similarly suggests that: 'Cold War and sexual adventures masked the fact that Bond was an imperial hero who provided a way for Britishness to continue to be defined in opposition to the 'dark' people of the world' (2003a, 136). Once again, however, the censor simply eradicates sensual or erotic language but does not address the racial overtones used to describe the character:

> Her lips were slightly separated from her teeth. Her nostrils started to tremble shakily. Her pupils shone through the diamond slots of her mask. . . . Her countenance was very sexual, almost bitchy. A *chienne*, it was the only thing he could say about her [My translation]. (Report 73-3461, File 10616-73, 1973)[3]

The fact that these racist comments are not censored in the Spanish translations might respond to the socio-political atmosphere that prevailed in the country. Franco's racial policy was similar, though not so extreme, to that of Hitler or Mussolini in the sense that the dictator's intentions were to uphold the ancient origins of the so-called 'Spanish race'. The animalized image of this black woman and how the censor disregards its pejorative implications point, therefore, to a reality that was deeply rooted in the subconscious of wide sectors of the Spanish population and which the State tried its hardest to maintain and strengthen.

Censorship, the State and the Manipulation of the Popular

Bond's reception in Spain thus echoes what happened in other countries – Ireland is a prominent example here – as censorship in both countries seemed to focus on sexual issues driven by moral and religious righteousness. These 'moral' preoccupations, however, were a mere front for a deeper rooted *political* motivation behind censorship. In Spain, all authors deemed politically suspicious by the authorities had to seek permission to print and circulate their work. This granted the board of censors the mechanisms – both licit and illicit – to approve or disapprove the publication of any written document. The process was systematic: all censors had to fill in a form that addressed a number of questions before eventually submitting their report. The content of these questions would read as follows: (1) Does it attack: the dogma, the morals, the Church or its priests, the regime or its institutions, the people who have worked for or collaborated with the regime? (2) The excerpts that are likely to be censored, do they qualify the work's overall content?

As can be perceived, censors had to pay close attention to whether or not the work that was under review showed a single trace of anti-Catholicism or criticism against the government. At the very beginning of Franco's dictatorship, censorship was ruthless and mutilated thousands of works that were 'only apparently' threatening for the country.[4] The number of taboo issues was countless but there were some such as communism, sex, heresy or atheism that were always crossed out in red. Related to this last question, Alberto Lázaro alludes to the 1938 Press Law passed in Spain in order to control and punish all those documents that sought to undervalue the prestige of the nation or to inculcate pernicious ideas in those that were categorized as intellectually weak (2004, 23). This law assumed that literature could contaminate the mind of readers since it could be used as a vehicle to transmit the values of the former Republican government, the communist ideals that were beginning to germinate in the incipient Soviet Union or any critical opinion about the Church.

Fleming's novels, as has been shown, were strictly censored when it came to *sexual* content. Nevertheless, censors did say very little, almost nothing at all, about their *ideological* background. Fleming's active participation in the British Intelligence Service and his inherent conservatism led him to approach Communism as a clear and present danger. As Umberto Eco brilliantly suggests, it is difficult 'to maintain that Fleming is not inclined to consider the British superior to all Oriental or Mediterranean races or that Fleming does not profess heartfelt anti-Communism' (2003, 45). Fleming's work manifests an unequivocal rejection of the Soviet Union and its socialist regime that must have thrilled the fascist regime in Spain. According to the majority of reports submitted by the Spanish censors, Fleming's positioning with respect to the USSR and the Communist threat was warmly welcomed as he was able to identify a common menace. Bond's actions were generally celebrated as he always succeeded in defeating communism, represented by the USSR and its satellite countries. In *From Russia with Love* (1957), in which Bond tries to overcome his Russian archenemy SMERSH, we can find the only moment in this series in which Franco's Spain is ever mentioned. Although the connotations are rather negative, there is no single comment about Spain being overtly labelled as a Fascist country. Nevertheless, it was not until the 1998 edition that the complete paragraph was included:

> We can discard Italy –argued General Vozdvishenski . . . They are active and intelligent, but they are harmless. They are only interested in their backyard,

the Mediterranean. The same could be said about Spain, except for the fact that its counterintelligence turns out to be a great hindrance for our Party. We have lost many great men at the hands of these fascists [My translation]. (41–2)

Censors thus found themselves navigating an ideological minefield as they glorified the accomplishments of a British secret agent who epitomized the values of a country that struggled against the Nazi-Fascist axis of which Franco was a widely known supporter.

Censorship has thus played an important part in the history of the popular success story that is the James Bond series. However, it seems that the response of the Spanish readership was remarkable, as the action-packed and thrilling Bond adventures appealed to a population condemned to passivity and backwardness by those in power. The success of these novels during Franco's dictatorship can be attested by their gradually increasing print-runs, which reached figures that can be compared to some of the most popular national and international writers. And who knows what their sales figures would have been like if they had been printed unaltered? According to the vast numbers of reports that were compiled on Fleming's works, Bond embodies most of the taboos that the Spanish censors categorized as dangerous and condemnable. But despite the arbitrariness of most decisions adopted by the members of the censorship board, the world of glamour and luxury James Bond represents was a source of fascination, or maybe simple escapism, for the Spanish readers.

At the beginning of this chapter, it was suggested that censorship has been an intrinsic part of the idiosyncrasy of most countries, even those that have more passionately defended their firm democratic stance and ideals. However, Ronald Paulson very illuminatingly points to the words of the Earl of Shaftesbury when he revolved around the controversial relation between censorship and satire, *ergo*, between the state and the literary realm. When Shaftesbury argued that 'the higher the slavery, the more exquisite the buffoonery' (1967, 264), he was implicitly assuming that, even though the mechanisms to mutilate, ban or exorcise a literary work could not be apparently avoided altogether, there were always formal and stylistic loopholes that allowed writers to avoid the pressures of censorship. This chapter has attempted to demonstrate, on the one hand, that Ian Fleming's James Bond novels were the object of severe persecution by the Spanish censors, but that, in the long run, they did not manage to restrict the growing popularity of the secret agent's adventures, on the other.

Censorship, in this sense, only operates effectively up to a certain extent, due to the conspicuous deficiencies and lack of reading comprehension among those who were designated to judge whether a book should be permitted or not. It is precisely the role of these censors that highlights the incongruities that underlie not only this very system but, broadly speaking, the essence of any dictatorial regime. The censors formed part of an extremely well-reputed minority that was surreptitiously appointed by the regime simply because they could uphold and preserve its ideological foundations and, more importantly, could be easily manipulated. In the hands of this group of 'dilettantes' lay the responsibility of supervising the cultural development of a country and promoting good reading practices among citizens. As Stuart Hall wisely suggests in one of his articles on George Orwell, it is precisely this 'concentration of power in the hands of a small elite, the breakdown of older, class-based social systems into new kinds of division between "élites" and "masses", the power of élites in manipulating mass consciousness through the use of authoritarian symbols' what censorship clings on to in order to empower and justify its legitimate right to control the population (1984, 235). Although sometimes understated, the relationship of the 'State' with culture and, more specifically, with 'popular culture' has always been driven by a need to control, regulate and filter any written document that might endanger the hierarchical structures that prevail in any country.

Notes

1. This paper has been elaborated thanks to the invaluable help of the staff at the Administration's General Archive (Alcalá de Henares, Madrid) and the financial support of the National Research project 'La familia disfuncional como efecto de la globalización en la producción narrativa y fílmica irlandesa (1980-2010) [FFI2011-23941]'.
2. It was stated above that the Spanish censorship was not characterized by its consistency. In Fleming's case, this is recurrently manifested in the different responses that his Bond novels had among censors. To follow with *Dr No*, we can see that, depending on the reader, the passages, words or sentences that were deleted differed a great deal. In the Catalan version of *Dr No*, published in the same year and also evaluated by the censorship board, all the excerpts that were considered morally unacceptable in the Spanish version were included without any

significant problem. To see this difference, it can worth reading the Spanish original words:

> 'Titubeando, Bond le dijo: "Nena, si no te metes en esa bañera, te daré unos azotes."' Sonriendo y sin pronunciar una palabra, obedeció. Una vez dentro extendiéndose en ella de cuerpo entero. El vello rubio de su cuerpo resplandecía a través del agua como moneditas de oro. Entonces, alzando la mirada, le dijo provocativamente: 'Tienes que lavarme. Yo no sé cómo se hace. ¡Anda, enséñame!' Desesperadamente, Bond le respondió: '¡Cállate de una vez Honey, y deja de tentarme! ¡Maldita sea! No es éste el momento de hacer el amor.'

3. The Spanish original version reads as follows: 'Tenía los labios ligeramente separados de los dientes. Las aletas de su nariz empezaron a agitarse temblorosamente. Sus pupilas relucían a través de las diamantíferas ranuras de su antifaz. Su rostro era muy sexual, casi perruna. . . . Una chienne fue el único calificativo que se le ocurrió a Bond.'

4. Censorship in Spain went through three main stages, starting in 1938. In 1966, Manuel Fraga Iribarne passed a New Press Law, which seemed to grant more freedom to writers. Finally, after Franco's death in 1975, censorship practically disappeared and the boards were progressively dismantled (Morales 2010, 12).

Works Cited

Amis, Kingsley (1965), *The James Bond Dossier*. London: Jonathan Cape.

Anonymous (n.d.), 'James Bond Novels that Were Edited, Censored and Banned'. *The Bondologist Blog*, http://thebondologistblog.blogspot.com. es/2012/08/james-bond-novels-that-were-edited.html, accessed 24 November 2010.

Arp, Robert and Kevin S. Decker (2006), 'That Fatal Kiss: Bond, Ethics and the Objectification of Women', in James B. South and Jacob M. Held (eds), *James Bond and Philosophy: Questions are Forever*. Chicago and La Salle: Open Court, pp. 201–14.

Baron, Cynthia (2003a), '*Dr No*: Bonding Britishness to Racial Sovereignty', in Christoph Lindner (ed.), *The James Bond Phenomenon: A Critical Reader*. Manchester and New York: Manchester University Press, pp. 135–50.

—(2003b), 'Under the Very Skirts of Britannia: Re-reading Women in the James Bond Novels', in Christoph Lindner (ed.), *The James Bond Phenomenon: A Critical Reader*. Manchester and New York: Manchester University Press, pp. 169–83.

Bennett, Tony and Janet Woollacott (2003), 'The Moments of Bond', in Christoph Lindner (ed.), *The James Bond Phenomenon: A Critical Reader*. Manchester and New York: Manchester University Press, pp. 13–33.

Berberich, Christine (2012), 'Putting England Back on Top? Ian Fleming, James Bond, and the Question of England'. *Yearbook of English Studies* 42, 13–29.

Black, Jeremy (2005), *The Politics of James Bond: From Fleming's Novels to the Big Screen*. Lincoln and London: University of Nebraska Press.

Chapman, James (2005), 'Bond and Britishness', in Edward P. Comentale et al. (eds), *Ian Fleming & James Bond: The Cultural Politics of 007*. Bloomington and Indianapolis: Indiana University Press, pp. 129–43.

Cisquella, Georgina, et al. (1977), *Diez años de represión cultural: La censura de libros durante la Ley de Prensa (1966-1976)*. Barcelona: Anagrama.

Cornellà-Detrell, Jordi (2013), 'The Afterlife of Francoist Cultural Policies: Censorship and Translation in the Catalan and Spanish Literary Market'. *Hispanic Research Journal* 14(2), 129–43.

Eco, Umberto (2003), 'Narrative Structures in Fleming', in Christoph Lindner (ed.), *The James Bond Phenomenon: A Critical Reader*. Manchester and New York: Manchester University Press, pp. 34–55.

Fleming, Ian (1998 [1957]), *Desde Rusia con Amor*. Barcelona: RBA.

Hall, Stuart (1984), 'Conjuring Leviathan: Orwell on the State', in Christopher Norris (ed.), *Inside the Myth. Orwell: Views from the Left*. London: Lawrence and Wishart, pp. 217–42.

Lázaro, Alberto (2004), *H.G. Wells en España: Estudio de los expedientes de censura (1939-1978)*. Madrid: Verbum.

Morales, Marisol (2010), 'Banned in Spain? Truth, Lies and Censorship in Kate O'Brien's Novels'. *Atlantis: The Journal of the Spanish Association of Anglo-American Studies* 32(1), 9–24.

Paulson, Ronald (1967), *The Fictions of Satire*. Baltimore: The Johns Hopkins Press.

Stock, Paul (2003), 'Dial "M" for Metonymy: Universal Exports, M's Office Space and Empire', in Christoph Lindner (ed.), *The James Bond Phenomenon: A Critical Reader*. Manchester and New York: Manchester University Press, pp. 215–31.

13

Subverting the Romance: The Fiction of Sarah Waters

Joanne Bishton

Introduction

With its emphasis on sexual difference, the very notion that romance should play a significant role in lesbian fiction may well be a source of surprise for readers of this chapter.[1] As has already been discussed in this book, romance, as a literary genre, is littered with heterosexist ideology and motifs that have contributed towards the Othering of the female form and female sexuality over a consistent period of time. Traditional romance prescribes a predominantly orthodox way of life that shores up the foundations of social grand narratives, like those of marriage and heterosexuality, and precludes any difference to these. As a consequence, as lesbian experiences fall beyond those of heteronormativity, it is reasonable and indeed relevant to question whether the genre of romance is at all suitable for lesbian re-appropriation.

Yet, in spite of these apparent impediments, critiquing lesbian lived experience via a fantasy of romance is a remarkably pertinent way to highlight the hierarchical nature of the ideological and social conventions of patriarchy. For instance, conventional romance privileges the qualities of youth and beauty within the gendered binary systems of masculinity and femininity. These prescribed value judgements form part of a standardized model of ideal romance, because, as Janice Radway says in her book *Reading the Romance*, they 'insure that the heroine and hero function as a single, dynamic centre of the novel' (1991, 123). This focus on the character development is important to readers, because ideal romance maps reality, as Radway also points out, 'the reader is permitted to live the heroine's relationship to the hero without distraction' (123). As a consequence, reading lesbian romance fiction highlights the limitations of patriarchy, because it is predicated on the interplay between ideas of power and submission, rather than equality. These positions are significant to the readings of regular themes of 'true love' and 'love at first sight' and are implicated in the assumption that heterosexual desire is the only means by which a woman can access a romantic 'happy ending'.

The 'love-hate' relationships of traditional romance may seem a naïve place from which to begin a critique of romance. After all, the genre's ability to move beyond such surface reading has already been eloquently expressed earlier in this book. Nevertheless, Radway makes it clear that female readers develop an emotional reliance on romance in a way that augments a certain 'cherry-picking' reading style. She states that '[women's] emotional dependence on romantic fiction is at least partially a function of their ability to restrict their reading to novels that focus only on a particular kind of interaction between heroine and hero' (119). Radway's study thus highlights the nurturing and reassuring capacity that romance offers women in the way that it returns them to a traditional version of patriarchy – boy meets girl, the overcoming of obstacles, the happy ending – that they both recognize and feel comfortable with. It is these emotional qualities of romance that are potentially the most compelling for its female readership.

Radway's research into the habits and expectations of romance readers emphasizes how women appear 'hardwired' into themes of love and desire. But this sense of pre-determinism does not mean that women are therefore passive readers. On the contrary, it appears that it is a 'fluid and active' reading process that holds much of its appeal for women, because as Radway points out, the final effects on the reader can 'neither be foreseen nor guaranteed in advance' (17). As readers of romance fiction, it is difficult to tell exactly how women respond to the regularity of themes offered by the genre or indeed whether 'the pressures exerted by developments in the larger culture' impose their own feminist demands onto the form (17). For example, are women using romance literature to work out their place in culture, or is it the text that is informing women of their social position? Do women read romance to locate their subjectivity or do they use the space of the text to challenge their assigned social positions? In order to answer these questions, we need to consider the consequences of this 'slippery' relationship between the text and the reader. The romance novel presents an ambiguous space that can be read as a site where the 'control over' female sexuality is played out. This, by its nature, provides the conditions where a potential challenge to normative behaviours can take place. As a consequence, readers can access the fluid and creative landscape of romance literature and generate acts of subversion.

Lesbian romance offers its readers the same level of emotional investment as the traditional romance.[2] But by telling a passionate story from the perspective of same-sex desire, it subverts the codes and conventions found in typical romances and re-casts female subjectivity. This chapter will examine the extent to which the lesbian figure re-scripts the submissive role of the traditional heroine by looking at Sarah Waters' three neo-Victorian lesbian romances. It will argue that the intimacy of the first-person narration brings Nancy's experience in *Tipping the Velvet* (1998) closer to the 'ordinary' reader's and in turn provides a sense of authenticity to any display of love. It will show how Nancy's sense of self enables Waters to subvert the orthodox representation of women being preternaturally nurturing. In challenging the assigned roles of women, this chapter will question the erotic responses conventional romances illicit from its readers. Taking examples from *Fingersmith* (2002) it will evidence how Waters subverts the economy of sex that is typically represented and in so doing, re-articulates the taboo of the abject body in order to re-situate the reader's pleasure. Finally, *Affinity* (1999) will be examined in order to discuss the way Waters revokes the heterosexist ideals of true love. Replacing the 'happy ending' scenario with rejection, Waters challenges the notion that the genre of romance has only one fulfilling ending.

The Protagonist

When women are represented in traditional romance fiction, they are usually accorded one of three roles: the heroine (the woman who shares 'true love' with the hero), the heroine's foil (who spends her time undermining the heroine in an attempt to distract the attention of the hero) and the love rival (a woman who is both alluring and hyper-sexual, known for her capacity to incite lust in men and envy in women) (Radway 1991, 133). Feminism recognizes this as a model of dependency that is based on sexual difference, as one that is focused on a lack of masculine qualities.[3] This is more specifically known as phallocentricism, where each of the 'occupied' positions of the woman is defined by and through her interactions with the hero. Such emotional and economic dependency presents a challenge for lesbian romance literature in terms of how to re-interpret the subjectivity of the desired object (the woman) when it has been so heavily encoded by a phallocentric world-view and when readers are also similarly indoctrinated. Even the assignation of the term 'heroine' to the female character is problematic for writers of lesbian fiction, because female subjectivity is usually only understood through male dominance. In this case, the heroine's experience of true love is completely reliant on the hero's capacity to provide emotional attachment.

One of the subtle implications of a system that has only one type of subjectivity is the way that it 'others' representations of women who cannot positively reinforce masculinity. Lesbian characters are notable minorities in many fictional genres, because, as Terry Castle's work in this area tells us, their shadowy presence is commonly cast out of normative society and forced to suffer a literary death for their 'unnatural' sexuality. As a consequence, writing a love story from the perspective of female same-sex desire addresses several important and related issues. Lesbian romance attempts to re-organize a woman's experience from a female-orientated point of view, by placing her at the centre of the text and not as a subsidiary of an economic exchange. It explores lesbianism in terms of creating a viable and visible social presence, while specifically showing her to be an autonomous subject in the way that it re-scripts her sense of self. As Castle suggests, '[lesbian romance] can play, obviously, a powerfully inspirational and self-affirming psychological function for members of minority groups' (2003, 1). This is because it confirms the status of a female-same-sex desire in a pejorative world order.

Tipping the Velvet (1998) is Sarah Waters' first novel to subvert the phallocentricism of romance. It is set in the latter part of the Victorian era, and explores the viability of same-sex desire against a historically specific time when lesbianism was outwardly and socially invisible.[4] In response to this historical anonymity, Waters seeks to move her story of love between women beyond the details of a coming-out narrative and guide her readers towards the prospect of a lesbian romance that is presented as a sustainable alternative to a typical heterosexual storyline. As a consequence, the first-person narration of the protagonist, Nancy Astley, accompanies the reader through a series of intimate and, at times, abusive lesbian relationships that provide the sense of maturity that typical coming-out stories lack. A brief synopsis of the text shows how *Tipping the Velvet* works towards creating a representation of viable same-sex desire, because it begins with an exploration of Nancy's feelings for Kitty Butler, her first lesbian love interest. Talking with her sister, Nancy states:

> 'When I see her . . . it's like – I don't know what it's like. It's like I never saw anything at all before. . . . She makes me want to smile and weep, at once. She makes me sore, here.' I placed a hand upon my chest, upon my breast-bone. 'I never saw a girl like her before. I never knew that there were girls like her. . . .' My voice became a trembling whisper. (Waters 1998, 20)

Nancy's unfamiliarity with the physical sensations of love, in the way that she cannot believe her eyes, feels a 'soreness' in her breast and 'trembles' attest to her innocence and frame her 'coming out' moment to her sister. She is palpably naïve in contrast to the self-sufficiency of the 'archetypal' heroine who does not suffer self-doubt.[5] Waters subverts the orthodox heroine figure and replaces it with an experience within the scope of the ordinary woman.

Waters uses Nancy's story to confront the idea that a woman's success in romance depends on her ability to demonstrate personal qualities that are beyond the 'average' in terms of their emotional and physical presence.[6] Yet, Radway's research in this very area highlights that most readers of romance are part of a standardized mainstream culture. Moreover 'romance reading [is] seen by women as a way of participating in a large, exclusively female community' (1991, 15). Whether the reading habits of this 'exclusive' group are acts of rebellion against the progressive feminist politics of the 1970s is difficult to tell. But what is clear is that reading heterosexual romance 'stitch[es] the reader ever more resolutely into the fabric of patriarchal culture' (15). In contrast, Nancy's initial candour is expressed in terms of its visceral connection with the audience, as all readers have access to the same range of emotions. Her feelings for Kitty are not motivated by personal gain: on the contrary, Nancy's only responsibilities are to herself. As a consequence,

Waters subverts the grand narratives of the traditional heroine, by enabling Nancy to author her own sexual awakening in a way that is both independent of a heterosexual storyline and presenting a woman who suffers self-doubt in a way that resonates with the ordinary reader's experience.[7]

Throughout the book, Nancy's sense of self matures. Waters expresses this development through her ever-increasing command of language. For instance, when her affair with Kitty moves from platonic to physical, Nancy suddenly sees the world through the eyes, both metaphorically and literally speaking, of the progenitor: 'Now suddenly, it was I who wooed it, me at whom it gazed in envy and delight. I could not help it: I had fallen in love with Kitty; now, *becoming* Kitty, I fell in love a little with myself' (Waters 1998, 126). It is interesting how Nancy is able to articulate the way she simultaneously assumes her place as an object of desire and the intensity that comes from owning the subjectivity of love. Being shown to occupy a dualism in this way conflates the dominant and submissive positions assigned by Western culture to gender. Such a didactic model is further revised in the way that Nancy owns the primacy of language through a first-person narration. Her repeated use of 'I' allows her to occupy the space of both the 'wooer' and the 'desired'.[8] This constant slippage between positions of subjugation and subjugated undermines the notion that gender is fixed, for it shows it to be capable of flux.

Waters uses this instability to subvert the dominant discourse of traditional romance when Nancy states:

> [t]his was a language not of the tongue but of the body, its vocabulary the pressure of a finger or a palm, the nudging of a hip, the holding or breaking of a gaze, that said, *You are too slow- you are too fast- not there, but here- that's good- that's better!*. (128)

The 'language of the tongue' represents patriarchal control, because power is maintained through the making and application of social law, which is disseminated through spoken and written language. Traditionally women have been excluded from this process. Waters refuses its authority here, because Nancy replaces it with the physical sensations of the body, as 'finger', 'hip' and 'eye' drive the intensity of passion. But more importantly, Waters uses the irregularity of this experience in terms of being '*too slow*', '*too fast*', '*not there*', '*but here*' to re-shape understanding of traditional romance. She removes the regularity of the models that Radway highlights as being the most compelling for women readers, such as the essentialism of true love, and empties them of meaning. This is because it is the 'language of the body' that achieves satisfaction, in terms of feeling 'good' and 'better', and not that of social expectation.

One of the ways that Waters has achieved success in subverting common themes of romance is how she re-imagines the cultural 'scripts' that have coded sexual behaviour.[9] She maintains this by charging her female characters with control over their own sexuality. In contrast to this, Radway highlights that heterosexual romance often leaves its readers unconvinced when it attempts to re-shape the masculinity of the hero by 'transforming [his] emotional indifference and sexual promiscuity into expressions of love, constant displays of affection, and the promises of marital fidelity' (1991, 127). Such acts of feminization, she sees, only serve to further entrench women in their social role of nurturer. Yet, perhaps more generally, they present further evidence of how gender is constructed from a set of debilitating heterosexual qualities.

In comparison to the hegemony of tradition, Nancy's character reconciles the masculine and the feminine in the way that she conflates the two. For instance, Nancy often appears masculine on occasions when she chooses to dress in male clothing or pursues her sense of social injustice. Yet, equally so, she appears feminine in her performances as Diana Leatherby's kept woman or 'tart' (Waters 1998, 248). But readers are reminded that '[a] double act is always twice the act the audience thinks it' (128). In other words, Waters highlights that looks can be deceptive and behaviours can be performed. Here, Waters shows that the most transgressive acts are those that are self-aware. Nancy understands what it is to be masculine and feminine and adapts her behaviour accordingly. Because of this she frees herself of the associated social restrictions. The advert for Mrs Best's lodger demonstrates this point entirely. The card reads: '*Respectable Lady Seeks Fe-Male Lodger*' (211). What appeals to Nancy is not the prospect of a place to stay but the 'hyphen,' as she says, 'I saw myself in it – in the hyphen' (211). The notion of existence goes beyond the confines of coded gender but is the reality of somewhere between the two.

Exploring the Erotic

As has been suggested, traditional representations of the female form undermine any ability to conceive women in terms of their autonomous sexuality. It has already been shown how heterosexual romance defines women according to the way they interact with the hero figure and, in turn, these 'qualities' are translated into the context of the ordinary, everyday by female readers. As Radway remarks, '[to] readers . . . the romantic universe is identical to the universe inhabited by real women' (1991, 188). But, this comment does not hint at the reasons why romance and reality need to be mirrored in this way. Is the genre of romance particularly successful because it offers its readers a sense of reassurance that comes from the familiarity of convention? Well, perhaps the answer is yes, when the model of female sexuality is based on the socially prized status of 'monogamous heterosexuality' (16). Even within the context of the growing popularity of erotic romance, according to the editorial guidelines given out by Mills and Boom, the sex is prescribed to fulfil the role of the 'lives of contemporary women' (cited in Radway 1991, 16). Consequently, sex is presented in the story to support the differences between the sexes.

This argument does not account for the mainstream success of Waters' erotic lesbian romances. If readers only read the romances that reflect their own sexuality, then, by virtue, Waters should only be popular with a lesbian audience. The fact that this is not the case suggests something quite unexpected and 'queer' is happening during the reading process. One way of seeking to answer this dilemma is to consider the way Waters subverts the erotic response of the reader. In normative society, the sexed body is contained because of a fear of abjection. The abject, or homosexual, body is perceived as a threat to the social order precisely because it defiles the laws of heteronormativity that maintain a gendered positionality.[10] Heterosexuality retains its prominence in society by demonizing homosexuality in ways that create a sense of suspicion in the general population. Even the most experimental erotic romances perpetuate these abject states, because they are driven by a desire to 'bind female desire to a heterosexuality constructed as the only natural sexual alliance' (Radway 1991, 16). Waters addresses the taboo of the abject by situating her characters outside of the social arguments that have traditionally seen them as deviant. In so doing, she questions the inherent pleasurable nature of heterosexuality.

One particular way that Waters recreates enjoyment for her readers is through the way she explores the abject body in contrast to men. *Fingersmith* (2002) contrasts the love affair between Maud Lilly and Susan Trinder with the faux romance between Maud and Richard Rivers. A triangle of deception is revealed during the plot, as Rivers, also known as Gentleman, attempts to use marriage to defraud Maud out of her inheritance. Susan joins Rivers in his crime, but Maud switches identity with Susan to avoid being committed to an asylum. Playing with a pun on the name 'gentleman', Waters shows that Rivers is *morally* bankrupt in the way his desire is motivated by greed. In contrast, Maud acts through love. She says:

> I meant to save her. Now I see very clearly what will happen if I do – if I draw back from Richard's plot. He will go . . . she will go and I shall be left. . . . Without Sue. And so you see it is love – not scorn, not malice; only love – that makes me harm her, in the end. (Waters 2002, 285)

In order for Maud to 'save' Sue, she would have to marry, but Waters shows that this is a corruptible act, because it is full of 'malice' and 'scorn', whereas acting in accordance with her sense of self is shown as an act of 'love.' In this respect the 'harm' that befalls Sue is caused by the corrosive nature of heterosexuality.

As Waters prioritizes the abject body over heterosexuality, she subverts the economy of sex shown in traditional romance fiction. Heterosexism depends upon its repudiation of homosexuality. But as Judith Butler suggests a text can re-articulate pleasure if it can show how patriarchy maintains its 'normative subject-position' through the abject body (1993, 112). As Maud is compelled by her fear of marriage to send Sue to the asylum, her abject body becomes a patriarchal prop used to confine women. As such, Waters uses the lesbian figure to re-focalize the reader.

As readers are given alternative ways of experiencing sexuality, Waters undermines the status quo of typical romance trajectories in terms of the marriage plot. Maud's inexperience in these matters, shown in her admission to Sue '"I wish you might tell me . . . what it is a wife must do, on her wedding-night!"' (2002, 139) presents Waters with an opportunity to re-write the polemics of the wedding night. For instance, when Maud complains that Rivers' kisses 'don't start [her] off' (141) she sets in motion a series of instructions that unleash the lesbian erotica of the book. Sue takes the lead to show Maud how to kiss, she says '[i]t was like kissing the darkness. As if the darkness had life, had a shape, had taste, was warm and glib' (141). Sue's description breathes life into the kiss and materializes the abject for the reader. Here, the 'darkness' is the outsider being invited in and given 'shape' and 'warmth'. Waters uses this example to re-position a woman's emotional response to a man. The metaphor of dance emphasizes the substitute marital sex act; Sue says, '"There are lots of ways to dance. You can only do this, one way"' (141). Waters is careful here not to privilege one version of sexuality over another. She shows that lesbianism is one of many possibilities. In this regard, Butler maintains that 'none of these positions would exist in simple opposition to normative heterosexuality' (1993, 109), because to do so would provide another, if different, sense of entitlement and this would weaken any potential that a new order might have to regenerate. Consequently, it is possible to see that Waters is opening up the potential to see homosexuality outside of its liminal, abject status.

Butler argues that if the abject is able to successfully transgress the norms of sexuality then the site of subversion has to have the necessary conditions for love (1993, 109). Waters' careful deconstruction of the façade of patriarchy has amply achieved this in *Fingersmith*, as Maud and Sue's affair was consummated on a 'faux' wedding night. Nevertheless, this perspective does not address the broader issue of why readers expect romance to offer a reassuring similarity to the world they occupy. Any critique of the effects of subversion ought to address the reading process too, especially when lesbian romance has crossed over into the mainstream. Eve Sedgwick offers a possible solution to this problem. She argues that the 'source' of a text is located somewhere between the 'text, the author and [her] oeuvre. In practice . . . it is a concept that enables the reader/critic to explore both text and characters as a site of relative autonomy with its own psycho-sexual economy' (2004, 183). In other words, Sedgwick suggests that readers can gain pleasure from the text itself, independent of established reality. In these terms, the text is able to tell its own story and readers are able to align their own viewpoint with that of the text. Thus a series of 'voices' becomes apparent; the text's, the author's, the reader's and those of the characters are the most obvious, but others will become evident too. Sedgwick's point is that they are seamless in the way they subsume one another. Such an affect has the potential to normalize the behaviour represented in the text, as no voice is exclusive. In light of this, the subverted romance becomes the mainstream representation of romance while it is being read. Readers gain pleasure not just from the active processes of subversion, but also from their 'temporary' re-orientation into the transgressive world of the text's story.

Failed Romance

If readers gain pleasure and satisfaction from 'ideal' romances because they reassure them of their place in the mainstream, then what happens when a romance fails? Does the failure of a romance spark fear in the reader, in the way that it highlights the vulnerability of women in patriarchy? Radway's study would certainly suggest this to be true (1991, 157). She highlights that the 'happy ending' scenario of ideal romances reveal a 'standard female development . . . [that leads] to emotional rewards' (157). Whereas failed romances can generate feelings of anger and bitterness towards the hero figure, precisely because of his inability to provide an appropriate response at the end of the romance. This detail unsettles the traditional world order of women readers. Radway argues that failed romances provide catharsis for women readers. The inept hero provides the vent through which women can release their repressed anger against their assigned role in society (158). If all romances were ideal in their endings women would suppress this angst, because a need for emotional satisfaction is a higher priority.

Waters' lesbian romance subverts the notion that 'happy endings' essentialize a woman's romantic experience, because she empties its mythical status of any meaning. She shows that the hero-heroine-dependant relationship is a hollow manifestation of a social illusion. *Affinity* (1999), for instance, foregrounds a story of obsession, coercion and deception. The tale revolves around Margaret Prior, a vulnerable gentlewoman, who becomes the inadvertent dupe in the love affair between murderer Selina Dawes and maid Ruth Vigers. Set within the confines of Millbank Ladies Gaol, Margaret happens upon the prisoner, Selina, and becomes increasingly beguiled by her story. Ultimately, though, it is the real lovers, who also happen to be the villains, who sail off together into the sunset, while the protagonist Margaret is left heartbroken.

In typical romantic fashion, Margaret begins to see saintly qualities in Selina, describing her 'hair . . . throat . . . wrists . . . mouth . . . flesh . . . like the signs of the stigmata on a saint' (Waters 1999, 163). Traditional heroines try to redeem the emotional failure of the hero by using their devotion in an attempt to transform his behaviour. But Waters inflates these qualities to the level of 'saint' in order to expose their artificiality. Indeed the pathos of this situation is more apparent as it becomes known that 'it was I [Margaret] who was changed, . . . It had worked upon me, secretly and subtly' (163). Waters shows how the pursuit to maintain the prospect of a 'happy ending' is a falsehood, because it is the heroine who alters her behaviour in order to satisfy the hero and not the other way around. Indeed this point becomes more apparent as the plot progresses and the crimes committed against Margaret become known.

Having realized that she has been cheated, Margaret declares, '[w]e were joined in the spirit and joined in the flesh – I was her own *affinity*. We had been cut, two halves together, from a single piece of shinning matter' (336).

Here Margaret again evokes a sense of the divine through her reference to her 'affinity' with Selina. Describing herself 'cut' from the same mould of 'shinning matter' invests godly qualities into their relationship and evokes the symbolism of the mythical sacrifice of a virginal female to the 'divine'. These exaggerated ideals cannot compensate for the cruelty shown towards Margaret by Selina and Ruth. Instead, Waters uses them to highlight the fascicle and hollow nature of the ideals that traditional romance invests heavily in. In this respect, Margaret's inability to intervene in the outcome of the plot exposes the dissatisfaction that arises from the emotional pursuit of a 'happy ending'.

Waters challenges the concept of the 'happy ending' by subverting the anxiety that readers can experience reading a failed romance. Selina and Ruth's escape revokes the morality of the ideal romance, because their crimes are rewarded by their freedom. Here Waters shows that the concept of 'true love' is not the panacea for 'happy ending' of social harmony but is, in fact, an unattainable status. This revokes the essentialism of traditional romance and shows that lesbian romance fiction is able to offer women an alternative emotional response.

Conclusion

Traditional romance coerces its readers into accepting the primacy of heterosexuality. Waters shows how lesbian romance can subvert this view by reinvigorating the arguments around gender and sexuality. In queering the conventional patterns of romance literature, she re-orientates a world that is presently predetermined and predictable. She achieves this perspective by querying the mythmaking that presents the female form as universalized. In so doing, the lesbian figure is re-focused for the reader and a new relationship dynamic is brought into view. This creative act evokes a sense of pleasure in the reader, as Waters proves that there are endless possibilities to romantic lived existence.

Notes

1. In order to avoid the contradictory meaning of lesbian sexuality in Western culture the term 'lesbian fiction' is used here in the context of fiction written about lesbian subjectivity and lived existence. Sarah Waters'

openness about her lesbian sexuality contributes towards a debate on what exactly constitutes lesbian fiction? As a genre, for instance, is it a body of work written by lesbians? Or, more specifically, is it fiction written about lesbian experience, without any consideration of the author's sexuality? This chapter reflects upon the subject matter within her fiction, rather than on her status per se. Further reading in this area could begin with Renée C. Hoogland's *Lesbian Configurations* (1997).

2. Here see the work of Paulina Palmer, particularly her chapter 'Girl Meets Girl: Changing Approaches to the Lesbian Romance' in Pearce, L. and Wisker, G. (eds) (1998), *Fatal Attractions: Rescripting Romance in Contemporary Literature and Film*.

3. For further reading on this issue, see the work of French feminists, in particular that of Luce Irigaray and Julia Kristeva.

4. There are many books available to help provide context for the Victorian period, but two are particularly useful here in combining both the Victorian era and the treatment of lesbianism during this time. Boyd, K. and McWilliam, R. (eds) (2007), *The Victorian Studies Reader* provides a sense of the cultural context in which the lesbian subject lived. Martha Vicinus' (1996), *Lesbian Subjects: A Feminist Studies Reader* presents an examination of lesbian subjectivity, defining her history and culture.

5. Within orthodox romances the archetypal heroine is someone who has to maintain the hero's attention in order to enable a successful union between the two. Radway argues that she has the tenacity to 'comprehend, anticipate, and deal with the ambiguous attentions of a man' (1991, 64). As a consequence, such a heroine has to be self-assured in order to carry the plot to its natural conclusion.

6. Following the perceived sexual revolution of the 1970s romance literature began to see the character of the heroine evolve. These women characters displayed the types of 'progressive' qualities expected of high-achieving women at this time.

7. Waters' Victorian fiction has a certain pedagogical feel to it, both in terms of educating the reader about the cultural history of the nineteenth century and in terms of calling on the scholarship of sexuality, feminism and queer theory. Cora Kaplan's book *Victoriana: Histories, Fictions, Criticism* (2007) delves into this relationship between contemporary authors of Victorian fiction with writings from the past. Similarly, Diana Wallace's text *The Woman's Historical Novel* (2005) explores the idea that sexuality is historically specific rather than being essential.

8. Traditional romance shores up the patterns and behaviours of patriarchy and this means that romantic heroines typically measure their own self-worth against the hero in order to conform to a cultural standard of love and desire.

9. See Lynn Pearce's (2004), *The Rhetorics of Feminism: Readings in contemporary cultural theory of the popular press* for further details.
10. Elizabeth Grosz' work on the abject is worth referring to here, particularly her 1989 book *Sexual Subversions*.

Works Cited

Boyd, K. and McWilliam, R. (eds) (2007), *The Victorian Studies Reader*. London and New York: Routledge.

Butler, J. (1993), *Bodies That Matter*. New York and London: Routledge.

Castle, T. (2003), *The Literature of Lesbianism*. New York: Columbia University Press.

Grosz, E. (1989), *Sexual Subversions*. Crows Nest, NSW: Allen & Unwin.

Hoogland, R. C. (1997), *Lesbian Configurations*. Oxford: Blackwell Publishers.

Irigaray, L. (1985), *Speculum of the Other Woman*, trans. Gillian Gill. Ithaca: Cornell University Press.

Kaplan, C. (2007), *Victoriana: Histories, Fictions, Criticism*. Edinburgh: Edinburgh University Press.

Pearce, L. (2004), *The Rhetorics of Feminism: Readings in Contemporary Cultural Theory of the Popular Press*. London and New York: Routledge.

Pearce, L. and Wisker, G. (eds) (1998), *Fatal Attractions: Rescripting Romance in Contemporary Literature and Film*. London, Stirling and Virginia: Pluto Press.

Radway, J. (1991), *Reading the Romance*. Chapel Hill and London: The University of North Carolina Press.

Vicinus, M. (ed.) (1996), *Lesbian Subjects: A Feminist Studies Reader*. Bloomington and Indianapolis: Indiana University Press.

Wallace, D. (2005), *The Woman's Historical Novel: British Women Writers, 1900-2000*. Basingstoke: Palgrave.

Waters, S. (1998), *Tipping the Velvet*. London: Virago.

—(1999), *Affinity*. London: Virago.

—(2002), *Fingersmith*. London: Virago.

14

The Hard-Boiled Detective: Dashiell Hammett

Bran Nicol

One way of decoding the familiar opposition between 'literary' fiction (or serious, enduring, prose works of art) and popular fiction ('pulp', 'trash', 'throwaway', entertainments) is on class grounds. Literary fiction is what educated people read, and it does them good to do so. Popular fiction, on the other hand, is what 'ordinary', working, people read, often literally as part of their working day – as they journey to work by train or tube. Popular fiction thus has its function: it takes its place in the daily grind, helping relieve the boredom of a necessary journey, or providing a moment of escapism amidst the monotony of ordinary existence. 'Literary' fiction, by contrast, is not functional, and this accounts for its value – unless we consider its function its supposed capacity to enrich our lives, or teach us something we did not already know.

In his attitude towards literature, the subject matter and style of his novels, his appeal to a mass readership, in his own 'blue-collar' credentials which smack of toil and hardship (an autodidact, an alcoholic, a worker in low-paid jobs), the American writer Dashiell Hammett (1894–1961) must be placed firmly in the 'popular fiction' camp. However, as I shall argue in this chapter, he occupies the position in such a way that it complicates the boundary between literary and popular fiction.

Hammett and Hard-Boiled Writing

Hammett is the undisputed pioneer of 'hard-boiled' detective fiction, one of popular fiction's most enduring modes of writing. Hard-boiled fiction is popular in that it has always sold in large numbers, and it also addresses, head-on, topics and issues that concern 'the populus', that is, most people. There are two ways critics have used the label 'hard-boiled' to describe fiction, and Hammett exemplifies each one. The first is thematic, to do with what distinguishes the fiction in terms of style and subject-matter. As the screenwriter and film director, Paul Schrader once put it, the hard-boiled story is distinguished by its presentation of 'a "tough", cynical way of acting and thinking which separated one from the world of everyday emotions – [it is] romanticism with a protective shell ... , [living] out a narcissistic, defeatist code' (1998, 56). Hard-boiled fiction deals with an unforgiving, recognizably modern, urban world and the ordinary, 'blue-collar' people who inhabit it, and who have been dealt a tough hand by life. While it is predominantly masculine, the hard-boiled world also includes women who are equally tough in that they too have to fight to survive, and whose straight-talking and overt sexual seduction matches the directness of the hard-boiled masculine predisposition towards violence.

The second way of defining hard-boiled fiction is to regard it as essentially American, and the response to particular social, political and economic conditions in the United States from the 1920s (see McCann 2000). Hammett, along with Raymond Chandler and James M. Cain, is part of the most famous trio of hard-boiled writers, a category also including other great writers of popular fiction, who have attracted less critical interest, such as Jim Thompson, David Goodis, Charles Willeford, Geoffrey Homes, Cornell Woolrich, Charles Williams, Leigh Brackett, Dorothy B. Hughes and Horace McCoy. The concentration of this kind of writing in American literature from the 1920s to the end of the 1950s – or from the eve of the Wall Street Crash in 1929 to the Cold War paranoia represented by the McCarthy trials in the 1950s, as Woody Haut has more poetically put it (1995, 6) – is why critics often refer to hard-boiled crime writing as a 'school'. Hard-boiled fiction could, more prosaically, be identified as fiction which began life as stories written for US 'pulp' magazines, such as *Black Mask* and *Dime Detective*, in the period from the 1920s to World War II. The post-war era saw the advent of the paperback (or 'pocket') book, a development in publishing which went hand in hand with the consolidation of the success of hard-boiled fiction. Rather than writing for magazines, major writers now produced work which appeared in paperback editions issued by publishers such as Pocket Books, Ace, Dell and Signet, and which attracted a mass readership.

Hammett's career and the rise of hard-boiled writing follow the same trajectory. His fiction initially appeared in journals such as *Black Mask* and was then published in paperback form. He exemplified the pulp writer, to the extent that he was one of the major writers in the sights of the paranoid US politician Senator Joseph McCarthy, who led the 'witch hunts' for 'un-American' figures in the 1950s, which sought to root out closet Communist sympathizers among America's cultural and political elite. McCarthy decided that Hammett's books were pro-communist and dangerous, given that they were on the shelves of so many private and public libraries, and he interviewed him in 1953. Most of all, though, what makes Hammett an exemplary hard-boiled writer is his style, more precisely his language. In his polemical apology for Hammett's writing, 'The Simple Art of Murder', published in 1950, Raymond Chandler accurately divined that, in contrast to the English armchair 'logic-and-deduction' thriller, 'Hammett gave murder back to the kind of people that commit it for reasons, not just to provide a corpse; and with the means at hand, not with hand-wrought duelling pistols, curare, and tropical fish. He put these people down on paper as they are, and he made them talk and think in the language they customarily used for these purposes. He had style, but his audience didn't know it, because it was in a language not supposed to be capable of such refinements' (1995, 894).

In *The Pursuit of Crime* (1981) Dennis Porter argues that Hammett – and Chandler in his own fiction – managed to produce a distinctively American literary language which functioned 'as an assertion of cultural emancipation and independent national identity' (1990, 83), especially in opposition to Britain, a literary colonizer of sorts. Hammett's language preferred 'directness over formality, lower-class speech over upper, popular over high culture, American forthrightness over English gentility' (88) – a stark contrast with the connotations of 'social conformity, circumspection and sobriety' (1991, 85) we find in the work of the quintessentially English crime writer Agatha Christie. Consider the opening line of Hammett's uncompromising first novel, *Red Harvest* (1929):'I first heard Personville called Poisonville by a red-haired mucker named Hickey Dewey in the Big Ship in Butte.' Yet Porter notes that, although it replicates the speech of real, uncomplicated working life, it is actually far more self-consciously aesthetic and surprising than Christie's 'predictable' choice of words: its rhetorical flourishes mean that Hammett's reader is forced 'to pay attention to his medium' (87). Porter pinpoints a contradiction which is central to understanding Hammett's place in modern American literature: on the one hand, defiantly American working class, on the other, studiously artistic, a worthy contemporary of the modernists and a precursor, in some ways, of sceptical postmodern approaches to detective fiction. I will return to this paradox in due course, but for now will consider the other main reason, besides his hard-boiled style, why Hammett is such a key writer of popular fiction.

Hammett and the Private Eye

Hard-boiled writers, Haut suggests, are literary 'workers', those who are not considered worthy of serious attention from mainstream criticism and who have less freedom to produce the kind of work they want than literary 'artists'. They are at the mercy of the market, 'subject to the stipulations of contracts and deadlines, to include requisite amounts of sex and violence' (1995, 3). Although Hammett, like many literary workers, had aspirations towards producing serious literary fiction, he was comfortable with this definition of authorship. He once described an author as a 'professional worker with words' (Panek 2004, 63). This differs drastically from the Romantic conception of the author as a person with a special gift which elevates him or her above ordinary men – an ideology which has proven remarkably persistent since the early nineteenth century.

Hammett's alignment with the literary worker was for more than philosophical reasons. He needed to write to make enough money to live. But, in a very real sense, his writing is yoked to his working life outside literature. From 1915 to 1922 Hammett worked as a private investigator for the famous Pinkerton's Detective Agency, and his experiences led to his invention of the iconic private eye figure, one of the most enduring character types in popular culture. Unlike other authors, even most other crime writers (the closest Agatha Christie came to crime was imagining the misuses of the poisons she saw on the shelves when she worked as a voluntary war-time nurse at Torquay hospital), Hammett actually lived the life he wrote about and lived in the kind of world he depicted in his fiction.

Each of Hammett's five novels is a detective story (though he may have been hard-boiled to the core, he was a remarkably versatile writer, and each of his novels differs markedly in style, veering from the harsh realism of *Red Harvest* to the psychological veracity of *Dain Curse* to the light-heartedness of *The Thin Man*). But he is best known for *The Maltese Falcon* (1930), the novel which, more than any other, can be regarded as responsible for elevating the figure of the private eye into the cultural consciousness.

Ostensibly *The Maltese Falcon* has a thriller plot which spins on the efforts of the private detective, Sam Spade, to solve the mystery surrounding the murders of two men: Floyd Thursby, a man he has been hired to find by the mysterious 'Miss Wonderly' who appears in his office at the start, and Miles Archer, Spade's own partner, who is shot while trying to track down Thursby. But this plot soon fades and is replaced by other mysteries. First, who is Brigid O' Shaughnessy, the alluring and dangerous woman (one of the prototypes of the *femme fatale*, a ubiquitous character-type in hard-boiled writing and the mode of film-making it inspired, *film noir*)? Secondly, where is the figurine of a black bird (hence the novel's title) which Spade is tasked to find by another mysterious client, Joel Cairo, and why is a gang of criminals so keen to find it? Both mysteries turn out to be connected to each other – thus suggesting the paranoid logic of the 'noir' plot, where everything seems to happen for a reason, and there are no such things as accidents. But even these mysteries pale beside the most significant source of intrigue in the novel: Spade himself, a character who dominates the action from start to finish.

Spade is a detective, but his work – as the novel reveals – is most unlike the kind of detective work performed by the hero of the 'logic-and-deduction' detective story, as perfected by Hammett's British contemporary Agatha Christie. Where Christie's Hercule Poirot is (like his ancestor Sherlock Holmes) a trustworthy, cerebral 'gentleman' detective, Spade is notable for his physicality, violent language and action, and his moral ambivalence. Spade's idealized, uncompromising toughness makes him just as unlike any *real* person as the cerebral 'armchair' detective. Nevertheless there remains something distinctively and appealingly human about his efforts to get to the bottom of corruption in the face of personal danger. As Nino Frank, one of the earliest commentators on noir, once said of the detective protagonists in film noir, Spade is unlike Holmes or Poirot in that he 'is not a mechanism but a protagonist' (2004, 16). His very humanness – and his immersion in a realistically drawn, crime-ridden world – was instrumental in his status as the prototype for the iconic twentieth-century figure of the private eye.

To understand how this happened we need to consider the influence of two interpretations of Spade, rather than his original portrayal in Hammett's text. Neither of these is completely true to the novel. Although *The Maltese Falcon* was successful, it was really the landmark film, produced in 1941 by John Huston, which propelled Hammett's figure of the private eye to fame. For decades the film was widely credited as the first example of *film noir* and is certainly the first portrayal of the private eye who was to become so ubiquitous in twentieth-century cinema (see Nicol 2013). More precisely, its appeal lies in the ability of Humphrey Bogart to inject his portrayal of Spade with sufficient charm and mischief to balance out the hard-nosed cynicism of Hammett's Spade.

Secondly, the impact of Spade results from his depiction in Chandler's 'The Simple Art of Murder'. Chandler's description of Hammett's private detective is often quoted: 'down these mean streets a man must go who is not himself mean, who is neither tarnished nor afraid. The detective in this kind of story must be such a man. He is the hero, he is everything' (1995, 997). While there is much accuracy in Chandler's description of Hammett's fiction, his essay is a polemical piece, partly interested in deriding the English 'country-house' tradition of detective fiction, and partly an exercise in subtle (and justified) self-promotion. Chandler was actively concerned with making the detective a transcendent figure. For all his admiration of the realism of hard-boiled fiction, he saw something timeless in the figure of the detective and in his own fiction drew parallels between private detective and the flawed hero of the romance (for example, the title of *The Lady in the Lake* [1943] is taken from Arthurian legend).

Strictly speaking, although the figure would not be what it is without *The Maltese Falcon*, the private eye is Chandlerian not Hammettian. Hammett's work is much less idealistic, much harsher and more violent, and Spade is a more morally ambivalent character. Throughout *The Maltese Falcon* he conducts simultaneous affairs with three women, including O'Shaughnessy whom he lets go to the gallows at the end, coldly calculating that this will ensure his own survival. The first paragraph of the novel describes him as a 'blond Satan' (Hammett 2002, 1). Rather than simply having a different interpretation of a case to that of the police, Spade is frequently in danger of being imprisoned, suspected of deliberately obstructing police investigations.

Even further from the romantic archetype was Hammett's first 'private eye' protagonist, The Continental Op. This character features in 28 short stories and in *Red Harvest*. Besides *The Maltese Falcon*, Spade only features in three other short stories. As the name suggests – Op stands for 'operative' – this is a portrait which goes even further from individualizing the private detective as a hero. Instead he is a worker. His name is devoid of the connotations which tend to attach themselves to literary detectives in the nineteenth and early twentieth centuries: investigating, penetrating and decoding (the term detective is derived from the Latin *dētegĕre*, to uncover, discover and reveal [OED; see Thompson 2007, 33]).

Although Hammett was crucial in the creation of the figure of the modern private eye – a modern knight, a questing Everyman – closer examination of how the figure is actually portrayed in his fiction tells another story, one which complements the importance of *work* in Hammett's biography and literary ethics. Private eyes are not 'individuals' in the way that ordinary people are. As a rule, they forfeit the things that make us individuals, such as desire, love and a private life in short, in order to fulfil the demands of their work (see Nicol 2013). The case is even more stark in Hammett. His 'Operative' is not given even the basic marker of individuality, a name. In a sense, the Op is not even a detective. His job is not so much to investigate and decode but to find solutions to problems. He is never elevated to a position above the morass of corruption and misery he investigates but remains fully – and consciously – down in the midst of it. He is 'morally ambiguous', as the historian Steven Marcus once remarked in a well-known introduction to a paperback collection of his stories: 'Which side was he on? Was he on any side apart from his own? And which or what side was that?' (1983, 198). Investigation is a job for the Op and no different from the kind of work which capitalism ensures people have to do: it is relentless drudgery and process, and its endpoint is imposing power over those who need to be policed. That the Op is part of the corruption is suggested by the fact that he becomes more and more violent, and more and more affectless as the body of work which features him grows.

Hammett's private eye – in the guise of Sam Spade and the Continental Op – does not represent the edified moral values Chandler's fiction yearns for. He stands simply for 'the job' itself – not even the economic independence it might lead to, but its mechanics, its procedure, the endless, unquenchable need to acquire 'the facts'. This is something Spade acknowledges in his final discussion with O'Shaughnessy, before sending her to her death. He tells her that he will not save her from the police even though he could, 'because I'm a detective and expecting me to run criminals down and then let them go free is like asking a dog to catch a rabbit and let it go. It can be done, . . . and sometimes it is done, but it's not the natural thing' (Hammett 2002, 226). Spade is referring to something *beyond* morality here, beyond even desire. As the canine comparison suggests, this is more like instinct.

The instinct makes itself felt in *Red Harvest* too, when Elihu Wilsson, the man who has invited the Op onto the case, tries unsuccessfully to get him taken off it. The Op forces Wilsson to keep him on, insisting that he will do 'a complete job or nothing' and telling him 'The check has been certified, so you can't stop payment. The letter of authority may not be as good as a contract, but you'll have to go into court to prove that it isn't' (Hammett 1982, 57). It is clear that the Op is driven not by the needs of the client but by the demands of the job. While this makes him effectively neutral (an advantage to the private detective) it also underlines the fact that the Hammettian detective does not adhere to a set of ethical precepts but to the principles of cold economics.

John Irwin has argued that one way of making sense of the hard-boiled tradition in fiction and film is to regard it as an assertion of the significance of *work* in the American psyche. The private detective, he suggests, is an embodiment of the 'desire for personal freedom' which 'has been central to American identity from the outset, since the pioneers set out to own and work their own land' (2006, 36). This is why 'a major thematic trajectory' in Hammett's and Chandler's fiction is the detective's movement 'from a salaried employee of a large private agency (the Continental Op and Spade) or of the DA's office (Marlowe) to being a self-employed, independent operator' (77). The upward movement of the private eye reflects the fact that 'the twentieth-century urban survival of that desire for a freedom grounded on economic independence has often been the attempt to control one's own destiny, be one's own boss, by owning one's own business' (36).

Hammett's Literariness

In his insistence that both writing and detection qualify as work not art, Hammett reinforced key elements of the hard-boiled ethic: blue-collar, defiantly popular, anti-Romantic. Chandler, whose own fiction reveals the 'Romanticism with a protective shell' identified by Schrader, claimed that this extended into an outright rejection of art 'I doubt that Hammett had any deliberate artistic aims whatever; he was trying to make a living by writing something he had first hand information about' (1995, 894). But it is not that simple. Hammett was a contemporary of the literary modernists, and the fact is that this most exemplary of literary 'workers' wrote popular fiction which revolved around themes we tend to regard as the province of literary art. Chandler himself notes the guile with which Hammett creates a style which seems to be unstylized – this is a skill which suggests a keen interest in the effects of how a story is told rather than an unquestioning indulgence in 'pure' narrative itself. More precisely, there is a prevailing self-reflexiveness about Hammett's work which parallels that of the modernists.

Hammett's fiction, especially when packaged in the lurid covers of pocket book editions, seems the epitome of popular fiction. But on closer inspection we see that it repeatedly draws on popular genres only to dissociate itself from them. *The Glass Key* (1931), for example, as its title suggests, is reminiscent of romance, but this is dispelled by its disturbingly violent story of political power (see Hall 1990). In the same spirit, *The Dain Curse* (1929) might be read as a parody of the 'logic-and-deduction' detective story. At one point near the end of the novel the Op gathers together the cast of suspects and dramatically reveals the killer's identity, only for him to be mistaken. The real revelation is that the Op has been unable to grasp all along the fact that the killer himself belongs to the Dain family.

Built in to Hammett's fiction, then, is an implicit critique of popular fiction which complements the most 'literary' version of the detective story, so-called 'metaphysical' detective fiction, a form which installs and subverts the conventions of the traditional form out of a postmodern preoccupation with fictionality (see Merivale and Sweeney 1999). In Hammett's case, however, the irony is doubled, as the subversion of genre is achieved not through a complex 'high-literary' style but in 'popular' prose.

Like the modernists and the postmodernists, Hammett's fiction is preoccupied with questions of narrative. *The Maltese Falcon*, for example, far more than anything else – more than crime, corruption or the state of early twentieth-century America – is about storytelling. From the outset its characters strategically use stories, most of which are obviously fake, to manipulate others – and this includes Spade himself. Brigid O'Shaughnessy is a veritable story-generating machine, but Spade immediately knows that her initial 'Miss Wonderley' tale is fake because he is blessed with a similar talent. Spade's own credentials as storyteller *par excellence* are clear throughout, especially in the chapter called 'Horse Feathers', named after the term used by Lieutenant Dundy to describe the lie Spade tells him. Interrogated by Dundy and his partner Polhaus after the detectives have caught them arguing furiously, Spade, Cairo and O'Shaughnessy each tell them a different story about what has happened. Spade's, surprisingly for a man we would assume is the most law-abiding of the three, is the most elaborate. He tells the police that what they have witnessed is a trick deliberately intended to mislead them. But although this enrages the police, who know they're being played for a fool, Spade's tactics work: Dundy's violent response, prompted by Spade's needling, prevents the detective from being questioned more seriously, and he is let off the hook.

More than showing how we use stories to construct reality, at points *The Maltese Falcon* also suggests that stories are essentially all we have: there is no stable reality. This is emphasized by one of the most famous and puzzling elements of *The Maltese Falcon*, what has become known as the 'Flitcraft parable'. In his first 'briefing' of his client/adversary Brigid O'Shaughnessy, Spade enigmatically chooses to sit her down and tell her a story about a man, Flitcraft, whom he was once tasked with finding. Spade discovered that Flitcraft fled from his humdrum life on a whim, after he had almost been killed when a beam fell suddenly from a building as he was walking by. The twist is that, having escaped, Flitcraft quickly settles down again into another version of exactly the same life in a different city. His reason is that his encounter made him feel 'like somebody had taken the lid off life and let him look at the works' (Hammett 2002, 63). This anecdote has no relevance to the plot of *The Maltese Falcon*. Rather it makes a point about living one's life according to a narrative. Flitcraft is compelled to reject the 'narrative' pattern – pre-scripted for him as it is for many others – by which one settles down into respectability, marries and has children, only to fall into it again. But it also shows that the entire story of the Maltese Falcon – a story which is unresolved, and which has nothing to do with the murder-mysteries at the beginning of the novel – is a similar diversion. We are placed in the position of the listening O'Shaughnessy and asked to draw conclusions from the narrative, as if the story of the Maltese Falcon will teach us something about our lives.

In reality, *The Maltese Falcon* is a remarkable, contradictory text: a plot-driven popular thriller, full of action, violence and sexual intrigue, but which resists final meaning and suggests that the value of narrative is not what it can reveal but how it can be *used*. This is revealed most starkly perhaps in Chapter 19, 'The Russian's Hand', which is structured around two strangely symmetrical episodes. The first is a rather distasteful scene – which was inevitably left out of Huston's otherwise faithful 1941 film version – in which

Spade forces Brigid to undress before him in the bathroom so he can find out if she is hiding a missing 1,000 dollar bill. It turns out that she isn't, a fact which emphasizes both Spade's capacity for sexual bullying and the fact that he is wrong in his deductions. The second scene comes soon after, and features the corpulent Gutman greedily unwrapping the package containing the Maltese Falcon, only to scrape back the veneer on the artefact to reveal lead underneath: it is a fake. Placed only pages apart, the chapter seems to be begging us to consider the parallels between the two episodes. There is the *femme fatale*, who is fake but whose substance, the source of her power, is not revealed by divesting her of her alluring veneer, and there is the Maltese Falcon, a fake object which has set in motion a chain of frenetic and violent events. Both are objects which set plots in motion – but these plots cannot be fathomed or decoded. The effect of the chapter is subtly to show us that *The Maltese Falcon* is about deception and the inability to uncover the truth, that if, like the characters, we are looking for truth, then we won't find it here. Its murder-mystery element is little more than a pretext than this enquiry into narrative.

Hammett's two most famous detectives, Spade and The Op, are both in the business of acquiring knowledge. That is a crucial part of the work of the private eye. Yet, in their cases, assembling the facts required to bring a criminal to justice is a long way from deduction or making sense of the mysterious world that envelops them – activities which are performed by other literary detectives. In fact, what is notable about Hammett's detectives is the fact that they do not read the world in the manner which is typical of the armchair detective. Rather than reading, they tell stories; they effectively *write* reality rather than interpret it.

For all its exemplary popular-fiction credentials, Hammett's writing, in other words, has a modernist sensibility: it shares modernism's concern with language, narrative, problematic redemption and closure, and repeatedly subverts the reality of its own storytelling. But this does not mean we can pin him down as a 'popular' modernist, for in other ways Hammett is most unlike his modernist contemporaries. In the end, he comes down on the side of the literary worker and not the artist. Writers like James Joyce and Virginia Woolf sought a way of convincing themselves and their readers that art could provide a kind of salvation in a godless world. They showed their characters experiencing 'epiphany' (a term borrowed, pointedly, from religious discourse), that is, made suddenly aware of the transcendent, aesthetic significance of an otherwise unremarkable mundane moment. In this way, the modernists – though atheist to the core – sought an escape from the workaday world. But this is not the same as Flitcraft's 'epiphany', which means precisely nothing – or if it means something, it is about the inevitably that one will always fall into the old same patterns of existence. Likewise, the elusive figurine of the Maltese Falcon, which – as the story tells us at considerable length in Chapter 13, 'The Emperor's Gift' – has obsessed many men and caused the deaths of others, signifies nothing. It may be a surprise that the excitement of Hammett's plots and the vitality of his language conceal such a bleak outlook on the world. But this is in keeping with hard-boiled fiction's determination to look unflinchingly at the inability of most ordinary people to find any meaning, escape or redemption in life other than the peculiar pleasures of reading and telling stories.

Works Cited

Chandler, Raymond (1995 [1944]), 'The Simple Art of Murder', in Frank McShane (ed.), *Chandler: Later Novels and Other Writings*. New York: Penguin Putnam, pp. 977–92.

Frank, Nino (2004), 'A New Kind of Police Drama: The Criminal Adventure', in Alain Silver and James Ursini (eds), *Film Noir Reader II*. New York: Limelight Editions, pp. 15–20.

Hall, Jasmine Yong (1990), 'Jameson, Genre, and Gumshoes: *The Maltese Falcon* as Inverted Romance', in Ronald G. Walker and June M. Frazer (eds), *The Cunning Craft: Original Essays on Detective Fiction and Contemporary Literary Theory*. Macomb, IL: Western Illinois University Press, pp. 109–19.

Hammett, Dashiell (1982), *The Four Great Novels: The Dain Curse, The Glass Key, The Maltese Falcon, Red Harvest*. London: Picador.

—(2002 [1929]), *The Maltese Falcon*. London: Orion Books.

Haut, Woody (1995), *Pulp Culture: Hardboiled Fiction and the Cold War*. London: Serpent's Tail.

Irwin, John (2006), *Unless the Threat of Death is Behind Them: Hard-Boiled Fiction and Film Noir*. Baltimore, ML: Johns Hopkins University Press.

McCann, Sean (2000), *Gumshoe America: Hard-Boiled Crime Fiction and the Rise and Fall of New Deal Liberalism*. Durham, NC: Duke University Press.

Marcus, Stephen (1983 [1974]), 'Introduction to *The Continental Op*', in Glenn W. Most and William W. Stowe (eds), *The Poetics of Murder: Detective Fiction and Literary Theory*. San Diego, CA: Harcourt Brace Jovanovich, pp. 197–209.

Merivale, Patricia and Elizabeth Sweeney (eds) (1999), *Detecting Texts: The Metaphysical Detective Story from Poe to Postmodernism*. Philadelphia: University of Pennsylvania Press.

Nicol, Bran (2013), *The Private Eye: Detectives in the Movies*. London: Reaktion.

Panek, LeRoy (2004), *Reading Early Hammett: A Critical Study of the Fiction Prior to The Maltese Falcon*. New York: McFarland.

Porter, Dennis (1990), 'The Language of Detection' [extract from *The Pursuit of Crime: Art and Ideology in Detective Fiction*], in Tony Bennett (ed.), *Popular Fiction: Technology, Ideology, Production, Reading*. London and New York: Routledge, pp. 81–93.

Schrader, Paul (1998 [1972]), 'Notes on *Film Noir*', in Alain Silver and James Ursini (eds), *Film Noir Reader*. New York: Limelight, pp. 53–63.

Thompson, Kirsten Moana (2007), *Crime Films: Investigating the Scene*. London and New York: Wallflower.

15

Violent Pleasures: War as Entertainment

Petra Rau

Crime fiction and war writing are the two genres that rely most heavily on violence, but they differ in the way in which violence is explained or justified. 'Golden Age' crime fiction revolved around individual psychopathologies and motivations that provided a mystery the detective had to unravel via a set of clues. The genre's various evolutions, from the hardboiled novel to contemporary Scandic Noir, increasingly suggest that the boundary between the legal and the illegal, the citizen and the criminal is hard to police (literally) because those who are in positions of authority – politicians, police officers, corporate executives – regularly resort to illegal means to shore up power and wealth without falling foul of the legal system. Therefore the ordinary citizen may resort to crime in order to obtain justice. In fact, violence is the means to redress the cleft between the law and justice.

War writing operates in a less grey-toned zone: military conflict is state-sanctioned violence and therefore does not require justification or explanation on an individual level. In war, the ordinary citizen is required to kill, particularly in conflicts that rely on large-scale conscription. Homicidal violence, a capital crime in civil society, becomes a means to conquer new territories, to forge a nation or defend its territory. Violence thus transcends base personal motivation (greed, jealousy, vengeance, lust) and is integrated into a narrative of heroism, valour and patriotic duty that can be shaped into national history, even national myth. (There is some crossover: Eric Ambler's and Alan Furst's novels use World War II as a backdrop for crime and espionage stories.) War writing, even when it is fundamentally opposed to military conflict, cannot avoid addressing the ideological links between the individual, the state and violence. Given the horrific cost of the world wars, we should perhaps ask why war writing should be popular at all, let alone be 'gripping' or 'entertaining'? What are the rules of this genre (if any), how do they evolve and what does this tell us about its appeal? Perhaps most pertinently, what cultural function does popular war writing perform for its readers?

Literary Wars

We might do well to remember that the *urtext* of Western literature is the story of a war, Homer's *Iliad* (ca. 800 BC), and that the literary canon of many Western cultures features at least one seminal text about war or a specific military campaign: Caesar's *Commentarii de Bello Gallico* (ca. 50 BC); *The Chanson de Roland* (ca. eleventh century) about the battle of Roncesvalles; Shakespeare's *Henry V* (1599); Grimmelshausen's *Simplicissimus* (1668) about the Thirty Years War; Stephen Crane's *The Red Badge of Courage* (1895) about the American Civil War; Alfred Lord Tennyson's 'The Charge of the Light Brigade' (1854) about the Crimean War; Emile Zola's *La Débâcle* (1892) about the Franco-Prussian war of 1870/1 or Leo Tolstoy's *War and Peace* (1869) which fictionalized Napoleon's campaign to conquer Europe. These texts are well known and often required reading on national curricula and university reading lists; but are they popular? Their canonization seems an indication of the writer's status or the significance of a war within a nation's history; the heftier narratives remind us through their monumental panorama that war writing has its origins in the epic. With the exception of

Grimmelshausen, none of these modern writers ever saw a battlefield, let alone battle. Rupert Brooke's poems were widely read and went into many editions during World War I. 'The Soldier' remains a staple of World War I poetry known by every A-level student in the UK, but one wonders to what extent his very limited exposure to battle enabled the grand pathos of his sonnets (compared to the more sardonic notes of Owen or Rosenfeld). If commercial success is an indication of a work's popularity, Crane is the only writer from the list above who qualifies.

In the twentieth century, literary war novels stood a better chance of being popular bestsellers or longsellers if they made a case *against* war (Sutherland 2007, 65), showing both its futility and the graphic realities of the horrendous physical conditions of mechanized warfare, unheroic death, the absurd bureaucracy attending war and the fallibility of military leadership. Needless to say these books were written by men who knew what they were talking about: Erich Maria Remarque's *All Quiet on the Western Front* (1929), Norman Mailer's *The Naked and the Dead* (1948), James Jones's *From Here to Eternity* (1951), Joseph Heller's *Catch-22* (1961), Kurt Vonnegut's *Slaughterhouse 5* (1969). These novels had tremendous impact in breaking a traditional pattern of representing war as a heroic endeavour of national duty and valiant masculinity. They refused to dignify military conflict by making sense of what they represented as mindless and brutalizing violence. They found favour with an increasingly sceptical reading public that had been exposed to the conditions of war on a much broader scale either as conscripted participants or via newsreel and TV reportage. Veterans found at least part of their experience acknowledged while non-combatants and subsequent generations gained a sense of the physical and psychological trauma of frontline action. It is hard to imagine a novel about a recent, modern war with similar impact: the point of drones is that they have no story to tell and they don't get traumatized.

War Writing and the Ordinary Soldier

The novels about the world wars cited above set a pattern that many subsequent war writers maintained – to show war from the point of view of the ordinary soldier (in popular fiction war still means combat and excludes the home front). Precisely what ordinary means in what type of war often constituted a point of interest for the readers of these books and accounted for their popularity: the first two books to reach one million paperback sales in Britain – Paul Brickell's *The Dambusters* (1951; filmed 1955) and Monsarrat's *The Cruel Sea* (1951; filmed 1953) – were war novels (Bloom 2008, 120). Similarly successful were Alexander Baron's *From the City to the Plough* (1948), Alistair MacLean's *The Guns of Navarone* (1957) and Nevil Shute's *A Town Like Alice* (1950, filmed 1956) and Christopher Landon's *Ice Cold in Alex* (1957; filmed 1958). Monsarrat wrote about the perils faced by the crew of the convoy ship *Compass Rose* in the U-Boat war in the Atlantic from the point of view of a professional sailor, the captain of a former merchant vessel. Baron fictionalized the D-Day landings in Normandy through the eyes of a private. Both writers chose 'ordinary' protagonists who have to accommodate themselves to conditions of war; both do their job as best they can; neither enjoys killing. The sales of these books were increased substantially by their film adaptations, most of them classics of British war films and television staples. Sue Harper (1997) has argued that the success of the films (and by implication, the success of the books) is rooted in the way in which they offered veterans a view of themselves on screen. To have their diverse experiences acknowledged (as navy, army and RAF personnel) and to show the home front how war might have shaped the soldier were adequate compensation for the narrative license and representational compromises writers and directors had to make. In other words, if the full reality of combat could not be shown, to suggest its emotional and psychological impact was sufficient to make films and books popular. And these often stood in for the stories men did not or could not pass on to the next generation. The curiosity of the postwar generation about their elders' experience also accounted for books about earlier periods to be highly successful, notably the Biggles' stories and C. S. Forester's Hornblower novels (1937–50), set during the Napoleonic Wars.

Forester's Horatio Hornblower is a classic serial hero whose career is mapped out by the series albeit not in strict chronological order. A doctor's son (read: middle-class), Hornblower rises through the ranks from midshipman to admiral. His achievement is due to personal merit rather than birth and privilege, and is made less straightforward by his anxieties. Whether set against a murderous bully, French villainy or the professional incompetence of his superiors, Hornblower prevails through his sense of duty, competence and integrity, but accident and fate also have their part to play. In essence, Forester used his hero to mythologize the virtues of the British naval tradition, and in the mid-century these remained remarkably constant. Both Forester and Monsarrat championed protagonists who were bound by craft and tradition and became leaders of men as a result of a test of character. Naive heroism is replaced by a focus on the corporate responsibilities of such ordinary men – their ability to forge and motivate a team; their knowledge of naval technology and seafaring that gains them institutional recognition and the respect of their subalterns. The critique of social class in these novels is also important and must have found a receptive mid-century audience no longer willing to accept conventional social divides after a total war they had fought as much against an enemy as for a better future.

Popular war fiction almost always relies on distancing: the war novel is by definition a historical novel. This genre always serves the interests of the present moment – so why would mid-century readers have wanted to read about the Peninsular or Napoleonic Wars? These conflicts, from which Britain emerged victorious, repelled a rival imperial nation and put its hubristic emperor in his rightful place (back on a small island). Such fiction reminded readers that the European continent had an irritating habit of producing pesky competition to British expansionist aspirations, all of them with impertinent invasion plans, be it from Spain, France or Germany. Yet it also reassured them that ultimately these continentals fall foul of the British habit of victory. The historical remoteness of these wars also allowed for a retrospective legitimization of military hegemony: it was not merely superiority in technology, strategy and resources that won wars but always also the hero's moral superiority (fair play, valour, chivalry, honour). Power still had to be dressed in, and harnessed to, responsibility; victory has to be deserved. Unlike historiography, fiction has greater freedom to celebrate 'glorious' history without seeming chauvinistic. This is essentially how national mythology works. In Forester's case, the Hornblower novels focused on the heydays of British military prowess that ensured the hegemony of the British over the French. The publication of these naval yarns, however, coincided with the nadir of the British Empire. Their continued popularity in the subsequent decades of decolonization might have been rooted in their double role of bolstering a retrospective imperialist mythology as well as offering the comfort of nostalgia in the light of a diminished global position.

One should not forget a curious phenomenon that does not easily fit into such a narrative of nostalgia: the tremendous popularity of Leo Kessler in the 1970s and 1980s. Kessler, a German pre-war emigrant, academic historian and journalist, wrote an impressive number of highly popular series about

World War II from the point of view of the ordinary German soldier. He could build on the success of Willi Heinrich, Sven Hassel and Hans Helmut Kirst whose global bestsellers were also adapted into film (*Cross of Iron, Wheels of Terror, 08/15* series, *The Night of the Generals*). Heinrich, Kirst and Hassel emphasized the distinction between fanatical ideologues and drafted soldiers to the extent that the latter could be seen as victims of war and Nazism. Kessler's 'band of brothers', however, were members of elite SS units, such as SS Battle Group Wotan under the fictional Colonel von Dodenburg. His Panzer division stalls the onslaught of the American army on Aachen in *The Devil's Shield* (1984), and the narrative point of view shifts between the bickering American leadership, German civilians in the besieged city and von Dodenburg's Panzer commanders. Kessler's SS troops are primarily skilled operators of military machinery who have become brutalized by war and fascism rather than the sadistic killers in black uniform that the 1970s' Italian art house cinema glamourizes. Kessler does not omit anti-Semitism nor does he miss opportunities for gratuitous sex scenes, but his potboilers do not have artistic pretensions and are written for a less innocent market that craves action, violence, realistic detail and sex rather than 'decent chaps'. Body horror is part of the grotesqueness war imposes. Since this war has been unleashed, and is being lost, by Nazi Germany, Hassel's troops experience a hell of their own making and only ever defer defeat. Hassel did for the war novel what Peckinpah did for film violence: he trusted that an audience who had the Vietnam war delivered daily to their TV screens knew that war was dirty.

Fictional War and its Audiences

War epics such as *The Iliad* and the medieval *chansons de geste* belong to the oral and performative traditions of courtly societies and cannot be called truly popular. After Scott's historical novels, war was popularized through a different genre: the adventure novel, often set in exotic or colonial spaces. Combat was the ultimate test of character for the protagonist, as either the rite of passage that turned the boy into a man or the event to which all previous scrapes had logically led. Because both adventure and war depend on agency, the authors, characters and audiences of such popular fiction are predominantly male. Charles Kingsley's *Westward Ho!* (1855) – written for an adult audience but very popular with boys – dramatized the sixteenth-century war with Catholic Spain. In it, Kingsley advocated muscular Protestant values and encouraged the fulfilment of Britain's imperial destiny: 'brave young England longing to wing its way out of its island prison, to discover and to traffic, to colonize and to civilize, until no wind can sweep the earth which does not bear the echoes of an English voice' (1855, vol. 1, 13). Later generations of Victorians read R. M. Ballantyne's adventure tales and G. A. Henty's war stories (often disseminated through the Sunday school movement) and would graduate to Rider Haggard's colonial romances, Kipling's stories of the Boer Wars and subscriptions to *Blackwood's Magazine*. The genre here is romance: the often strenuous reality of life in utterly foreign climes is rarely dwelt upon in terms other than blithe optimism, nor is the gruesome reality of battlefield combat represented in all its bloody detail. Death, when it comes, is swift. Increasingly, these stories glorified martial spirit as part of English national character. Highly formulaic, these books offered their male readers an entirely homosocial fictional diet that naturalized both imperialism and combat as logical outlets for healthy, muscular British masculinity. The Victorian conflation of adventure and combat into heroic manliness is important because it lays the foundation for all later phenomena that represent war as exciting or ennobling. This is the mythology that the twentieth-century anti-war novel has to debunk but that resurfaces with stubborn regularity in a variety of entertainment media.

After World War II, neither imperial destiny nor belligerent masculinity appears to be credible as ideological underpinnings for juvenile literature, and yet there is a medium that dramatizes simple heroics for a young(ish) audience – the war comic. On both sides of the Atlantic, war comics emerged in the 1950s and remained a staple of juvenile literature throughout the 1970s (Paris 2000, 230ff). D. C. Thomson's *Commando* is still being published in the UK today and compilation volumes are readily available. The vast majority of these comics dealt with World War II, again in an entirely homosocial context. War is reliably an environment – in fiction – in which men are among themselves and rarely troubled by domestic trivialities or the demands of women. As Michael Paris has noted, the comics barely feature civilians, the home front, women or children, let alone the moral complexities of controversial military strategies such as Hiroshima or Dresden. The Holocaust or political persecution are entirely absent as are indeed the brutal realities of the battlefield (2000, 232). In fact, the episodic nature of a comic narrative reduces the war to endless missions completed by a small group of soldiers who are intensely patriotic but utterly apolitical. The reader is left entirely ignorant of the collateral effects of combat on the civilian population which constitute the majority of victims in World War II and since. This is very conventional localized warfare in which the British are unfailingly victorious against clichéd Nazis or Japanese enemies.

The educational value of such limited representation ostensibly consists in detailed instruction about military technology. *Commando's* issues were always prefaced by a detailed drawing of, say, a Tommy-gun, a specific RAF plane or a tank model that played a prominent role in the subsequent narrative. The fondness with which elderly and middle-aged men wax lyrical about these comics (Riches 2004) suggests how formative they were, and how their unfailing emphasis on British bravery and courage might have informed the longevity of World War II in the cultural memory in the UK among generations who never saw a Tommy-gun in real life, let alone fired one. The height of popularity of World War II comic from the mid-1960s throughout the 1970s succeeded messier colonial 'emergencies' in real life (notably in Kenya and Malaya) and coincided with the Vietnam war and the peace movement. Compared with those protracted and controversial forays into exotic territory, World War II offered a simpler story, and – importantly – the possibility of survival, heroism and victory.

Film and TV adaptations with major stars contributed substantially to the high sales of mid-century war novels. Gregory Peck played the lead in Raoul Walsh's 1951 adaptation of *Captain Horatio Hornblower* in an era where cinema fell in love with the epic and need not yet fear competition from ubiquitous domestic TV screens. Hornblower's longevity continues with a recent multi-part TV dramatization (1998–2001) and inevitable release as DVD box-set. Forester's imitators benefited from his legacy and from this pattern of book-to-film and book-to-script marketing. Peter Weir adapted Patrick O'Brian's Jack Aubrey series (1969–89) as *Master and Commander* (2003), starring Russell Crowe. Bernard Cornwell's Sharpe novels (1981–2006) were also made into TV dramas (1993–7). These novels could still tap into post-imperial nostalgia and satisfy a desire for fictional combat that the Cold War spy thriller's mind games could not really service. The adaptations, however, made the most of the popular taste for period drama and the new possibilities of computer-generated action sequences and special effects.

The return of the big screen epic in the first decade of the twenty-first century is notable, as is the widespread success of belligerent videogame entertainment. CGI has made combat and its body horror eminently feasible and watchable whether in antiquated form (*Troy*, *300*), as slow-motion fantasy gorefest (HBO's *Game of Thrones*) or as sci-fi battle against cyborgs and aliens (*Battlestar Galactica*). This may strike us as a curious phenomenon given how alien violent combat is to most Western audiences' quotidian life: war happens elsewhere and to other people. Its ostensible improbability perhaps constitutes the near-exotic appeal of both war fiction and war games – a different form of distancing. Precisely because war does not happen to us we can play at it and immerse ourselves in a fictional fantasy of belligerent adventure. It is perhaps rather alarming to know that real-life combatants use war simulation games as training, leisure activity and to alleviate (!) post-traumatic stress. One might want to ask whether this is not an indication of the extent to which such entertainment naturalizes violence. Roger Stahl has called the visual habituation to combat through entertainment 'militainment' (2010, 6). For him, such violent pleasures lessen the male citizens' opposition to military conflict because they translate state violence into an object of pleasurable consumption. True, first-person shooter games such as *Call of Duty* or *Medal of Honour* (whose titles suggest war is a valorous pursuit) may attract a different age-group from, say, *Commando* comics or the war novels of Cornwell and O'Brian. Yet while the medium changes, the principle of ideological conditioning in favour of war *because it is exciting to fight the bad guys* remains relatively unchanged from the Victorian juvenile war tale to the modern first-person shooter.

History and Body Horror: Cornwell's Contemporary Bestsellers

If Forester and O'Brian championed the navy, Bernard Cornwell's Sharpe series features an infantry officer. His serial hero, however, is a less anxious specimen of masculinity, which accounts for a greater degree of unapologetic violence in Cornwell's books. Their pattern is in many ways as episodic as that of *Commando* comics: a mission or battle per instalment, structured around a key protagonist and a small group of men. Having exhausted the Regency period Cornwell has branched out into early modern history. His novel *Azincourt* (2008) dramatizes a legendary battle in the Hundred Years War from the point of view of an ordinary soldier, the longbowman Nicholas Hook, who participates in Henry V's campaign in Northern France.

Agincourt, as John Keegan sums up, 'is an episode to quicken the interest of any schoolboy ever bored by a history lesson, a set-piece demonstration of English moral superiority and a cherished ingredient of a fading national myth. It is also a story of slaughter-yard behaviour and of outright atrocity' (2004, 79). In a nutshell, 'Agincourt' is history-as-body horror elevated into ideological essence. Received wisdom about this battle has it that the English contingent was reduced to about five or six thousand archers and a thousand armed men, standing against a French force of 25,000 armoured men-at-arms (Keegan 2004, 88). The odds seemed overwhelmingly against the English but they won.

As in the Sharpe novels, the protagonist participates in 'glorious' history. Little time is lost with contextualizing Henry V's spurious claim to the French throne. Cornwell's interest revolves around the technology of the longbow that ensured Henry's victory at Agincourt, and in the physical and material reality of medieval warfare. Indeed the technological detail must compensate for the simplistic characterization and predictable plot: the hero of *Azincourt* is the longbow rather than the longbowman:

> Hook ran his hand down the wood, feeling its swell and fingering the small ridges left by the bowyer's float, the drawknife that shaped the weapon. The stave was new because the sapwood, which formed the back of the bow, was almost white. In time, he knew, it would turn to the colour of honey, but for now the bow's back, which would be farthest from him when he hauled the cord, was the shade of Melisande's breasts. The belly of the bow, made from the trunk's heartwood, was dark brown, the colour of Melisande's face, so that the bow seemed to be made of two strips of wood, one white and one brown which were perfectly married, though in truth the stave was one single shaft of beautifully smoothed timber cut from where the heartwood and sapwood met in the yew's trunk. (2009, 97)

With all this feeling and fingering going on, eventual combat becomes a form of sexual release. Note how awkwardly the factual information sits next to the focalization ('In time, he knew . . .'). Such intrusive explanatory passages are of course for the reader's benefit.

> 'Kill them!' Sir John bellowed. 'Kill them! Kill them! Kill them!' That was when the battle joy came to him, the pure joy of being a warlord, armoured and armed, dangerous and invincible. He used the poleaxe's hammerhead to beat down armoured enemies. The hammer did not need to pierce armour, few weapons could, but the weight alone could stun a man and one blow was usually sufficient to put a man down or cripple him. (400)

The gorefest of siege and battle is always accompanied by an impromptu mini-lesson in medieval weaponry as if the 'action' needed an instructive voice-over from a seasoned representative of the local re-enactment society or a television historian. There is plenty of 'telling' and not an awful lot of 'showing', which someone less fascinated by the medical traumaturgy of military combat and keener on fast-paced action might find a little trying. Cornwell's narratorial intrusions sit alongside the unreconstructed 'battle joy' that permeates the book in its paradigmatic scenes of the sacking of a town, a drawn-out siege, army movement and the final battle – a taxonomy of medieval warfare situations. Hook observes the massacre of Soissons from a hiding place inside the town: he sees war turn into anarchy against the civilian population. This is contrasted with the siege of Harfleur during which he is part of the attacking army. Weakened by diminishing resources and dysentery, the English forces ultimately conquer the town but Henry has mercy on its inhabitants. The Anglo-Saxons can afford to be more civilized because they enjoy some advantages. Their national unity enables the wearing of a sort of uniform (everyone wears the same St George's surcoat and is easily recognizable). They also benefit from active leadership: '[The king] was there, in the fight, and Hook felt a surge of pride that England had a fighting king and not some half-mad monarch who circled his body with straps because he believed he was made of glass' (252).

War is not the only occasion for violence in a feudal age. Beginning with the scenes in rural England, Cornwell describes a society in which violence is part of the civilian's experience, be it in family feuds or in religious persecution. Women are routinely threatened with rape (in fact they only appear as queen, rape victim or rescued damsel-turned-lover). Good leadership is always supported by military competence and creates loyalty but it is not the sole prerogative of the aristocracy. Hook receives a promotion as a result of his courage and achievements. Cornwell is also careful to contrast the courtly rules of chivalry that apply to staged tournaments with the slaughter of actual battle. And social position determines survival: unlike ordinary soldiers, wealthy knights can be captured and ransomed. The gain of the common warrior is far from noble: loot in any shape is part of the soldier's spoils and motivation.

Jerome de Groot has pointed to the significance of the maps included in Cornwell's books as part of their claim to realism (2010, 84). They underline the specificity of topography and terrain for the plot, and emphasize the historical facts the fiction dramatizes. The paperback edition of *Azincourt* includes ancillary material ('Behind the Battle') that shores up the seriousness of historical fiction but actually undermines the novel's ability to speak for itself. 'Behind the Battle' includes a note by Cornwell in which he passes his verdict on the recent discussion among historians about the actual number of combatants involved, suggesting less discrepancy between the two warring sides. He rejects fresh assessment in favour of received wisdom out of a 'gut instinct' about contemporary (i.e. fourteenth-century) reaction to the battle. Cornwell's interest lies not in the complexity of historical interpretation of source material, or in a rewriting of a well-known narrative, but in national myth. History's contradictions and vicissitudes are ironed out into simplified, emotionally satisfying essences for the purpose of shoring up a narrative of collective identity. In the case of *Azincourt*, the superiority of the common longbowman over the armour-plated knight on horseback is more to do with British skill and French stupidity than with the accident of weather: both horses and armour-clad knights are virtually immobilized in a muddy, sodden field. Cornwell happily takes sides: 'I don't feel sorry for the French, but the horses' (2009, n.p.). The battle of Agincourt is by no means as strategically significant in the Hundred Years War as the battles of Crécy or Poitiers (Tuchman 1978, 583–4), but it lends itself to a David-and-Goliath narrative of national heroism that must have been a propaganda gift to the English king. Shakespeare's St Crispin's speech from *Henry V* is naturally included in the ancillary material as is an author interview:

> This was an English team, there were very few foreigners playing for us. There were a handful of Welsh, and a handful of Gascoignes, and a couple of Flemings, but really this was an English team, no foreign born football players . . . it's part of our national myth. All countries live by myths and Agincourt is there very much in the centre of our myth, as is Trafalgar, as is Waterloo, and the one thing they all have in common is that it's the French. I suppose that we tend to define ourselves in our history against the French, they're the real neighbours, they're the ones you have to beat, they're the real rivals. It's a rivalry that went on for over a thousand years. (Cornwell 2009, n.p.)

This interpretation of English (as opposed to British) history rings of nostalgia for the habit of victory and for an identity uncomplicated by the modern realities of immigration and multiculturalism. Cornwell's version of history does not reach into the twentieth century when the Germans replace the French; when military victory depends on powerful Allies (and when myth has to transform debacles into stories of resilience); when the Suez crisis seals the end of imperialist ambitions; and when 'beating the French' just means another rant about EU legislation. Cornwell's focalizers historicize and legitimize anti-French sentiment as if a modern novelist were not capable of representing 'the other side' or problematizing the English king's claim to the French throne. It is perhaps apposite here to ask whether the *popular* war novel is primarily about conflict or primarily about national myth, with the small 'band of brothers' representing the nation and its values. This is where the bestselling war novel and the popular anti-war novel differ most strongly. In the latter, combat does not signify anything but mindless slaughter; the individual is subsumed by history rather than becoming an agent in it. In the former, state-ordained violence is made to mean something, however retroactively: heroic masculinity, national character, glorious history. Here the soldier's contribution or sacrifice has a part to play in the outcome:

> 'From this day to the ending of the world,
> But we in it shall be remembered – We
> few, we happy few, we band of brothers' (Shakespeare 2008, IV, 3).

The popularity of the historical war novel in Britain has as much to do with the 'habit of victory' at the core of 'glorious' history as with the 'invention of tradition', and it is more palatable to rejoice in victory if technological and strategic prowess are clothed in moral superiority or some sort of destiny. More recent wars – the Falklands, Iraq, Afghanistan – have not (yet) generated bestselling fiction that features modern combat. Over 90 per cent of the victims of modern war are now civilians, which suggests that the definition of what a war novel traditionally features (soldiers in combat) simply no longer credibly represents the reality of warfare.

Works Cited

Bloom, C. (2008), *Bestsellers: Popular Fiction Since 1900*, 2nd edn. Basingstoke: Palgrave.

Cornwell, B. (2009), *Azincourt*. London: Harper.

Groot, J. de (2010), *The Historical Novel*. London: Routledge.

Harper, S. (1997), 'Popular Film, Popular Memory: The Case of the Second World War', in M. Evans and K. Lunn (eds), *War and Memory in the Twentieth Century*. Oxford: Berg, pp. 163–77.

Hassel, S. (1978 [1957]), *The Legion of the Damned*. London: Corgi.

Keegan, J. (2004 [1976]), *The Face of Battle: A Study of Agincourt, Waterloo and the Somme*. London: Pimlico.

Kessler, L. (1998 [1974]), *The Hawks of Death, The Devil's Shield.* London: Futura.

Kingsley, C. (1855), *Westward Ho!* 2 vols. Leipzig: Bernhard Tauchnitz.

Paris, M. (2000), *Warrior Nation: Images of War in British Popular Culture, 1850-2000.* London: Reaktion.

Riches, A. (2004), *When the Comics Went to War: Comic Book War Heroes.* Edinburgh: Mainstream.

Shakespeare, W. (2008 [1599]), *Henry V*, ed. Gary Taylor. Oxford: Oxford University Press.

Stahl, R. (2010), *Militainment, Inc.: War, Media and Popular Culture.* London: Routledge.

Sutherland, J. (2007), *Bestsellers: A Very Short Introduction.* Oxford: Oxford University Press.

Tuchman, B. (1978), *A Distant Mirror: The Calamitous 14th Century.* Harmondsworth: Penguin.

16

Popular Vampires: The Twilight Effect

Neil Campbell

Without the dark, we'd never see the stars.

(Meyer 2009a, 204)

We stood there for a moment, remembering. Though the memories were human and clouded, they took over my mind completely.

(Meyer 2011, 445)

The re-emergence of popular vampire stories from the USA can be understood using Gilles Deleuze and Félix Guattari's claim that 'It is in war, famine and epidemic that werewolves and vampires proliferate' (1988, 243). Under conditions of crisis and anxiety, they suggest, humanity questions its motives, relations and beliefs, testing and re-imagining them through the prism of fantasy, horror and the inhuman. In post-9/11 American culture, doubts and fears accrued to shake the very foundations of US security, self-assurance and national identity, and by meditating upon aspects of otherness, social dread and cultural evolution, it certainly felt its boundaries were under threat. Nina Auerbach famously argued that 'every age embraces the vampire it needs' (1995, 145) and Teresa Goddu remarked in response to this idea, '[t]he vampire reflects national moods and, hence, tells us who we are' (1999, 126). It is around these intersections of crisis, national mood and the revamping of the vampire narrative that this chapter examines the *Twilight effect* and discusses how Stephenie Meyer's phenomenally successful saga 'reflects national moods and, hence, tells us who we are'.

American Return

Faced with the 'crisis' of 9/11 and the subsequent 'War on Terror', *Twilight* can be read as a fiction of return, reprocessing fears triggered by the communal fragility felt within the American nation as its fundamental values were suddenly jeopardized from dangerous outside forces. In Meyer's fictional world, America is tested, its values re-examined and its people reckoned with through the dark mirror of vampires and werewolves. However, through this confrontation, and as Fred Botting once wrote of the Gothic, emerges 'a powerful means to reassert the values of society, virtue and propriety: transgression, by crossing the social and aesthetic limits, serves to reinforce or underline their value and necessity, restoring or defining limits' (1996, 7). This process of reassertion is central to the *Twilight* saga, reacting to transgressive forces by reinvoking traditional orders of family, territorialism, morality and restraint within the wider context of American national identity. If, as Mark Edmundson believes, the 'Gothic woke its eighteenth-century readers up . . . roused them from the smug self-assurance often induced by enlightenment rationalism', and did so via 'the night side of life . . . with fears and desires that enlightened reason had banished' (1997, 9), then *Twilight* seeks to put back some reassuring 'sparkle' through its recuperation of vampirism as the expression of lost or superseded values. As Edmundson further argues, specifically in relation to the USA, 'the Gothic mind is antithetical to all smiling American faiths' (5), and conventionally, as Goddu adds, 'the gothic disrupts the dream world of national myth with the nightmares of history [and] discloses the instability of America's self-representations' (1997, 10). The eternal promise of America, contained in its 'national myth' of democracy, entrepreneurialism, freedom, family and youthful vigour, has been arguably corrupted and tarnished by rapid cultural, social and political change as well as by the kinds of external threats epitomized by 9/11.

Indeed, this is precisely how the saga begins, with the stark warning from Eden itself: 'But of the tree of knowledge of good and evil, Thou shalt not eat of it: For in the day that thou eatest thereof thou shalt surely die' (Gen. 2.17). The moral crisis of *Twilight* is the threat of social breakdown, of families split apart and scattered, of a loss of moral compass and, above all, of the failure of national mythologies and ideals when pitted against threats from both inside and outside. In *Eclipse*, Bella Swan, Meyer's teenage heroine, feels unsettled because, as she puts it, it was as if 'all the patterns were broken' (2009b, 344). Thus what the novels perform across the whole saga is, ultimately, an elaborate attempt to banish the darkness and rekindle the lost values embedded in an earlier, mythic vision of America; a new Eden reborn out of the woods, no longer of Puritan New England, but Forks, Washington. As Leslie Fiedler once explained, 'the American writer inhabits a country at once the dream of Europe and a fact of history; he lives on the last horizon of an endlessly retreating vision of innocence – on the "frontier", which is to say, the margin where the theory of original goodness and the fact of original sin come face to face' (1960, 27). Here, in this 'inconsequential town', the battle is over good and evil, over a 'vision of innocence' and 'original goodness', at the very frontier of American culture, in the wilderness 'clearing' transposed to the twenty-first century Pacific Coast.

Curiously, however, that goodness is articulated and enacted through the force of history surging back into the present, not to disrupt it in the same way as the Gothic is often seen to do, but rather to act as a 're-memorying' of forgotten ideals. It is the ageless Cullen vampire family in the saga who reminds contemporary, broken America of its original optimistic values and in so doing offer up what Victoria Nelson has termed 'The new "bright" Gothick' in which 'if we want to get to heaven, monsters and demi-goddesses can help show us it is right here on earth' (2012, 19). As Goddu put it, 'The gothic can strengthen as well as critique an idealized national identity' (1997, 10), and the *Twilight* saga is always concerned with strengthening communal identity through gestures of return, restraint and restoration – a kind of rebirth of wonder.

As Catherine Spooner points out, Meyer was not the first to alter such perceptions, since Anne Rice's *Vampire Chronicles* (1976–2003) fuelled the 'popular preoccupation with vampires ... providing ... an interior life and constructing them to resemble celebrities in whose lifestyles her readership can sustain a vicarious interest' (2006, 51). Increasingly, this resulted in a 'domestication' or 'mainstreaming' (Nelson 2012, 130) of the vampire in recent times (see Gordon and Hollinger 1997; Spaise 2005), most noticeably in Charlaine Harris's Sookie Stackhouse novels (2001–) and the subsequent *True Blood* television series (2008–). In this newer configuration, the vampire disturbs previously clear distinctions between themselves and humans, creating the fuzzy borderland explored so thoroughly in the *Twilight* saga.

Meyer makes humanity perpetually vulnerable to the invasion by outside forces (here thirsty vampires and avenging Volturi), just as the 9/11 attacks changed the dynamics of American invincibility and forced some reconsideration of how to respond to external threats to sovereignty. Under such conditions of precarity, as Judith Butler has argued, violent assertion is the usual mode of response, however, such vulnerability might also result in an alternative, more measured reaction based on 'another vision of the future than that which perpetuates violence in the name of denying it' (Butler 2006, 18). At a key moment in the showdown with the Volturi in *Breaking Dawn*, Aro says 'Only the known is safe. Only the known is tolerable. The unknown is . . . a vulnerability' (Meyer 2011, 665). Butler argues that it is precisely by embracing vulnerability that we comprehend more fully our 'socially constituted bodies, attached to others' and through this understand our 'fundamental dependency and ethical responsibility' to others (2006, 20, 22). Rather than violence as the only recourse to being made vulnerable, Butler argues for a politics based on mutual recognition and an understanding of the precariousness of life, and Meyer's novels can be seen to embrace these ideas.

Ironically, of course, it is the immortal Cullens who become Meyer's vehicle alerting humanity to such values, and it is to this group of heroes and new gods that the novels look for leadership. It is the undead who announce the fragility of our humanly vulnerable and contingent lives, having learnt to abstain from blood drinking and as a result become 'civilized', able 'to form bonds based on love rather than survival or convenience' (Meyer 2009b, 378). As Edward Cullen puts it, vampires are like a 'living stone – hard and cold . . . we are set the way we are, and it is very rare for us to experience a real change' (Meyer 2009c, 444). Out of this strange mixture, however, Meyer reinvents a quasi-politics and ethics of non-violent negotiation based on reimagined American values enacted by these new gods of the wilderness.

But, ultimately, this coldness and inability to feel 'real change' in Meyer's vision undermines the political potential of Butler's work, leaving a community that is static, unfeeling, detached and conservative.

In many respects, Meyer's Mormon faith may have fed this desire to re-engage with what for many in twenty-first century USA would be seen as lost values. Many critics have argued that Mormonism is *the* American religion, containing within it a spiritual vision of the nation and its purpose in the world. As Stephen Mansfield reported, 'Mormons believe that the nation is divinely ordained . . . the Constitution . . . drafted under divine guidance, and that the US will play a predestined role during the millennial reign of Christ' (2012, n.p.). Thus, Mormons became 'champions of the American vision' with the *Book of Mormon* as an elaborate allegory of America: not as a book of revelation but a tale of the nation spiritualized by its 'author' Joseph Smith's inventive mind combining Old Testament ideas and American realities to create a mystical version of early history wherein American values defined God's kingdom on Earth; its effective Manifest Destiny. Indeed, Meyer has commented that 'Unconsciously, I put a lot of my basic beliefs into the story. Free agency is a big theme, as is sacrifice' (Glaister 2008, n.p.).

American Place

Despite the reach of the *Twilight* books, there is something fundamentally American about them, beginning early on with the setting which takes Bella from 'Paradise Valley', Phoenix, Arizona, to Forks, Washington. In a sense, from one frontier to another, from sunlight and warmth to 'gloomy, omnipresent shade' dominated by rain and cloud (Meyer 2009a, 3) where Bella faces the 'forks' in her life path from which she must choose a direction and a destiny. Immediately, she says, 'You could never see the sky here; it was like a cage' and consequently her journey becomes a 'personal hell on Earth' (10, 23). As the books unravel, of course, her divine comedy is a journey through this Hell to a new Paradise found through love and sacrifices with Edward.

The mythic landscape of Forks is deliberately otherworldly: the Olympic Peninsula with its mist-shrouded Mount Olympus – home of gods and mythic creatures; Port Angeles, the landing place of angels; La Push Reservation with its Native American tribal werewolves, and the dark woods and deep waters surrounding it all. It is in these sacred spaces that Meyer's renewal of American values takes place. In *New Moon*, she writes,

> What kind of place was this? Could a world really exist where ancient legends went wandering around the borders of tiny, insignificant towns, facing down mythical monsters? . . . Was there anything sane or normal at all, or was everything just magic and ghost stories? (2009b, 259)

In the spirit of fantasy, as described by Rosemary Jackson, such created worlds of otherness are 'compensatory' because they 'fill up a lack, making up for an apprehension of actuality as disordered and insufficient' (1981, 174). Bella is drawn into this world because her own is 'disordered and insufficient'; she feels clumsy and incongruous, rejected by her mother and awkward with her father, and yet, as ever, throughout the saga, this mystery of otherness reconnects her with primal forces and values. Thus the 'green maze' of the forest or the meadow where Bella and Edward kiss take on magical, Edenic qualities: 'small, perfectly round, and filled with wild-flowers', 'a magic place full of light . . . lit by sunshine and the sparkle of his skin' (Meyer 2009a, 226; 2009b, 171–2). Here she feels a different order emerging: 'Nothing had changed in this forest for thousands of years, and all the myths and legends of a hundred different lands seemed much more likely in this green haze than they had in my clear-cut bedroom' (2009a, 119).

If external space is reshaped as transformative and Edenic, banishing the dark threat of traditional Gothic tales, then so too is internal space such as the Cullens' house (Meyer 2009a, 280) which typifies the anti-Gothic position of the novels. Although secluded in the dark forest and, therefore, externally resembling a cliché of the Gothic lair, the inside of the house is a contradictory space where the absence of 'coffins . . . piled skulls in the corners . . . [and] cowebs' is commented on by Bella (287). The Cullens' spatial territory resembles their codes of existence; light, open and airy, 'painted a soft, faded white' (281); like a 'McMansion located on an estate outside of town', as Nelson puts it (2012, 135).

The American New World setting is thus critical to Meyer's *revamped* vampires and referred to through a number of cultural markers in the novels, such as Bella's discovery that 'Vampires like baseball', because as Edward comments, 'It's the American pastime' (2009a, 303). Similarly, when Bella puzzles over Edward's identity, she draws on her American cultural context for a parallel: 'I had been vacillating during the last month between Bruce Wayne and Peter Parker' (77). Later Edwards retorts, 'What if I'm not a superhero? What if I'm the bad guy?' (79). This becomes a running joke, for example, when Bella comments later that she does not always want to be Lois Lane, but would rather like to be Superman (413). Tellingly, these references demonstrate how Meyer has indeed created a new breed of superheroes, or gods, to both save humans and show them how to live differently and better.

Equally important to this redefining of community values throughout the novels is the celebration of wealth and consumption identified with the Cullens' ability to 'predict trends in the stock market' (2009b, 12) and its transference onto Bella in the last book of the series with her 'acceptance into an Ivy League college', with the 'shiny black credit card that felt red-hot in [her] back pocket' (2011, 4), and the Mercedes Guardian she drives. Such signs of conspicuous consumption are part of Meyer's larger vision of the Cullens as central to a metaphorically reimagined community, a 'tapestry of family and friends' with different races, languages and myths 'interlaced' (2011, 486–7), creating a hybridized utopia. In this portrait of the world, werewolves and vampires, Native and Euro Americans work together for the common good. Their collision of legends permits a double tale to emerge throughout the saga of Edward and Jacob, which by *Breaking Dawn* has become an emblematic alliance against the Volturi to save their common (American) territory. Thus the personal family narrative extends outward from Bella's dysfunctional family to embrace a dream of a wider community in which she imagines herself part of a 'strange collage' of Jacob's world and hers, with 'the bobbing heads of two small, black-haired children' (2009c, 469), while simultaneously incorporated into the Cullens' vampire coven. This blending of family and community visions is seen too at La Push Reservation when Bella is drawn to Emily's warm kitchen as 'a friendly place, bright with white cupboards' like a 'romantic movie . . . it sang out with joy and life and true love' where she was 'scrubbing at a spotless floor . . . tugging a string of wool through an ancient loom, and always cooking' (2009b, 293, 308). This mirrors her response to the clean lines and airy spaciousness of the Cullen house in the first novel. Bella's dream is to somehow coexist between these worlds, rather like her desire to have both Edward and Jacob in her life throughout the saga. Symbolically and more dramatically, however, it represents Meyer's ideal America summed up in Bella's response to the possibility that Edward might be a vampire: 'It doesn't matter to me what you are' (2009a, 161).

By the final book of the saga, *Breaking Dawn*, the landscape has become almost entirely symbolic as Meyer removes the action from the 'real' America of Forks, high school and family homes to mythic, emblematic space like 'Isle Esme' where Bella is transformed to 'woman' and then to vampire, to be, like Edward, 'frozen in his seventeen year old perfection' (2011, 14). Here the imagery is of the Fountain of Youth associated in American myth with Ponce De Leon's Bimini and now reimagined as Bella's space of change, with its 'beach glowing pale in the light of the moon', 'gentle swells' and 'weightless current' (71, 77) that invite her to her sexual awakening in the ocean.

However, her return as a vampire is to the American world of the Cullens' designed wilderness and the 'cottage room' with its deliberate echo of the frontier reimagined as an 'eclectic' (443) *House and Home* version of the *Little House on the Prairie*: 'The floor was a crazy quilt of smooth, flat stones ... exposed beams ... the walls were warm wood ... the beehive fireplace in the corner held the remains of a slow flickering fire' (443). As always, however, this is a mythic and magical space 'where you just expected Snow White to walk right in with her apple in hand, or a unicorn to stop and nibble at the rosebushes' (444). From the transformative Paradise isle to the elaborate remodelled frontier America, Meyer places Bella into a parallel reality where conventional dark Gothic spaces are undone and with it traditional expectations of the vampire: 'Edward had always thought that he belonged to the world of horror stories. Of course, I'd known he was dead wrong. It was obvious that he belonged *here*. In a fairy tale' (444). At such moments, Meyer completes her experiment by not simply transforming her heroine, but also in changing her readers' vision of the USA reborn out of a mythically remembered past through 'a backward version – in effect, a reversal' of the Gothic (Nelson 2012, 146).

American Youth

If the novels transpose the vampire story into a 'cottage room' in a forest, or into small town America with the Cullens' suburban gated community, then it also favours the archetypal environment of the mainstreamed Gothic learnt from *Buffy the Vampire Slayer*, the high school. It is no surprise that the finale of *Twilight* is the all-American Prom with its self-reflexive references to being 'like a horror movie waiting to happen' or to *Carrie* (Meyer 2009a, 422, 424), as well as to other teen dramas familiar to its target Gen X/Y audience. In fact, crucial to understanding the saga's impact and popularity is to recognize its use of and appeal to a youthful audience schooled in popular culture. Thus Meyer shifts the vampire narrative within the generic framework of the youth text, and in particular the teen angst high school drama (*Pretty in Pink* and *My So Called Life* meets *Carrie* and *The Faculty*). *Buffy* had already proven that there was a market for this type of domestication taking vampires from the shadow world of Transylvania or even the gloomy New Orleans of Anne Rice's novels, to the sunlit, small town of Sunnydale, which, as it transpires, was sitting on top of a Hellmouth. As Spooner argues, *Buffy* 'maps the traumas of teenage existence back onto those of Gothic fiction so that high school is literally hell . . .' (2006, 115). In *Twilight* the social crises being responded to are always, in part, derived from these earlier works with their intense anxieties of teendom: of fitting in and being popular, body image, the containment of family and the allure of relationships and sexuality. Of course, in Meyer's world this teen angst is relativized through Bella's contact with Edward so that the everyday becomes increasingly extraordinary. Suddenly the teen world of being 'free to pout and mope' (2009a, 127) is set against choices of life and death, and battles over good and evil, past and future. The saga enacts a psychodrama whereby youth is reimagined *outside* of traditional youth culture so that Meyer interrupts adolescent thoughtlessness and solipsism, like Bella's initial efforts to use the 'shattering beats' through her headphones to make it 'impossible . . . to think' (113), and reconnects her with the existential world of agency, responsibility and mortality. The novels refute this youthful exclusion of the world and bring it crashing into Bella's life through the Cullens forcing her to confront the meaning of time and change, bringing an extraordinary seriousness involving constant discussions over ethics, moral dilemmas and sexual boundaries. In truth, the books talk a lot and shift the emphasis of much youth culture away from *doing* to *pondering*.

Thus Bella, the awkward high school heroine, embodies these tensions; being independent and wilful and yet strangely uncertain of herself and only too willing to accept the traditional roles of swooning, rescued damsel or domestic carer to her inadequate father Charlie. In keeping with the books' interest in recuperating traditional values, it is not surprising that, despite her outward suggestion of independence and feminist rhetoric, Bella is a conservative figure prone to what she calls '*Anne of Green Gables* flashbacks' in which she imagines herself 'in a long skirt and high-necked lace blouse with my hair piled up on my head' (2009c, 246). Through such moments, the novels locate Bella in the past, fulfilling the role expected of women *before* feminism: 'A world where it would surprise no one if I wore his ring on my finger. A simpler place, where love was defined in simpler ways. One plus one equals two . . .' (288). The 'simpler place' evoked here is the lost time that the novels reclaim through the immortal Cullens, representing an idealized timeless moment of myth and fantasy that will eventually, in the course of the four novels, become Bella's world as well.

Central to this 'simpler place' is how teen sexuality is reorganized in the novels, perhaps echoing the pamphlet *For the Strength of Youth* given to all Mormons as a guide to the teachings of their faith. Meyer's Mormonism constructs the novels' moral tone, since desire, though constantly, and often explicitly apparent, is always thwarted by control, repression and fear. In this sense she explores teenage sexuality, one of the staple themes of American youth texts since the 1950s, through Bella's 'restless craving' and the subsequent 'strange new intensity' (2009a, 192, 202) she feels for Edward, a power like 'unexpected electricity' making her 'blood electric in [her] veins' (122, 191).

Meyer, however, sees the transformative quality of desire and the energy and strength gained through abstinence, harnessed to a communal purpose rather than selfish pleasure. The lesson is learnt through Carlisle Cullen, an 'ethical vampire' (Nelson 2012, 135) who tells Edward of his struggle 'to perfect his self-control' in order to apply himself to more auspicious goals like 'saving human lives' in 'the New World' (Meyer 2009a, 297). Self-control and the curbing of individual appetites constitute Meyer's sense of familial and communal care reconfiguring, like Carlisle's dream, a (new) New World in which, ironically, what it might mean to be *truly* human is revealed through vampires: 'you're resurrecting the human in me, and everything feels stronger because it's fresh', claims Edward (2009a, 265). The Cullens, therefore, become Meyer's exemplar for 'essential humanity' because they have learnt a type of transcendent new faith, 'to rise above – to conquer the boundaries' and thereby, to achieve a fuller realization of what humanity should and could be (268).

Thus Meyer rewrites teenage sexuality as 'courtship' and slow exploration; a kind of addicted romance replacing the frenetic fumbling of high school dating: 'I wish you could feel the complexity . . . the confusion . . . I feel', says Edward (243). In fact, the mid-section of *Twilight* becomes a treatise on the nature of romance and love presenting arguments for old-fashioned moralities about waiting, contrasted with its more popular image in cinema and fiction: 'It's incredible isn't it, the difference between reading about something, seeing it in the pictures, and experiencing it?' (264). Edward sums it up as 'I wrestled all night, while watching you sleep, with the chasm between what I knew was *right*, moral, ethical, and what I *wanted*' (265).

The rewards for such 'wrestling' and abstinence, the novels suggest, is immortal perfection like that achieved by Bella, who once transformed to a vampire claims she 'had found [her] true place in the world, the place I fit, the place I shined' (2011, 485). With extraordinary powers of mind and body, she reaches the 'conditions both of pre-Fall Paradise and of Swedenborgian-Spiritualist heaven, where celestial sexuality is an exalted alchemical wedding that reunites the world and the two sexes' (Nelson 2012, 146).

The United Nations of Vampires

As we have seen, Meyer's novels work by *interrupting* the everyday human world with extraordinary events that transport readers away from it in order to return *differently*. These spiritual shifts lead towards what Nelson calls 'the new supernatural' (2012, xi), as well as relating nostalgically to political and moral values derived from a precise past American vision. Thus the domesticated is interrupted, as is the world of school and teenage anxieties – classes, Proms, baseball games, meals, shopping trips and many other quotidian moments – so that during the hiatus, we are forced to review and even challenge our thinking and expectations of such ordinary scenes. Bella puts it well in *Eclipse*, 'In my head, everything spun and shifted, rearranging so that things that had meant one thing before, now meant something else' (2009c, 259). As a result of these interruptions, the saga imagines a remoralized USA reappropriating values associated with the mythic origins of the nation and its subsequent rise to power. In a self-reflexive moment in *Breaking Dawn*, Jacob notes that 'Like this wasn't real. Like I was in some sort of Gothic version of a bad sitcom' (2011, 170). In many respects the *Twilight* saga is exactly this; a Gothic version of a bad sitcom reacquainting its readers with values one might associate with a retrofitted *Father Knows Best* or *The Adventures of Ozzie and Harriet* from the political consensus of 1950s' USA. For, as Nelson argues, there is always a sense of 'reversal' at work in Meyer's sense of faith, a return to some imagined mythic time 'to accommodate the spiritual needs of its consumers' (2012, 262). Politically and culturally this is apparent in the 'Gothic sitcom' played out across the quartet of novels and best explored through the vampire Garrett's key speech during the final showdown with the Volturi in *Breaking Dawn*.

Appropriately, he is an American revolutionary, a 'patriot' (Meyer 2011, 668) who states explicitly to Aro 'This won't be the first time I've fought to keep myself from a king's rule. Here's to freedom from oppression' (659). Speaking for those gathered in the clearing, a veritable United Nations of Vampires, Garrett universalizes traditional American values endorsed in Meyer's books; standing up against oppression for freedom, overturning tyranny and supporting the dominant structures of community and family. As he says of the Volturi, 'Witness now as they seek flimsy excuses to continue their true mission. Witness them struggle to find a justification for their true purpose – to destroy this family here' (666). The 'invasion' of these outsiders is opposed by a new errand in the wilderness; a counter-mission defined through the 'power' of the Cullens and their 'intense family binding' as Garrett terms it (666). Having put aside the darkness of the vampire's Gothic past, he tells us, 'in return . . . they have found something worth even more perhaps than mere gratification of desire . . . the peaceful character of this life of sacrifice . . . [and] no thought of domination' (666). Out of personal struggle emerges Meyer's political vision of a reborn New World optimism, potentially multi-ethnic and harmonious, moral and virtuous, but only maintained by the constant policing of its borders against the threat from the outside.

In truth, Meyer's work charts a trajectory rooted in Mormon Americanism and a faith tied to unchanging traditional values emblematized through the immortality of the Cullens' static relationship to the past – 'set the way we are' – in which, as Edward says to Bella, the result is like 'leaving time behind' (2009c, 246). Butler argues that too often in American history, as indeed after 9/11, there was a demand for action to 'restore the loss or return the world to a former order, to reinvigorate a fantasy that the world formerly was orderly' (2006, 29–30). In the end, this is also the problem with Meyer's 'action' and her novels' return to fundamental American values, since contained within them are also conservative, retrograde notions of power and gender relations, family dynamics and social hierarchy that constitute another type of myth or 'fantasy' to 'return the world to a former order' and to rediscover what Bella calls 'a simpler place'. Despite the non-violent ethics that the books ultimately support, where alliance, treaty, negotiation, 'forgiveness' and 'witness' (Meyer 2011, 48, 667) overcome the threats of brutal war, there is still an uncomfortable stasis in the politics of the *Twilight* saga, living only in the frozen past holding fast to the timeless, immortality of values that perhaps would benefit from the antagonistic struggles that contingency, the precariousness of life and all its inherent vulnerabilities actually bring; something the immortal Cullens and, ultimately, the *transformed* Bella Swan, can never truly comprehend.

Ultimately, Meyer's revamped vampire is a device, a dark prism through which to view what it means to be human and to present a particular political vision of a reimagined American moral leadership moving inexorably towards 'The Happily Ever After' (Meyer 2011, 688). In Bella's words, who, by the end of the saga, has turned away from her humanity, 'Without the dark, we'd never see the stars' (2009a, 204). But perhaps that ought to read 'stars and stripes'?

Works Cited

Auerbach, N. (1995), *Our Vampires, Ourselves*. Chicago: University of Chicago Press.

Botting, F. (1996), *Gothic*. London: Routledge.

Butler, J. (2006), *Precarious Life: The Powers of Mourning and Violence*. London: Verso.

Deleuze, G. and Guattari, F. (1988), *A Thousand Plateaus*. London: The Athlone Press.

Fiedler, L. (1960), *Love and Death in the American Novel*. New York: Stein and Day.

For the Strength of Youth, (no author) at https://www.lds.org/youth/for-the-strength-of-youth/sexual-purity?lang=eng.

Glaister, D. (2008), 'Mormon who put new life into vampires', http://www.guardian.co.uk/books/2008/jul/20/news.booksforchildrenandteenagers, accessed on 27 November 2012.

Goddu, T. (1997), *Gothic America: Narrative, History, and Nation*. New York: Columbia University Press.

—(1999), Review Essay, 'Vampire Gothic'. *American Literary History* 11(1), 125–41.

Gordon, J. and Hollinger, V. (1997), *Blood Read: The Vampire As Metaphor in Contemporary Culture*. Philadelphia: University of Pennsylvania Press.

Jackson, R. (1981), *Fantasy: The Literature of Subversion*. London: Routledge.

Mansfield, S. (2012), 'Mormonism's American Values', http://usatoday30.usatoday.com/news/opinion/forum/story/2012-09-09/mormon-american-values-romney/57719056/1, accessed on 18 October 2012.

Meyer, S. (2009a [2005]), *Twilight*. London: Atom Books.

—(2009b [2006]), *New Moon*. London: Atom Books.

—(2009c [2007]), *Eclipse*. London: Atom Books.

—(2011 [2008]), *Breaking Dawn*. London: Atom Books.

Nelson, V. (2012), *Gothika: Vampire Heroes, Human Gods, and the New Supernatural*. Cambridge, MA: Harvard University Press.

Spaise, T. L. (2005), 'Necrophilia and SM: The Deviant Side of *Buffy the Vampire Slayer'*. *Journal of Popular Culture* 38(4), 744–62.

Spooner, C. (2006), *Contemporary Gothic*. London: Reaktion Books.

17

Rewriting Popular Classics as Popular Fiction: Jane Austen, Zombies, Sex and Vampires

Ben Dew

It is a truth universally acknowledged that a reader in possession of a good Jane Austen novel must be in want of (many) more such stories: this, it would seem, is the mantra of the industry that has sprung up around Austen's fiction in recent years. Austen herself must be held partially responsible for her publishing legacy; not only did she create works with a unique capacity to inspire devotion, but by dying at the relatively young age of 42, with only six completed novels to her name, she ensured (albeit unwittingly) that demand for her fiction would always outweigh supply. Authors and publishers have done their best to redress this imbalance, providing a startling array of prequels, sequels and adaptations of her texts. These works now have a considerable heritage of their own. The first attempts at expanding Austen's *oeuvre* came from two of her nieces, Catherine Hubbeck and Anna Austen Lefroy, who used Austen's unfinished novels *The Watsons* and *Sanditon* as starting points for their respective literary endeavours (Lynch 2005, 161). Sybil Brinton's 1914 work, *Old Friends and New Fancies,* however, is the first true sequel, beginning at the end of *Pride and Prejudice* and using characters from all of Austen's works. Numerous writers have followed in Brinton's wake, and while the twentieth century was by no means lacking in Austen adaptations, the growth of print-on-demand technology and the increasing popularity of e-readers have enabled a dramatic increase of their number in recent times. The most notable feature of this body of work is, perhaps, its size; since the millennium, for example, more than a hundred different writers have produced versions of *Pride and Prejudice,* between them publishing well in excess of 200 novels. Of these authors, nine (at least) have written six or more such works. In attempting to inspire various combinations of tears, fear, laughter and sexual arousal, these texts have frequently taken a good deal of liberty with Austen's story. Elizabeth has become the slayer of aliens, zombies and vampires, while Darcy has been re-imagined as, among other things, King Arthur, a rock star and a small woollen puppet.[1]

Despite such diversity and, on occasions, bizarreness, it is possible to identify a number of trends among *Pride and Prejudice* adaptations. The vast majority of the writers (in excess of 90 per cent) are female. Darcy appears to be the principal point of interest for many of them; of the 200 adaptations consulted, a third contain references to Darcy in their title, while only 5 per cent mention Elizabeth (either as Elizabeth Bennet or Mrs Darcy). The novels themselves are also similar in structure and are the product of four basic narrative strategies, sometimes used in isolation, sometimes in combination. The most common sort of transformation involves a simple expansion of the story in the form of a sequel or, more rarely, a prequel to the original tale. Closely related to this approach is 'the variation', a work which alters a single element of the original story and, through imagining the consequences of this change for the novel's characters, constructs an alternative narrative. The core premise of such narratives, which are a standard feature of the 'fan-fiction' genre, can be expressed through a 'what if' statement. Examples include: Ola Wegner's (2010) *Deception* (what if another wealthy and attractive man had appeared in Elizabeth's life after the ball at Netherfield?); Alexa Adams's (2010) *First Impressions: A Tale of less*

Pride and Prejudice (what if Elizabeth and Darcy had fallen in love at the Netherfield Ball?) and Ann Herendeen's rather more ambitious (2010) *Pride/ Prejudice* (what if Elizabeth and Darcy had been bisexual, attracted to both each other and Charles Bingley and Charlotte Lucas respectively?). The appeal of such continuations is easy to see; not only do they enable both readers and authors to spend more time with much-loved characters, but they also provide an opportunity for writers to reinterpret Austen's plot for a twenty-first century audience. Indeed, many 'variations' use their 'what if' premise to imagine Austen's characters embarking upon more illicit romantic escapades and resisting the moral and sexual codes which shaped their behaviour in 1813. Such a procedure is particularly significant given Austen's own approach to mass-market literature. Austen was clearly indebted to the popular sentimental tradition of writing, which came to the fore in the latter half of the eighteenth century. However, as Judy Simons has argued, she 'subverts the plot of the popular novel . . . placing shady intrigue and sexual threat in the background, whilst the routine fabric of daily life becomes the stage for playing out the real horrors . . . which confront young women in Regency England' (2009, 470). Modern writers of variations, in a sense, reverse this process, subverting Austen's domestic narratives and, like their popular predecessors, placing 'shady intrigue' centre stage.

A third type of adaptation is based around a shift in narrative focalization. Such a device can be used in a variety of ways. Some writers simply alter the point of view and provide versions of the novel narrated from a different perspective (generally that of Darcy). Others expand the story of a more minor character, seeking to give renewed literary life to (among others) Wickham, Georgiana Darcy, Lydia and Mary Bennet and Charlotte and Maria Lucas.[2] The final, and perhaps the most interesting, type of adaptation transplants the action of *Pride and Prejudice* to a different cultural milieu. Examples include Lev Raphael's *Pride and Prejudice: The Jewess and the Gentile* (2011), Lavinia Angell's *The Sheik of Araby: Pride and Prejudice in the Desert* (2010) and most famously, Helen Fielding's *Bridget Jones' Diary* (1996), which traces the eponymous heroine's various romantic entanglements in 1990s London. Other writers dramatically transform the Regency England Austen used as her setting through the addition of aliens, vampires, werewolves and zombies. Such shifts not only dramatically alter the social norms with which the novels are concerned – perhaps most significantly by making violent death as common an occurrence as romance – they also bring Austen's canonical text into close contact with a range of narrative tropes and conventions from less conventionally 'literary' forms of writing. This case study will focus on three such adaptations: Seth Grahame-Smith's *Pride and Prejudice and Zombies* (2009), Amy Armstrong's work of erotic fiction *Pride and Prejudice: A Clandestine Classic* (2012) and Amanda Grange's *Mr Darcy, Vampyre* (2009). While these works use a range of the techniques and approaches discussed above, all seek to fuse Austen's writing with a genre of popular fiction. Such a move, I argue, necessitates reflection on the relative statuses of 'popular' and 'canonical' literature, and the nature of the relationship between them.

Zombies

Pride and Prejudice and Zombies is premised on the notion that Hertfordshire has been over-run by hordes of the undead; consequently, the Bennet sisters face the dual challenges of finding suitable husbands and keeping themselves, and their friends and family, alive in the face of zombie attacks. The novel is not a work of original fiction, but rather a 'mash-up', which employs the same 61-chapter structure as *Pride and Prejudice*, and combines sections of prose from Austen with additions from Grahame-Smith. Such a technique allows Grahame-Smith to exploit popular assumptions about both Austen's writing and zombie fiction. Indeed, the juxtaposition of the two genres is the source of much of the book's humour. Its front cover, for example, utilizes William Beechey's *Portrait of Marcia Fox*, an image of a pretty, young Regency woman, frequently employed on the dust-jackets of Austen's novels.[3] In this case, however, the artist, Doogie Horner, has made some dramatic modifications; the lower half of Fox's jaw has been made skeletal, her eyes have been given a sinister red glow and generous daubs of dark red blood have been applied to her pristine white dress and neck. The text itself provides a narrative equivalent of this representation, moving abruptly between images of 'ultra-violent zombie mayhem' and 'classic regency romance' (Austen and Grahame-Smith 2009, title page). During the Meryton ball, for example, an attack from two 'female dreadfuls' cracks the skull of one of the guests 'like a walnut . . . sending a shower of dark blood spouting as high as the chandeliers' (Austen and Grahame-Smith 2009, 14). Almost immediately, however, Grahame-Smith reverts to Austen's account, simply placing the phrase 'apart from the attack' to her observation that 'the evening passed off pleasantly for the whole family' (2009, 16). Ultimately, Grahame-Smith shows that the Bennet family are rather more concerned by who-danced-with-who at the ball, than the violent death of one of their neighbours.

The insertion of disembodied creatures into Austen's narrative is accompanied, somewhat ironically, by an increased focus on the body and its various excretions. Often this takes the form of a reification of characters' social and mental anxieties; thus Mrs Bennet's 'nerves' are given a physical representation through her habit of vomiting, while the loss of liberty Wickham experiences from his forced marriage to Lydia is accompanied by a loss of control over his bowel movements. Elsewhere, blood and brains are splattered indiscriminately over the living and living dead alike. The body is further emphasized by the text's bawdiness. Testicular punning is a defining feature of Elizabeth and Darcy's courtship; at Netherfield, the two giggle over the merits of public and private balls (2009, 73), Elizabeth and Lydia later lament that there are hardly any balls to be had in Meryton (2009, 175), while at Pemberley Elizabeth returns the lead ammunition she has borrowed with the phrase: 'Your balls, Mr Darcy' (2009, 205). The theme is developed during the visit to Pemberley when Mrs Gardiner observes of Darcy that: 'there is something of dignity in the way his trousers cling to those most English parts of him' (2009, 206). Such references exploit a number of conflicting assumptions about Austen's work. On the one hand, despite the efforts of generations of academics, Austen has never entirely shaken off the reputation she acquired in the Victorian era, and her novels are still viewed as providing, in Anthony Trollope's words, 'a sweet lesson of homely, household, womanly virtue' (Trollope, in Southam 1987, 8). On the other hand, however, television and film directors have often sought to uncover a latent sexuality within Austen's work. This salaciousness has been widely commented upon, and much of the press reaction to the hugely successful 1995 BBC adaptation of *Pride and Prejudice* noted screen-writer Andrew Davies' preoccupation with heaving Regency cleavages and the non-too-subtle allure of Darcy's trousers (see Sales 1996, 227–39). Grahame-Smith is clearly aware of both the 'polite' Austen and the 'prurient' one, and takes delight in both emphasizing the propriety and refinement of her fictional world and, simultaneously, violating it.

Such an approach ensures that the relationship between *Pride and Prejudice and Zombies* and *Pride and Prejudice* without zombies is a complex one. To an extent, Grahame-Smith removes much of the restraint that characterizes Austen's writing. This is particularly true in his use of violence. In allowing Mary Bennet to grab a fork and attack Mr Collins, Elizabeth to smash Darcy's head against a mantelpiece and Darcy to beat Wickham lame, the text releases some of the lingering resentment and aggression that remains hidden beneath the original's surface. Indeed, such passages capture the 'id' of *Pride and Prejudice*'s characters, with the polite and civilizing influence of Austen's 'super-ego' removed. The novel is also, to borrow a term from Mikhail Bakhtin, fundamentally 'carnivalesque' in character (1984a and 1984b). Like the carnival, and those literary works which took it as a model, Grahame-Smith's writing combines the lofty with the low, and uses parody and an emphasis on the body to bring an exalted object (in this case a canonical literary text) down to earth. If read in this manner, *Pride and Prejudice and Zombies* could be conceived as destabilizing the boundary between popular and literary writing and, through doing so, providing an attack on a fundamentally conservative 'high' or 'official' culture. To pursue this line of argument too far, however, would be a mistake. The book's aim, as its blurb states, is to transform 'a masterpiece of world literature into something that you'd actually want to read'. Underlying such an objective, and the novel more generally, are a series of assumptions about the literary and the popular, with the former presented as serious, cerebral, pious and a little dull and the latter as comic, fun and subversive. Placing zombies in an Austen novel is a worthwhile endeavour because it enables Grahame-Smith to exploit the comic potential of the division between these categories. Such a move, however, serves to confirm, rather than question, the gap between 'high' and 'low' culture.

Sex

While Grahame-Smith's 'mash-up' technique is also employed within *Pride and Prejudice: A Clandestine Classic*, its author, Amy Armstrong, provides a rather different sort of textual insertion. The novel's starting point is a premise common in *Pride and Prejudice* 'variations': what if Elizabeth and Darcy had allowed their passion for one another to spill out – metaphorically and, on occasions, literally – before the novel's conclusion? This idea is explored through a succession of erotically charged scenes: Elizabeth and Darcy have a series of vivid sexual fantasies about one another, enjoy a passionate embrace when Elizabeth is at Netherfield and engage in oral sex at the Netherfield Ball. Elizabeth finally loses her virginity during the visit to Hunsford. Such additions not only turn *Pride and Prejudice* into a work of soft-core pornography, but also enable it to become a reflection on the nature of sexual desire in Georgian England. The text's primary subject is the tension between its characters' natural passions and the restrictive social environment in which they live. Elizabeth is presented as an individual overtly preoccupied with her own sexuality; however, although her imagination and body lead her in one direction, she constantly fears the judgements of others. Consequently, she spends much of the novel questioning the propriety of her actions and worrying about her capacity to 'prevent herself from doing the very thing which society told her she should not, as a lady, desire, certainly not outside the sanctity of marriage' (Austen and Armstrong 2012, 944–5). Similarly, Darcy conceives of himself as a 'slave to society's rules and tenets' (1224) and tries, albeit with very little success, 'to rein in his treacherous thoughts and remain stoic' (1225–6).

Such a structure not only gives Armstrong's sex scenes an illicit quality well suited to the 'romantic' genre in which she is writing, but also emphasizes the bond between Elizabeth and Darcy. These individuals, Armstrong reminds us, are united not just by their desire for one another, but also by their anxieties concerning, and ultimate rejection of, repressed and repressive attitudes towards sex. The novel's interest in the relationship between individual and societal attitudes towards desire also allows new approaches to Austen's characters to be developed. One of the key challenges Armstrong faced was maintaining a clear differentiation between Wickham and Darcy. An erotic *Pride and Prejudice* would seem to require that Elizabeth and Darcy engage in a series of pre-marital sexual dalliances; however, there is a real danger that if Darcy is allowed to seduce Elizabeth, their relationship will come to resemble Wickham's (in Austen's eyes) sordid affair with Lydia. Armstrong is clearly alert to this, even allowing Elizabeth to reflect on the similarities between her own situation and that of her youngest sister. However, any sense of moral equivalence between Darcy and Wickham is eliminated through the text's emphasis on Darcy's 'politeness'. Thus, while Armstrong's regular references to her protagonist's physical strength and his tendency to grunt and growl alluringly when in a state of physical excitement serve to emphasize his masculinity, he is also shown to be a considerate and well-mannered lover. During their encounter at the Netherfield Ball, for example, Darcy promises 'upon [his] honour' not to do anything to Elizabeth that she does not 'explicitly want' (2140). While Elizabeth's 'honour' may be compromised by the events that follow, Darcy sticks to his word. Similarly, when Elizabeth decides 'to welcome [Darcy] inside her' at Hunsford Parsonage, she knows that, despite his considerable state of 'fervour', her lover 'would not press her if she changed her mind' (3755–6). Elizabeth is also conscious that it is not her own conduct that separates her from Lydia, but that of Darcy. If he, Elizabeth observes to herself, had not been 'such a gentlemen', she could, after all, 'so easily be in her sister's place' (5538–9). Armstrong, therefore, provides a distinctive notion of gentlemanliness, associating it not so much with virtue and propriety, but rather considerateness and discretion in the face of a judgemental society.

Armstrong's aim in her work, as her attempt to reconcile politeness with pornography implies, is to create smooth transitions between the nineteenth and twenty-first century sections of text. Two further techniques help her to achieve this. First, Armstrong adds long sections of interior monologue to the story, which allow Darcy and Elizabeth, using the standard language and tropes of literary erotica, to reflect on the events and characters Austen describes. During their first meeting, for example, we are informed that the heat in Darcy's eyes 'warmed Elizabeth's body, making her tingle and rousing her own clandestine desires' (297). Darcy also notes Elizabeth's allure, and imagines kissing her 'mouth-wateringly fleshy' lips while 'his hands did things to her body he was sure she had never dreamed possible' (645–6). Such passages ensure that rather than being taken by surprise, both characters and readers are well prepared for the novel's numerous sexual encounters; the reader is also by this time intimately acquainted with the idiom in which these scenes are to be described. Secondly, while sticking to the basic plot, as the 'mash-up' approach compels her to do, Armstrong alters the relationships between the novel's protagonists. Like a number of Austen's novels, *Pride and Prejudice* is based on a mistaken judgement on the part of the heroine. Elizabeth is initially repulsed by Darcy's manners and is attracted to Wickham's behaviour and person. Much of the story is concerned with the consequences of this judgement and the process through which it is reversed. Armstrong, however, largely abandons this structure. Despite her dislike of Darcy's haughtiness, Elizabeth is, as we have seen, immediately and deeply attracted to him; for Wickham, by contrast, her feelings are insipid at best. Consequently, rather than showing the value of 'second attachments' (as Austen had done), Armstrong's novel emphasizes that her characters' spontaneous desire for one another is based on a fundamental compatibility. Indeed, the narrative's plot is concerned with both the means through which the rational thought processes of the protagonists 'catch up' with their desires and the actions that characters have to perform to make their desires socially acceptable. Such devices enable *Pride and Prejudice* to function, essentially, as a work of erotic fiction and, as a result, Armstrong's approach is in sharp contrast to that of Grahame-Smith. *Pride and Prejudice and Zombies* is concerned with the disjunction between the 'popular' and the 'literary' and seeks to emphasize the incongruity of finding zombies in an Austen novel. Armstrong's text, however, does everything possible to reduce the gap between Austen and erotic fiction. Indeed, the tagline for the 'clandestine classics' series, 'the classic revealed', not only hints at the amount of flesh that will be on show, but also implies that beneath their prudish exteriors, major literary texts have a decidedly erotic core waiting to be uncovered.

Vampires

A third approach to the relationship between Austen and popular modes of fiction is to be found in Amanda Grange's *Mr Darcy, Vampyre*. This sequel to *Pride and Prejudice* opens with Elizabeth and Darcy's wedding, and it goes on to narrate their honeymoon tour around Europe. The trip is not a happy one for Elizabeth. Darcy is cold and aloof and shows no interest in her sexually, while his friends are distant and mysterious. Seeking the aid of a friendly Italian prince, Elizabeth decides to return to England. The prince, however, betrays Elizabeth to a vampire, who not only attempts to induct her into the vampire cult by sucking her blood, but also reveals the reason for Darcy's odd behaviour: he too is an immortal whose conscience makes him unwilling to feed on humans. The remainder of the novel is concerned with the married couple's attempt to free Darcy from the vampire curse, success in which enables them to consummate their marriage, and return to a life of normality at Pemberley. Through structuring her narrative in such a manner, Grange is able to use its vampire premise to repeat (albeit post-marriage) the basic plot of *Pride and Prejudice*. While Elizabeth is, perhaps, more conscious of it second time around, her task in both novels is essentially the same: to free herself from the influence of an alluring but deceitful man (Wickham/the Prince), uncover the reasons for Darcy's odd behaviour and, through doing so, gain an understanding of his true merit. This process enables Darcy to achieve contentment at a personal, familial and social level and, consequently, to fulfil his allotted role in life as a land-owning English gentleman. Grange's text demonstrates, therefore, that many of the patterns of behaviour Austen describes can, perhaps rather surprisingly, be explained using the conventions of vampire fiction. As a result, rather than simply transforming *Pride and Prejudice* into a work of genre fiction (as Armstrong has done), Grange uses her sequel to explore the links between Austen and the vampire tradition and, through doing so, emphasizes the parallels between a canonical and a non-canonical form of writing.

Grange, like Grahame-Smith, also draws fruitfully on ideas and images associated with adaptations of Austen's works. Indeed, rather in the manner of a film director over-indulging in sumptuous Regency-looking outfits and locations, her prose lingers – in a way that Austen's does not – on the clothes that her characters wear and the rooms they visit. For example Mme Rousel, one of Darcy's cousins, is introduced with an elaborate description of her appearance and attire in which the narrator's gaze moves from her hair – 'piled on her head with and secured by a long mother-of-pearl pin' – through the 'small frills' which passed for sleeves and the sheer fabric of her skirt, to the 'gold sandals' on her feet and the 'dark red shawl' draped across her knees (Grange 2009, 40). Grange's attitude towards such images is distinctly ambivalent. On the one hand, the novel's obsession with luxurious fabrics supports its key conceit: that while the appearances of the people Elizabeth and Darcy encounter are superficially impressive, their artifice hides a darker truth. Indeed, the glittering but fundamentally unnatural and soulless salons of continental Europe, devoid (like a vampire) of any evidence of age and wear, only serve to emphasize the more homely charms of England. True contentment, it is implied, is to be found in a 'living and breathing home' like Longbourne, with its 'scuffed and worn' furniture (218). On the other hand, however, Grange takes too much pleasure in descriptions of European fashion and upholstery for such a critique to be entirely effective. As much as critiquing excessive refinement, her writing, through describing it at such length, celebrates it, providing a sort of textual version of a BBC costume drama.

Grange also draws directly upon costume drama's most celebrated scene, the meeting in Davies' 1995 BBC adaptation between Elizabeth and Darcy after the latter has just emerged from a cooling swim in the lake at Pemberley. Playing with such associations, Grange gives her protagonists a lake scene of their own. While in the Alps, Elizabeth spies her husband taking an early morning dip; rather than simply observing him, however, she discards her clothes and joins him. The two then enjoy a rare moment of passion that is only interrupted by the unexpected arrival of Lady Catherine de Bourgh. Such water-based encounters constitute a significant feature of the text. Despite the difficulties of the first days of their marriage, Darcy and Elizabeth's affection is briefly rekindled as Elizabeth becomes 'mesmerised' by her husband's touch when they are on the deck of the ship taking them to France (30). Water is also significant in the final chapter of the novel. In a scene that draws heavily on the Indiana Jones film franchise, Darcy and Elizabeth find themselves under an ancient Roman villa, first decoding enigmatic inscriptions on stone tablets and later facing a watery death in a rapidly flooding cavern. The key moment comes when Darcy and Elizabeth, the waters rising rapidly around them, enjoy what they believe will be a final kiss. However, rather than prefiguring death this embrace leads to new life; the flood soon relents and the waters wash away Darcy's fang marks and restore his human identity. The associations being made here are quite straightforward. Land (particularly 'foreign' land) is associated with unnatural forms of formality and restraint; water, by contrast, is associated with intimacy, sexual liberty and the natural cycle of life. It is noteworthy that in developing and exploiting this imagery Grange uses characters from Austen and images and ideas from both Hollywood action adventure and costume drama.

Conclusion

Academic criticism has often taken a rather scornful approach to literary adaptations of Austen's work. Deirdre Shauna Lynch, for example, has labelled this body of work 'universally derivative' (2005, 161), while Judy Simons, despite praising some of the more 'sophisticated transpositions', notes that many Austen sequels are merely 'crude continuations of the original' (2009, 471). For the student of literature, however, the significance of these works lies not so much in their merit or lack of merit, but rather in their role and status within modern literary culture. A useful way of theorizing this culture is to be found in the account of poly-systems developed by the Israeli theorist Itamar Even-Zohar (1979). For Even-Zohar, literary poly-systems are characterized by their stratification and are composed of a centre (the canonical texts approved by 'official' culture) and a periphery (less highly regarded works such as popular forms of literature, and children's writing). Canonicity, Even-Zohar maintains, can be of two types, the static and the dynamic. The former refers to a text that is 'accepted as a finalized product and inserted into a set of sanctified texts literature (culture) wants to preserve' and the latter to 'a certain literary model [which] manages to establish itself as a productive principle' and shapes new types of writing (1990, 19). The survival (or not) of a system will be determined by the constantly changing relationship between the 'centre' and the 'periphery'. Thus although, at one level, Even-Zohar sees central and peripheral works as rivals, it is the dynamic tension between them that enables a literature to prosper. As he notes, 'when there is no "sub-culture," or when it is not allowed to exert real pressures on "high"/official/canonized culture, there is little chance of there being a vital "high" culture' (1979, 296).

While it is difficult to imagine any of the works discussed in this chapter entirely displacing Austen from her place within 'official culture', the study of these novels is important in the sense that it allows us to understand more about the structure of the Anglophone literary poly-system. To an extent, such an investigation further demonstrates the ways in which 'centre' and 'periphery' can enjoy a reciprocal relationship with one another. The 'peripheral' works discussed here are evidence of the dynamic canonicity of *Pride and Prejudice*, a novel which continues to act as a model for countless literary and cinematic adaptations. Moreover, by drawing on Austen's work, these re-imaginings emphasize its importance, and, thereby confirm its status as a key part of the 'static' canon. Indeed, the 'static' element of *Pride and Prejudice*, the original text of the novel, might be seen to be 'kept alive' by the readers who are drawn to it after encountering one of the text's many adaptations. Such adaptations also allow Evan-Zohar's model to be developed further. It is very difficult for any modern reader to come to Austen without preconceptions; the ways in which television directors, Austen's family and designers of university syllabi (among others) have represented her inevitably shape and mould our understandings. Indeed, one of the most noteworthy features of modern Austen 'rewritings' is their self-conscious exploitation of popular images of, and ideas about, her work. As a consequence, such texts are adaptations of both *Pride and Prejudice* itself, and what might be called the '*Pride and Prejudice* phenomena', the mass of cultural baggage that has attached itself to the novel over the past 200 years. The relation between centre and the periphery, therefore, is a complex one: the more 'central' a text becomes, the greater the periphery it spawns, and the more that periphery controls our engagement with the centre.

Notes

1. See (respectively): Pinnock 2011; Grahame-Smith 2009; Jeffers 2009; Dixon 2011; Rigaud 2011; Wang and Wang 2012.
2. Grange 2011; Elliott 2011; Odiwe 2008; Aitken 2011; Burris 2009; Becton 2011.
3. Beechey's painting was the first portrait to grace the cover of an Austen novel, the 1966 edition of *Emma* (see Gilbert 2008).

Works Cited

Adams, A. (2010), *First Impressions: A Tale of Less Pride & Prejudice*. Parker, CO: Outskirts Press.

Aitken, V. (2011), *Mary Bennet's Chance*. Brighton: Pen Press.

Angell, L. (2010), *The Sheik of Araby: Pride and Prejudice in the Desert*. Seattle, WA: Create Space.

Austen, J. and Armstrong, A. (2012), *Pride and Prejudice: Clandestine Classics*. Lincoln, UK: Total E-Bound Publishing.

Austen, J. and Grahame-Smith, S. (2009), *Pride and Prejudice and Zombies*. Philadelphia, PA: Quirk Books.

Austen, J. and Raphael, L. (2011), *Pride and Prejudice: The Jewess and the Gentile*. New River, AZ: Booknook.biz.

Bakhtin, M. (1984a [1965]), *Rabelais and His World*, trans. H. Iswolsky. London: Wiley.

—(1984b [1929]; rev. and trans. 1973), *Problems of Dostoevsky's Poetics*, trans. C. Emerson. Minneapolis and London: University of Minnesota Press.

Becton, J. (2011), *Maria Lucas: A Short Story*. Charlotte, NC: Whiteley Press.

Brinton, S. (1914), *Old friends and New Fancies: An Imaginary Sequel to the Novels of Jane Austen*. London: Holden & Hardingham.

Burris, S. (2009), *An Unlikely Missionary*. Scenery Hill, PA: Double Edge Press.

Dixon, P. O. (2011), *He Taught Me To Hope: Darcy and the Young Knight's Quest*. Seattle, Washington: Create Space.

Elliott, A. (2011), *Georgiana Darcy's Diary: Pride and Prejudice continued*. n.p.: Wilton Press.

Even-Zohar, I. (1979), 'Polysystem Theory'. *Poetics Today* 1(1/2), 287–310.

—(1990), 'Polysystem Theory'. *Poetics Today* 1(1), 9–26.

Fielding, H. (1996), *Bridget Jones' Diary*. London: Picador.

Gilbert, D. (2008), 'From Cover to Cover: Packaging Jane Austen from Egerton to Kindle'. *Persuasions on-line* 29(1). Retrieved from http://www.jasna.org/persuasions/on-line/vol29no1/gilbert.html.

Grange, A. (2009), *Mr Darcy, Vampyre*. Naperville, IL: Sourcebooks.

—(2011), *Wickham's Diary*. Naperville, IL: Sourcebooks.

Herendeen, A. (2010), *Pride/Prejudice: A Novel of Mr. Darcy, Elizabeth Bennet, and their Forbidden Lovers*. New York: Harper.

Jeffers, R. (2009), *Vampire Darcy's Desire*. Berkley, CA: Ulysses Press.

Lynch, D. S. (2005), 'Sequels', in J. Todd (ed.), *Jane Austen in Context*. Cambridge: Cambridge University Press, pp. 160–8.

Odiwe, J. (2008), *Lydia Bennet's Story*. Naperville, IL: Sourcebooks.

Pinnock, J. (2011), *Mrs Darcy vs. the Aliens*. Cromer: Proxima/Salt.

Rigaud, H. L. (2011), *Fitzwilliam Darcy; Rock Star*. Naperville, IL: Sourcebooks.

Sales, R. (1996), *Jane Austen and Representations of Regency England*. London: Routledge.

Simons, J. (2009), 'Jane Austen and Popular Culture', in C. Johnson (ed.), *A Companion to Jane Austen*. Oxford: Blackwell, pp. 467–77.

Southam, B. (1987), *Jane Austen: The Critical Heritage, volume 2, 1870-1940*. London: Routledge.

Wang, J. and Wang, H. (2012), *Jane Austen's Pride and Prejudice: Cozy Classics*. Vancouver: Simply Read Books.

Wegner, O. (2010), *Deception: A Tale of Pride and Prejudice*. Seattle, WA: Create Space.

18

Edu-Biz: The Worlds of Learning and Writing – A Writer's Perspective

Carl Tighe

Knowledge of the literature of the past is essential to any writer. However, while writers are aware of texts other than their own, and are particularly aware of the writing out of which their own has grown, they are not concerned with the 'place' in the canon or the critical interpretation of finished texts which have already achieved publication. Creative Writing is concerned with making what the Italian poet Julius Caesar Scaliger (1484–1558) called 'imaginative interventions' in the present (Scaliger 1561). Creative Writing is concerned with what will be written, what is being written, how a creative idea will be shaped and expressed, how it will get out into the world. Creative Writing – in addition to pondering the nature of humanity and interrogating the peculiar activity we call writing as an essential part of its daily business – is the midwife of new texts: it is concerned with planning and drafting of creative work, the process of bringing new work into existence, with the act of making, with solving particular creative problems, the difficult business of bringing feelings, states of mind, ideas and ways of seeing into the world and with finding effective forms. Inevitably there is a link between the popularity of Creative Writing courses, the nature of popular fiction, the function of the market and the dream of writing.

Creative Writing clearly has its own historical, philosophical and theoretical elements to discover, recover and burnish: but in addition it attempts to affect awareness of feelings, the way people organize their thought and view their life. It attempts to bring into being new products of the mind, new ways of seeing and understanding, to say things never thought or said before – or if not, then to say things again but better fitted for contemporary readers.

One of the major questions the traditional study of literature often misses out, but which Creative Writing can address, is the issue of the social role and social function of the writer as a creative and interpretive intellectual. And from this recognition other questions grow. What is writing? What do writers do? What does writing do? How do they represent the world in words? Why do writers write? Who is their audience? What might their audience expect of them? And once asked these questions open up debates of considerable complexity which for some unravel the dream of writing, if not in the dawning realization that their talent is limited, then in the patience-frazzling realities of the cultural climate – publishing, marketing and second guessing what the public will want to read.

In the UK Creative Writing first made an appearance in 1970 at the University of East Anglia, and since then it has assumed almost mythic status due to the critical and popular success of alumni such as Rose Tremain, Anne Enright, Kazuo Ishiguro and Ian McEwan. Over the next two decades Creative Writing established a modest presence in undergraduate studies (usually as part of an English degree) at several British universities: after Derby University pioneered a stand-alone undergraduate degree in 2000, six other UK universities also developed degrees in the subject, and by 2008, it was offered as a degree component at 20 British universities. The National Association of Writers in Education website lists 421 Higher Education Creative Writing courses (see www.nawe.co.uk). Creative Writing is The Open University's most popular module. PhDs in the subject have started to appear. At British universities there are now over 5,000 students studying Creative Writing at undergraduate level – that is more than the number studying English Language (*Student Record 2003-08*, 2009). The subject is well established in the USA, Canada, Australia and New Zealand, and it has begun to establish itself in universities in India, Poland, Italy, Romania and elsewhere. These are confirmations that the subject is popular, is re-creating a distinct place for itself within the academy and in the public imagination, and is developing its own presence and agenda of study.

There are several current ideas about what Creative Writing at university might be. One popular view is that Creative Writing is simply Life Writing, something that allows people to write out their experience and which encourages *catharsis* (the purging of emotion). The most extreme form of this view sees Creative Writing as a kind of Art Therapy, an academic variety of care in the community. While most tutors acknowledge a therapeutic element to the subject, this is not the main thrust of Creative Writing within universities. Indeed, tutors usually try to persuade students to move beyond the safety of autobiography, however therapeutic, to put their revelations into fictional or poetic form, to develop narratives that are more than 'the way it actually happened', to think themselves into someone else's life and feelings, to take an imaginative leap out of their own skin and develop a cloak for their experience.

It is often assumed that Creative Writing is something anyone can do, that 'we all have one novel in us'. Usually this is accompanied by the explanation that Creative Writing is merely 'free' or 'personal' expression, that we only have to emote on paper, write 'what we feel', and that a student can never 'get it wrong'. This view is not something that tutors easily accommodate: those who come to the subject with this idea usually come to grief very quickly. It is often something of a shock to discover that Creative Writing is a subject which sets standards – and not only in terms of literacy, academic performance, satire or witty observation of social *mores*. Because, in practical educational terms, the subject insists on moving students towards professional standards of presentation, writing, spelling, organization, planning, reading, engagement and expression, Creative Writing can do things, including combating plagiarism, that now give traditional academic subjects real difficulties (see McCrory 2001).

Creative Writing within the university plays a broad role, not as Arts Therapy, a service unit for Dyslexia, Remedial Academic Support, nor even as a part of Adult Literacy, but simply in its own right. Perhaps the most important and the easiest to understand of the various erroneous views of Creative Writing is the one that sees it simply as 'part of English'. This, for people who remember 'doing' poetry at school, makes a kind of sense. But while there is clearly a great deal of common ground and productive cross-over between the two subjects, the work, agenda and practices of English teachers are very different from those of Creative Writing teachers. Both subjects are concerned with general cultural values, the interpretation of experience, and with words and language: but after this they part company. The difference in aims and methodology of the two subjects is almost total and it is important to distinguish between the *work* of English and the *work* of Creative Writing.

English emerged as a literature in the fourteenth century and as a university subject was accepted in Cambridge with some reluctance in the 1860s (Potter 1937; Tillyard 1955; Mulhern 1979). For many years the subject struggled to gain acceptance from the more established disciplines, which considered it to be the equivalent of 'geography or forestry', a subject for those who were not intellectually equipped to study the more serious subjects (see Alvarez 2005, 81). The study of English was planned at Cambridge University in 1917 and started at around the time of the 1918 Armistice. The Cambridge English syllabus stopped at around 1830 and English staff, mainly part-time 'freelance' lecturers, at first allied themselves with the Classics and Philology by setting about Anglo Saxon and Medieval texts in the hope that this would give the subject some academic credibility; they dabbled with philosophy, history and religion in developing an interpretative methodology and then, in the developing intellectual foment that followed World War I, took up from Matthew Arnold the battle for culture. They claimed to be 'central' to national cultural life and the moral health of English society and set about ranking texts in order of 'moral seriousness'. In the years 1926–7, English was ratified as a degree course and a centralized Faculty structure established to administer and teach it. Throughout the 1930s and 1940s as more UK English departments opened up, the subject fought a desperate battle to establish the idea that it was something more than 'a charming parasite' or a training ground for book reviewers (Leavis 1948). By the mid-1970s, the avenues of exploration outlined by F. R. Leavis, Q. D. Leavis, L. C. Knights and those gathered around the journal *Scrutiny* were largely exhausted or simply by-passed by new ideas from the European mainland, and the 1990s saw English enter what is now referred to as the 'the Culture Wars' in which the canon was contested, the literary application of Political Correctness was investigated and increasingly English devoted itself to literary theory, which seemed somehow more serious, more tangible, more academic than any previous version of the subject.

Creative Writing confronts literary theory in general with the awkwardness of its existence and its practicality, but of the canon it has particular questions: where does the canon leave the contemporary would-be popular writer? Does the 'accepted literary canon' actually represent us? Do we have a responsibility to tradition or to the identity that goes with certain traditions?

Should writers be concerned with tradition? Does tradition affect them at all? Can writers ignore tradition? Are we part of a tradition of writing just because of the language that history handed us? Who among our predecessors do we look to, have time for, reread, admire and argue with? Who do we dismiss? In what areas do we share things? In what ways are our aims common? What binds us to the writers of the past? Are we doing something that develops an idea they started? Or are we doing something entirely new? In an age dominated by Hollywood, TV soaps and a commercial, rather than a literary, market for writing, is it possible to do something new? And if we do something new, will we find a publisher or a market for it?

To put it bluntly, when looking at the orthodox literary canon – at how we are represented in terms of our identity and culture – the contemporary writer asks whether what they are asked to study and respect is not still merely a list of books mainly by dead, white, upper middle class, English males, but also what the canon has to do with what they want to write and read now. And this in turn raises questions about identity, privacy and choice; about the fragmentation of society, the privatization of experience and the nature of community; and about the 'core values' of education and the nature of education itself. Rick Gekoski opened up some of these issues when he wrote:

> I lived through a time when it was great to read. There were so many books that you *had* to read, which would have been read by everyone you knew. Not merely read, through, but digested and discussed. We formed not merely our opinions but ourselves on them. It was a common culture – or more accurately, a common counter-culture – which included music, art and film. Within our middle-class, educated world there was a canon, which wasn't limited to Shakespeare, Jane Austen and Scott Fitzgerald. You could assume people around you had read a lot of contemporary books: if they hadn't, it occasioned not merely puzzlement, but disapproval. So: if we asked a bunch of literate university students today what they had read, what they had *all* read – what would be the answer? I suspect the answer would be: nothing. Not that young people don't read, but they don't read together. They haven't got, as we had, a common culture. (Gekoski 2010)

It is possible to see now that Creative Writing, by restoring and reasserting itself within the academy, is fulfilling some part of the inner reflection on, and training for, citizenship that the ancients so valued and which is reflected in so many classical texts. For classics scholars the study and practice of Rhetoric and Poetics (from which in part the idea of teaching Creative Writing descends) was what was once termed 'a liberal education'

(Glover 1953). By helping to create the 'classics of tomorrow' within the modern academy Creative Writing quietly, in its own way, and by a completely different route, has begun to find, revive and extend the idea of 'the classics', to challenge, revitalize, review, renew and develop the idea of national (and international) literature and the canon, and to reassert a standard-setting civic role for literature such as the ancients believed in and which distinguished literary critics, writers, thinkers, scholars and teachers as diverse as Matthew Arnold, Cardinal Newman, Antonio Gramsci, Leon Trotsky and F. R. Leavis once sought for the study of Literature.

I am often asked what is the relationship of Creative Writing to the canon, and how exactly does the subject prepare young writers for particular markets, and how many writers do you actually produce? These are interesting questions, but they seem to suppose one standard answer, when in fact every university course and teacher is different. But also perhaps it is unfair to look at the subject in these terms – would we ask how many Renaissance Dramatists an English department produces, how many Native Americans American Studies produces, or how many MPs result from Politics degrees? Creative Writing recruits some students who have read a lot, who are serious about writing and who want to write professionally, but like most subjects it also has many more students who simply want a degree and have no intention of taking their studies further.

Creative Writing certainly urges student-writers to consider the market for their writing, but the main struggle is to hone the student's critical/creative skills and to accommodate them to working in workshops, critiquing each other's work in creative and supportive ways. Discussion of the market in this environment is mainly to point out the literary standards and styles that apply, to give students something to aim at, and to warn that the market is in a constant state of flux and totally unpredictable in terms of what kinds of writing will succeed. The idea that luck, contacts, good looks and persistence do not play a part, or that a particular genre or good writing alone will be sufficient, would be seriously misleading.

Another question I am asked is whether we have special assignments where students learn how to write in specific genres. The answer to this is a clear 'No' – and for good practical reasons. While we do address questions of genre, writing for a particular genre (cowboy, romance, sci-fi, horror, fantasy, teen-fiction and their various cross-over hybrid forms) demands massive preparation and in-depth reading: teaching such a course would involve similar labour. In writing a historical novel, for example, the writer might be involved in reading equivalent to a PhD over several years. This is clearly something that cannot be accommodated on a one semester course. Also, on most degrees within any given cohort there is unlikely to be sufficient number of students interested in any one genre to run a module. It is a simple, financial problem. If a team were to offer a course on, say, writing Romantic Fiction, it would not recruit enough students to pay the tutor's fees. Of course if the team were to offer a course on Twilight/Werewolf/Un-dead/Vampire writing, the response might be different. Or at least, this year and possibly next year it might recruit, but then the fashion would change, the demand would shift. Even at Masters Level writing workshops are general, catering for as many possibilities and personal tastes as is practicable, and students are encouraged to develop the type of genre and writing that interests them.

Are students taught about the publishing world and its many demands? Yes, but the publishing world is itself constantly responding to reader demands, sales, marketing, economic predictions, etc., and UK publishing, for the last 20 years, has been in the throes of rationalization, where publishers are not being bought up but have been trans-atlanticized, globalized and e-booked, so second guessing the publishing world is not something that could easily be taught by tutors whose skill lies in writing. In the face of rapid global change, personal experience of a writer is often more useful to students than a trend analysis. That said, however, writers – as part of 'popular culture' – are more recognized and accommodated by universities than was once the case: many universities now try to recognize the most successful local writers with honorary degrees; almost all universities run a careers and employability day to which Creative Writing teams contribute: they also invite local writers, agents, publishers and successful ex-students employed in the creative industries and literature development to return and talk about their experiences. Writers and publishers are now less shy of holding literary events – readings, talks, book launches – in universities.

Do writers take publishing trends into account? Yes, particularly those engaged in writing for a particular genre. Literary writers, however, seem to take much less note of these things and are driven by their own inner demons, tastes and observations. But student-writers, in my experience, are hardly aware of trends at all. And if they are, the process of writing a novel or producing a collection of poems or stories is so long (minimum 2 years) that by the time they have produced something in response to a particular trend, the trend has moved on, mutated, changed into something else. At the same time it has to be said that literary trends are more often the accident of coincidental publication – publishers thinking alike – and copying the success of others, than they are the product of writers setting the lead.

Of course, all writers respond to the market. But it is a free market. There can be no promise of success even for those who write superbly and get straight 'A' grades. To all these questions tutors of writing would say their primary task is to concentrate on getting the student to write well, to write better, to aim at standards where publication might be possible. While it is good to have an eye on the target market, the business of agents, publication and markets are not something that can easily be addressed on a *writing* course. And to offer more than this, to direct students precisely towards a particular market with the promise of publication, to offer even a hint of success in such an unpredictable area, would be to open up a whole range of discontent.

An undergraduate writing course (as with any other degree course) is only an introduction to the subject. It can do little more than acquaint students with the basics, making them more aware of what they need to do if they are to succeed, making them more aware of what it takes to write well; it will introduce them to the tools they need to develop and explore for themselves once they leave university. And to reiterate an earlier point, even if graduates from Creative Writing do not go on to literary success, they are nevertheless more aware of writing and its difficulties, more aware of the literary world, more aware of the canon and contemporary writing and more aware of the possibilities for further reading. As in every other subject, how students engage with the skills on offer, how they apply their talent after the course has finished, how they sift the trends of popular fiction is entirely up to them. At the back of our mind there is always the creeping suspicion that we assume a hunger for education that might not exist, that we assume writing is an ambition with a shaping social role when really students have a very different agenda.

A student who arrives at university with a well-stocked mind and a bookshelf full of well-thumbed novels stands a far better chance of identifying and breaking into their market than the average undergraduate who arrives having read only a few selected literary passages in an 'A' level anthology. And whatever the well-prepared student learns at university, they will be much better placed to take advantage of it in turning themselves into a professional writer than the student who simply wants to know what they need to do to pass the module. In the current educational and economic climate, teaching writing feels like the pessimism of the intellect and the optimism of the will, as Antonio Gramsci used to say. But perhaps it was never any different.

With these things in mind what a writer-teacher brings to the subject in terms of personal experience is vitally important. For me the prime ingredient of any writing course is not a grasp of genre or a sense of style, or even an ambition to write popular novels – though all these things help. What I seek to develop in student-writers – whatever the module or the genre – is an awareness of words, the stock of words, what is in words, our precise choice of words, what we can do with words. Every year as a writer and teacher, I ask Creative Writing students: What do writers do when they write? Usually, as soon as the question is asked, a chasm of uncertainties opens up. What do we mean by *writer*? We all write, so in what way is what a writer writes different from what a non-writer writes? Why? Who says? And so on. To a certain extent the question has faced writers down the ages and it is exactly the kind of open-ended conundrum you might expect in a university. But it is not an idle question, and over the last few years the question has been increasingly focused for me, not by disinterested academic speculation, but by current events.

One of the most important things writers of all political persuasions do is direct us to think about how words are used and what is in words. Dictionaries tell us the meaning of words in the past, at particular moments in time, but writers tell us about the inner life of our language, about what is happening to words now. Because language and words are tied to issues of identity, perception, ambition and ideas of community, writing is much more likely than other art forms to be judged, not only in artistic terms but also in moral and political terms. The Nobel Prize-winning Bulgarian writer, Elias Canetti was very aware that the content of words shifted through time and daily usage: he was aware that just because a word once had a particular content or meaning it did not mean that it would always have that same meaning or content. He said that to notice changes in meaning and to make use of these changes was to be an 'earwitness', and this, he said, was a writer's duty (Canetti 1987).

Lewis Carroll was another writer who studied language very carefully: he loved to play with words and was aware of the arbitrary nature of meaning. In *Alice Through the Looking-Glass* (1871), Humpty Dumpty explains to Alice that although we get birthday presents once a year we could get un-birthday presents on the other 364 days of the year. He ends his explanation ends with: 'There's glory for you!'

> 'I don't know what you mean by "glory"', Alice said.
>   Humpty Dumpty smiled contemptuously. 'Of course you don't – till I tell you. I meant "there's a nice knock-down argument for you!"'
>   'But "glory" doesn't mean "a nice knock-down argument",' Alice objected.

'When I use a word,' Humpty Dumpty said, in rather a scornful tone, 'it means just what I choose it to mean – neither more nor less.'

'The question is,' said Alice, 'Whether you can make words mean so many different things.'

'The question is,' said Humpty Dumpty, 'which is to be master – that's all.'

Alice was too much puzzled to say anything; so after a minute Humpty Dumpty began again: 'They've a temper, some of them – particularly verbs: they're the proudest – adjectives you can do anything with, but not verbs – however, I can manage the whole lot of them! Impenetrability! That's what I say!'

'Would you tell me, please,' said Alice, 'what that means?'

'Now you talk like a reasonable child,' said Humpty Dumpty, looking very much pleased. 'I meant by "impenetrability" that we've had enough of this subject, and it would be just as well if you'd mention what you mean to do next, as I suppose you don't mean to stop here all the rest of your life.'

'That's a great deal to make one word mean,' Alice said in a thoughtful tone. (Carrol 1970, 267–9),

Generally, unlike Humpty Dumpty, writers work with a language which, while it is constantly changing and responding to social pressures, is given. For example, although we now avoid using it, at one time the word 'nigger' was in common use. Neither Agatha Christie nor Joseph Conrad saw anything wrong in using the word in their book titles – *Ten Little Niggers* (1939) and *The Nigger of the 'Narcissus'* (1897). The word also appears in the works of Charles Dickens, G. B. Shaw, D. L. Sayers, Mark Twain, Rider Haggard, D. H. Lawrence, Ernest Hemingway, Carson McCullers and even US President Woodrow Wilson. Enid Blyton's story 'The Three Golliwogs' has characters named Golly, Woggie and Nigger. It would be very difficult to wipe this from the language or delete these books from the literature. It would also be a falsification of the past and the language of the past.

Now, although the British National Party and National Front, KKK, White Supremacists in the southern states of the USA and white separatists in South Africa still use the word, and Quentin Tarrantino and Spike Lee often have black characters in their films use the word, it has not been socially permissible to use this word for some years, and in the United States, there has been pressure to remove all books containing the word from schools and libraries. Now it is often referred to simply as 'the n-word'. From being *the* word to describe black people, the taboo on its use is now so strong that even an informed discussion about its origins, history, spelling and changing function can hardly take place. An actor is reported as saying:

> The N-word. I don't use it . . . ever . . . I don't want *anybody* to use it. If somebody uses that word towards me, I'm going to take issue with it because it's not a definition of me. I don't think it gives anybody any power over me to use that word; in fact, I think if you use that word towards me, you've lost all power. Once you've used that word towards me, I know exactly who you are and I'll crush you. No question, no ifs, buts or maybes. (Hattenstone 2003, 17)

And when the actor Michael Richards was recorded abusing a black heckler in the audience with the words: 'you fucking nigger' the furore which followed was as much about the racist epithet as about the problem of trying to report and discuss the incident without repeating what had been said (Mayes 2006, 33). But if we cannot air-brush this word entirely from the present, we certainly cannot make it vanish from the past either. It is important if we want to chart race relations in USA, the history of the anti-slavery movement, the issues of the American Civil War, the history of jazz, blues and rock and roll, the musical achievement of Elvis Presley, population shifts and urban and industrial development in the USA, the history of the KKK, or even slavery and the histories of Bristol and Liverpool.

This example, contentious as it might be, shows that it is important for writers to follow the shifts in the language since these represent changes in understanding and social relations. Conrad, Christie, Blyton, McCullers and the others did not avoid the word – indeed, there was no reason for them to think they should – and there were few alternative words available to them. None of them could have predicted a shift in sensibility that would make that word unacceptable within a few decades. And when, in the 1970s, John Lennon said 'Woman is the nigger of the world' he was making use of this change to highlight a different shift in perception. And this is not disinterested academic speculation limited to some ivory tower: all the writers mentioned in the preceding five paragraphs were the popular writers and leading cultural figures of their day, and most are included in the canon.

Writers often see their work as a struggle to understand what is happening to words, to reveal some of the hidden possibilities. My way of thinking about words is the mantra:

> Writing tells us what is happening to words
> Words tell us what is happening to feelings
> Feelings tell us what is happening to people

For all writers the conscious creation of new work entails the choice of words, and that means dealing with two contradictory impulses. The first is the temptation to use words as they are given, to set down only words which are current, which do not cause problems, which can be easily absorbed, which do not challenge. This is, I think, to see the writer merely as part of the entertainment industry and to accept the idea that the writer can make no meaningful intervention in the world. The second, opposite impulse, is to seek out and make use of words to probe meaning, to make it obvious how words change, are changed, are compromised in daily use, to reveal what is often hidden in words. A writer must always choose between these two possibilities, must always choose between 'servility and insolence' (Sontag 1982, 190). For a writer to say what they hear, to record what is happening to words, to be an *earwitness,* will always be characterized as an act of treachery, sedition, opposition or aggression by those who do not want these things observed, recorded, represented in words or dragged to light.

For a young poet, novelist or short story writer perhaps working on their first volume, this kind of discussion can be helpful. To know that this is what other writers have been thinking about is reassuring, creative and generative. To engage in discussion of these topics with others is an act supportive of professional solidarity. But the relationship between this discussion, popular literature and the would-be popular writer can be quite strained. I am aware, for example, that for the student who 'just wants to write' or who just wants know what they need to do to pass the module, this kind of exchange can be baffling. And this is not helped by the context, where university attention is fixed on recruitment, retention and results, since this discussion and this level of discussion are hardly on the 'event horizon'.

Creative Writing is relentlessly contemporary, that is its nature, and so inevitably tends towards the popular. Even so, while a writer like Kazuo Ishiguro is often touted as the successful product of such a course, the number of graduates and postgraduates emerging from university writing courses in the UK is still tiny, and their impact is still limited. But as a writer-teacher I am also aware that by equipping those who want to write we are changing – perhaps with glacial slowness – our literary culture. We are reducing the 'beginners tax' new writers pay by being unaware of the 'world of words', the way the writing business operates and the way writing – with its emphasis on what is in words – can work in the wider community.

Works Cited

Alvarez, A. (2005), *The Writer's Voice*. Bloomsbury: London.

Canetti, E. (1987), *The Conscience of Words & Earwitness*. London: Picador.

Carrol, L. (1970), *The Annotated Alice*. Harmondsworth: Penguin.

Gekoski, R. (30 October 2010), 'Asks if There was a New Canon', 'Guardian Books Blog', *The Guardian*, 21.

Glover, T. R. (1953), *The Ancient World*. Harmondsworth: Penguin.

Hattenstone, S. (7 June 2003), 'Doing the Right Thing'. *The Guardian Weekend*, 17.

Leavis, F. R. (1948), *Education & the University: A Sketch for an English School*. London: Chatto & Windus.

Mayes, I. (27 November 2006), 'A Word for Word Account of Racist Abuse'. *The Guardian*, 33.

McCrory, M. (2 November 2001), 'Strategies for Checking Plagiarism in a Creative Writing Programme', seminar paper: English Subject Centre Conference on Plagiarism, University of Liverpool.

Mulhern, F. (1979), *The Moment of 'Scrutiny'*. New Left Books: London.

Potter, S. (1937), *The Muse in Chains*. London: Cape.

Scaliger, J. C. (1561), *Poetices libri septem: Ad Sylvium filium*. A. Vincentius: Lyon.

Sontag, S. (1982), *A Susan Sontag Reader*. Harmondsworth: Penguin.

Tillyard, E. M. W. (1958), *The Muse Unchained: An Intimate Account of the Revolution in English Studies at Cambridge*. London: Bowes & Bowes.

Afterword:
The Future of the Popular

Christine Berberich

The preceding chapters have highlighted and celebrated the diversity that is generally encompassed by the term 'popular fiction'. Popular writing is heavily genre-oriented – but the seven genre chapters have outlined that there is no such thing as a 'typical' crime novel or a stereotypical horror story. While it is a characteristic of 'genre novels' to share certain traits, the chapters on Romance, Adventure Writing, Science Fiction, Crime and Horror Writing, Children's Literature and the Graphic Novel have shown that there are subgenres and sub-sub-genres to these umbrella terms, and that genres have remained alive precisely because of their ability to adapt and reinvent themselves according to the wishes and demands of the 'market'. The chapter on the twentieth-century ideological background to popular fiction that preceded the genre chapters has set out that this market might, in fact, be manipulated by its producers: by the publishing industry and, importantly, those in power who control it. Popular fiction, as Clive Bloom has argued, 'covers a wide range of ideological (especially sociological, political and aesthetic) areas' (2002, 17) and as such it has, always and inevitably, been contested and politicized: for Scott McCracken, popular fiction is representative of social conflict as it 'acts as a medium through which the social contradictions of modernity can be played out' (1998, 6). But there are many other ideological tensions at play, too: readers want to be amused, stimulated, thrilled, puzzled, entertained – in short: escape their mundane everyday lives; writers want to express themselves and also, potentially, their world views while, simultaneously, sell books to be able to make a living from writing; publishers want to make a profit and dominate the market. All these various demands seem almost irreconcilable. The constant and ever-expanding profit-driven marketing that surrounds everyday life and, especially, our consumption of popular culture certainly has considerable influence on the production of popular fiction. Bestsellers immediately spawn copy-cat publications that show similar content traits but that also, externally, *look* similar – a successful cover design for one text is replicated for the next. The unexpected summer 2012 bestseller *The One-Hundred Year-Old Man Who Climbed Out of the Window and Disappeared* by the Swedish novelist Jonas Jonasson, with its distinctive turquoise, black and white cover depicting a little old man scuttling away with a large suitcase seen through a window, saw follow-up publications such as Catharina Ingelman-Sundberg's 2014 novel *The Little Old Lady Who Broke All the Rules* with a very similar cover design, this time in purple, black and white, and depicting a, yes, little old lady scuttling away on a Zimmer frame, seen through a *broken* window. Jonasson's own follow-up novel to *The One-Hundred-Year-Old Man*, to be released with much hype and advance publicity in spring 2014, and entitled *The Girl Who Saved the King of Sweden*, has a virtually identical cover design, down to the same font and the same arrangement of the long title down the length of the book. On the strength of just one successful novel, Jonasson has thus become, or rather *been turned* into, his own successful brand that, in turn, influences other writers and their novels, not only in terms of their content but also in terms of the paratext of their cover design.

Despite this clear evidence for market manipulation and the power of marketing, Chapter 2 concluded on the warning note that the ideological, hierarchical rule over the popular culture market might not be as clear cut as many cultural commentators believe. In the long run, it is still the consumer who actively seeks out individual texts – and others of the same ilk, provided s/he liked them in the first place. Scott McCracken has pointed out that 'popular fiction may use simple forms, but if these simple forms are to win an audience, they must be able to address that audience's concern' (1998, 11). This comment echoes the words of an earlier cultural commentator, Stuart Hall, who stated that 'If the forms of provided popular culture are not purely manipulative, then it is because, alongside the false appeals, the foreshortenings, the trivialization and short circuits, there are also elements of recognition and identification, something approaching a recreation of recognisable experiences and attitudes, to which people are responding' (1981, 233). Audience recognition and, importantly, *interest* in the topics raised by popular fiction are thus of paramount importance. Readers need to be able to recognize themselves and their concerns in their reading matter; otherwise they will not become involved. And this is where, inevitably, the problem with market manipulation and control lies: popular culture, as John Fiske has shown, 'is always difficult mountainous territory for those who wish to control it' as 'the economic needs of the industries can be met only if the people *choose* their commodities' (1989, 104–5, emphasis mine). The same, inevitably, goes for the political or ideological content of popular culture – it can only be understood, heeded, absorbed if it is, actually, consumed. For McCracken, 'popular fiction . . . has always provided a structure within which our lives can be understood' and 'has the capacity to provide us with a . . . temporary sense of self' (1998, 2), and herein lies the success of popular culture: it reflects our contemporary, everyday world but simultaneously works as a form of escapism by offering us a few hours away from that very everyday life, by presenting us with fantasy worlds or happy endings, by letting us forget for a while or, alternatively, by letting us become involved. So even though it has become institutionalized to a certain extent, it also offers a multitude of possibilities for each individual reader.

These possibilities are not only due to the diverse subject matter and the many different genres and subgenres of popular fiction that allow different worlds for different readers to escape to. The continuous and continuing success of popular fiction also lies in its ability to constantly reshape the actual reading experience. As Bloom has convincingly shown, 'all literature works, on one level or another, on precedent (tradition); and popular fiction is the area where it is necessary to reinvent the precedents that were most successful' (2002, 17). If we go back full circle to Boris Akunin's popular Erast Fandorin series that opened this collection, it is clear to see how Akunin uses literary precedent. His novel *Leviathan* (2004) is almost entirely set on board the steamer 'Leviathan' during its voyage through the Suez Canal. But it is not only this iconic setting that pays homage to Agatha Christie's classic *Death on the Nile* (1937), but also Akunin's small cast of characters that, in typically Christie-esque manner, try to divert suspicion away from themselves and on to their fellow travellers. His suave sleuth Erast Fandorin himself ('that starched collar sticking up like alabaster, that jewelled pin in the necktie, that red carnation . . . in the buttonhole, that perfectly smooth parting with not a single hair out of place, those carefully manicured nails, that narrow black moustache that seemed to be drawn on with charcoal' [Akunin 2004, 26]) is a nod to Christie's dapper and slightly foppish Hercule Poirot who, on first appearance, is described as a 'quaint dandified little man' who 'carried himself with great dignity', with a 'very stiff and military [moustache]' and an 'almost incredible' neatness of attire, to whom 'a speck of dust would have caused . . . more pain than a bullet wound' (Christie 2013, 23). The intertextuality in Akunin's novel is evident – but is not vital for understanding or, crucially, enjoying the text. But it is a perfect example of what Bloom terms 'the art of literary repetition, homage and pastice' (2002, 24) in popular culture.

Popular fiction thus offers a variety of readings and interpretations. Fiske points out that 'the texts of popular culture . . . are full of gaps, contradictions, and inadequacies. It is what aesthetic criticism would call its "failings" that . . . allow [the popular text] to "speak" differently in different contexts, in different moments of readings' (1989, 125). For Fiske, popular fiction does not have the simple, straightforward message that its critics claim it has; instead, it leaves gaps and spaces that allow it to be read in many different ways, interpreted variously, depending on experience, prior literary knowledge and political awareness. Ian Fleming's popular James Bond novels, for example, might be read as pure escapism, conjuring up a fantasy world of spies, fast cars, gadgets and beautiful women. This is certainly a message that has been perpetuated through their film adaptations from the 1960s onwards to the present day that have turned the Bond brand into a still flourishing franchise: new films still come out and usually come hand-in-hand with many and very diverse advertising campaigns trying to sell Bond's favourite drink, the 'authentic Bond watch', or luring potential buyers with the prospect of driving 'his' car. Ian Fleming himself had asserted that his books were 'written for warm-blooded heterosexuals in railway trains, airplanes or beds' (Fleming 1963, 14) – that is as *entertainment*, rather than anything to be taken seriously, or with any kind of political or ideological message. However, Juan Elices' Chapter 12 has shown that an allegedly 'innocent' and apolitical popular text can become highly charged material in a different country and a different social and political context. Different readings and attitudes can thus interpret the same novels as politically highly (in?)sensitive texts, for instance asserting an imperial role for Britain that has long been superseded by political realities on the world stage and stubbornly clinging to a fast disappearing hegemonic-patriarchal-colonial life-style. For some readers, this interpretation might then still tickle their fancy or tick some reactionary-nostalgic boxes; for others, it might leave a sour aftertaste to a previously escapist and indulgent reading experience (see also Berberich 2012).

Power is thus a vital component in any discussion of popular fiction that should neither be ignored nor sidelined. But it is not necessarily only the straightforward manipulative control of those in power over the masses. Popular fiction, in turn, has power and consequently can be, and has been, used to subvert the status quo and to challenge authority and the alleged 'norm' of social conventions; it might not always do so in an obvious or straightforward manner but, instead, approaches sensitive topics creatively, stealthily and metaphorically, allowing its readers once more space to interpret and to think, to challenge and subvert things for themselves. Bloom's comment that popular writing 'always includes imagination, negotiation and *refusal* and allows minority groups . . . to negotiate their space in contradiction to the *vox populi*' (2002, 28), already cited in Chapter 2, is again relevant, as it can, ultimately, be seen in all the chapters of this collection. To name but two examples, in Chapter 9 on the relatively recent genre of the graphic novel, for example, Monica Germanà shows how texts often debased and derided as 'comics' tackle difficult and challenging historical themes (such as, for instance, Art Spiegelman's *Maus* that offers an entirely new approach to second-generation Holocaust narratives) or sensitive social-cultural issues (in the case Marjane Sartrapi's *Persepolis* that illustrates a woman's struggle to find a personal space and identity as a liberated and emancipated female during Iran's cultural revolution). Similarly, and as Joanne Bishton's Chapter 13 has shown, Sarah Waters subverts the classic conventions of the Romance to raise the profile of and, effectively, empower lesbian writing. For Fiske, popular fiction thus comprises 'text[s] of struggle between forces of closure and openness, between the readerly and the producerly, between the homogeneity of the preferred meaning and the heterogeneity of its readings' (1989, 125). Any given text has, inevitably, an *intended* meaning. But not every reading experience is the same: every engagement with a text varies from reader to reader, and so popular fiction, free of the potentially inhibiting label of 'literary classic' that *must* be appreciated, offers its readers the freedom to roam within the text, to fill in potential gaps, to imaginatively invest in it and draw from it whatever conclusions they wish.

This might then be what Walter Benjamin referred to when he talked about 'the greatly increased mass of participants' (1978, 239). Writing with great foresight as early as the 1930s, Benjamin felt that 'the distinction between author and public is about to lose its basic character. . . . At any moment the reader is ready to turn into a writer' (232). This comment seems particularly pertinent in the opening decades of the twenty-first century. We no longer solely rely on bookshops or libraries to provide new fuel for our reading passions. Instead, readers now take up televised book-group recommendations, peruse internet sites, download books on their e-readers to carry entire libraries on small electronic devices or listen to an audio-book while driving. New and enticing reading matter is now, literally, often only a mouse click away. Just as the nineteenth-century lending library, as Chris Pittard has shown in Chapter 1, has helped change the actual *format* of the novel, from the formerly popular three-volume form to the more easily lendable one-volume one, twenty-first century digital developments see an increasing 'liberation' of (popular) fiction from its traditional 'medium', the book, towards something more virtual, something we can access online, on the move, without being encumbered, as some people might see it, with a heavy book. This potentially makes the engagement with popular fiction both easier and more all-encompassing and inclusive. And with this new accessibility also come new forms of active participation: publishers provide online discussion forums; customers provide feedback and reviews of their latest purchases via Amazon; budding writers take to the internet in their droves to publish regular blogs that, they hope, will lead to their big break into the world of authorship. Increasingly, first-time authors rely on on-demand publishing via the internet, with services such as Createspace that do not only allow aspiring authors to upload their manuscripts but also give them complete control over the design, from font and colour options to the finishing of the page, cover design etc. Once the 'virtual' book has been created and uploaded it is available as a print-on-demand service, available through a variety of online services but also more traditional book retailers. The same service, incidentally, is available for music uploads and the creation of CDs, thus allowing a wider and wider base to participate in the production and dissemination of popular culture in various forms and manifestations. And while popular fiction thus produced might, ultimately, fail to tap into the *mass* market or reach bestseller status, it still effectively means that its authors can make some headway and find an opening into a notoriously difficult market, as, increasingly, traditional publishers keep an eye on those e- and on-demand publications to source potential future authors for their own catalogues. And, maybe, in light of this Richard & Judy's call for new authors discussed and challenged in Chapter 2 is not quite so problematic after all. Yes, the choices made in the selection of the 'best' new novel might not be entirely transparent and objective; maybe the sponsors W. H. Smith and Thornton's have their business interest at heart. But maybe their popular programme really does want to open itself up to more active participation by the very people it targets. Maybe it is, after all, a public-minded initiative rather than a cynical and calculating marketing strategy.

Regardless of the conclusion we might eventually arrive at, one thing is certain: 'popular' is, and always has been, a contentious term, open to a multitude of approaches. So maybe we ought to, in conclusion, revisit the definition of 'popular' put forward in the Introduction: 'belonging to the people', 'widely-favoured' or 'well-liked' on the one hand, 'low', 'base' and with 'a strong sense of setting out to gain favour' on the other, with popular culture, in particular, identified not by the people but by those trying to influence and manipulate them (Williams 1976, 198–9). The chequered history of twentieth-century popular culture certainly seems to imply the latter approaches to the popular: the abuse of power, the manipulative element of it that seems to condemn its consumers to a streamlined, a trivialized and institutionalized diet of conformist sub-cultural matter. This is a trend that can certainly still be seen in the early decades of the twenty-first century: in the marketing and pushing of certain material at the expense of other; in the many copy-cat productions of surprising bestsellers; in the similar cover designs, created especially to lure readers with the promise of more reading of the same kind they enjoyed before; in the plethora of seemingly mindless material we are fed on a daily basis, and by a variety of media. But, alongside this, there are also the many promising signs: the increased participation of the public in the production of culture on the internet, for example, and the increasing interest that the industry shows in this. This shows that the 'popular' element to (as in: the people's interest and investment in) popular culture is still there and, potentially, on the increase again. Because of this, popular fiction will continue to constantly reinvent itself and be re-invigorated, and will always serve as an important social and cultural document of its time.

Works Cited

Akunin, Boris (2004), *Leviathan*. London: Weidenfeld & Nicolson.

Benjamin, Walter (1978 [1936]), 'The Work of Art in the Age of Mechanical Reproduction', in Hannah Arendt (ed.), *Illuminations*. New York: Schocken Books, pp. 217–51.

Berberich, Christine (2012), 'Putting England Back on Top? Ian Fleming, James Bond and the Question of England'. *Yearbook of English Studies* 42, 13–29.

Bloom, Clive (2002), *Bestsellers: Popular Fiction since 1900*. Basingstoke: Palgrave Macmillan.

Christie, Agatha ([1920] 2013), *The Mysterious Affair at Styles*. London: Pan Books.

—([1937] 2014), *Death on the Nile*. London: Harper Collins.

Fiske, John (1989), *Understanding Popular Culture*. London: Routledge.

Fleming, Ian (1963), 'How to Write a Thriller'. *Books and Bookmen* (May), 14.

Hall, Stuart (1981), 'Notes on Deconstructing "the Popular"', in R. Samuel (ed.), *People's History and Socialist Theory*. London: Routledge & Kegan Paul, pp. 227–40.

McCracken, Scott (1998), *Pulp: Reading Popular Fiction*. Manchester: Manchester University Press.

Williams, Raymond (1976), *Keywords: A Vocabulary of Culture and Society*. London: Fontana/Croom Helm.

Index